Legal Transplants

Legal Transplants

An Interdisciplinary Approach

MATHIAS SIEMS

Professor of Private Law and Market Regulation,
European University Institute, Florence, Italy

OXFORD
UNIVERSITY PRESS

OXFORD
UNIVERSITY PRESS

Great Clarendon Street, Oxford, OX2 6DP,
United Kingdom

Oxford University Press is a department of the University of Oxford.
It furthers the University's objective of excellence in research, scholarship,
and education by publishing worldwide. Oxford is a registered trade mark of
Oxford University Press in the UK and in certain other countries.

Published in the United States of America by Oxford University Press
198 Madison Avenue, New York, NY 10016, United States of America.

British Library Cataloguing in Publication Data
Data available

Library of Congress Control Number: 2025948364

ISBN 9780198884125

DOI: 10.1093/9780191991981.001.0001

Printed and bound by
CPI Group (UK) Ltd., Croydon, CR0 4YY

MIX
Paper | Supporting
responsible forestry
FSC® C013604

The manufacturer's authorized representative in the EU for product safety is
Oxford University Press España S.A. of Parque Empresarial San Fernando de Henares,
Avenida de Castilla, 2 – 28830 Madrid (www.oup.es/en or product.safety@oup.com).
OUP España S.A. also acts as importer into Spain of products made by the manufacturer.

Preface

Sherlock Holmes and Dr Watson went on a camping trip. After a good meal and a bottle of wine, they lay down for the night and went to sleep.

Some hours later, Holmes awoke and nudged his faithful friend. 'Watson, look up at the sky and tell me what you see.' Watson replied, 'I see millions and millions of stars.'

'What does that tell you?' Watson pondered for a minute. 'Astronomically, it tells me that there are millions of galaxies and potentially billions of planets. Astrologically, I observe that Saturn is in Leo. Horologically, I deduce that the time is approximately a quarter past three. Theologically, I can see that God is all powerful and that we are small and insignificant. Meteorologically, I suspect that we will have a beautiful day tomorrow. Why, what does it tell you?'

Holmes was silent for a minute, then spoke. 'Watson, don't you see it? Some bastard has stolen our tent.'[*]

The literature on legal transplants provides some parallels to this joke. Similar to the response by Dr Watson, there is no shortage of perspectives, but it also seems that something important may be missing. This book aims to present a nuanced and fair analysis of the use of, and literature on, legal transplants. However, beyond exploring many details, it also aims to shift the debate in two important ways. First, it suggests that research and practice of legal transplants cannot, and should not, draw on legal scholarship only. There is a rich literature in other disciplines on topics such as policy transfer, cultural transfer, entangled history and diffusion of ideas that closely connect to the notion of legal transplants. As this book will show, interdisciplinarity is also needed as we explore questions such as 'why do legal transplants take place?', 'how do they work?', and 'should they regularly happen as a means of law reform?'. Second, in responding to these questions, this book aims to make a strong case for legal

* Adopted from https://users.ox.ac.uk/~peter/humour/holmes.html, http://www.laughlab.co.uk/ and https://www.newyorker.com/magazine/2002/11/11/science-of-humor-laughter accessed 21 October 2025.

transplants. In other words, it will show that legal transplants do happen frequently, that they often do work, and that they should indeed be a main tool for lawmakers. This position does not dispute valid criticism expressed in the literature. However, this book aims to challenge the view that any problems or concerns should lead to a new legal isolationism.

This book is targeted at a wide audience. It aims to appeal to legal scholars and other lawyers, which includes those who have an interest in comparative law but also others as legal transplants play a role in all domestic legal systems in the world. As the concept of legal transplants can also be applied to the spheres of international and transnational law, scholars of these fields of law can also benefit from this work. Moreover, as this book aims to show that the topic of legal transplants is closely related to research in other academic fields, such as history, international relations, development studies, institutional economics, and political science, it also aims to appeal to researchers in these fields.

Chapters of this book have been presented at lectures and workshops at Universidad Adolfo Ibáñez in Santiago di Chile, Victoria University of Wellington, University of Siena, Sapienza University of Rome, Bocconi University in Milan, and the European University Institute in Florence: I am very grateful for these invitations and the constructive comments on my ideas. In particular, I would like to thank Rafael Bezerranunes, Tania Groppi, Patrícia Jerónimo, Nicola Lupo, Federico Mucciarelli, Matteo Nicolini, Jasminka Pecotić Kaufman, Sky Ma, Sabrina Ragone, Amnon Reichman, Sapna Reheem Shaila, Thomas Streinz, and Elizabeth Trujillo and for their detailed comments on the draft version of the full manuscript. I also warmly thank the (former) EUI PhD students Dominik Dworniczak, Katarina Lundahl, Dorota Nowacka, Carolina Paulesu, and Onur Ucarer who helped me with the research on the non-Anglophone literature on legal transplants, Pedro José Mercado Jaén who assisted me with the bibliometric analysis, and Niall O'Shaughnessy for proofreading and linguistic suggestions. Last but not least, I thank Oxford University Press for supporting this book project.

Mathias Siems
Florence, Italy
January 2026

Contents

Figures

Tables

Abbreviations

ADR	Alternative Dispute Resolution
AI	Artificial Intelligence
ATJ	Andean Tribunal of Justice
CEE	Central and Eastern Europe
CSR	Corporate Social Responsibility
EBRD	European Bank for Reconstruction and Development
ECJ	European Court of Justice
EU	European Union
G20	Group of Twenty
GDP	Gross Domestic Product
GDPR	General Data Protection Regulation (EU)
ICJ	International Court of Justice
IMF	International Monetary Fund
IR	International Relations
JSTOR	Journal Storage (database)
LLM	Master of Laws
M&A	Mergers and Acquisitions
MNE	Multinational Enterprises
NGO	Non-governmental Organisation
OECD	Organisation for Economic Development
PECL	Principles of European Contract Law
PRC	People's Republic of China
QCA	Qualitative Comparative Analysis
SJD	Doctor of Juridical Science
UN	United Nations
UNCITRAL	UN Commission on International Trade Law
UNIDROIT	International Institute for the Unification of Private Law
WTO	World Trade Organization

1

Introduction

A. Motivation and main idea of this book

More than fifty years ago, Alan Watson's *Legal Transplants: An Approach to Comparative Law* was published.[1] Watson's analysis of legal transplants was strongly influenced by his background as a Scottish legal historian with an interest in Roman law, in particular analysing the reception of Roman law in Scotland and continental Europe. The subsequent literature has broadened the scope of analysis to many further aspects. For example, it has discussed how legislative drafting can contribute to the design of effective legal transplants, what role courts have in applying the transplanted rules (or even in engaging in transplants themselves), and whether the diverse understanding and application of rules in the transplant country poses a challenge to the notion of legal transplants.[2]

It is timely to revisit the notion and use of legal transplants. In recent years, the use of the term 'legal transplants' in the literature has increased considerably.[3] Substantive reasons also point towards possible changes in the way transplants are understood and used. For example, in today's world of plural legal orders, the 'foreignness' of legal transplants differs from plain transplants between two countries.[4] It is also clear that political, economic, social, and technological changes influence the use and evaluation of legal transplants. For example, geopolitical trends, such as shifting power dynamics between the US, Europe, and China, and the globalisation of businesses and law firms mean that today's landscape is very different from the time in which Watson's book was published.[5]

[1] Alan Watson, *Legal Transplants: An Approach to Comparative Law* (Edinburgh: Scottish Academic Press, 1974; Athens, GA: University of Georgia Press, 2nd edn, 1993).
[2] See the discussion of these topics in Chapter 3 at Section B 2 (for the role of courts), Chapter 5 at Section B 2 (for challenges to this notion), and Chapter 7 at Sections B 1 and C 1 (a) (for the role of legislative drafting).
[3] See the bibliometric analysis in Chapter 2 at Section C.
[4] See eg Chapter 3 at Section C and Chapter 5 at Section C 1, 2 (a), and 3 (b).
[5] See eg Chapter 4 at Section B 3.

Legal Transplants. Mathias Siems, Oxford University Press. © Mathias Siems 2026.
DOI: 10.1093/9780191991981.003.0001

Another motivation for revisiting uses of legal transplants is that many recent discussions connect this topic to the literature in other academic fields, such as history, international relations, development studies, institutional economics, and political science. For example, this includes questions such as: how have legal transplants been used in transition economies and post-conflict societies as means of legal reform? Are legal transplants in the Global South a continuation of forms of neo-imperialism by countries of the Global North? Can it be shown empirically that the transplantation of certain foreign legal models has a positive economic effect in transplant countries? And what is the relationship between the topic of legal transplants and the literature on policy diffusion and policy transfer? As indicated in the sub-title, this book is particularly interested in these interdisciplinary connections.

While much of the current legal literature on this topic has a positive focus, this book also deals with the normative arguments vis-à-vis the use of legal transplants. Of course, this normative debate does not exist in a vacuum. Thus, in the progression of the following chapters, the following interconnected points will be made. First, the term 'legal transplants' is frequently used in the literature, today often disregarding Watson's narrow position (Chapter 2). Second, applying a wide notion of 'law', legal transplants capture a variety of phenomena, which also shows the openness and flexibility of this concept (Chapter 3). Third, while legal transplants take place due to a variety of reasons, there is a trend towards voluntary transplants (Chapter 4). Fourth, legal transplants generally 'work' even if they are modified in their host environment (Chapter 5). Fifth, in many instances, it is desirable to use a legal transplant (Chapter 6). Sixth, it is possible to provide guidance on how the design of legal transplants should be pursued (Chapter 7).[6]

The overall point this book aims to make is therefore that there is *a case for legal transplants*. As we will see throughout this book, this point is made against the backdrop of many equally strong criticisms, such as that transplants are 'impossible', more akin to 'irritants', forms of 'legal imperialism', or 'cultural appropriation'.[7] Thus, while this book critically analyses the literature on legal transplants, it also has the normative ambition to show that, in today's world, laws should not be insulated from outside legal influence. Moreover, beyond

[6] For more details on this positive-normative narrative see Section D.

[7] Pierre Legrand, 'The Impossibility of Legal Transplants' (1997) 4 *Maastricht Journal of European and Comparative Law* 111; Gunther Teubner, 'Legal Irritants: Good Faith in British Law or How Unifying Law Ends Up in New Divergences' (1998) 61 *Modern Law Review* 11; James A Gardner, *Legal Imperialism: American Lawyers and Foreign Aid in Latin America* (Madison, WI: University of Wisconsin Press, 1980); Sally E Merry, 'Law, Culture, and Cultural Appropriation' (1998) 10 *Yale Journal of Law and Humanities* 101.

the risk of using transplants too rarely, it provides suggestions on how to use transplants in a correct manner (ie it addresses the risk of using transplants wrongly).

This introductory chapter proceeds in Section B with an introduction to the meaning and scope of the term 'legal transplants'. Section C explains the relationship between this book and the existing literature in law and other fields. Section D outlines the subsequent chapters of this book.

B. What are 'legal transplants'?

Today, the term 'legal transplant' is used widely; yet, as explained in this section, the literature also suggests many other terms to denote this phenomenon. Applying a pragmatic understanding of the term 'legal transplants', this section then presents five motivational examples in order to illustrate the wide scope of the notion of legal transplants employed in this book.[8]

1. The 'battle of metaphors'

In the so-called 'battle of metaphors',[9] this book uses the term 'legal transplant' as the main metaphor. Some authors prefer other terms, while some also propose that different terms may be used for different categories. The main other terms suggested are legal reception, borrowing, diffusion, mimesis, transfer, import, export, migration, copying, imitation, adoption, influence, circulation, cross-fertilisation, translation, irritation, and contamination.[10] Yet, as we will see, none of them are without problems.

The initial problem with the word 'transplant', as with words such as 'transfer' and 'migration', is that it would imply that the transplanted law has been removed from the origin unit and that it can only be used by one transplant unit,

[8] Notably, applying a wide notion of 'law', as further explained in Chapter 3.

[9] Vlad Perju, 'Constitutional Transplants, Borrowing, and Migrations' in Michel Rosenfeld and András Sajó (eds), *The Oxford Handbook of Comparative Constitutional Law* (Oxford: OUP, 2012) 1304, 1306.

[10] See eg David Nelken, 'Legal Transplants and Beyond: Of Disciplines and Metaphors' in Andrew Harding and Esin Örücü (eds), *Comparative Law in the 21st Century* (The Hague: Kluwer, 2002) 19, 30–1; David Nelken, 'Beyond the Metaphor of Legal Transplants?: Consequences of Autopoietic Theory for the Study of Cross-Cultural Legal Adaptation' in Jiří Přibáň and David Nelken (eds), *Law's New Boundaries: The Consequences of Legal Autopoiesis* (Dartmouth: Ashgate, 2001) 265, 272–82; Andrew Harding, 'The Legal Transplants Debate: Getting Beyond the Impasse?' in Vito Breda (ed), *Legal Transplants in East Asia and Oceania* (Cambridge: CUP, 2019) 13, 27.

which is evidently not the case. The words 'copying', 'imitation', and 'mimesis' do not face these problems; yet, they seem to imply that the law in question will be identical in both units. However, apart from situations where the transplant unit copies a precise legal text, it is more common that it modifies the object to its own needs. This modification can also be an objection against the term 'legal transplant' if one considers such transplants as being akin to organ transplants;[11] yet, if one follows the original definition of a transplant which is to 'lift and reset a plant in another soil',[12] a greater degree of change may be implied given that a plant may well develop differently in a foreign climate, soil, etc.[13]

Nevertheless, some argue that words may be preferable which, contrary to words such as 'transplant' or 'export', also capture situations where law has travelled in an 'unplanned or even accidental fashion'.[14] For example, this would suggest words such as legal 'influence', 'inspiration', 'cross-fertilisation', 'circulation', 'diffusion', 'irritation', or 'contamination'. The final two of these words, however, face the challenge that they imply an, a priori, negative normative assessment. By contrast, words such as 'influence' or 'diffusion' would be more inclusive and neutral. Like other terms, such as 'migration' and 'transfer', they may also have the advantage of not assuming that legal transplants are 'socially easy'.[15] However, the broadness of many of these more inclusive terms can be a problem. They may be overinclusive as almost all social phenomena are somehow related to each other. Moreover, any bibliometric search of terms such as 'legal influence' or 'legal transfer' would lead to many hits that capture other phenomena, notably certain forms of 'influence' and 'transfer' on whatever topic that are not 'illegal' (say, referring to a legal transfer of property as opposed to an illegal one, such as the transfer of a stolen item).

[11] H Patrick Glenn, 'On the Use of Biological Metaphors in Law: The Case of Legal Transplants' (2006) 1 *The Journal of Comparative Law* 358, 362.

[12] https://www.merriam-webster.com/dictionary/transplant accessed 22 October 2025.

[13] For a similar argument see TT Arvind, 'The "Transplant Effect" in Harmonization' (2010) 59 *International & Comparative Law Quarterly* 65, 66 ('Much as winemakers claim that a grape variety transplanted outside its native *terroir* produces a different wine notwithstanding that it remains the same plant, a transplanted law often functions in a different way in its new home.'). More sceptical about this 'horticultural metaphor': Gary Watt, 'Comparison as Deep Appreciation' in Pier Giuseppe Monateri (ed), *Methods of Comparative Law* (Cheltenham: Edward Elgar, 2012) 82, 91–6. For situations with changes to both legal and horticultural titles: Matteo Nicolini, 'Horticultural Titles: Seeds, Gardens, and English Law in Seventeenth-century Virginia Plantations' (2025) *Law and Humanities*, https://doi.org/10.1080/17521483.2025.2566558.

[14] Mathias Reimann, 'Comparative Law, An Overview of the Discipline' in Konrad Zweigert and Ulrich Drobnig (eds), *International Encyclopedia of Comparative Law, Volume II: Chapter 4* (Leiden: Brill, 2020) para 4-347; also Nelken (n 10) (2001), 276 and 281 (distinguishing between mechanical, organic, and discursive metaphors).

[15] Günter Frankenberg, 'Constitutions as Commodities: Notes on a Theory of Transfer' in Günter Frankenberg (ed), *Order From Transfer: Comparative Constitutional Design and Legal Culture* (Cheltenham: Edward Elgar, 2013) 8.

Some works also discuss whether certain terms may have an 'exporter' or 'importer' bias. For example, it is said that 'diffusion' is too focussed on the origin country (or the donor or exporter), which is misleading for situations where ideas do not spread from a single source or centre.[16] By contrast, terms such as 'borrowing' and 'reception' refer to an active position of the transplant country (or the recipient or importer). Yet, such an active position is not always present as scholarship also refers to 'imposed transplants'.[17] But then, terms which refer to neither of the two units, such as 'migration', may also be problematic as they may imply that 'legal elements cross boundaries on their own'.[18] Thus, again, there is no term that is without its shortcomings.

Finally, in languages other than English, some authors distinguish between terms, for example, using variants of the term 'transplant' as referring to the copying of specific legal norms, as distinguished from more general influence.[19] However, authors from different countries (and/or different languages) also have different general preferences. These have been explored in a separate journal article, which provides the following summary: in French, the dominant concept is *transfert de droit*, but *circulation de droit* and *acculturation juridique* are also frequently utilised.[20] In the German and Turkish literature, translations of the term reception, namely *Rezeption* and *hukuk resepsiyonu*, are used in the majority of contributions. In the Italian literature, the term *circolazione* is the most frequently used concept, with *trapianto* also regularly employed. In the Polish and Spanish language literature, translations of 'legal transplants'—'*transplanty prawne*' and '*przeszczepy prawne*' in Polish and '*trasplante jurídico*' and '*trasplante legal*' in Spanish—are most widely used.[21] This article also shows that the use of a particular term is sometimes related to the respective substantive analysis: for example, the term 'reception' is likely to be used by recipients of transplants, which matches its use in Turkey, while

[16] Esin Örücü, 'A Synthetic and Hyphenated Legal System: The Turkish Experience' (2006) 1 *The Journal of Comparative Law* 261, 264 (thus, 'to talk of "infusion of law" would be more apt in this case').

[17] Margit Cohn, 'Legal Transplant Chronicles: The Evolution of Unreasonableness and Proportionality Review of the Administration in the United Kingdom' (2010) 58 *American Journal of Comparative Law* 583, 591. See also Chapter 3 at Section D 1.

[18] Reimann (n 14).

[19] Eg, in Polish: Tomasz Czech, *Konsorcjum kredytowe* (Warsaw: LexisNexis, 2011) section 1.1; in Finnish: Heikki ES Mattila, 'Reseptio, Resipiointi, Omaksuminen' (*The Helsinki Term Bank for the Arts and Sciences*, 2015), available at https://tieteentermipankki.fi/wiki/Oikeustiede:reseptio accessed 22 October 2025; Tuula Linna, 'Transplantti—metafora, mutta mistä?' (2010) 5 *Lakimies* 835.

[20] See also the themes of the XIIIth Congress of Comparative Law, held in Montreal in 1990 on 'Circulation des modèles juridiques' and the XVIIIth Congress of Comparative Law in 2010, held in Washington, DC on 'Legal Culture and Legal Transplants', translated as 'La culture juridique et l'acculturation du droit'.

[21] Dominik Dworniczak and others, 'The Notion of Legal Transplants Beyond the Anglosphere: Decentring the Debate' (2025) 16 *Transnational Legal Theory* 357, 368–9.

'transfer' is a term related to the donor and correlated with the use of this term in France.[22]

As this book is written in English, it follows the bibliometric findings of Chapter 2, which show that the term 'legal transplant' has won the day in Anglophone legal scholarship.[23] Such a pragmatic approach can also refer to the observation that, in any case, metaphors are 'by their very nature [. . .] neither true nor false, only more or less useful'.[24] Indeed, it may be said that, whatever skewed connotations the term legal transplant may have, today's literature simply uses it in a generic manner. In other words, we may have a case where a metaphor has reached the stage of becoming a concept.[25] The examples of the next subsection also aim to show that it is possible to understand the term 'legal transplant' in a wide manner.

2. Motivational examples

In the literature, it is rightly said that starting a discussion of legal transplants with a 'bottom-up view' is preferred to the use of a 'grand transplant theory'.[26] In this subsection, five examples aim to illustrate that a range of topics and subtopics can be part of a modern canon of legal transplants. In doing so, this subsection also aims to preview some main points of discussion that feature in this book. The choice of the five examples follows key streams of the literature on legal transplants and related concepts. Thus, this choice should not be read as implying that other cases may not also be important, or even more important, when it comes to particular aspects of legal transplants, as indeed many further examples will follow in the subsequent chapters of this book.

First, 'German law in Japan' is largely a product of the transplantation of the German codes on criminal law, criminal procedure, civil law, civil procedure, commercial law, and bankruptcy law at the turn of the twentieth century.[27] It

[22] ibid, 374–5.

[23] See Chapter 2 at Section C.

[24] Nelken (n 10) (2001), 274.

[25] For this point see Nicholas Onuf, 'Polemics: Fitting Metaphors—The Case of the European Union' (2010) 18 *Perspectives* 63, 65 ('metaphors are concepts in the making'; 'concepts are generalized, conventionalized and naturalized metaphors').

[26] For these terms: Mathias W Reimann, 'A Bottom-up View of Legal Transplants' (review of Jens Drolshammer & Rolf Weber, *Wie das Recht auf Reisen geht* (Bern: Stämpfli, 2019))' (2020) 68 *American Journal of Comparative Law* 689; Nursel Atar, 'The Impossibility of a Grand Transplant Theory' (2019) 4 *Ankara Law Review* 177. See also Michele Graziadei, 'Comparative Law as the Study of Transplants and Receptions' in Mathias Reimann and Reinhard Zimmermann (eds), *The Oxford Handbook of Comparative Law* (Oxford: OUP, 2nd edn, 2019) 442, 445–54 (starting with 'classical cases').

[27] For a list of the precise laws see J Mark Ramseyer, 'Mixing-and-Matching Across (Legal) Family Lines' (2009) *BYU Law Review* 1701, 1709–10.

is fairly uncontroversial to call this case a 'legal transplant', and it is also frequently mentioned by contemporary authors writing about other cases where countries had the aim to 'modernise' their laws.[28] This example also illustrates some of the complicating factors which are indeed typical for many legal transplants. Japan did not simply translate and copy the German codes but made some adjustments, taking into account laws of other countries (eg, France), while subsequent developments have led to further modifications, notably with profound US influence after the Second World War.[29] It has also sometimes been doubted whether the imported law is really effective (eg, given low rates of litigation in Japan); yet, it is clear that the contemporary Japanese legal system is not merely a 'façade of Western law'.[30] Finally, while the Japanese case is typically portrayed as a voluntary legal transplant, it followed the pressure by Western powers to reopen Japan to international commerce;[31] thus, as we will also see in other examples, both voluntary and involuntary factors often interact.

Second, 'English (or British) law in India' was imposed on the local population in various stages: initially by the British East India Company followed by more centralised control, in particular after the direct rule from 1858 to 1947 (the 'British Raj').[32] For such cases, some authors prefer terms such as 'imposition'; yet, the majority view accepts that there can also be 'involuntary legal transplants'.[33] In substance, the transplantation of English law to India was wide-ranging as it concerned not only specific legal rules but also the establishment of courts and other state institutions. This does not mean that the transplanted law was left unchanged: for example, as a means to facilitate the transplant process, in India and other British colonies, the case law was often codified.[34] After the end of British colonialism, the Indian legal culture

[28] This will be discussed elsewhere in this book in further detail, eg, Chapters 4 at Section B 2, Chapter 5 at Section C 4 (b), and Chapter 6 at Section B 1.

[29] See eg Ramseyer (n 27); R Daniel Kelemen and Eric C Sibbitt, 'The Americanization of Japanese Law' (2002) 23 *University of Pennsylvania Journal of International Law* 269. In addition, George Mousourakis, *Traversing Legal Traditions: Perspectives on Comparative Law and Legal History* (Cham: Springer, 2nd edn, 2025) 328–38 refers to the prior reception of Chinese law.

[30] As stated by Henry W Ehrmann, *Comparative Legal Cultures* (Englewood Cliffs, NJ: Prentice Hall 1976) 47. For a discussion of the litigation rate in Japan see Mathias Siems, *Comparative Law* (Cambridge: CUP, 3rd edn, 2022) 188–90.

[31] For references to this history see Luke Nottage, 'Development of Comparative Law in Japan' in Mathias Reimann and Reinhard Zimmermann (eds), *The Oxford Handbook of Comparative Law* (Oxford: OUP, 2nd edn, 2019) 201, 202–3.

[32] See eg Jean-Louis Halpérin, 'Western Legal Transplants and India' (2010) 2 *Jindal Global Law Review* 14; Ronald J Daniels, Michael J Trebilcock, and Lindsey D Carson, 'The Legacy of Empire: The Common Law Inheritance and Commitments to Legality in Former British Colonies' (2011) 59 *American Journal of Comparative Law* 111 (comparing eight former colonies).

[33] For details see Chapter 3 at Section C 1.

[34] See eg Werner Menski, *Comparative Law in a Global Context* (Cambridge: CUP, 2nd edn, 2006) 242, 464.

has retained close ties with English legal culture, in particular in its case law and also due to the retention of the English language as the main language of Indian courts.[35] The majority of comparative lawyers have therefore no hesitation calling India today a 'common law country', while a minority view points towards the lasting influence of local and religious laws.[36]

Third, 'foreign case law in the Constitutional Court of South Africa' is used here as an example of cross-border judicial dialogue as a legal transplant. Some of the literature does not speak about legal transplants in such cases but rather emphasises that courts 'merely' consider foreign judgments as akin to other non-binding sources of inspiration.[37] In the South African case, we have the rare situation that the 1996 Constitution itself specifies that the court 'may consider foreign law' when interpreting human rights.[38] In practice, this happens frequently, often with references to legal rules and case law from both civil and common law countries (as well as international law, if applicable);[39] in contrast to the previous two examples, there is also some exchange of ideas among countries of the Global South.[40] While it is thus permissible that the South African Constitutional Court considers foreign case law, there have also been cases where its justices rejected the relevance of foreign precedent.[41] In other countries, notably in the US, it is even more controversial whether courts should make use of judicial legal transplants;[42] thus, this case also serves as

[35] For the decision to retain the common law see Marc Galanter, 'The Aborted Restoration of "Indigenous" Law in India' (1972) 14 *Comparative Studies in Society and History* 53. For the case law see KG Balakrishnan, 'The Role of Foreign Precedents in a Country's Legal System' (2010) 22 *National Law School of India Review* 1. See also H Patrick Glenn, *Legal Traditions of the World* (Oxford: OUP, 5th edn, 2014) 312–13 (for interaction between case law and Hindu law).

[36] For the minority view see Menski (n 34) 203; also MP Singh and Niraj Kumar, *Indian Legal System: An Enquiry* (New Delhi: OUP, 2019) xxix–xxx (stating that some features are from the common law but others 'closely resemble other legal families, such as the codes and general impetus to codify (as in the case in the civil law system), customary legal systems based on Hindu and Islamic law, and the presence of state-acknowledged systems of tribal law'). For mainstream classifications of legal families see eg Siems (n 30) 82–109.

[37] Explicitly: Andrew Novak, *Transnational Human Rights Litigation: Challenging the Death Penalty and Criminalization of Homosexuality in the Commonwealth* (Cham: Springer, 2019) 123.

[38] Section 39(1)(c) of the Constitution of the Republic of South Africa 1996. For other countries see the references in note 90 of Chapter 7.

[39] See eg Jacob Foster, 'The Use of Foreign Law in Constitutional Interpretation: Lessons from South Africa' (2010) 45 *University of San Francisco Law Review* 79; Christa Rautenbach and Lourens du Plessis, 'In the Name of Comparative Constitutional Jurisprudence: The Consideration of German Precedents by South African Constitutional Court Judges' (2013) 14 *German Law Journal* 1539; Christopher Roberts, *Foreign Law? Congress v. the Supreme Court* (El Paso: LFB Scholarly Publishing LLC, 2014) 150–62.

[40] For examples of successful global judicial dialogue challenging the death penalty and the criminalisation of homosexuality in Commonwealth countries see Novak (n 37).

[41] See the discussion in Gábor Halmai, 'The Use of Foreign Law in Constitutional Interpretation' in Michel Rosenfeld and András Sajó (eds), *The Oxford Handbook of Comparative Constitutional Law* (Oxford: OUP, 2012) 1328, 1345–6.

[42] The US Supreme Court is divided on whether to refer to foreign case law in the interpretation of the US Constitution: see eg *Roper v Simmons* 125 SCt 1183 (2005); *Lawrence v Texas* 123 SCt 2472

an example of the more general debate of whether or not transplants should take place.

Fourth, 'EU-modelled regional courts in Latin America' are used here as an example that has not only been discussed by legal scholarship but also relates to the literature in political science and international relations on regional policy diffusion. Moreover, it serves as an illustration of the growing field of legal transplants at the levels of regional, transnational, and international law.[43] In the present case, the influence of the model of the Court of Justice of the EU on the Andean Tribunal of Justice has been contrasted with the diffusion of 'softer' forms of dispute resolution (eg, the WTO system).[44] In this example, it is uncontroversial that the EU served as a model, and this is also the case for the general design (not all details) of the Andean Community and other regional organisations in Latin America and elsewhere.[45] Since regional co-operation is largely a deliberate act, it also raises the question of whether legal transplants should be used in the design of regional structures—or, more generally, how transplants relate to the field of legislative drafting.[46] At the same time, the apparent use of the EU as a model raises the issue, also more generally, of whether both the debate and the use of legal transplants have a 'Eurocentric bias'.[47]

Fifth, the example of 'anti-smoking policies in US cities/states' derives from studies in political science. This research, published in articles from the mid-2000s, found, for instance, some competition among proximate cities, imitation of larger cities, and a snowball effect of local policy adoptions to the state

(2003); *Foster v Florida* 537 US 990 (2002); *Atkins v Virginia* 536 US 304 (2002). In other countries, many senior judges have, in principle, endorsed the possibility of considering arguments from foreign case law, see references in Siems (n 30) 113–14.

[43] This also connects to the growing field of 'comparative international law', ie attempts to find connection and synergies between comparative law and international law; see generally Mathias Siems, 'Comparative International Law: State of the Art' in Robert Schütze and Mathias Siems (eds), *Comparative International Law: Foundations and Critique* (Oxford: Hart Publishing, 2026) 3.

[44] Karen J Alter and Laurence R Helfer, *Transplanting International Courts: The Law and Politics of the Andean Tribunal of Justice* (Oxford: OUP, 2017). See also Karen J Alter, 'The Global Spread of European Style International Courts' (2012) 35 *West European Politics* 135 (identifying eleven functioning copies of the ECJ).

[45] See eg Tobias Lenz, *Interorganizational Diffusion in International Relations: Regional Institutions and the Role of the European Union* (Oxford: OUP, 2021); Thomas Risse, 'The Diffusion of Regionalism' in Tanja A Börzel and Thomas Risse (eds), *The Oxford Handbook of Comparative Regionalism* (Oxford: OUP, 2016) 87; Mario Telò, Louise Fawcett, and Frederik Ponjaert (eds), *Interregionalism and the European Union: A Post-Revisionist Approach to Europe's Place in a Changing World* (Farnham: Ashgate, 2015); Philippe De Lombaerde and Michael Schulz (eds), *The EU and World Regionalism: The Makability of Regions in the 21st Century* (Farnham: Ashgate, 2009).

[46] Tobias Lenz and Gary Marks, 'Regional Institutional Design' in Tanja A Börzel and Thomas Risse (eds), *The Oxford Handbook of Comparative Regionalism* (Oxford: OUP, 2016) 513 as well as Chapter 7.

[47] Frequently discussed in comparative law: see Siems (n 30) 96, 132, 163, and 327. For literature on the possible model role of the EU see n 208 of Chapter 4.

level.[48] Here too, its inclusion within the research on legal transplants can offer some new perspectives. To start with, it is interesting to note that this research deals with units below the country level as well as transplants between units from different levels. Such forms of transplants are less commonly researched in legal scholarship; yet, they feature, for example, in political science and geography.[49] As these latter fields do not typically phrase their topics in legal terms, this research also offers an opportunity to reflect, for example, on the relationship between law and policy, and on the way law may also be created at a local (or informal, contractual, etc) level.[50] Finally, it is noteworthy that this line of research is often of a quantitative and causal nature. This is uncommon for traditional legal research on this topic, but this may well change if we assume a closer interaction with other social sciences.

C. Relationship to existing literature

Chapter 2 will present a bibliometric assessment of the way the term 'legal transplant' and related concepts have been used in the literature. The purpose of the present section is, therefore, not a general review of the literature on legal transplants. Rather, it has the more specific aims, first, to relate this book to other books on legal transplants (as well as related concepts) and, second, to provide an introduction to research from other academic disciplines considered in this book.

1. Books on legal transplants and related concepts

Many authors only cite the book by Alan Watson as a book specifically dedicated to legal transplants.[51] However, the research conducted for the purposes

[48] Charles R Shipan and Craig Volden, 'The Mechanisms of Policy Diffusion' (2008) 52 *American Journal of Political Science* 840; Charles R Shipan and Craig Volden, 'Bottom-up Federalism: The Diffusion of Antismoking Policies from U.S. Cities to States' (2006) 50 *American Journal of Political Science* 825; Fabrizio Gilardi, Charles R Shipan, and Bruno Wüest, 'Policy Diffusion: The Issue-Definition Stage' (2021) 56 *American Journal of Political Science* 21.

[49] In political science, the first key study on US states was Jack L Walker, 'The Diffusion of Innovations among the American States' (1969) 63 *The American Political Science Review* 880. In geography there is now a large field of urban policy mobilities, see Section C 2.

[50] See Chapter 3 at Section B 1.

[51] Eg Pier Giuseppe Monateri, *Advanced Introduction to Comparative Legal Methods* (Cheltenham: Edward Elgar, 2021) 91; Uwe Kischel, *Comparative Law* (Oxford: OUP, 2019) 143–4; Peter de Cruz, *Comparative Law in a Changing World* (London: Routledge Cavendish, 3rd edn, 2007) 510–13.

of this book found more than ninety books that have variations of the term 'legal transplant' or related concepts, such as 'legal borrowing', 'reception of law', or 'legal migration', in the title. The list of all of the titles is provided in Annex 1. This collection also includes books that use translated versions of these terms in other languages than English, notably in French, German, Italian, and Spanish. Publications in these other languages can be interesting as transplants may be discussed in different ways in different places. As found in another publication, many authors take examples from their own country's history as a starting point. For example, in the Spanish and French language literature, the cases of colonial transplants are often reflected in critical perspectives on legal transplants. By contrast, the German, Turkish, and Polish literature are typically more influenced by cases of voluntary transplants which are reviewed in a more technical nature, while the extensive Italian literature discusses transplants from various perspectives (doctrinal, historical, critical, etc), possibly due to comparative law being a mandatory subject for a law degree in Italy.[52] However, despite these variations, the following overview will show that, across countries, the vast majority of these more than ninety books have a focus on specific examples of legal transplants. Thus, beyond illustrating the many possible further examples of legal transplants, this section aims to show that there is not a comparable single-authored monograph published in English which addresses general questions of legal transplants.

A first group of existing books are best understood as specific case studies. Some of them focus on the present law of one country or other legal unit, namely, books on commercial law transplants in Vietnam, judicial reforms in Taiwan, the post-communist import of law by the Hungarian Constitutional Court, the influence of foreign human rights case law in the UK, transplants in Nepalese law, and—in the German literature—transplants in German corporate law, Mexican property law, and Thai constitutional law.[53] Further books focus on specific examples that go beyond one country or other unit. They deal with transplants in insolvency law and competition law in Asia, the transplantation of Muslim marriage in Western Courts, the mimetic evolution of the European Court of Justice, the movement of legal ideas as a contribution to Europeanisation, the Andean Tribunal of Justice as an example of transplants of international courts, the protection of the Himalayas through transplants of international law, as well as further topics in the German and Italian literature.[54] Other books

[52] For all these points see Dworniczak and others (n 21) 386–7.
[53] References in Annex 1, Category 1, also referring to two books published in Italian and Portuguese.
[54] References in Annex 1, Category 2.

are case studies of historical transplants, here often using the term 'reception'. These address British West Indian slavery laws as legal transplants, transplants in early twentieth-century China, transplants in Taiwan under Japanese colonial rule (1895–1945), the reception of Western law in Egypt (1875–1952), the nineteenth century interaction of transplants with local traditions in Hawaii, the reception of English commercial law in Malaysia, as well as a number of further topics in books published in German, Italian, and Turkish.[55] In this regard, it is also noteworthy that the book about the Malaysian transplant preceded Watson's book by a decade and that, in the German literature, the first book with the title 'Rezeption' goes back to the year 1905.[56]

Second, some books combine multiple case studies, for example, about transplants in various countries of a particular region, transplants in various countries in a particular area of law, transplants that all involve the same origin or transplant country, or particular transplanting institutions (eg, courts). The fact that there are multiple case studies means that these books sometimes include some general discussion about legal transplants. These books are generally written by one or two authors and deal, again, either with the present or the past. As regards books that mainly focus on the present law, we have books on transplants of corporate governance regimes to South Asia, the transplantation of EU law in CEE, abusive forms of constitutional borrowing, the judicial recourse to foreign law, the transplantation of problem-solving courts, and—in the French, German, and Italian literature—books on the international influence of French and Swiss law and transplants of US criminal law and criminal procedure in Europe.[57] In the historical variant, books deal with a comparison of transplants in the Ancient Roman and British Empires, the reception of English law abroad, as well as Watson's book, which despite its broad title, is mainly an analysis of the diffusion of Roman law.[58]

Another group of books of multiple case studies are edited collections. Some of them have fairly general titles, namely books on 'The Transfer of Institutions', 'Transfrontier Mobility of Law', 'Adapting Legal Cultures', 'Law and Development and the Global Discourses of Legal Transfers', 'Comparative Law in Legislative Drafting', 'The Diffusion of Law', and 'Comparisons in

[55] References in Annex 1, Category 3.
[56] For further historical discussion see Chapter 2 at Section B 1.
[57] References in Annex 1, Category 4.
[58] References in Annex 1, Category 5 (a) with (b) for translations of Watson's book.

Legal Development';[59] yet here too, if at all, only some of their chapters reflect on legal transplants or related concepts at a general level. Further edited books can again be divided into those that deal with today's law and historical cases. In the contemporary category, there are, for example, books on different aspects of legal transplants in constitutional law, private law transplants in Eastern Europe, imitation and innovation of legal education in Asia, and transplants in East Asia and Oceania;[60] historical books deal with the reception of continental ideas in common law countries (1820–1920), the reception of Roman law by Jews and other minorities in the Roman empire, and legal transfers in the British Empire.[61]

Third, a search for books on legal transplants at a general level produces fewer results.[62] There is no published book in English, but a valuable Czech PhD thesis written in English on the 'success in legal transplanting'.[63] Two published German PhD theses deal with, respectively, theoretical-methodological complexities of transplants and present an analysis of their typologies; thus, different from the Czech thesis, the main focus is here on the positive (non-normative) understanding of legal transplants. An edited Spanish-language book addresses the topic of legal theory and legal transplants. In this book, various authors discuss the Spanish-language publication of a doctorate thesis from Harvard on the reception of legal theories in Latin America; thus, in the edited Spanish-language book, there is also a strong focus on Latin America (and thus, it could also be classified as belonging to the second category above). As a final example, a French book on the reception of foreign private law as a phenomenon of legal sociology discusses many key aspects of legal transplants; yet, having been published in 1975, it does not consider Watson, nor the subsequent critiques by Legrand and other scholars.

Finally, the search for books on legal transplants or related legal concepts in the title produced some books that turned out to be written by authors from other disciplines, notably political science and history. These books deal with constitutional borrowings by Weimar Germany and the French Fifth Republic, the cross-border diffusion of health, family, and employment laws, the rule-of-law diffusion between the African Union and the Organization of American

[59] References in Annex 1, Category 6 (a) (some with more specific sub-titles). Similarly, the two books published in Italian and French, see (b) and (c).

[60] References in Annex 1, Category 7 (a). In addition, see ibid (b) to (d) for books published in German, Spanish, and French.

[61] References in Annex 1, Category 8 (a). See also ibid (b) for a German book on legal transfers in history.

[62] For references to the following books see Annex 1, Category 9.

[63] By contrast, unpublished PhD theses which deal with particular cases studies of transplants have not been included in Annex 1.

States, the reception of law in Frisia in the late Middle Ages, and the circulation of Islamic law across centuries.[64] Thus, similar to the books in the first and second categories above, these books are specific in their scope. They also point towards the possible benefits of considering research outside the field of legal scholarship.

2. Research in other academic disciplines

In an article on 'Social Science and Diffusion of Law', William Twining criticises Watson's research on legal transplants as 'generalisations [which] are not backed up by empirical evidence' while observing that 'almost all social science diffusion research has been empirical'.[65] Thus, Twining proposes to take a more interdisciplinary perspective, a view shared by other authors such as David Nelken and Günter Frankenberg.[66]

Indeed, it makes sense to consider a variety of other disciplines in deepening the understanding of legal transplants from both a positive and a normative perspective. A simple way to screen the possible interaction between research on legal transplants and related research from other fields is a Google Scholar search of journal articles from any academic discipline. This leads to a fairly diverse list of non-law journals that mention the term 'legal transplant(s)' with the fields most frequently represented being business and economics, sociology, political science, and history.[67] To be sure, this does not capture publications where other disciplines use their own terminology to refer to phenomena that legal scholars would call 'legal transplants'. In other words, it is also worth examining how concepts of other disciplines intersect with the notion of 'legal transplants'.

The closest 'siblings' to research on 'legal transplants' are the overlapping fields of 'policy transfer' and 'policy diffusion'. There are a number of books on these topics, some also with other terminologies such as policy circulation

[64] References in Annex 1, Category 10.

[65] William Twining, 'Social Science and Diffusion of Law' (2005) 32 *Journal of Law and Society* 203, 212 and 230.

[66] David Nelken, 'Towards a Sociology of Legal Adaptation' in David Nelken and Johannes Feest (eds), *Adapting Legal Culture* (Oxford: Hart Publishing, 2001) 7 (the book's goal was 'to bring together a range of international scholars with different disciplinary loyalties [. . .]'); Günter Frankenberg, 'Preface' in Günter Frankenberg (ed), *Order from Transfer: Comparative Constitutional Design and Legal Culture* (Cheltenham: Edward Elgar, 2013) xii, xiv (introducing the book as 'an interdisciplinary project').

[67] For details see Chapter 2 at Section D 2.

or lesson drawing.[68] However, key discussions have also been in journal articles. The main authors are: Richard Rose (publications since 1991) on policy learning; David Dolowitz and David Marsh (since 1996), Mark Evans (since 1999), and Diane Stone (since 1999) on policy transfer; as well as Beth Simmons (since 2004), Fabrizio Gilardi (since 2005), and Charles Shipan and Craig Volden (since 2006) on policy diffusion.[69] In a nutshell, the main difference is that 'policy transfer' is mainly about qualitative case studies with a particular focus on actors and processes, and 'policy diffusion' research is typically about quantitative studies aiming to understand patterns.[70]

Further literature can be found in related fields of policy research. For example, there are books with the titles 'institutional mimetism' and 'institutional transplantation'.[71] These books are similar to 'policy transfer'; yet, potentially, they have a wider scope as they also cover informal institutions. Another line of research, mainly from geography, examines policy mobilities and assemblages with a key interest in the way policies are locally modified.[72] By contrast,

[68] Osmany Porto de Oliveira (ed), *Handbook of Policy Transfer, Diffusion and Circulation* (Cheltenham: Edward Elgar, 2021); Tim Legrand, *The Architecture of Policy Transfer: Ideas, Institutions and Networks in Transnational Policymaking* (London: Palgrave, 2021); Laure Delcour and Elsa Tulmets (eds), *Policy Transfer and Norm Circulation: Towards an Interdisciplinary and Comparative Approach* (London: Routledge, 2019); Magdaléna Hadjiisky, Leslie A Pal, and Christopher Walker (eds), *Public Policy Transfer: Micro-Dynamics and Macro-Effects* (Cheltenham: Edward Elgar, 2017); Richard Rose, *Learning from Comparative Public Policy* (London: Routledge, 2005); Mark Evans (ed), *Policy Transfer in Global Perspective* (Aldershot: Ashgate, 2004); Richard Rose, *Lesson-Drawing in Public Policy: A Guide to Learning Across Time and Space* (Chatham: Chatham House, 1993).

[69] The years refer to the first of a series of publications by these authors, namely: Rose (n 68); David Dolowitz and David Marsh, 'Who Learns What from Whom: a Review of the Policy Transfer Literature' (1996) 44 *Political Studies* 343; Mark Evans and Jonathan Davies, 'Understanding Policy Transfer: A Multi-Level, Multi-Disciplinary Perspective' (1999) 77 *Public Administration* 235; Diane Stone, 'Learning Lessons and Transferring Policy across Time, Space and Disciplines' (1999) 19 *Politics* 51; Beth A Simmons and Zachary Elkins, 'The Globalization of Liberalization: Policy Diffusion in the International Political Economy' (2004) 98 *American Political Science Review* 171; Fabrizio Gilardi, 'The Institutional Foundations of Regulatory Capitalism: the Diffusion of Independent Regulatory Agencies in Western Europe' (2005) 598 *The Annals of the American Academy of Political and Social Science* 84; Charles R Shipan and Craig Volden, 'Bottom-up Federalism: The Diffusion of Antismoking Policies from U.S. Cities to States' (2006) 50 *American Journal of Political Science* 825.

[70] See David Marsh and Jason C Sharman, 'Policy Diffusion and Policy Transfer' (2009) 30 *Policy Studies* 269 (also encouraging closer interaction between these fields). But see also the qualitative study by Kurt Weyland, *Bounded Rationality and Policy Diffusion: Social Sector Reform in Latin America* (Princeton, NJ: Princeton University Press, 2006).

[71] Yves Mény (ed), *Les politiques de mimétisme institutionnel: La greffe et le rejet* (Paris: L'Harmattan, 1993); Mamadou Dia, *Africa's Management in the 1990s and Beyond: Reconciling Indigenous and Transplanted Institutions* (Washington, DC: World Bank, 1996); Willem Martin de Jong, *Institutional Transplantation: How to Adopt Good Transport Infrastructure Decisionmaking Ideas from Other Countries?* (Delft: Eburon, 1999); Martin de Jong, Konstantinos Lalenis, and Virginie Mamadouh (eds), *The Theory and Practice of Institutional Transplantation: Experiences with the Transfer of Policy Institutions* (Deventer: Kluwer Academic Publishers, 2002).

[72] Eg, Eugene McCann and Kevin Ward, 'Policy Assemblages, Mobilities and Mutations: Toward a Multidisciplinary Conversation' (2012) 10 *Political Studies Review* 325; Jamie Peck, 'Geographies of Policy: From Transfer-Diffusion to Mobility-Mutation' (2011) 35 *Progress in Human Geography* 773.

international relations, global policy analysis, and European studies often address at the 'macro-level' how states interact with each other, as well as international and regional organisations, with the potential of policy transfers beyond their borders.[73]

Related research can also be found in cultural studies, anthropology, and sociology. Here, the debate is often framed in what has been known as 'Galton's problem'. It derives from a disagreement between Sir Edward Tylor and Francis Galton at an event in 1888: Tylor presented his anthropological research in order to show deep commonalities between cultures, but Galton objected that these similarities could equally be due to cross-cultural borrowing.[74] At a similar point in time, the French sociologist Gabriel Tarde published a book, which, in the English translation, is called the 'laws of imitation', both addressing the imitating behaviour of individuals and society at large.[75] Further key publications occurred in the second part of the twentieth century: Everett Rogers' book on the 'diffusion of innovations', originally published in 1962, aimed to develop general insights into the emergence and diffusions of new technologies;[76] an influential 1983 article by Paul DiMaggio and Walter Powell used the term of 'institutional isomorphism' to analyse why organisations tend to become more and more similar;[77] and, in 1990, an article by Pierre Bourdieu reflected on the international circulation of ideas and their reinterpretation in the host country.[78]

Historical research is relevant for legal transplants as many of its case studies are about historical events (see the previous subsection) and thus often require a deep historical understanding of the phenomena in question. Moreover, there are growing lines of research on 'entangled history' and 'transnational history' which cover phenomena that may overlap with legal transplants.[79] For

[73] See Legrand (n 68) 5–7; Hadjiisky and others, 'Introduction: traversing the terrain of policy transfer: theory, methods and overview' in Hadjiisky (n 68) 3–4, 8–13.

[74] Edward B Tylor, 'On a Method of Investigating the Development of Institutions; Applied to Laws of Marriage and Descent' (1889) 18 *The Journal of the Anthropological Institute of Great Britain and Ireland* 245 (with Galton's objection at 268). See also Raoul Naroll, 'Galton's Problem: The Logic of Cross Cultural Analysis' (1965) 32 *Social Research* 428.

[75] Gabriel Tarde, *Les lois de l'imitation* (Paris: Félix Alcan, 1890), translated as Gabriel Tarde, *The Laws of Imitation* (New York: Henry Holt and Company, 1903).

[76] Everett M Rogers, *Diffusion of Innovations* (New York: Free Press of Glencoe, 1962; 5th edn, 2003).

[77] Paul J DiMaggio and Walter W Powell, 'The Iron Cage Revisited: Institutional Isomorphism and Collective Rationality in Organizational Fields' (1983) 48 *American Sociological Review* 147.

[78] As republished in Pierre Bourdieu, 'Les conditions sociales de la circulation internationale des idées' (2002) 145 *Actes de la recherche en sciences* 3.

[79] See eg Michael Werner and Bénédicte Zimmermann, 'Beyond Comparison: Histoire Croisée and the Challenge of Reflexivity' (2006) 45 *History and Theory* 30; Pierre-Yves Saunier, *Transnational History* (London: Red Globe Press, 2013). The former has its origins in the historical research on 'cultural transfer', notably Michel Espagne and Michael Werner (eds), *Transferts. Les relations interculturelles dans l'espace franco-allemand (XVIIIe et XIXe siècle)* (Paris: Editions Recherche sur les

deep research into specific phenomena, it has also been suggested that scholarship should cross 'the divide between area studies scholarship and comparative legal studies'.[80] Indeed, as area studies are interdisciplinary in nature, it is bound to include legal phenomena which legal scholars would call 'legal transplants'.

Linguistics and psychology are particularly suitable for research that aims to understand the nuances of the transplant process. As law is typically phrased in words, it is clear that legal transplants often face the challenge that the words of the new law may distort the original meaning;[81] yet, comparative linguistics may also be used to show how languages interact in more or less complex ways.[82] Psychology is said to help with 'fundamental clarifications about cognition, imitation, improvisation, emulation, adaptative learning' (etc) in understanding cultural and legal diffusion.[83] It can also provide insights at the 'micro-level' into when and how individuals learn from others in a social context.[84]

Finally, research from a variety of fields can contribute to the question of whether or not legal transplants should be used. On the empirical side, some economic research identifies laws that help countries economically and may thus justify transplanting these rules.[85] Development studies may address similar questions; yet, here, the emphasis is often on aims other than economic growth, particularly in contemporary research.[86] A further related discipline is post-colonial studies, in particular if one aims to identify cases where transplants should not happen due to continuing power imbalances between countries from the Global North and Global South.[87] Another perspective can

civilisations, 1988). Another term used is that of 'cultural mobility', Stephen Greenblatt (ed), *Cultural Mobility: A Manifesto* (Cambridge: CUP, 2010).

[80] Michael Ng, *Legal Transplantation in Early Twentieth-Century China: Practicing Law in Republican Beijing (1910s-1930s)* (London: Routledge, 2014) 117–18.

[81] For example, this has been argued about the Japanese constitution: see Kyoko Inoue, *MacArthur's Japanese Constitution* (Chicago, IL: University of Chicago Press, 1991).

[82] See William Labov, 'Transmission and Diffusion' (2007) 83 *Language* 344; also Heikki E Mattila, *Comparative Legal Linguistics* (Farnham: Ashgate, 2nd edn, 2013) 17, 147–51, 357–59 (on interaction between legal languages).

[83] Graziadei (n 26) 458.

[84] The classical work is Albert Bandura, *Social Foundations of Thought and Action: A Social Cognitive Theory* (Englewood Cliffs, NJ: Prentice Hall, 1986).

[85] See eg Katharina Pistor, Martin Raiser, and Stanislaw Gelfer, 'Law and Finance in Transition Economies' (2000) 8 *Economics of Transition* 325.

[86] See eg Emil Dauncey, Vandana Desai, and Robert B Potter (eds), *The Companion to Development Studies* (London: Routledge, 4th edn, 2024) (with chapters on development as freedom, culture, development ethics, civil society, environmental interests, social movements, etc).

[87] See eg Judith Schacherreiter, 'Postcolonial Theory and Comparative Law: On the Methodological and Epistemological Benefits to Comparative Law through Postcolonial Theory' (2016) 49 *Verfassung und Recht in Übersee* 291.

be offered by ethics and moral philosophy as it may identify 'good rules' that are worth transplanting.[88] For practical issues, research on legislative drafting can be helpful if the decision to transplant a particular rule needs to be implemented in a way that works well in the transplant country.[89]

In sum, all of these lines of research show that research from other fields than law should play a key role in any discussion about legal transplants. Thus, in this book, such research features in all of its chapters as it aims to integrate it into the key discussions about legal transplants (rather than providing separate chapters dedicated to particular disciplines).

D. Outline of chapters

This book deals with legal transplants at different levels of analysis: descriptive, explanatory, and prescriptive.[90] Thus, it has a both a positive and a normative dimension with chapters 2 to 5 being mainly interested in the positive side of the argument, and chapters 6 to 9 moving to the normative one.[91] This analysis incorporates the literature on legal transplants but also considers that the topic of legal transplants connects to discussions in other academic fields such as political science, economics, sociology, and history. Thus, while this book is partly a book about the state of the art of this literature, each of its chapters also provides its distinct contributions to this debate.

Chapter 2 is entitled 'A Bibliometric Assessment of the Use of the Term "Legal Transplants"'. It aims to assess whether certain assumptions about the use of this term hold up to a bibliometric assessment. It does so by showing time-series on the evolution of this and related terms. Furthermore, the combined use of the term with certain keywords presents an evaluation of the substantive orientation of the literature. It finds that the term 'legal transplants' is more and more frequently used in the literature, today often disregarding Watson's narrow position. It also shows a broadening of the literature on legal transplants, for example its connection with topics of international law and interdisciplinary perspectives. Finally, the chapter observes, however, that

[88] Notwithstanding its limits: see eg Mark Osiel, *The Right to Do Wrong: Morality and the Limits of Law* (Cambridge, MA: Harvard University Press, 2019).

[89] See eg Nicola Lupo and Lucia Scaffardi (eds), *Comparative Law in Legislative Drafting: The Increasing Importance of Dialogue Amongst Parliaments* (The Hague: Eleven, 2014).

[90] For a similar approach see Mark Evans, 'Understanding Policy Transfer' in Mark Evans (ed), *Policy Transfer in Global Perspective* (Aldershot: Ashgate, 2004) 10, 13 ('description—how policy transfer is made; explanation—why policy transfer occurs; prescription—how policy transfer should be made').

[91] This does not imply that there is a strict 'is/ought' divide, see Chapter 6 at Section C 1 (b).

most of the current literature on legal transplants and policy diffusion/transfer does not consider the respective other line of research.

Chapter 3 presents 'An Anatomy of Legal Transplants' that goes beyond the motivational examples of the present chapter. This anatomy has the main categories 'object of the transplant', 'relevant units', and 'transplantation' and uses them to identify the interactions between the origin and transplant unit (thus, aiming to avoid either an 'exporter' or an 'importer' bias, noted in the present chapter). This chapter shows that legal transplants capture a variety of phenomena. Thus, the approach adopted in this book is different from that which regards the term 'legal transplant' as narrowly referring to the copying of near-identical codified rules only. Overall, the chapter concludes that the concept of legal transplants is practically useful given its high degree of openness and flexibility.

Chapter 4 asks the question 'Why Do Legal Transplants Take Place?'. It distinguishes between the classical debate about the motivations for legal transplants and the 'causes of causes' leading to legal transplants. The presentation of 'causes of causes' uses flow charts in order to illustrate and discuss the complexity of the causal network. This shows that legal transplants take place due to a variety of reasons, some deliberate ones, but also due to other causal factors (in particular, noting the role of agents). On a positive note, the chapter concludes that there is a trend towards voluntary transplants, often following a reasonable evaluation of the advantages and disadvantages of the transplanted law.

Chapter 5 addresses the question 'Do Legal Transplants "Work"?'. The debate on this topic is often portrayed in a binary way as a disagreement between optimists and pessimists. Yet, it is more plausible to generally agree with the intermediate position that much depends on the way transplants are adjusted to fit in their host environment. Specifically, this chapter presents three ways transplants may or may not work, namely according to the categories 'knowledge and understanding of the law', 'compliance and enforcement', and 'desired societal influence'. Examining these aspects in detail, it is also the aim of this chapter to show the circumstances that determine 'how' transplants work. It concludes that legal transplants generally 'work', in particular if they are modified in a smart manner.

In Chapter 6, this book turns to the normative question 'Is it Desirable to Use Legal Transplants?'. It explains that some authors express general tendencies on whether transplants should take place. However, in order to provide a more valid assessment of transplants, it is preferable to consider the law and circumstances of each case. For this purpose, the chapter notes that 'is' and 'ought' arguments are often closely entangled. On this basis, it evaluates the criteria of legitimate interest, suitability of the transplant, principled objection, and balancing. Overall, the chapter concludes that often the desirability of legal transplants can be affirmed and thus lawmakers should be open to their use.

This leads to the question of Chapter 7 'How Should the Design of Transplants be Pursued?'. This chapter reviews the literature that has suggested various steps and categories in answering this question. It also provides its own suggestions on the way the search and design of legal transplants should be pursued. Specifically, the chapter provides twelve recommendations which can be applied to many cases of legal transplants. Overall, this chapter notes that, while the 'foreignness' of a transplanted law can increase the risk of failure, if done intelligently, the experience of the transplant in the origin unit can reduce any risks that the enactment of the new law entails.

Chapter 8 summarises the contribution other disciplines than law can, and should, make to the literature on legal transplants. It also reiterates the main substantive argument of a case for legal transplants and what this may mean for future research and practice.

2

A Bibliometric Assessment of the Use of the Term 'Legal Transplants'

A. Introduction

What should be the historical starting point for an analysis of the literature on legal transplants? It is often said that legal transplants have a long history. For example, the Babylonian Code of Hammurabi of the seventeenth century BC is revealed to display strong Sumerian influences,[1] Aristotle referred to comparative constitution-making of the city-states of Ancient Greece,[2] Roman law is said to have been a multicultural product of African, Semitic, and Mediterranean civilisations,[3] and Islamic law has its roots in Roman, Persian, Byzantine, Talmudic, and customary Arab law.[4] Thus, it seems right to say that 'every legal system contains imported elements'[5] and that law's evolution 'has always been externally influenced'.[6]

Yet, the actual debate about legal transplants is often seen as a phenomenon of the last fifty years only. For example, it is claimed that Alan Watson 'gained world fame with his book *Legal Transplants: An Approach to Comparative Law*, as the inventor of the term and concept of legal transplants which became omnipresent in legal literature until today',[7] and that the 'technical concept itself of a "legal transplant" was proposed by the Scottish/American comparatist,

[1] Ernst Levy, 'The Reception of Highly Developed Legal Systems by Peoples of Different Cultures' (1950) 25 *Washington Law Review* 233.

[2] Mark Evans, 'Introduction: Is Policy Transfer Rational Policy-making?' in Mark Evans (ed), *Policy Transfer in Global Perspective* (Aldershot: Ashgate, 2004) 1.

[3] Pier Giuseppe Monateri, 'Black Gaius: A Quest for the Multicultural Origins of the "Western Legal Tradition"' (1999) 50 *Hastings Law Journal* 1.

[4] Khaled Abou El Fadl, 'The Islamic Legal Tradition' in Mauro Bussani and Ugo Mattei (eds), *The Cambridge Companion to Comparative Law* (Cambridge: CUP, 2012) 295.

[5] Ugo Mattei, Teemu Ruskola, and Antonio Gidi, *Schlesinger's Comparative Law* (New York: Foundation Press, 7th edn, 2009) 240.

[6] Margit Cohn, 'Legal Transplant Chronicles: The Evolution of Unreasonableness and Proportionality Review of the Administration in the United Kingdom' (2010) 58 *American Journal of Comparative Law* 583, 628.

[7] Sima Avramović, 'In Memoriam Alan Watson (1933–2018)' (2018) *Annals of the Faculty of Law in Belgrade International Edition* 177, 178.

Legal Transplants. Mathias Siems, Oxford University Press. © Mathias Siems 2026.
DOI: 10.1093/9780191991981.003.0002

Alan Watson, who is the founder and best-known representative of this intellectual movement'.[8] However, some authors also express some doubts about the relevance of the debate on 'legal transplants' today. While the penultimate sentence included the words that they are 'omnipresent in legal literature until today', another article suggests that the 'interest in the topic seems to have waned, perhaps because, for the time being, it seems that there is little left to be said'.[9]

Thus, this raises a number of questions which are of key relevance to the following chapters of this book: how important is the topic of legal transplant today, and how does it relate to the popularity of related concepts such as policy transfer and policy diffusion? How much is this research due to Watson's influence and, more specifically, is it the case that today's research goes beyond Watson's approach in discussing transplants across the legal field and with connections to research of other disciplines?

This chapter presents a bibliometric assessment of these and related questions. To set the scene, Section B provides an overview of the origins of the terms 'legal transplants' and related concepts. Subsequently, Section C displays and discusses the findings on the evolution of the use of these terms across time, and Section D does so for their substantive use.[10] Section F concludes.

B. The origins of the term 'legal transplants' and related concepts

1. Alan Watson, his contemporaries, and predecessors

Alan Watson's book on Legal Transplants was published in the first edition in 1974.[11] The main text was unchanged in the second edition, published in 1993, though it includes an eleven-page afterword.[12] In the original preface, Watson states that the 1974 book derived from a seminar delivered at the University of

[8] AA Saparova, 'Legal Transplants: Nature and Structure of Content' (2015) 10 *The Journal of Comparative Law* 93, 94.

[9] Mathias Reimann, 'A Bottom-up View of Legal Transplants' (book review of Jens Drolshammer and Rolf Weber, *Wie das Recht auf Reisen geht* (Stämpfli, 2019)) (2020) 68 *American Journal of Comparative Law* 689, 680.

[10] Unless stated otherwise, the search underlying the following data was conducted in the last week of December 2024.

[11] Alan Watson, *Legal Transplants: An Approach to Comparative Law* (Edinburgh: Scottish Academic Press, 1974).

[12] Alan Watson, *Legal Transplants: An Approach to Comparative Law* (Athens, GA: University of Georgia Press, 2nd edn, 1993).

Virginia in the autumn of 1970 as well as further talks in the subsequent three years. In a later comment, however, he explained that, having received negative feedback from many friends on the draft manuscript, he initially did not publish the book for five years;[13] so apparently, a draft of the main text was already written in the late 1960s.

In the same period, several other publications dealt with the same topic. Three articles from 1968, 1969, and 1972 discussed examples of 'reception' and 'legal importation',[14] while the 1970 Congress of the International Academy of Comparative Law included a general session on 'The global reception of foreign law'.[15] Moreover, in 1973 and 1974, two other legal scholars explicitly referred to the notion of legal transplants, namely John Beckstrom writing about the 'Transplantation of Legal Systems'[16] and Otto Kahn-Freund writing about the 'problem of transplantation' in the context of 'uses and misuses of comparative law'.[17] Beckstrom and Kahn-Freund did not refer to Watson's work-in-progress (as it was), nor did Watson refer to Beckstrom and Kahn-Freund in his afterword from 1993. Beckstrom's article has also largely been neglected in the academic literature, while Kahn-Freund's article is frequently cited, though usually not for its small section on legal transplants.[18]

In substance, it is worth noting that most of Watson's book does not deal with the notion of 'legal transplants' as such but rather contains historical case studies on the way Roman law has been influential in various places at various points in time. However, the initial reviews of Watson's book focussed on his more contentious general statements that legal transplants are not only widespread but fairly 'easy', in particular that they do not depend on similar social, political, and economic conditions between the origin and the transplant

[13] Alan Watson, 'The Birth of Legal Transplants' (2013) 41 *Georgia Journal of International and Comparative Law* 605, 607.

[14] William B Stoebuck, 'Reception of English Common Law in the American Colonies' (1968) 10 *William and Mary Law Review* 393; Robert B Seidman, 'The Reception of English Law in Colonial Africa Revisited' (1969) 2 *Eastern Africa Law Review* 47; Robert C Pozen, 'Public Corporations in Ghana: A Case Study in Legal Importation' (1972) 3 *Wisconsin Law Review* 802.

[15] The proceedings have not been published as a whole but for some information see 'Huitième congrès international de droit comparé (Pescara, 29 août-5 septembre 1970)' (1970) 22 *Revue internationale de droit compare* 731.

[16] John H Beckstrom, 'Transplantation of Legal Systems: An Early Report on the Reception of Western Laws in Ethiopia' (1973) 21 *American Journal of Comparative Law* 557.

[17] Otto Kahn-Freund, 'On Uses and Misuses of Comparative Law' (1974) 37 *Modern Law Review* 1, 5. Cf also John W Cairns, 'Watson, Walton and the History of Legal Transplants' (2013) 41 *Georgia Journal of International and Comparative Law* 637, 643 ('One suspects that Kahn-Freund was pleased with his metaphor of transplantation, and disappointed to find that the same metaphor was employed at length in Alan's book and featured in the title.').

[18] A Google Scholar search for Beckstrom's article shows ninety-nine citations; the one by Otto Kahn-Freund shows 1618 citations out of which 774 mention also the term 'legal transplants'. For the precise search terms see Annex 2.

country. In this regard, the main reaction of the five book reviews published in the mid-1970s was one of scepticism, namely that Watson was criticised as being a legal positivist who disregarded the importance of socio-legal research.[19]

Neither these book reviews nor Watson himself claims that he was the first person who had observed that lawmakers often borrow laws from other countries. Watson cites, for example, Jeremy Bentham's writing 'Of the Influence of Time and Place in Matters of Legislation' from the early nineteenth century which includes the phrase of 'Transplanting Laws',[20] an article by Frederick Walton from 1927 on 'The Historical School of Jurisprudence and Transplantations of Law',[21] an article by Albert Kocourek on 'Factors in the Reception of Law' from 1935,[22] a statement by Roscoe Pound from 1938 that the 'history of a system of law is largely a history of borrowings of legal materials from other legal systems',[23] a number of papers presented in 1955 at a colloquium in Istanbul on the problem of the reception of foreign laws,[24] and book chapters from the 1960s by Guido Tedeschi and Alan Gledhill on legal reception in India and Israel.[25] It is also noteworthy that Watson himself was, apparently, uncertain about how to call the phenomenon under investigation: while his book is entitled 'legal transplants', the text also refers to the terms (legal)

[19] Book reviews of Alan Watson's 'Legal Transplants: An Approach to Comparative Law' by Marc Ancel (1975) 27 *Revue internationale de droit comparé* 303; Charles Maechling (1974–75) 15 *Virginia Journal of International Law* 1037; RB Seidman (1975) 55 *Boston University Law Review* 682; Anon (1975) 27 *Stanford Law Review* 1208; Otto Kahn-Freund (1975) 91 *Law Quarterly Review* 292.

[20] Jeremy Bentham, 'Of the Influence of Time and Place in Matters of Legislation' in John Bowring, *The Works of Jeremy Bentham, Volume i* (Edinburgh: William Tate, 1838–1843) 169, 172, also cited in Watson (n 12) p 35. See also Andrew Huxley, 'Jeremy Bentham on Legal Transplants' (2007) 2 *The Journal of Comparative Law* 177.

[21] FP Walton, 'The Historical School of Jurisprudence and Transplantations of Law' (1927) 9 *Journal of Comparative Legislation and International Law* 183 cited in Watson (n 12) 100.

[22] Albert Kocourek, 'Factors in the Reception of Law' (1935) 10 *Tulane Law Review* 209, cited in Watson (n 12) 93 (in a republished version from 1938).

[23] Watson (n 12) 22 cites, for example, Roscoe Pound 1951 ('history of a system of law is largely a history of borrowings of legal materials from other legal systems . . . .'), which goes back to Roscoe Pound, *The Formative Era of American Law* (Boston: Little, Brown & Co, 1938) 94.

[24] The papers of the conferences have mainly been published in *Annales de la Faculté de Droit d'Istanbul*, volume 5 (1956), available at https://dergipark.org.tr/en/pub/iuafdi/issue/706 accessed 22 October 2025, while a selection of papers (and some translations into English) were also published in *International Social Science Bulletin*, volume 9 (1957). Watson (n 12) 93, 97, 98, cites the *Annales*, notably Max Rheinstein, 'Types of Reception' (1956) 5 *Annales de la Faculté de Droit d'Istanbul* 31. A further meeting on reception of Western law in India took place in Barcelona in 1956, see the report by Kurt Lipstein in (1957) 9 *International Social Science Bulletin* 85.

[25] Alan Gledhill, 'Reception of English Law in India' in William B Hamilton (ed), *The Transfer of Institutions* (Durham, NC: Duke University Press, 1964) 165, cited in Watson (n 12) 35; Guido Tedeschi, 'On Reception and on the Legislative Policy of Israel' in Guido Tedeschi and Uri Yadin (eds), *Studies in Israel Legislative Problems [Scripta Hierosolymitana, 16]* (Jerusalem: Hebrew University, 1966) 11, cited in Watson (n 12) 95.

borrowing, influence, and reception[26] without offering an explicit assessment on which of those terms may be most appropriate.

Thus, it is clear that Watson did not 'invent' the idea of, or even the term, legal transplants. As we have seen, this honour may be granted to Bentham. It is also possible that others may have used this term, or related ones, prior to Bentham. For example, reference has been made to Thomas Hobbes, writing in the 1620s, that 'As we may see where there are several plantations by one people, they severally give different orders and customs according to the intent and purpose of the first planters.'[27] However, comparing Watson's to these prior publications, it can be established that these earlier works have not been cited frequently in the literature.[28] Thus, there is some justification to focus on Watson's book for the purposes of this chapter.

In substance, it is suggested here that Watson's book has been a key fixture in the debate on legal transplants due to three factors. First, he was the first author to provide a book-length treatment of 'legal transplants'. Second, as the subtitle of his book illustrates, he proposed that research on legal transplants should be researched and taught as the key topic of comparative law. Third, he expressed the provocative view that legal transplants can be studied as a purely legal phenomenon as they often occur independently of the social, political, and economic context of the countries involved.[29]

2. Relationship to literature published in other languages

Watson's book on legal transplants had some impact beyond the English-speaking world. Notably, this can be seen in some publications in other languages which explicitly use the English term 'legal transplant',[30] while other

[26] Watson (n 12) 22 (borrowing of materials), 39 (influence), 44 (reception), 95 (legal borrowing).

[27] Huxley (n 20) 182.

[28] For example, a search with Google Scholar only shows twenty-eight cites for Bentham's *Of the Influence of Time and Place in Matters of Legislation*; Walton's 'The Historical School of Jurisprudence and Transplantations of Law' only has forty-three citations. For the precise search terms see Annex 2.

[29] Cf also Mathias Reimann, 'Comparative Law, An Overview of the Discipline' in Konrad Zweigert and Ulrich Drobnig (eds), *International Encyclopedia of Comparative Law, Volume II: Chapter 4* (Leiden: Brill, 2020) para 4-336 (Watson's success due to the 'provocative' and 'dramatically exaggerated fashion' of his view).

[30] Eg, in German: Gudula Deipenbrock, 'Legal Transplants?—Rechtsvergleichende Grundüberlegungen zum technischen Rechtsnormtransfer' (2008) 107 *Zeitschrift für Vergleichende Rechtswissenschaft* 343; Holger Fleischer, 'Legal Transplants im deutschen Aktienrecht' (2004) *Neue Zeitschrift für Gesellschaftsrecht* 1129; in Polish: Paulina Bieś-Srokosz, 'Legal transplants w prawie administracyjnym' (2020) 30(1) *Roczniki Nauk Prawnych* 21; Jagoda Szpak, 'Kontrowersje wokół zagadnienia "legal transplants"' in Mirosław Sadowski and Piotr Szymaniec (eds), *Prace z zakresu integracji europejskiej oraz nauk penalnych* (Katedra Doktryn Politycznych i Prawnych Wydziału Prawa, Administracji i Ekonomii Uniwersytetu Wrocławskiego, 2011) 53; in Spanish: Jim Ramírez

publications prefer translated versions of this term, such as *Rechtstransplantate* in German,[31] *trapianto giuridico* in Italian,[32] *tra(n)splante jurídico* in Spanish,[33] and *transplantacji prawa* in Polish.[34]

However, Watson's impact on this non-Anglophone literature should not be overstated. First, as already mentioned in the previous chapter, this literature often employs other terms than that of a transplant to describe the same phenomenon: in French, these are often variants of the terms 'transfer' and 'acculturation', in Italian and French variants of 'circulation', and in German and Turkish variants of 'reception'.[35]

Second, in many of the publications in other languages, Alan Watson is not cited. Notably, in Turkish scholarship, Watson is not a major scholarly figure representing this notion given the long tradition of publications on the Turkish reception of Western law in the nineteenth century and then in the 1920s,[36] also with early publications by Turkish authors in other languages.[37] As regards other languages more generally, only around a quarter of publications on transplants or related concepts in French and Polish cite Watson, whereas it is around half for publications in German, Italian, and Spanish.[38]

Third, a good deal of non-Anglophone publications preceded Watson's book. Notably, this is the case for publications on the 'reception' of laws.[39] Here,

Figueroa, 'Legal culture and legal transplants. A propósito de la recepción del precedente vinculante en el sistema jurídico peruano' (2018) 73 *THEMIS Revista de Derecho* 27; in Italian: Jihane Benarafa, *Il Takaful oltre il legal transplant: l'etica islamica difronte al rischio assicurativo* (Turin: Giappichelli, 2024); in Swedish: Jens Andreasson, 'Inlösen, äganderättsövergång och "legal transplants"' (2005) 5 *Svenskt Juristtidning* 522.

[31] Gebhard M Rehm, 'Rechtstransplantate als Instrument der Rechtsreform und -transformation' (2008) 72 *Rabels Zeitschrift für ausländisches und internationales Privatrecht* 1.

[32] Luca Ettore Perriello, 'Trust e trapianti giuridici' (2017) *Contratto e impresa/Europa* 638. See also the translation Alan Watson, *Il trapianto di norme giuridiche: un approccio al diritto comparato* (Naples: Edizioni Scientifiche Italiane, 1984).

[33] Daniel Bonilla Maldonado (ed), *Los mandarines del derecho: Trasplantes jurídicos, análisis cultural del derecho y trabajo pro bono* (Bogota: Siglo del Hombre Editores, 2017); Christian J Backenköhler Casajús, 'Transplante jurídico' (2019) 17 *EUNOMÍA. Revista en Cultura de la Legalidad* 262.

[34] Iwona Szymczak, 'Dobór ekwiwalentnych rozwiązań prawnych w procesie transplantacji prawa' (2015) 77(4) *Ruch Prawniczy, Ekonomiczny i Socjologiczny* 29.

[35] See Chapter 1 at Section B 1, based on Dominik Dworniczak and others, 'The Notion of Legal Transplants Beyond the Anglosphere: Decentring the Debate' (2025) 16 *Transnational Legal Theory* 357.

[36] Dworniczak and others (n 35) 370–1. For elements of continuity between the Ottoman Empire and the Republic of Turkey see Ceyhan Muhammed, 'Continuity and Change: The Missed Historical Background of the Turkish Legal Revolution' (2022) 13 *Turkish Historical Review* 67.

[37] See the contributions by Ferit Ayiter and others in (1956) 5 *Annales de la Faculté de Droit d'Istanbul* 93, as well as Hıfzı Velidedeoğlu, 'Les facteurs de codification dans l'Empire ottoman et les causes de la réception du code civil suisse par la Turquie républicaine' (1961) 11/16-17 *Annales de la Faculté de Droit d'Istanbul* 21.

[38] Based on the more than 500 publications analysed in Dworniczak and others (n 35).

[39] A term also frequently used in the older Anglophone literature, see references in nn 1, 14, 16, 22, 24, and 25.

we find many publications in the first decades after the Second World War. The previous chapter already cited three books published in German from 1955 to 1970 on specific case studies of legal reception.[40] Journal articles by the Hungarian-French scholar Imre Zajtay published in both French and German in 1957 and in French, German, and Turkish in 1970 and 1971 provide general discussions on the reception of law.[41] There is also a Polish article on the reception of German law in Poland and Lithuania from the 1960s.[42] Some publications also date back prior to the Second World War. Apart from three German books, cited in the previous chapter,[43] there is, for instance, a French journal article from 1938.[44] One of the German books, which in translation has the title 'The causes of the reception of Roman law in Germany', indicates on the first page that in the period from 1860 to 1880 the question of the reception of Roman law in Germany had been discussed in great detail;[45] notably, the work by Rudolf von Jhering can be seen as endorsing the incorporation of foreign ideas into German law.[46] Going even further back, via Google Books, it is possible to find a book from 1787 that mentions the reception of law in Germany.[47] There is also a Polish publication from 1808 that uses the word 'copying' in explaining the diverse origins of Lithuanian and Polish laws.[48]

Fourth, as regards more recent literature, the three main books on legal transplants and related concepts published in French, German, and Italian are from 1975, 1981, and 2000. The 1975 book by Athanase Papachristos on legal

[40] See Dahm, Schumacher, and Kitagawa, cited in Annex 1, Category 3(b).

[41] Imre Zajtay, 'La réception des droits étrangers et le droit comparé' (1957) *Revue Internationale de Droit Comparé* 690; Imre Zajtay, 'Die Rezeption fremder Rechte und die Rechtsvergleichung' (1957) 156 *Archiv für die civilistische Praxis* 361; Imre Zajtay, 'La Reception globale des droits étrangers' in *Études de droit contemporain* 31–40 (Travaux et recherches de l'Institut de droit comparé de Paris, v XXXIII, 1970); Imre Zajtay, 'Zum Begriff der Gesamtrezeption fremder Rechte' (1970) 170 *Archiv für die civilistische Praxis* 251; Imre Zajtay, 'Yabancı Hukukun Tüm Olarak İktibası' (1971) 37 *Journal of Istanbul University Law Faculty* 309. See also Imre Zajtay, 'Reception of Foreign Laws and Unification of Law' (1975) 35 *Louisiana Law Review* 1117.

[42] Józef Matuszewski, 'Recepcja prawa niemieckiego w Polsce i na Litwie' (1966) 20(9) *Sprawozdania z Czynności i Posiedzeń Naukowych Łódzkiego Towarzystwa Naukowego* 1.

[43] See von Below, Michaelis, and Coing, cited in Annex 1, Category 3(b).

[44] Andreas B Schwarz, 'La réception et l'assimilation des droits étrangers' in *Recueil d'études en l'honneur d'Edouard Lambert*, tome II (Paris: LR Sirey, 1938) 581–90.

[45] Georg von Below, *Die Ursachen der Rezeption des römischen Rechts in Deutschland* (Berlin: R Oldenbourg, 1905) VII ('Nachdem einige Jahrzehnte lang, etwa von 1860–80, die Frage nach den Ursachen der Rezeption des Römischen Rechts in allgemeinen Erörterungen mit Eifer behandelt worden war, . . . '). See also Kurt Lipstein, 'Conclusions' (1957) 9 *International Social Science Bulletin* 70 ('to most students of legal history, the word reception is connected with the reception of Roman law in Western Europe between 1100 and 1600.').

[46] Further discussed in Chapter 6 at Section B 1.

[47] Wilhelm Gottlieb Tafinger, *Ueber die Bestimmung des Begrifs der Analogie des Teutschen Privatrechts und der Grundsäze* (Ulm: Wohler, 1787) 83, 157–8.

[48] Tadeusz Czacki, *Czy prawo rzymskie było zasadą praw litewskich i polskich? I czy z połnocnemi narodami mielismy wiele wspolnych praw i zwyczaiow? Rosprawa czytana w Krzemieńcu na otwarciu roku szkolnego 1808. w Gimnazyum Wołyńskiem* (Vilnius: Józef Zawadzki, 1809).

reception as a phenomenon of legal sociology is the one that is most general in nature; yet, the 1981 book by Ernst Hirsch on reception as a social process (as applied to Turkey) and the 2000 book by Elisabetta Grande on imitation and law (as applied to transplants in criminal procedure) also contain, in addition to case studies, general discussions on the feasibility and desirability of legal transplants today.[49] However, if one examines the impact of these three books in the Anglophone literature, it is rather modest with three, twenty, and twenty-three citations on Google Scholar, compared to 2,520 for Watson's book.[50] Thus, this confirms that, even for an international topic such as legal transplants, it is not the case that literature easily permeates national and linguistic borders.[51]

To conclude, Watson's book on legal transplants has had some impact beyond the English-speaking world, but other publications and concepts also played an important role. Furthermore, Watson's view that legal transplants should become the main concern of comparative law cannot be observed in French, German, and Italian textbooks of comparative law as most of them focus on legal families.[52] Thus, again, Watson's general impact should not be overstated.

C. Evolution of use of the term 'legal transplants' and related terms across time

1. General evaluation showing increased use

The strengths and weaknesses of bibliometric methods are widely known and discussed.[53] Their main advantage is that they can provide answers to these questions that go beyond anecdotal examples. Among its shortcomings are the gaps of databases, the limitations of search functions, the risks of false positives and negatives, and the corresponding (and inevitable) subjectivity of some of

[49] Athanase C Papachristos, *La réception des droits privés étrangers comme phénomène de sociologie juridique* (Paris: LGDJ, 1975); Ernst Hirsch, *Rezeption als sozialer Prozeß: erläutert am Beispiel der Türkei* (Berlin: Duncker & Humblot, 1981); Elisabetta Grande, *Imitazione e diritto: ipotesi sulla circolazione dei modelli* (Turin: Giappichelli, 2000).

[50] As of 3 January 2025, using the option 'search English pages'. See Annex 2.

[51] For a similar conclusion see Dworniczak and others (n 35) 386–7.

[52] See Mathias Siems, 'Book Review of *Rechtsvergleichung* (Uwe Kischel)' (2017) 65 *American Journal of Comparative Law* 462.

[53] See eg Alois Matorevhu 'Bibliometrics: Application Opportunities and Limitations' in Otávio José de Oliveira (ed), *Bibliometrics: An Essential Methodological Tool for Research Projects* (London: IntechOpen, 2024) 3, 12–13; John L Worrall and Ellen G Cohn, 'Citation Data and Analysis: Limitations and Shortcomings' (2023) 39 *Journal of Contemporary Criminal Justice* 327.

Table 2.1 Overview of corpora used in this chapter

Database	Sub-category	Possible further variants
Google Books Ngram	English language	scaled by all books or other sub-groups
Google Scholar	[no further restrictions]	includes variants of terms (using 'OR')
Google Scholar	use in source: 'journal' OR 'review'	includes variants of terms (using 'OR'); scaled by publications that include 'law' AND 'legal'
Google Scholar	use of word in title	includes variants of terms (using 'OR')
Westlaw 'World Journals'	use of word in five instances	includes variants of terms (using 'OR'); scaled by publications that include certain terms
JSTOR	[no further restrictions]	includes variants of terms (using 'OR')

the choices a researcher makes. To reduce these risks, the quantitative evaluation of the literature on legal transplants is based on multiple databases and search options, as shown in Table 2.1.

First, Google Books Ngram is a convenient tool to conduct such a search in books. It covers a wide range of books, and there are also some prior examples that have used Ngrams in legal scholarship.[54] Of course, any search across time needs to consider that the number of books (and, possibly, the proportion of published books included in Google Books) has increased over time. Thus, all of the following Ngram results are relative ones, ie they show the use of a certain term as a percentage of all books or another sub-group of books.

Figure 2.1 is based on a search that accounts for two factors: first, while the term 'legal transplant' is the 'classical' one, following Watson's terminology, it is also worth considering the variations 'law transplant' and 'transplantation of law'. Second, Google Books Ngram allows the option to add '_INF' to the search term which leads to the inclusion of different endings of the term, for example, 'legal transplant' and 'legal transplants'.[55] Figure 2.1 shows that 'legal

[54] Eg, Cameron Shackell and Lance De Vine, 'Quantifying the Genericness of Trademarks Using Natural Language Processing: An Introduction with Suggested Metrics' (2022) 30 *Artificial Intelligence and Law* 199; Kenneth A Adams, 'Interpreting and Drafting Efforts Provisions: From Unreason to Reason' (2019) 74 *Business Lawyer* 677, 699, 701; Catalina Goanta, 'Big Law, Big Data' (2017) *Law and Method*, available at https://doi.org/10.5553/REM/.000029 accessed 22 October 2025.

[55] For the options of Google Books Ngram see https://books.google.com/ngrams/info accessed 22 October 2025.

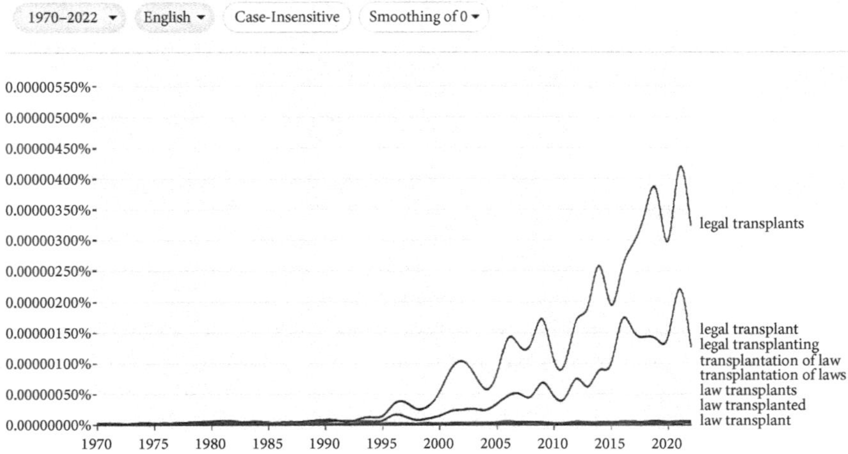

Figure 2.1 Use of variants of the term 'legal transplants' (Google Books Ngram)

transplants' has been the most commonly used term and that all of the terms have become more frequently used, in particular since the 2000s.

Figure 2.2 controls for the fact that the number of books on 'law' and 'comparative law' may have in varied over time. The curve that controls for 'law' books is very similar to the general one (Figure 2.1), in particular as both show a fairly consistent general rise.[56] Controlling for 'comparative law' shows a general rise too,[57] but also that the use has fluctuated between 8 and 14% in the last ten years. This can be seen as evidence that legal transplants play some role in comparative law today; yet it may also be interpreted as challenging Watson's ambition that legal transplants should become the main topic of comparative law.

Second, Google Scholar is convenient to use and fairly comprehensive in the coverage of different sources, but it also has some limitations. On the plus side, it enables the usual tools of Google, for example, strings and options (such as AND or OR). In the present case, it was therefore possible to use a formula that covers various forms of references to legal transplants (namely: 'transplantation of law' OR 'transplantation of laws' OR 'law transplants' OR 'law transplant' OR 'legal transplant' OR 'legal transplants' OR 'legal transplantation'

[56] Note that this is scaled by 1/1000 to fit it on the same chart as the one for 'comparative law'. See also the search terms in Annex 2.

[57] For a similar finding see the time series of the use of the term 'legal transplants' in the *American Journal of Comparative Law* by Toby S Goldbach, 'Why Legal Transplants?' (2019) 15 *Annual Review of Law and Social Science* 583, 588.

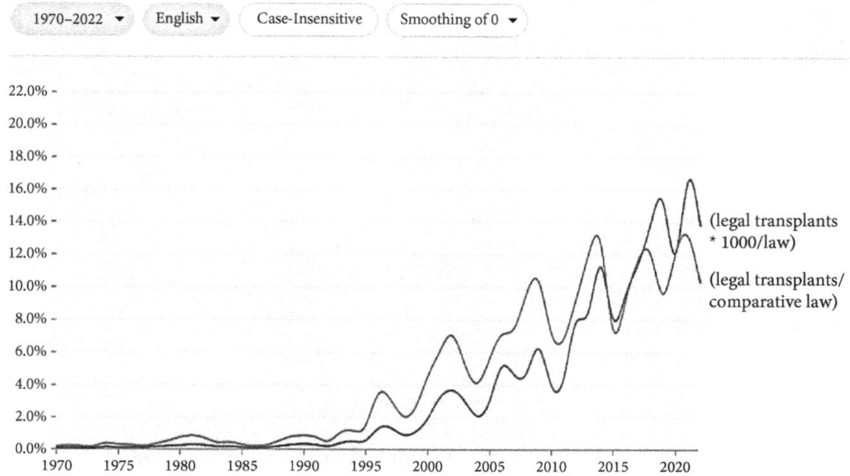

Figure 2.2 Relative use of term 'legal transplants' in books with 'law' and 'comparative law' (Google Books Ngram)

OR 'legal transplantations'). The following search also ticked the box 'include citations' which refers to sources where 'Google knows that a resource exists (because some other source cited it) but they can find no web resource to match it'.[58]

In detail, without further restrictions, this search leads to 14,600 hits up to 2023[59] with only twenty-seven of those prior to 1970, ninety-seven in the 1970s, 182 in the 1980s, 669 in the 1990s, 3,670 in the 2000s, 8,270 in the 2010s, and 4,610 from 2020 to 2023. If one restricts the search to any of these words included in the title of the publication, the results are as following: two prior to 1970, twenty-three in the 1970s, eight in the 1980s, fifty in the 1990s, 191 in the 2000s, 410 in the 2010s, and 165 from 2020 to 2023—in total 849.[60]

These first findings with Google Scholar thus show again that the use of the term 'legal transplants' (or their variants) has increased substantially over time, in particular in recent years. As to the limitations of these findings, to start with, Google Scholar is not fully consistent in the extent to

[58] For this function see Randy L Miller, 'An Introduction to Google Scholar' (2019), available at https://core.ac.uk/download/pdf/213463845.pdf.

[59] The year 2024 was not included as data for this year would be incomplete given that Google Scholar publications for this year are unlikely to be complete until late 2025.

[60] For the precise search terms see Annex 2.

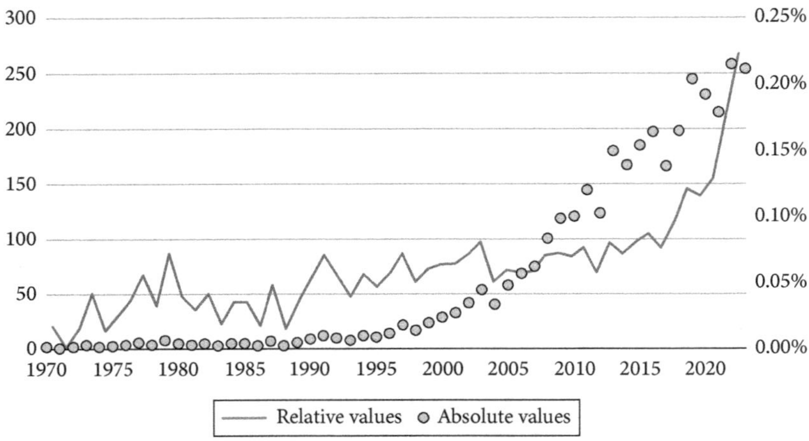

Figure 2.3 Google Scholar time trend for journal articles on 'legal transplants' (or variants)

which it includes sources that would not be classified as academic publications. It is also possible that some papers appear multiple times if there has been a modification of the title from the working paper to the published version. Moreover, it is a limitation to only use the absolute number of hits without considering the increase of materials in Google Scholar over time.

For the purposes of Figure 2.3, the Google Scholar search has thus been limited to sources that include 'journal' or 'review' in the title in order to reduce the risk of overinflating the number of hits due to non-academic sources or multiple hits of the same piece. Moreover, the results are presented in a way that includes both the absolute and relative values. The relative values consider publications with 'law' and 'legal' in the text (the cumulative search is used here to reduce the risk of false positives).[61] It can be seen that the relative values also rise across time; yet a steeper rise only appears in the last five years. As for the other searches conducted with Google Scholar, this search includes variants of the phrase 'legal transplants' and, explicitly checking these variants, it is found that the phrase 'legal transplant(s)' accounts for 67% of the hits, 'legal transplantation(s)' for 23%, 'law transplant(s)' for 6%, and 'transplantation of law(s)' for 4%.

[61] For the precise search terms see Annex 2.

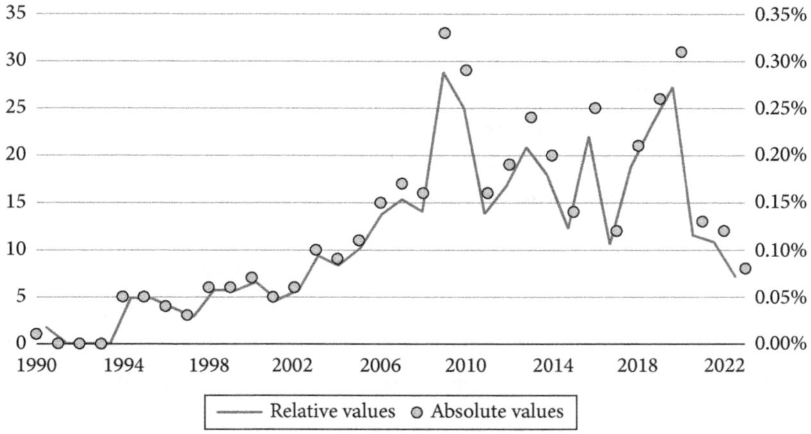

Figure 2.4 Westlaw time trend for journal articles on 'legal transplants' (or variants)

Third, Westlaw provides a further opportunity to examine trends, with some advantages but also some disadvantages. Searching Westlaw can show specifically how often in law journals the term 'legal transplants' has been used. The following is based on the Westlaw category of 'World Journals'. Yet, even in this category, US law journals are dominant. This can be seen in a simple general search for 'legal transplants' (and their variants, as above) which shows 2,267 hits for US journals and 367 hits for international journals.[62]

For the purposes of this chapter, a key advantage of Westlaw (also as compared to other law databases such as Hein Online or JSTOR) is that it is possible to specify that a certain word or phrase needs to be mentioned multiple times in the article. Thus, it enables a search for articles that deal with legal transplants in detail rather than relying on other proxies, such as whether the term is used in the title (see above for Google Scholar). Figure 2.4 therefore reports the number of articles that mention the term 'legal transplants' (or their variants) at least five times,[63] both displaying the absolute hits and scaled in % by all Westlaw journal articles. This figure starts in the 1990s as, prior to

[62] Search on 10 January 2025. When conducting a search on Westlaw, it reports two categories of results: 'United States Journals' and 'International Journals'. However, there is some overlap between these categories, as some of the international journals are also included in the US journals. Consequently, the total results figure reported by Westlaw after each search is not entirely accurate, as it includes these duplicate entries. To reduce the overreporting of the number of hits, the following results were manually analysed to remove duplicate publications. For the precise search terms see Annex 2.

[63] For the formulas see Annex 2.

that, only two Westlaw articles fulfil the 'five times' requirement.[64] The general trend is again upwards, though, given the lower number of observations, with more outliers than in Google Scholar.

Further analysis with Westlaw has imposed the additional requirement that articles also mention the term 'comparative law' at least five times. This leads to a similar time-trend as displayed in Figure 2.4, only with a reduction of the numbers by around 35 to 40%. In average, according to those calculations, 12.15% of these comparative law articles published between 2010 and 2023 include the topic of legal transplants, and thus at a similar level as in Google Books Ngrams (see Figure 2.2, above). Here too, we can therefore conclude that legal transplants play a key role in comparative law, while not dominating the field.

2. Related terms and their use

It was already mentioned that some legal scholars prefer other terms than that of 'legal transplants'.[65] Some of these terms are unsuitable for bibliometric research as they can also refer to phenomena which are not equivalent to legal transplants (eg, legal transfer, legal influence, legal export/import, legal borrowing); some other terms are also excluded here as they are only used very rarely (eg, legal mimesis, legal cross-fertilisation). The following thus focusses in its first part on just the two main 'competitors' of the term legal transplant: legal reception and legal diffusion (including variants of these terms).

Figure 2.5 shows that, since the mid-1990s, the term 'legal transplants' has been more frequently used than reception or diffusion, also considering variants of these terms.[66] In previous years, however, the competition was more open. According to Figure 2.6 (here limiting the search to the four main variants), the term 'reception of law' was the most popular one for most of the period from 1950 to 1995. Thus, only two decades after the publication of Watson's book, 'legal transplants' became the main term to describe the phenomenon discussed here.

[64] The first one was Alan Watson, 'Legal Change: Sources of Law and Legal Culture' (1983) 131 *University of Pennsylvania Law Review* 1121.
[65] See Chapter 1 at Section B 1.
[66] For the precise search terms of Figures 2.5 and 2.6 see Annex 2.

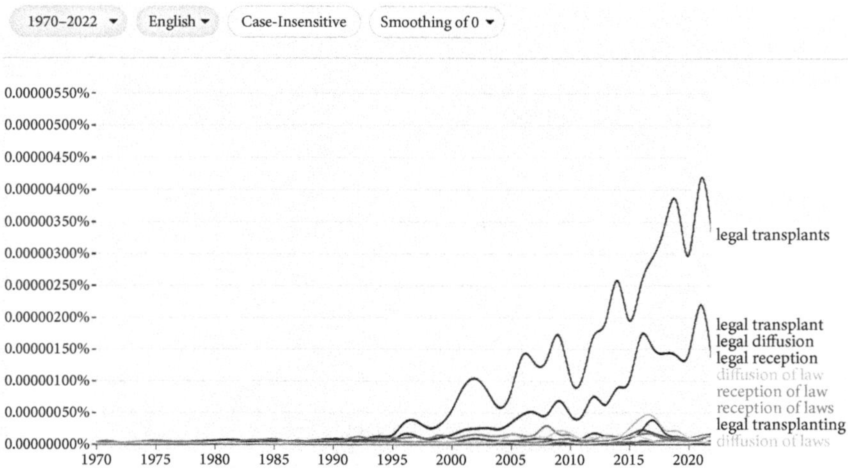

Figure 2.5 Google Books Ngram time trend with comparison of related legal terms (1970–2022)

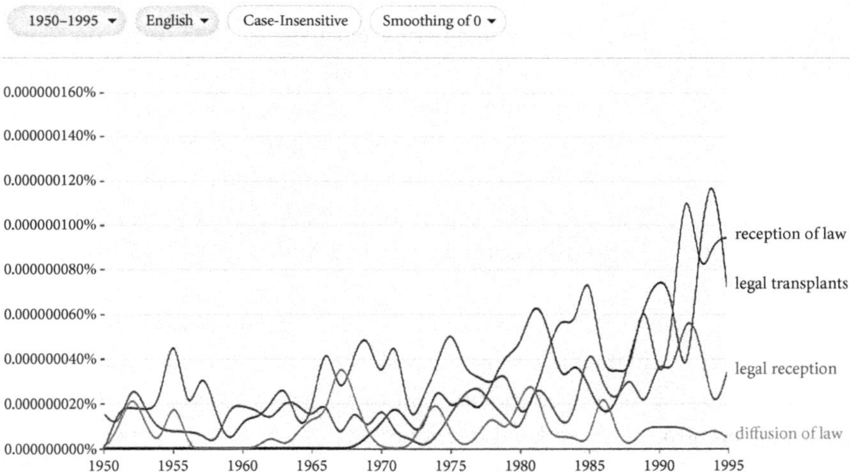

Figure 2.6 Google Books Ngram time trend with comparison of related legal terms (1950–1995)

Considering the period from 1970 to today, Google Scholar and Westlaw confirm this result.[67] A Google Scholar search for legal transplants (or variants of it) in sources with 'journal' or 'review' in the title (as in the previous section)

[67] For the precise search terms see Annex 2.

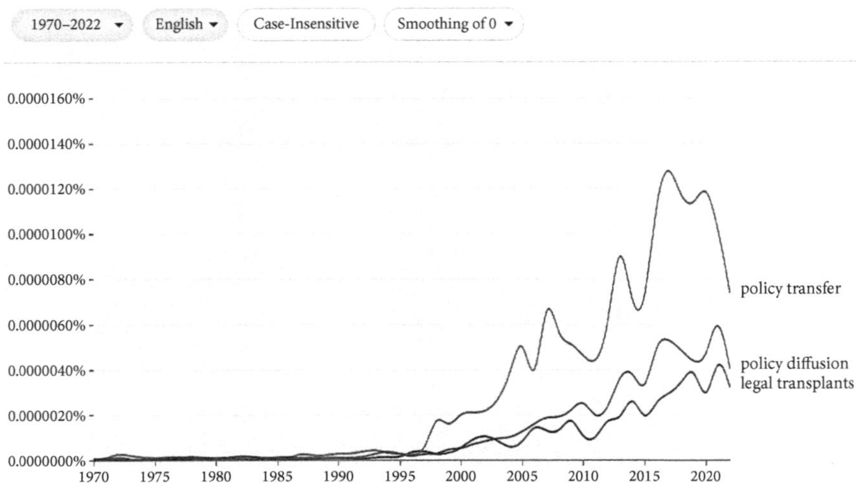

Figure 2.7 Google Books Ngram time trend with comparison to policy transfer and diffusion

leads to a total number of 3,390 hits between 1970 and 2023. With the same method, 'legal reception', 'reception of law', and 'reception of laws' have been used 396 times and 'legal diffusion', 'diffusion of law', and 'diffusion of laws' 320 times. With Westlaw, it is again possible to impose the requirement that a certain term needs to be mentioned at least five times in a particular article. Here, compared to the 387 hits for 'legal transplants' (or variants), there are only fifteen hits for 'legal diffusion' (or variants) and two for 'legal reception' (or variants).

The terms 'policy transfer' and 'policy diffusion' from political science and related fields are similar to 'legal transplants'.[68] Of course, though being similar, these terms do not fully overlap with that of a legal transplant; for example, consider a situation where a legal transplant is used to merely implement the same policy in a better way than the previous rules.[69]

Figure 2.7 shows that the popularity of 'policy transfer' and 'policy diffusion' also rose around the year 2000 and that these terms have become (even) more frequently used in books from any field than the term 'legal transplants'. In Google Scholar, the 3,485 hits for legal transplants are also superseded by the 5,840 hits for 'policy transfer' and the 5,180 hits for 'policy diffusion'

[68] See Chapter 1 at Section C 2.
[69] See also the discussion of the object of legal transplants in Chapter 3 at Section B.

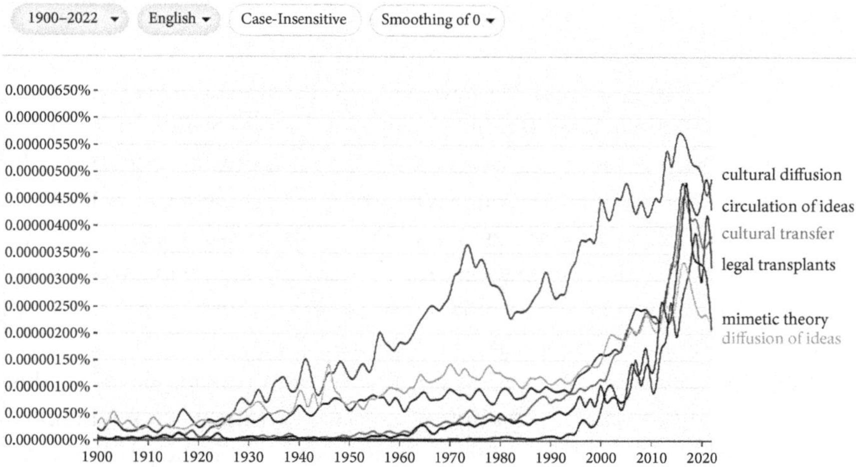

Figure 2.8 Google Books Ngram time trend with comparison to further related non-legal terms

(including the variants 'diffusion of policy' or 'diffusion of policies'). However, using Westlaw—and thus again limiting the search to law articles, and then again applying the five-word restriction—the term 'legal transplants' is by far more popular with 288 hits as compared to nineteen and forty-eight hits for the other two terms. Thus, it is clear that the legal literature is more inclined to use and discuss the concept of legal transplants than the related phenomena of policy transfer/diffusion.[70]

Figure 2.8 presents a comparison with three further terms from other fields: 'cultural diffusion', 'cultural transfer', 'circulation of ideas', 'diffusion of ideas', and 'mimetic theory'.[71] It uses the start year 1900 in order to show that these non-legal terms already gained in popularity earlier than those of legal transplants, policy transfer, and policy diffusion. Of course, these terms also refer to broader phenomena which go beyond laws and policies. Thus, it can be said that the cross-border influence of ideas and culture has been discussed for a long time, while its application to law and policy is a more recent phenomenon.

[70] For this point see also Section D 2.

[71] See also Chapter 1 at Section C 2 (for cultural studies and history), as well as Chapter 4 at Sections B 2 (for mimetic theory), and C 3 (a) and (d) (for cultural transfer and diffusion).

3. Interpretation

The foregoing analysis shows that prior to the 1970s there have been few uses of the term 'legal transplants' and that, even after the publication of Watson's book, the use of this term had been rather limited until the mid-1990s. It may be suggested that Alan Watson's idea started to become more influential afterwards as scholars discussed the feasibility of transplanting rules in post-communist and other transition economies.[72] A visible sign of this trend may have been that a group of legal scholars from Serbia set up a foundation and website to celebrate and promote the work of Alan Watson.[73]

However, according to the findings of this section, the popularity of the terms 'policy transfer' and 'policy diffusion' also rose at the same point in time. Indeed, other literature confirms these trends. According to the policy literature, for example, a tipping point for the 'movement of public policies crossing borders' was the 'fall of the Berlin Wall, when policies would no longer circulate inside the closed circuits',[74] and it is said that 'interest in policy transfer has exploded' since the mid-1990s due to an 'increased sense of the interdependence and permeability of domestic policy regimes' as regards topics such as financial crises, climate change, and development policy.[75] Furthermore, it is suggested in the legal literature that the growing volume of legal transplants in the late twentieth century was due to factors such as growing similarities between societies and cultures and increased interactions between legal systems, including regimes of global governance.[76]

Thus, a plausible interpretation is that across the social sciences (including political science and law), a common interest in this topic emerged in the mid-1990s. Watson's influence may merely have been that legal scholars phrased

[72] See eg Beata Kviatek, *Explaining Legal Transplants: Transplantation of EU law into Central Eastern Europe* (Nijmegen: Wolf Legal Publishers, 2015); Christa Jessel-Holst, Rainer Kulms, and Alexander Trunk (eds), *Private Law in Eastern Europe: Autonomous Developments or Legal Transplants?* (Tübingen: Mohr Siebeck, 2010); John Stanley Gillespie, *Transplanting Commercial Law Reform: Developing a Rule of Law in Vietnam* (Aldershot: Ashgate, 2006); John Jupp, 'Legal Transplants as Solutions for Criminal Law Reform in Post-Intervention States: Afghanistan's Interim Criminal Procedure Code 2004' (2013) 61 *American Journal of Comparative Law* 51.

[73] At the time of writing the website is http://awf.ius.bg.ac.rs/ accessed 29 November 2025, while the original one was http://web.archive.org/web/20160321095907/http://alanwatson.org/. For a Polish interview with Watson explaining his fame in Serbia see Alan Watson and Maciej Jońca, 'Zapożyczenia to droga, na której rozwija się prawo' (2012) 12/1 *Zeszyty Prawnicze* 181.

[74] Osmany Porto de Oliveira, 'A Prelude to Policy Transfer Research' in Osmany Porto de Oliveira (ed), *Handbook of Policy Transfer, Diffusion and Circulation* (Cheltenham: Edward Elgar, 2021) 1.

[75] Magdaléna Hadjiisky, Leslie A Pal, and Christopher Walker, 'Introduction: Traversing the Terrain of Policy Transfer: Theory, Methods and Overview' in Magdaléna Hadjiisky, Leslie A Pal, and Christopher Walker (eds), *Public Policy Transfer: Micro-Dynamics and Macro-Effects* (Cheltenham: Edward Elgar, 2017) 1, 2.

[76] Reimann (n 29) para 4-345.

this debate under the heading of 'legal transplants' and not other terms such as legal diffusion or legal reception. Similarly, this terminological path dependence seems to account for the preferences of using 'legal transplant' and not 'legal transplantation' in emphasising the object and not the process of this phenomenon (here too, different from the terms policy diffusion and transfer).[77]

This section has also shown that use of the term 'legal transplants' features in the comparative law literature in around 10–12% of the articles published in recent decades. Yet, they have not become the main topic of comparative law, as proposed by Watson. Indeed, this finding can also be confirmed in major handbooks of comparative law which typically include one, but not more, chapters on legal transplants.[78] The analysis in the next section of this chapter evaluates the substantive use of the term 'legal transplants', which also provides the opportunity to revisit the topics of this section, such as the influence of Watson and the cross-disciplinary interest in legal transplants.

D. Substantive use in law journals and elsewhere

1. Combined use of 'legal transplants' with keywords

As mentioned earlier in this chapter, Alan Watson is often portrayed as the founding father of the study of legal transplants, despite the fact that the concept was also used by Otto Kahn-Freund at the same time and, earlier on, by Jeremy Bentham and others.[79] Thus, the first part of this subsection examines how often these three authors have been mentioned in publications on legal transplants. The fourth author included is Pierre Legrand, given that his 1997 article on 'The Impossibility of Legal Transplants' has become a key point of reference for a sceptical position.[80] Specifically, it has been examined whether papers that contain the term 'legal transplant' also mention the names of these

[77] For details on objects and process see Chapter 3 at Sections B and C.

[78] Eg Michele Graziadei, 'Comparative Law as the Study of Transplants and Receptions' in Mathias Reimann and Reinhard Zimmermann (eds), *The Oxford Handbook of Comparative Law* (Oxford: OUP, 2nd edn, 2019) 442; Jörg Fedtke, 'Legal Transplants' in Jan M Smits (eds), *Elgar Encyclopedia of Comparative Law* (Cheltenham: Edward Elgar, 2nd edn, 2012) 434; Vlad Perju, 'Constitutional Transplants, Borrowing, and Migrations' in Michel Rosenfeld and András Sajó (eds), *The Oxford Handbook of Comparative Constitutional Law* (Oxford: OUP, 2012) 1304; Mariana Mota Prado, 'Diffusion, Reception and Transplantation' in Peter Cane and others (eds), *The Oxford Handbook of Comparative Administrative Law* (Oxford: OUP, 2020) 255. However, Mathias Siems and Po Jen Yap (eds), *The Cambridge Handbook of Comparative Law* (Cambridge: CUP, 2024) contains two chapters.

[79] See Sections A and B 1.

[80] Pierre Legrand, 'The Impossibility of Legal Transplants' (1997) 4 *Maastricht Journal of European and Comparative Law* 111. For Legrand's criticism see also Chapter 5 at Section B 2.

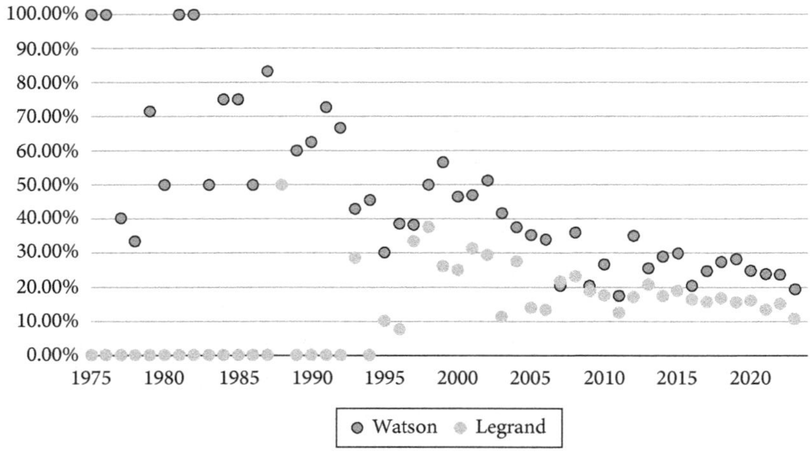

Figure 2.9 Google Scholar search for Watson/Legrand and legal transplants

four authors. Thus, the search in this corpus is conducted for their names, specifically their last names. Potentially, this could lead to false positives (eg, citations to other authors with the last names 'Watson' or 'Legrand'); yet, checking a sample of citations, this risk was found to be negligible.

In Google Scholar (as in the previous section, with the sources 'review' or 'journal' and including variants of the phrase 'legal transplants'), Watson is cited in 984 of the 3,485 publications (28.24%), Legrand in 575 (16.50%), Kahn-Freund in 223 (6.40%), and Bentham in 151 (4.33%).[81] Tracking the top two authors over time, Figure 2.9 shows that Watson was often cited in more than 50% of the articles until the mid-1990s; yet, as the topic of legal transplants became more appealing to a wider audience (see the previous section), this number dropped to less than 25% with Legrand following closely behind him. A limitation of this method is that it includes articles that only make casual references to legal transplants. With Westlaw, it is again possible to add the requirement that articles mention 'legal transplants', or variations thereof, at least five times.[82] Then, Watson is cited in 302 of the 387 articles (78.04%), Legrand in 173 (44.70%), Kahn-Freund in 105 (27.13%), and Bentham in 25 (6.46%). Here, Watson has also retained a high proportion of references in recent articles that discuss legal transplants: for example, between 2020 and 2023, Watson is cited in fourty-four of sixty-three articles (69.84%).

[81] For the precise search terms see Annex 2.
[82] For the precise search terms see Annex 2.

Does this mean that Watson's view on legal transplants is (still) strongly endorsed in the literature? It is suggested here that this seems unlikely. As the frequent references to Legrand also indicate, both Watson and Legrand are often portrayed as being at the extreme ends in their positions on this topic. Thus, many citations are by scholars who cite both to set the scene for taking an intermediate position.[83]

Another question is how 'deep' Watson has been cited in the literature. It can be hypothesised that many of the recent citations of Watson do not engage with his arguments in detail but simply refer to him as a short-hand reference for the notion legal transplants. To investigate this point, the fifty-one Google Scholar citations of Watson for the year 2021 have been examined by hand. For four of those, it was not possible to access the actual publication. Thus, this left forty-seven publications: out of those only fourteen (29.79 %) cited Watson's book with a precise page number, twenty-one (44.68 %) cited the book as a whole, four (8.51 %) cited other writings by Watson,[84] and eight (17.02 %) did not contain an actual reference to publications by Watson.

Thus, given that there is only a weak focus on Watson's actual research, the next part of this subsection explores whether publications on legal transplants may also have other substantive focal points as Watson. For example, does the literature focus on particular areas of law? Is it now closely linked to discussions in international law? Is it not the historical perspective (as in Watson) that is at the fore but a political or economic one? And is there a focus on particular countries or regions?

First, it has been examined whether there is an even or uneven use according to areas of law. Table 2.2 displays this information for data collected with Google Scholar (again, with the sources 'review' or 'journal' and considering variants of the phrase 'legal transplants') and Westlaw (here, again, with imposing the requirement that a term is used five times). The marker terms are the ones of the areas of law.[85] While this may over- or underreport the absolute numbers for all areas of law, the main points of interest are, in any case, the relative values, namely the comparison with all articles and the ranking of the areas of law. Here, it is revealing that 'private law' is the area with the relatively most frequent use of legal transplants as well as the top area of law. Thus, the

[83] See also Chapter 5 at Sections B 3 and C.

[84] One citation each to: Alan Watson, *Society and Legal Change* (Edinburgh: Scottish Academic Press, 1977); Alan Watson, 'Legal Transplants and Law Reform' (1976) 92 *Law Quarterly Review* 79; Alan Watson, 'Aspects of Reception of Law' (1996) 44 *American Journal of Comparative Law* 335; and Alan Watson, 'Comparative Law and Legal Change' (1978) 37 *Cambridge Law Journal* 313.

[85] For the precise search terms see Annex 2.

Table 2.2 Area of law search for 'legal transplants' (or variants)

	Google Scholar			Westlaw		
	(i) all	(ii) legal transplants	(ii) of (i)	(i) all	(ii) legal transplants	(ii) of (i)
'criminal law'	144,000	887	0.62%	12,340	38	0.31%
'public law'	87,400	804	0.92%	6,180	28	0.45%
'constitutional law'	45,600	782	1.71%	10,972	39	0.36%
'private law'	35,800	1,210	3.38%	4,905	76	1.55%
'commercial law'	18,100	647	3.57%	2,425	30	1.24%

debate on legal transplants has, to some extent, followed the traditional focus of comparative law on private law topics.[86] However, legal transplants are also discussed in articles (as well as in books)[87] of other areas of law. Indeed, the subsequent chapters will repeatedly return to the view of some authors that different areas of law pose different questions to the use of legal transplants.[88]

Second, both Google Scholar and Westlaw have been searched for the terms 'comparative law', 'international law', 'transnational law', 'EU law', and 'European law'.[89] The results are that for Google Scholar, out of 3,485 hits, 2,200 also mention 'comparative law', 1,750 also 'international law', 387 also 'transnational law', and 807 also EU or European law. For Westlaw, out of 387 hits, 229 also mention (five times) 'comparative law', 118 also 'international law', ten also 'transnational law', and twenty-eight also EU or European law. Thus, this shows, unsurprisingly, that articles on legal transplants also refer to discussions of comparative law. Yet, while Watson had no particular interest in international, transnational, and European law, the current literature often relates legal transplants to these levels of law.[90]

Third, using the same corpus and method, a search for 'history', 'politics', 'economics', and 'sociology' leads to the result that for Google Scholar out of

[86] For example, in Konrad Zweigert and Hein Kötz, *An Introduction to Comparative Law* (Oxford: Clarendon, 3rd edn, 1998), whose English title omits this focus of the original German version: Konrad Zweigert and Hein Kötz, *Einführung in die Rechtsvergleichung auf dem Gebiete des Privatrechts* (Tübingen: Mohr Siebeck, 3rd edn, 1996). See also Mathias Siems, *Comparative Law* (CUP, 3rd edn, 2022) 34 (discussing the view that private law is particularly suitable for a functional comparative analysis).

[87] See Chapter 1 at Section B 1.

[88] See Chapter 4 at Section C 3 (d), Chapter 5 at Section C 4 (a), Chapter 6 at Section C 4 (a), and Chapter 7 at C 3 (d).

[89] For the precise search terms see Annex 2.

[90] See further Chapter 3 at Section C 2.

3,485 hits for the phrase legal transplants and its variants, 2,630 also mention 'history', 1,960 also 'politics', 1,800 also 'economics', and 909 also 'sociology'. For Westlaw, out of 387 hits, 283 also mention (five times) 'history', 122 also 'politics', eighty-four also 'economics', and twenty-five also 'sociology'. Thus, the first three non-law categories are fairly close. The relevance of history is not a surprise given that legal transplants often relate to particular historical events. However, the fact that politics and economics are also frequently mentioned is revealing as it shows that, today, legal transplants are more frequently discussed in an interdisciplinary manner. Reflecting on Watson's interest in Roman law, it has also been calculated that 'Roman law' is mentioned 548 times (Google Scholar) and thirty-five times (Westlaw). To contrast this with a term related to politics and economics, this is exceeded by the term 'World Bank'[91] which is mentioned 711 times (Google Scholar) and forty-eight times (Westlaw). Thus, here too, it can be seen that the research on legal transplants has moved in new directions.

Fourth, Table 2.3 displays how far law articles dealing with a particular country discuss legal transplants. It is based on Westlaw only as with Google Scholar any results may be diluted by general 'fads and fashions' unrelated to any preference to discuss legal transplants in the legal context of a particular country. Using again the 'five-words threshold',[92] the absolute ranking of countries mentioning legal transplants has, as the top countries, mainly large countries and/or countries of the developed world.[93] This is likely to be due to the fact that these countries are frequently mentioned in law review articles anyway. Thus, it is more meaningful to rank countries by their propensity to refer to legal transplants in all articles that deal with a particular country. Table 2.3 shows the top twenty-five of such a ranking for all countries that have at least ten articles that discuss legal transplants, given that for countries with fewer such articles the results would often be driven by single observations.[94]

In substance, the prevalence of the US and many European countries in Table 2.3 can be explained by the model function of their laws for other countries. Yet, the European countries in this table also include Russia, Poland, and Ukraine which are likely to be discussed as receivers of legal transplants after the fall of communism. Moreover, the inclusion of seven Asian, five Latin

[91] For this topic, see Chapter 4 at Section C 3 (b) and Chapter 6 at Section B 2.

[92] For the precise search terms see Annex 2.

[93] The top ten are: United States (238), China (108), Germany (95), Japan (81), France (78), Canada (55), India (49), United Kingdom (43), Russia (37), Italy (33).

[94] For example, this includes Nepal (2 out of 470 = 0.43%), Romania (6 out of 1,077 = 0.56%), Albania (2 out of 416 = 0.48%), Kazakhstan (3 out of 528 = 0.57%).

Table 2.3 Top 25 countries with frequent discussions of 'legal transplants' (or variants)

Countries	% of (i) of (ii)	(i) legal transplant	(ii) all country	Continents
United States	1.42%	238	16,775	North America
China	0.85%	108	12,720	Asia
Germany	0.83%	95	11,407	Europe
Japan	0.74%	81	10,988	Asia
France	0.68%	78	11,430	Europe
Taiwan	0.67%	31	4,648	Asia
Colombia	0.58%	18	3,129	South America
Italy	0.57%	33	5,802	Europe
Singapore	0.47%	27	5,698	Asia
Venezuela	0.47%	10	2,138	South America
Spain	0.47%	27	5,771	Europe
India	0.45%	49	10,941	Asia
Russia	0.45%	37	8,286	Europe
Poland	0.45%	12	2,693	Europe
Canada	0.40%	55	13,631	North America
Israel	0.39%	33	8,538	Asia
Argentina	0.38%	20	5,212	South America
United Kingdom	0.37%	43	11,756	Europe
Ukraine	0.37%	9	2,448	Europe
South Africa	0.34%	21	6,243	Africa
Chile	0.32%	13	4,020	South America
Brazil	0.32%	21	6,644	South America
Egypt	0.30%	9	2,987	Africa
Belgium	0.28%	9	3,209	Europe
Turkey	0.27%	10	3,690	Asia
Netherlands	0.26%	15	5,783	Europe

American, and two African countries confirms that, in contrast to Watson's focus on Roman law in the Western world, the literature on legal transplants has now a global reach. Notably, this list includes many countries that are often seen as typical cases of transplant countries (Japan, Singapore, India, Israel, South Africa, Turkey, etc). The second rank of China is also noteworthy. Thus, it has been calculated how the 108 citations to China and legal transplants distribute over time: these are predominantly found in recent years, which makes sense given the increase of Western-type transplants in Chinese law, with the percentage of all articles on legal transplants referring to China exceeding 30% in the 2010s and 2020s (so far).[95]

2. Analysis of types of journals

Information on the types of journals in which articles on legal transplants are published is a further means to examine the focus of publications on legal transplants. For the purposes of Figure 2.10 and Table 2.4 this has been done with Google Scholar (only), given that for the Westlaw corpus it is in any case clear that this would be dominated by US law reviews.

With Google Scholar, a broad search for 'legal transplants' (or equivalent terms) (with the restriction source 'journal' or 'review', as above) produces too many hits to be checked manually. Thus, 2020 has been chosen as a sample year which led to 193 publications. According to Figure 2.10, the majority of these publications are in law journals (including journals that include 'law &', other topics such as law & society, or law & economics), while 20% of publications that mention 'legal transplants' are from a variety of other journals covering a number of other disciplines from both social sciences and humanities.

In order to examine publications that deal with legal transplants in more detail, Table 2.4 is based on the articles that have 'legal transplants' (or equivalents) in the title, selecting as a sample the years 2010 to 2021. Out of the journals in which the ninety-seven articles have been published, the American Journal of Comparative Law leads the list of nine articles. It publishes topics from any country of the world; thus, its top ranking does not indicate any particular thematic orientation but is simply due to it being the most established journal of comparative law today. This is different for the Asian and Chinese journals which also feature highly in the list. Specifically for China, it is interesting to note that the ninety-seven articles include seventeen articles in journals by Chinese universities.

For further evaluation, the list of journals has been searched for particular marker terms. Searching for the names of continents in the names of the journals, ten journals have 'Europe' in the title, ten 'America', nine 'Asia', and one 'Africa'. The low number for 'Africa' may be due to the fact that African

[95] The precise data are: pre 1990s: 0; 1990s: 5 out of 27 = 18.52%; 2000s: 21 out of 114 = 18.42%; 2010s: 61 out of 179 = 34.08%; 2020 to 2024: 21 out of 63 = 33.33%.

Figure 2.10 Journals with articles on 'legal transplants' (2020)

scholarship uses other theoretical frameworks (such as post-colonialism[96]) to discuss the history and continued presence of legal transplants in African countries. Searching for 'comparative', 'international', 'historical' (or 'history'), and variants of 'law and society' in the titles, 'comparative law' leads with twenty-two of the ninety-seven articles. This is followed by nine for 'international', six for 'law and society', and four for 'historical' (or 'history'). Thus, here too, this shows a link to topics of international law, while it is also clear that these numbers leave out further journals that discuss international law but do not have 'international' in the journal title.

[96] Some research also links this topic to legal transplants: see eg Matteo Solinas, 'The Nature of Legal Transplants—Inspirations from Postcolonial Scholarship' (2017) 22 *NZACL Yearbook* 179; Jedidiah J Kroncke, 'Legal Innovation as a Global Public Good: Remaking Comparative Law as Indigenization' in Philipp Dann, Michael Riegner, and Maxim Bönnemann (eds), *The Global South and Comparative Constitutional Law* (Oxford: OUP, 2020) 110.

Table 2.4 Journals with articles with 'legal transplants' in title (2010–2021)

Citations	Journals
9	American Journal of Comparative Law
4	Asian Journal of Comparative Law Asian Journal of Law and Society ISAIDAT Law Review
3	Chinese Journal of Comparative Law
2	European Review of Private Law Hague Journal of the Rule of Law Jindal Global Law Review Journal of Northeast Agricultural University Review of European Administrative Law The International Review of Intellectual Property and Competition Law
1	African Human Rights Law Journal; American Journal of Legal History; Annual Review of Law and Social Science; Australian Journal of Asian Law; Australian Journal of Corporate Law; Brooklyn Journal of International Law; Cambridge International Law Journal; Chinese Journal of Systems Science; Common Market Law Review; Comparative Law Review; Electronic Journal of Comparative Law; European Journal of Comparative Law and Governance; European Law Journal; European Journal of International Law; European Review of Contract Law; Flinders Law Journal; German Law Journal; International Journal of the Legal Profession; Jersey and Guernsey Law Review; Journal of Beijing University of Aeronautics and Astronautics; Journal of East China University of Science and Technology; Journal of Guangxi University for Nationalities; Journal of Indonesian Economy and Business; Journal of Wuhan University of Science and Technology; Journal of Competition Law and Economics; Journal of Dalian Maritime University; Journal of Fuyang Teachers College; Journal of Industrial Ecology; Journal of Jiamusi Education Institute; Journal of Kufa legal and political science; Journal of Law, Technology and Public Policy; Journal of Legal Studies 'Vasile Goldiş'; Journal of Liaoning Administrators College of Police; Journal of Qiqihar University; Journal of Shijiazhuang University; Journal of Sichuan Police College; Journal of Southwest University of Political Science; Journal of Zhengzhou University of Aeronautics; Kyiv-Mohyla Law and Politics Journal; Law & Society Review; Maastricht Journal of European and Comparative Law; Nanjing University Law Review; New Zealand Journal of Public and International Law; Padjadjaran Journal of Law; PalArch's Journal of Archaeology of Egypt; Queen Mary Journal of Intellectual Property; Review of Central and East European Law; Romanian Review of Private Law; Russian Journal of Legal Studies; Singapore Academy of Law Journal; Statute law review; The Estonian Historical Journal; The Journal of Business Law; The Legal History Review; The Rabel Journal of Comparative and International Law; The Journal of Legal History; The Journal of Specialised Translation; Uniform Law Review; University of Queensland Law Journal; UNTAG Law Review; Veteran Law Review

Table 2.5 Disciplinary distribution of terms in journals (JSTOR)

	(i) 'legal transplant(s)'		(ii) 'policy transfer' or 'policy diffusion' (or variants)		combined search for (i) and (ii)		(iii) all articles
	all	% of (iii)	all	% of (iii)	all	% of (iii)	all
Political Science	278	0.026%	1,595	0.151%	1,857	0.176%	1,053,314
Law	893	0.134%	222	0.033%	1,057	0.159%	665,651
Public Policy & Administration	7	0.005%	553	0.369%	560	0.374%	149,817
International Relations	34	0.010%	480	0.139%	510	0.148%	345,066
Business	53	0.007%	419	0.053%	469	0.059%	791,462
History	246	0.015%	180	0.011%	413	0.025%	1,663,072
Sociology	36	0.006%	359	0.064%	390	0.069%	563,466
Economics	56	0.007%	294	0.039%	342	0.045%	761,237
Education	18	0.002%	269	0.028%	287	0.030%	946,590
American Studies	2	0.00%	228	0.048%	230	0.048%	476,181

While searches with Google Scholar are convenient, it does not include the option to distinguish between different disciplines. By contrast, JSTOR includes the categorisation of journals into academic disciplines (while also allowing that a journal is catalogued in several disciplines simultaneously). Table 2.5 reports the findings for the ten disciplines that use the terms 'legal transplants', 'policy transfer', and 'policy diffusion' most frequently. It shows that the term of 'legal transplants' is predominantly used in Law, where it accounts for 0.322% of the total hits, with significant distance followed by Political Science (0.063%) and History (0.035%). Conversely, 'policy transfer/diffusion' demonstrates a broader appeal, with a notable presence in Public Policy & Administration with 0.887% of the total hits, followed by Political Science (0.363%), International Relations (0.334%),[97] Sociology (0.147%), and Business (0.127%).

These numbers highlight the multidisciplinary nature of policy transfer/diffusion as compared to the more domain-specific usage of legal transplants.

[97] A search of the total number of publications catalogued under both Political Science and International Relations on JSTOR reveals that 22.83% of the publications appear in both categories, indicating a significant overlap between the two disciplines. The overlap between Political Science and other disciplines like Law (3.72%) or Public Policy and Administration (2.39%) is significantly lower. For the specific search function see Annex 2.

It also evidences the fragmentation of academic disciplines. Thus, while Figure 2.10 included some journals outside law which used the term 'legal transplants', Table 2.5 shows that the vast majority of authors who write about policy transfer/diffusion do not consider the literature on legal transplants. Likewise, while the literature on legal transplants has become more open (as shown in the previous subsection), most legal scholars do not consider the related literature on policy transfers/diffusion.

It was already mentioned in the first chapter of this book that research on legal transplants can benefit from closer alignment to these other disciplines.[98] The data of Table 2.5 also show that there is significant potential to align the literature on legal transplants closer to these other disciplines. According to Table 2.5, when combining a search for both terms Public Policy & Administration leads the field by some distance, followed by Political Science, Law, and International Relations. As in the previous section,[99] it can again also be shown that the growth in academic publications is most pronounced for policy transfer/diffusion as the JSTOR publications grew from 128 hits pre-1990 to 166 in the 1990s, 983 in the 2000s, 1,981 in the 2010s, and 288 in the 2020s. By contrast, the term 'legal transplants' shows a more gradual trajectory, with eighty-eight hits pre-1990, increasing to 106 in the 1990s, 299 in the 2000s, 463 in the 2010s, and seventy-one in the 2020s.

3. Interpretation

The bibliometric results of this section show that Watson still plays some role in the discussion on legal transplants today. However, the literature has also diversified in new directions. The clearest example of the reduced impact of Watson is that Roman law plays little role in today's discussions about legal transplants. Indeed, as found in the previous section,[100] the rapid increase of interest in legal transplants in the last twenty years is only weakly related to Watson's original idea. Rather, we have seen that legal transplants are often (simply) a convenient general concept to describe and discuss the diffusion of legal rules and concepts across countries.

In this section, wide academic use of legal transplants has been found, for example, in its prevalence across many areas of law, as well as in the way it is

[98] See Chapter 1 at Section C 2.
[99] See Section C 2.
[100] See Section C 3.

today often linked to topics of international law. This finding is confirmed by further literature that discusses, for example, whether there may be transplants of international courts,[101] and whether domestic rules and institutions could diffuse 'upwards' as a 'vertical legal transplant'.[102] A further broadening concerns the geographic scope. Legal transplants are a popular concept in examining the use of foreign models in developing and transition economies. China and other Asian countries are now frequently mentioned as examples of legal transplants, which, beyond journal articles, can be seen in many recent book publications.[103] In particular, with respect to law in China, legal transplants feature frequently, both in the Western literature (as accessed by Westlaw) and in journal articles published by Chinese universities in English.

While Watson took a largely legal perspective, this section has shown that some of the literature on legal transplants now discusses legal transplants in an interdisciplinary manner. This can also be seen in specific examples: for instance, the political dimension arises in discussions about legislative drafting and legal transplants,[104] and research in law and economics examines the effect of legal transplants.[105] However, the findings of this section also noted the further potential to more closely align the research on legal transplants with the large fields of research in other disciplines, notably on policy transfer and policy diffusion.

E. Conclusion

This chapter provided a bibliometric assessment of the use of the term 'legal transplants' and related terms in the literature. Such a quantitative method is

[101] Karen J Alter and Laurence R Helfer, *Transplanting International Courts: The Law and Politics of the Andean Tribunal of Justice* (Oxford: OUP, 2017).

[102] For example, this has been discussed for the migration of the principles of reasonableness and proportionality to international investment law and the procedure of amicus curiae participation at the European Court of Human Rights. See Valentina Vadi, *Proportionality, Reasonableness and Standards of Review in International Investment Law and Arbitration* (Cheltenham: Edward Elgar, 2018); Anna Dolidze, 'Bridging Comparative and International Law: Amicus Curiae Participation as a Vertical Legal Transplant' (2015) 26 *European Journal of International Law* 851.

[103] For examples see the books by Gillespie, Nicholson, Chisholm, Khanal, Kaneko, Ng, Wang, Harding and others, and Breda, cited in the Annex 1.

[104] Eg Helen Xanthaki, 'Legal Transplants in Legislation: Defusing the Trap' (2008) 57 *International and Comparative Law Quarterly* 659; Nicola Lupo and Lucia Scaffardi (eds), *Comparative Law in Legislative Drafting: The Increasing Importance of Dialogue Amongst Parliaments* (The Hague: Eleven, 2014).

[105] Eg Peter Grajzl and Valentina Dimitrova-Grajzl, 'The Choice in the Lawmaking Process: Legal Transplants vs. Indigenous Law' (2009) 5 *Review of Law and Economics* 615; Daniel Berkowitz, Katharina Pistor, and Jean-François Richard, 'Economic Development, Legality, and the Transplant Effect' (2003) 47 *European Economic Review* 165.

not the only way to analyse this topic—and the other chapters of this book indeed use other methods. It also faces the challenge of subjectivity given that, in any bibliometric assessment, many choices need to be made; yet the fact that different corpora have led to very similar results gives confidence that the findings of this chapter are fairly robust.

A first main finding has been that legal transplants are an increasingly popular topic, notably with a rise in popularity since the mid-1990s and in particular in recent years. This finding also provides a first note of caution as regards the importance of Watson's contribution to legal transplants. Watson used this term in his 1974 book; yet, the recent literature, while it may still cite Watson in a superficial manner, is the result of more recent trends that make this topic attractive. This can also be confirmed by the growing popularity of the related concepts of 'policy transfer' and 'policy diffusion' in political science and other fields, while most of the existing literature on legal transplants does not consider this research.

A second main finding of this chapter is that today's literature on legal transplants has many different focal points, showing that legal transplants are understood as phenomena that are relevant in many different contexts. They also extend to any area of law, are often discussed in connection with international law and make reference to countries across the world. Despite the aforementioned limitations to cross-disciplinary dialogue, some authors also discuss legal transplants in an interdisciplinary spirit. Thus, there is clear general broadening of the scope of legal transplants in the literature.

For this book, these findings justify both the topicality of the topic of legal transplants and its wide understanding. The subsequent Chapter 3 aims to map how the increased scope of legal transplants can be presented as an anatomy of legal transplants. Furthermore, as this chapter found that other disciplines than law discuss even more frequently concepts such as policy and cultural transfer and diffusion, Chapters 3 to 7 will explain in the introductory sections which of these other disciplines can contribute to the question raised in the respective chapter and then incorporate these insights into the subsequent analysis.

3
An Anatomy of Legal Transplants

A. Introduction

Some of the current legal literature includes various taxonomies of legal transplants. For example, Margit Cohn distinguishes transplants according to categories such as type of influence, exporter, adopted norms, etc.[1] William Twining also identifies various categories but then distinguishes all of them under the perspective of a 'standard case and some variants'.[2] Similarly to the latter distinction, Cohn also explains that there has been a change in the way transplants are used: they 'are no longer adoptions of entire systems of law in a top-down fashion initiated by colonial forces. Instead, they come in different shapes and sizes, take place serially, and originate in a variety of sources.'[3]

In the literature on policy transfers, the debate has evolved along similar lines though with a stronger emphasis on the role of the agents of the transfer process. Categories include, for example, 'objects, levels, agents, arenas, destinations, directions, and forces'[4] or forms (coercive, negotiated, voluntary), scope (temporal and spatial organisation), agents/actors, objects, degrees (copying, adaptation, hybridization, inspiration).[5] There is also a parallel to the distinction between more and less typical cases: according to Diane Stone and colleagues, the 'conventional cases' of policy transfer are, for example, based on the assumptions that their use concerns policies of developed states and technocratic knowledge; yet, today they often also occur, for example, in

[1] Margit Cohn, 'Legal Transplant Chronicles: The Evolution of Unreasonableness and Proportionality Review of the Administration in the United Kingdom' (2010) 58 *American Journal of Comparative Law* 583; Margit Cohn, 'Legal Transplants: A Theoretical Framework and a Case Study from Public Law' in Mathias Siems and Po Jen Yap (eds), *The Cambridge Handbook of Comparative Law* (Cambridge: CUP, 2024) 426.

[2] William Twining, 'Diffusion of Law: A Global Perspective' (2004) 49 *The Journal of Legal Pluralism and Unofficial Law* 1; William Twining, 'Social Science and Diffusion of Law' (2005) 32 *Journal of Law and Society* 203; William Twining, *General Jurisprudence: Understanding Law from a Global Perspective* (Cambridge: CUP, 2009) 279.

[3] Cohn (2010) (n 1) 628.

[4] Osmany Porto de Oliveira, 'A Prelude to Policy Transfer Research' in Osmany Porto de Oliveira (ed), *Handbook of Policy Transfer, Diffusion and Circulation* (Cheltenham: Edward Elgar, 2021) 1, 7.

[5] Katja Bender, Sonja Keller, and Holger Willing, 'The Role of International Policy Transfer and Diffusion for Policy Change in Social Protection—A Review of the State of the Art' (IZNE Social Protection Working Paper 14/1, 2014) 11–12.

Legal Transplants. Mathias Siems, Oxford University Press. © Mathias Siems 2026.
DOI: 10.1093/9780191991981.003.0003

'complex transnational networks' and through 'subaltern exercises of power and resistance'.[6]

This chapter draws on both streams of literature, however, with a modified approach. Its main part (Sections B to D) is structured according to the object of the transplant, the relevant units, and the transplantation itself. These categories resemble some categories of prior research. However, this chapter then always distinguishes between the origin and the transplant unit and how variables of these two units interrelate. The following therefore shows matrices that display more complex categories of these relationships, also indicating to what extent typical cases of legal transplants can be categorised. This interaction between the origin and the transplant unit also sets the scene for the analysis of the subsequent Chapter 4, notably how influential agents are in determining whether and how legal transplants take place.

B. Object of the transplant

Figure 3.1 displays the eight objects discussed in this section. The first subsection outlines these categories while the second one deals with the relationship between origin and transplant unit as regards these objects. At the outset, it should also be noted that these eight objects are used here as a starting point as they reflect frequent divisions in the literature; yet they are not necessarily independent of each other. For example, codified rules may reflect a particular legal idea or policy, or a particular transplant may concern a mixture of different objects. Notably, within Figure 3.1, a graphic distinction is made between the first four categories that reflect a division into sources of law, while the second four categories are based on other notions related to law that can be the object of a transplant.

1. Categories

It seems obvious to say that 'legal transplants' need to be about the 'law'. However, it is far less clear what 'law' may include as authors in legal theory and legal philosophy take many different positions as to the nature of law.[7] For

[6] Diane Stone, Osmany Porto de Oliveira, and Leslie A Pal, 'Transnational Policy Transfer: The Circulation of Ideas, Power and Development Models' (2020) 30 *Policy and Society* 1, 2–4.

[7] Thus, some comparative law books cover the question 'what is law?' in some detail, see Geoffrey Samuel, *An Introduction to Comparative Law Theory and Method* (Oxford: Hart Publishing, 2014) 121–51.

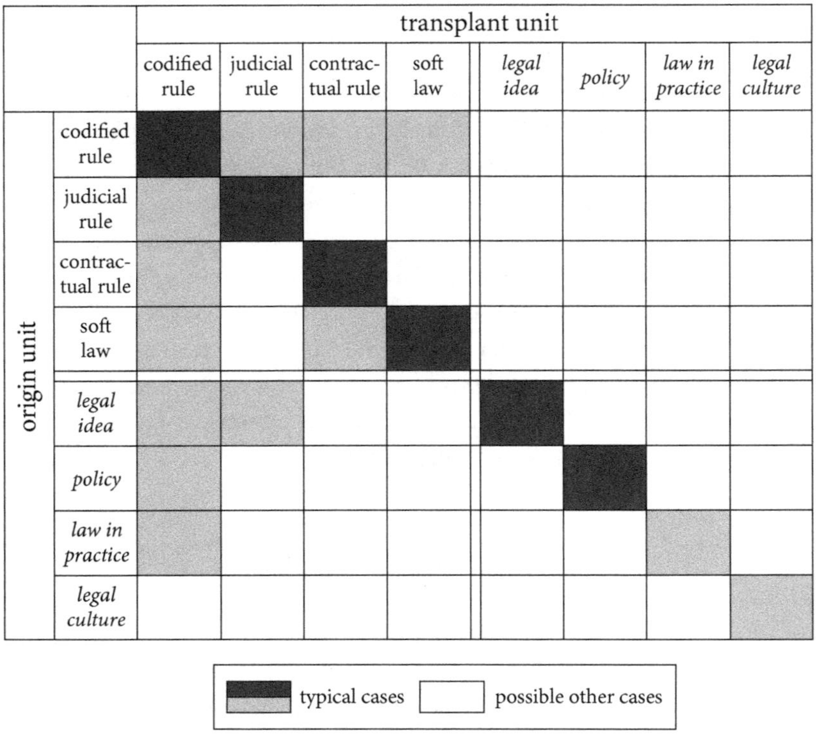

Figure 3.1 Categories of transplants based on the object

present purposes, a pragmatic and wide approach is adopted, following similar positions of other publications on legal transplants. For example, both Max Rheinstein and William Twining refer to 'legal phenomena' in order to cover a wide range of objects.[8] David Nelken writes that transplants can concern 'various elements of legal culture' such as legal norms, salient features of legal institutions and of their infrastructure, social behaviour in using and not using law, types of legal consciousness in the legal profession and in public,[9] and Neli Frost uses a socio-legal paradigm of law to include 'not only state laws and institutions, but also a diffusion of standards, regulations, soft-law, treaties,

[8] Max Rheinstein, 'Types of Reception' (1956) 5 *Annales de la Faculté de Droit d'Istanbul* 31, 36; Twining (2004) (n 2) 17.

[9] David Nelken, 'Towards a Sociology of Legal Adaptation' in David Nelken and Johannes Feest (eds), *Adapting Legal Culture* (Oxford: Hart Publishing, 2001) 7, 25.

customs and international agreements'.[10] Reference can also be made to the notion of legal pluralism as it has emerged since at least the 1980s.[11]

The category of a 'codified rule' in Figure 3.1 is in today's world fairly self-explanatory. As a possible object of a legal transplant, it can be about a particular provision of a statute, but it can also concern an entire act or code. As this section merely aims to identify possible objects, it is left open who drafted the codified rule (eg, territorial states, international organisation, sub-state units); thus, Figure 3.1 refers to origin and transplant units (not origin and transplant countries) while the subsequent Section C will then distinguish between different types of units.

The 'judicial rule' is the natural equivalent to the codified rule in countries with the notion of 'case law' (ie typically common law countries). However, it is also meant to refer to judicial rules of countries where court judgments 'merely' have a persuasive power as, in practice, this can be as important as in the former countries.[12] Likewise, and similar to the previous category, the judicial rule includes rules by any judicial body, for example also international courts and arbitral tribunals.

The category 'contractual rule' covers all of such contractual rules, regardless of their precise legal nature. Some civil codes explicitly state that contracts have the force of law,[13] but there can also be non-binding contractual rules such as letters of intent (or, else, those may be seen as 'soft law', see the subsequent category). Contractual rules, as understood here, can also be those of organisations, for example, the articles of associations or bylaws of companies or other private and public bodies.

The notion of 'soft law' derives from international law; yet it can also be applied to domestic rules. While there is no commonly agreed definition, it is clear that soft law needs to be understood 'in opposition to hard law and non-law'.[14] More specifically, some authors refer to legal norms that do not have the form of a source of law, while others include all legal norms which are not enforceable (even if they are in the form of a formal legal source).[15] Prominent examples are voluntary codes of conduct, such as corporate governance

[10] Neli Frost, 'Transnational Corporations as Agents of Legal Change: The Role of Corporate Social Responsibility' (2016) 5 *Cambridge Journal of International and Comparative Law* 502, 512.

[11] The classical work is John Griffiths, 'What is Legal Pluralism?' (1986) 18 *The Journal of Legal Pluralism and Unofficial Law* 1.

[12] Mathias Siems, *Comparative Law* (Cambridge: CUP, 3rd edn, 2022) 66.

[13] Such as article 1103 of the French Code Civile and Article 1372 of the Italian Codice Civile.

[14] Fabien Terpan, 'The Definition of Soft Law' in Mariolina Eliantonio, Emilia Korkea-aho, and Ulrika Mörth (eds), *Research Handbook on Soft Law* (Cheltenham: Edward Elgar, 2023) 43, 44.

[15] See eg Laszlo Blutman, 'In the Trap of a Legal Metaphor: International Soft Law' (2010) 59 *International and Comparative Law Quarterly* 605; John Cerone, 'A Taxonomy of Soft Law: Stipulating a Definition' in Stéphanie Lagoutte, Thomas Gammeltoft-Hansen, and John Cerone (eds), *Tracing the Roles of Soft Law in Human Rights* (Oxford: OUP, 2016) 15.

codes,[16] that encourage but do not oblige companies to follow certain good practices. Following the notion of legal pluralism, another example is how in the law of assisted suicide, besides the positive criminal and medical law, guidelines of medical associations and public prosecutors are translated into social practice.[17] Some authors also regard indicators, such as comparative indices of the rule of law, governance, and corruption, as a form of 'soft law', while others also acknowledge at least their 'law-like' features.[18]

The category 'legal idea' is included here to cover substantive elements of the law that are not explicitly found in precise legal rules. Thus, these ideas may be about concepts that synthesise a particular set of rules (eg, the principles of good faith, the principle of proportionality). They may also go beyond precise legal rules as far as they are of a more normative nature (eg, legal certainty, the rule of law). The term 'legal idea' has been chosen as an umbrella term in order to capture phenomena that may also be known by other terms, such as legal principle,[19] general principles of law,[20] legal topoi,[21] or legal system.[22]

By contrast, the category 'policy' is motivated by the literature on policy transfer and policy diffusion.[23] In a nutshell, a policy is understood to be a 'course or principle of action adopted or proposed by an organization or individual'.[24] Thus, it can be about policies by governments or other public bodies (ie public polices) or other entities or persons (eg, organisational policies), also in the international sphere. It can also cover diverse substantive topics as the policy literature includes sub-fields such as social, health, education, and foreign policy. All of this can be reflected in specific legal rules; yet, a focus on policies provides a different perspective as the rule focus of legal scholarship.

[16] See the collection at https://www.ecgi.global/content/codes accessed 22 October 2025.

[17] John Griffiths, Heleen Weyers, and Maurice Adams, *Euthanasia and Law in Europe* (Oxford: Hart Publishing, 2008).

[18] See eg Mauro Bussani, Sabino Cassese, and Marta Infantino, 'Quantification of Performance as a Regulatory Technique: A Comparative Appraisal' in Mauro Bussani, Sabino Cassese, and Marta Infantino (eds), *Comparative Legal Metrics: Quantification of Performances as Regulatory Technique* (Leiden: Brill, 2023) 323, 352–3; Mathias Siems and David Nelken, 'Global Social Indicators and the Concept of Legitimacy' (2017) 13 *International Journal of Law in Context* 436.

[19] See eg Ronald M Dworkin, 'The Model of Rules' (1967) 35 *University of Chicago Law Review* 14; Humberto Ávila, *Theory of Legal Principles* (Dordrecht: Springer, 2007).

[20] Guido Alpa, 'General Principles of Law' (1994) 1 *Annual Survey of International and Comparative Law* 1; Giorgio Gaja, 'General Principles of Law', in *Max Planck Encyclopedia of Public International Law* (2020), available at https://opil.ouplaw.com/abstract/10.1093/law:epil/9780199231690/law-9780199231690-e1410 accessed 22 October 2025.

[21] Theodor Viehweg, *Topik und Jurisprudenz* (Munich: CH Beck, 5th edn, 1974).

[22] Claus-Wilhelm Canaris, *Systemdenken und Systembegriff in der Jurisprudenz* (Berlin: Duncker & Humblot, 1969).

[23] See generally Chapter 1 at Section C 2.

[24] https://policy-insider.ai/glossary/ accessed 22 October 2025.

'Law in practice' (or 'law in action') is a common phrase to draw a distinction to the 'law in the books' (ie statutory and case law).[25] Today, the interest in the law in practice is often associated with the overlapping fields of legal realism, law and society, socio-legal, and empirical legal studies. Examples include the practical operation of courts and other enforcement practices, the compliance with legal rules, legal education, and the legal profession. All of these elements are usually not a mere reflection of the law in the books; thus, research on the law in practice often raises the question about the general relationship between law and society.[26]

Finally, 'legal culture' is a term that may include a variety of elements. In what follows, it is understood as referring to the attitudes of the general public as well legislators, judges, and practising lawyers towards the law (ie the external and the internal legal culture).[27] It also includes informal types of social control and dispute resolution, the habits and attitudes underpinning them, as well as the possibility of customary legal rules.[28] All of these elements may be relevant at various scales (international, regional, national, sub-national, etc). There is also the view that relates the notion of legal cultures to that of legal families (ie common law, civil law, etc),[29] while it may be more accurate to say that legal families are a conglomerate of all of the categories outlined here.

2. Relevance and interactions

The categories of the previous subsection form the basis to categorise legal transplants according to their objects. The following takes the respective object in the origin unit as a starting point and then discusses how far it is typically the case that, in the transplant unit, the transplant is reflected in the same object or whether it may be transformed into a different one. This evaluation is based on existing cases of legal transplants but also their discussion in the literature. Figure 3.1 summarises these typical cases while clarifying that other transformations may also occur.

[25] It goes back to Roscoe Pound, 'Law in Books and Law in Action' (1910) 44 *American Law Review* 12.

[26] Further discussed in Chapter 5 at Section B.

[27] It goes back to Lawrence M Friedman, *The Legal System: A Social Science Perspective* (New York: Russell Sage Foundation, 1975).

[28] See the discussion in Siems (n 12) 174–7.

[29] Csaba Varga, 'Comparative Legal Cultures: Renewal by Transforming into a Genuine Discipline' (2007) 48 *Acta Juridica Hungarica* 95.

For the case of *codified rules* in both units a number of further distinctions can be made. Silvia Ferreri and Larry DiMatteo distinguish between cases where (i) a country adopted an entire 'code' (citing as examples the adoption of the Swiss Civil Code by Turkey and the German one by Japan), (ii) the transplantation of a more distinct law (citing as an example the adoption of French sales law by Louisiana), and (iii) the adoption of more specific legal rules (citing as an example the adoption of the German 'defence of security' in Chinese contract law).[30] Going even further into the details of specific legal rules, it can be examined how far particular phrases or sentences have been copied verbatim by the transplant unit.[31] Other distinctions are, for example, in which areas of law legal transplants are most likely to occur, and how far they require a technological, contextual, or ideological perspective.[32] Another distinction may be between rules of constitutional law, ordinary statute law, and secondary administrative rules,[33] also with the possibility that transplants move, for example, from constitutional rules in the origin country to ordinary statute law in the transplant country.

Considering the transplantation of codified rules to other categories, there are at least three situations where this is fairly typical (see the shadings in Figure 3.1). First, codified rules may be adopted in another country's case law: for example, this happens in a situation where a country codifies details of certain general rules (eg, good faith, directors' duties, proportionality) which can then be used as guidance in the courts of a country without such codification.[34] Second, contractual rules may adopt rules codified from another country; for example, parties may adapt their contracts to the rules of a foreign country in order to make it easier to follow the same rules as in contracts with parties from that country.[35] Third, it is possible that codified rules become soft law in another country, for example,

[30] Silvia Ferreri and Larry A DiMatteo, 'Terminology Matters: Dangers of Superficial Transplantation' (2019) 37 *Boston University International Law Journal* 35, 54.

[31] For an example, see Dionysia Katelouzou and Mathias Siems, 'The Global Diffusion of Stewardship Codes' in Dionysia Katelouzou and Dan Puchniak (eds), *Global Shareholder Stewardship: Complexities, Challenges and Possibilities* (Cambridge: CUP, 2022) 631.

[32] Otto Kahn-Freund, 'On Uses and Misuses of Comparative Law' (1974) 37 *Modern Law Review* 1, 6; Twining (2009) (n 2) 286. For areas of law see also Chapter 4 at Section C 3 (d).

[33] For this distinction, as applied to transplants, see Daphne Barak-Erez, 'The Institutional Aspects of Comparative Law' (2009) 15 *Columbia Journal of European Law* 477.

[34] See eg Court of Appeal of the Supreme Court of New South Wales, *Deputy Commissioner of Taxation v Dick*, 3 August 2007, 226 FLR 388, paras 107–8 (referring to the codification of directors' duties in UK Companies Act 2006, s 172(1)).

[35] Ronald J Gilson, 'Globalizing Corporate Governance: Convergence of Form or Function' (2001) 49 *American Journal of Comparative Law* 329, 346–50 (as 'convergence through contract'). See also Roman Uliasz, 'The Transplantation of Legal Concepts by Means of Language: A Private Law Perspective' (2023) 12 *Cambridge International Law Journal* 266, 279–84 (on transplantation by international commercial contracts).

where in the latter country there is agreement on the usefulness of these rules but not their mandatory nature.[36]

For *judicial rules* in both units, there is today a large body of literature that discusses examples of judicial dialogue and cross-citations.[37] The first chapter of this book already referred to South Africa where foreign case law is an accepted source of interpretation.[38] Elsewhere, judges have expressed the view that there is at least a flow of ideas within legal families. For example, the former French judge Guy Canivet relates foreign citations in France to the role of legal families and similar levels of economic development.[39] For the UK, a book by the late Lord Bingham explains how UK judges have considered decisions from other common law jurisdictions, but occasionally also from further afield (while also noting that, as far as the law is codified, the 'judge is unlikely to gain much help from other jurisdictions').[40] But common law judges have also discussed whether the bond between their jurisdictions may have weakened. In the well-known UK case of *Donoghue v Stevenson*, the House of Lords considered US case law, but even then indicated that 'though the source of the law in the two countries may be the same, its current may well flow in different channels'.[41] There is also some explicit backlash against the use of foreign case law, in particular in the US, as discussed later in this book.[42]

The transfer of foreign case law to codified norms is sometimes said to be unlikely. According to Ernst Hirsch, case law cannot be received due to its thousands of volumes of text.[43] Yet, transplantations of distinct judicial rules can be transformed into codified legal rules. An old example is the codification of some of the common law rules in colonial India, with those codified rules then also being

[36] For example, while the US listing rules of the NYSE had requirements of some board members being independent since 1966, the UK Code of Best Practice 1992, s 2.2 (as well as subsequent rules) only introduced those as a form of soft law.

[37] See eg Mads Andenas and Duncan Fairgrieve (eds), *Courts and Comparative Law* (Oxford: OUP, 2015); Elaine Mak, *Judicial Decision-Making in a Globalised World* (Oxford: Hart Publishing, 2013); Tania Groppi, Marie-Claire Ponthoreau, and Irene Spigno (eds), *Judicial Bricolage: The Use of Foreign Precedents by Constitutional Judges in the 21st Century* (Oxford: Hart Publishing, 2025); Project on 'Cross-Citations between Supreme Courts in Europe', http://cross-citations.blogspot.com/ accessed 23 October 2025.

[38] See Chapter 1 at Section B 2.

[39] Guy Canivet, 'The Practice of Comparative Law by the Supreme Courts: Brief Reflections on the Dialogue Between the Judges in French and European Experience' (2006) 80 *Tulane Law Review* 1377.

[40] Tom Bingham, *Widening Horizons: The Influence of Comparative Law and International Law on Domestic Law* (Cambridge: CUP, 2010). But see also John WF Allison, *A Continental Distinction in the Common Law* (Oxford: OUP, 1996) 27 (transplant of public/private law distinction from civil law by English courts despite not acknowledging it).

[41] *Donoghue v Stevenson* [1932] AC 562, 576 (per Lord Buckmaster).

[42] See Chapter 6 at Sections B 2 and C 1 (b) and 4 (a).

[43] Ernst Hirsch, *Rezeption als sozialer Prozeß: erläutert am Beispiel der Türkei* (Berlin: Duncker & Humblot, 1981) 15.

transplanted to other parts of the British empire.[44] Today, we can for example observe that the business judgment rule of US corporate law has found its way into codifications in continental Europe.[45]

The transplantation of a *contractual rule* is feasible as far as mandatory laws do not hinder the implementation of the aspired contract design.[46] It has been discussed in a number of examples, such as elements of M&A agreements in Germany and India that resemble those of the US[47] and indigenous community-corporate mining agreements that took the model of Canadian contracts.[48] An Italian publication also mentions the contractual models of franchising, factoring, and leasing as examples that have crossed borders (often even retaining their English names).[49] For contractual rules in particular, it is also possible to observe transplants within one country: for example, US data show how exclusive forum provisions to multiforum shareholder litigation have been gradually adopted in corporate charters and bylaws by most major US corporations.[50]

Contractual rules can also become codified laws. As for typical cases, Natasha Affolder writes that 'this is evident in the area of investment contracts, where contractual provisions on natural resource development, taxation provisions or transparency, and anti-corruption language may require changes to domestic legislation' but then also provides a detailed example from the way conservation contracts influence environmental law.[51] As legal transplants can concern any units (discussed in the next section), it is also possible that such a transplant occurs within the same country: for example, in the evolution of

[44] Jean-Louis Halpérin, 'Western Legal Transplants and India' (2010) 2 *Jindal Global Law Review* 14.

[45] Julia Told, 'Business Judgment Rule: A Generally Applicable Principle?' (2015) *European Business Law Review* 713, 727–8.

[46] For a difficult case see Luca Enriques, Casimiro Antonio Nigro, and Tobias H Tröger, 'Can U.S. Venture Capital Contracts Be Transplanted into Europe? Systematic Evidence from Germany and Italy' (LawFin Working Paper No 58, 2025), available at https://ssrn.com/abstract=5287685 accessed 23 October 2025. More positive: Peter Agstner, Antonio Capizzi, and Paolo Giudici, 'Le partecipazioni privilegiate del venture capitalist' (2025) 70/2-3 *Rivista delle società* 200, 238–40.

[47] Heike Schweitzer, 'Private Legal Transplants in Negotiated Deals' (2007) 4 *European Company and Financial Law Review* 79; Afra Afsharipour, 'Legal Transplants in the Law of the Deal: M&A Agreements in India' in Claire A Hill and Steven Davidoff Solomon (eds), *Research Handbook on Mergers and Acquisitions* (Cheltenham: Edward Elgar, 2016) 445.

[48] Natasha Affolder, 'Looking for Law in Unusual Places: Cross-Border Diffusion of Environmental Norms' (2018) 7 *Transnational Environmental Law* 425, 430–7.

[49] Ugo Mattei, 'Circolazione dei modelli giuridici' in *Enciclopedia del diritto, Annali I* (Milan: Giuffrè, 2007) 173, 174. For the linguistic element see also Maurizio Lupoi, 'Profili (anche linguistici) dei flussi giuridici' (*Accademia della Crusca*, 20 July 2002), available at https://accademiadellacrusca.it/it/contenuti/profili-anche-linguistici-dei-flussi-giuridici/1 accessed 23 October 2025.

[50] Roberta Romano and Sarath Sanga, 'The Private Ordering Solution to Multiforum Shareholder Litigation' (2017) 14 *Journal of Empirical Legal Studies* 31.

[51] Affolder (n 48) 433, 437–42.

capital markets law, it happened that private stock exchange listing rules (ie the contract to get admitted to a particular stock exchange) gradually became codified in binding legislative rules.[52]

While *soft law* has not been a key concern in the original literature on legal transplants,[53] it is now more frequently discussed. For example, publications deal with the way multinational enterprises (MNEs) transplant the use of codes of conduct in creating 'special legal zones',[54] how labour standards set by such codes of conduct are an example of the diffusion of self-regulatory norms by private actors,[55] how codes on corporate social responsibility (CSR) form a well-connected citation network,[56] and how the international master agreement on derivative trading has influenced its Chinese counterpart (including the way Chinese courts align the interpretation of its terms to the former agreements).[57] As soft law can have different forms and shapes, it is also possible that, in such cases, soft laws change, for example, that codes drafted by a private body in one country are enacted by a government-sponsored body in another country.[58]

Further typical variants of this literature include situations where soft law becomes 'hard law' as codified or contractual rules. This happened in the examples that some transnational CSR codes have become part of supply contracts as well as some legislative initiatives,[59] that the OECD Guidelines on financial education have been incorporated into Columbian law and practice,[60] and that informal

[52] John C Coffee Jr, 'The Rise of Dispersed Ownership: The Roles of Law and the State in the Separation of Ownership and Control' (2001) 111 *Yale Law Journal* 1.

[53] See Chapter 1 at Section B 2.

[54] Tomaso Ferrando, 'Private Legal Transplant: Multinational Enterprises as Proxies of Legal Homogenisation' (2014) 5 *Transnational Legal Theory* 20.

[55] Jodi L Short, 'Transplanting Law in a Globalized World: Private Transnational Regulation and the Legal Transplant Paradigm' in Francesca Bignami and David Zaring (eds), *Comparative Law and Regulation: Understanding the Global Regulatory Process* (Cheltenham: Edward Elgar Publishing, 2016) 430.

[56] Oren Perez and Ofir Stegmann, 'Transnational Networked Constitutionalism' (2018) 45 *Journal of Law and Society* S135; Oren Perez, Reuven Cohen and Nir Schreiber, 'Governance Through Global Networks and Corporate Signaling' (2019) 13 *Regulation & Governance* 447.

[57] Mark Hsiao, 'From the Global ISDA Master Agreement to the Chinese version of NAFMII: A Standard form Contract as the Source of Legal Transplant, Irritation, and Integration' (2024) 15 *George Mason International Law Journal* 1.

[58] For example, this has happened for Stewardship Codes, see Katelouzou and Siems (n 31). For another example, see Katarzyna Chałaczkiewicz-Ładna, Irene-marie Esser, and Jonathan Hardman, 'Lost in Transplantation? The Challenge of Deploying "Comply or Explain" in Scottish Higher Education Governance' (2026) 30 *Edinburgh Law Review* 25.

[59] Chang-hsien Tsai and Yen-nung Wu, 'What Conflict Minerals Rules Tell Us about the Legal Transplantation of Corporate Social Responsibility Standards without the State: From the United Nations to the United States to Taiwan' (2018) 38 *Northwestern Journal of International Law & Business* 233.

[60] Felipe A Galvis Castro, 'Derecho internacional de la educación financiera: importación e implementación en Colombia' (2017) 38 *Revista de Derecho Público* 2.

environmental standards have migrated to both legislation and contract.[61] Often such hardening of soft law occurs if the transplant country lacks the economic or social pressure that makes soft law an effective tool in the origin country. Another example is that of indicators as a form of 'soft law' as many of them explicitly aim to be transposed into domestic law.[62]

Legal ideas are similar to any other ideas which diffuse into a new environment.[63] The comparative law literature has discussed, for example, the reception of continental ideas in the common law world,[64] the idea of having a codified state law,[65] the Western model of human rights,[66] the ideal of the rule of law,[67] the transparency of public administration,[68] and the interchange of legal languages[69] as examples of legal transplants. Legal ideas may also be 'mere' academic ideas: for example, this can refer to research on citation networks in legal academia,[70] and the way theories of justice operate across different cultures.[71] Specific examples of research on the transfer of legal theories are from Japan[72] and Latin America.[73] The latter research was put at the centre of interest by Diego Eduardo López Medina: he argues that the European legal influence on Latin America is mainly felt in transplants of legal theory; yet,

[61] Affolder (n 48).

[62] See the examples in Siems (n 12) 371–2.

[63] See Chapter 2 at Section C 2.

[64] Mathias Reimann (ed), *The Reception of Continental Ideas in the Common Law World: 1820–1920* (Berlin: Duncker & Humblot, 1993). See also Allison (n 40).

[65] Jean-Louis Halpérin, 'The Concept of Law: A Western Transplant?' (2009) 10 *Theoretical Inquiries in Law* 333.

[66] Siems (n 12) 340–7. Specifically for human dignity: Alberto Oehling de los Reyes, 'El concepto constitucional de dignidad de la persona: forma de comprensión y modelos predominantes de recepción en la Europa continental' (2011) 91 *Revista Española de Derecho Constitucional* 135.

[67] Till Patrik Holterhus (ed), *The Law Behind Rule of Law Transfers: On Rule Based Interactions of Legal Orders in a Globalized World* (Baden-Baden: Nomos, 2019); Katarzyna Górka, *Jawność posiedzeń Sejmu i Senatu oraz jej ograniczenia w Konstytucji RP* (Warsaw: CH Beck, 2014) (for post-communist Poland).

[68] Alban Spielkamp, *Dialogische Rechtsentwicklung im europäischen Verwaltungsrecht: Strukturen transnationaler Rechtsrezeptionen am Beispiel der Verwaltungstransparenz* (Tübingen: Mohr Siebeck, 2025) 292.

[69] Barbara Pozzo, 'Comparative Law and Language' in Mauro Bussani and Ugo Mattei (eds), *The Cambridge Companion to Comparative Law* (Cambridge: CUP, 2012) 88, 90–4.

[70] Basil Markesinis, *Comparative Law in the Courtroom and Classroom: The Story of the Last Thirty-Five Years* (Oxford: Hart Publishing, 2003) 75–155 and 261–4.

[71] Man-Chung Chiu, 'Going Beyond Globalization and Localization: Articulating a Theory of Justice in Han-Chinese Culture' (2010) 21 *Law and Critique* 93.

[72] See Chapter 5 at Section C 2 (b).

[73] See the subsequent footnote and, eg, Daniel Bonilla Maldonado (ed), *Teoría del derecho y trasplantes jurídicos* (Bogota: Siglo del Hombre Editores, 2009); Mario Alberto Cajas Sarria, 'Usos locales de Tratados de Legislación Civil y Penal de Jeremy Bentham en los inicios de la República' (2010) 34 *Revista de Derecho* 21, 25; Juan Jorge Almonacid Sierra, 'Insumos para la cimentación de la historia del derecho comercial colombiano a través de la teoría del transplante [sic] jurídico' (2007) 20 *Pensamiento Jurídico*, available at https://revistas.unal.edu.co/index.php/peju/article/view/38631 accessed 23 October 2025.

these theories have often been made 'impure' in 'local reception sites' while local jurists still pay lip service to their original universal meaning.[74]

A potentially complex situation can arise when ideas become part of the codified or judicial rules of the transplant unit. In this regard, Ernst Hirsch even takes the view that this should be the main way we understand legal reception, namely that the object of a transfer is a particular 'legal thought' which, as a social process, then reappears in a modified form in the other country.[75] Similarly, Thomas Wilhelmsson phrases the dynamic process of Europeanisation in private law as a case of a movement of legal ideas,[76] Andrew Harding suggests that 'largely in practice we are talking about the transplantation of a legal idea, not a law as such',[77] and Alejandro Nieto refers to a transplant of the inspiring principles of the law ('its spirit') as a case of 'integrative reception'.[78] Such perspectives can also be supported by the functional method of comparative law, namely that different countries follow the same idea but may do so with somehow different rules.[79] As regards judicial rules, the literature on judicial dialogue too has shown how courts adopt 'doctrinal constructions' or other legal ideas from other domestic or international courts.[80]

The transplantation of *policies* is the main topic of the literature on policy transfer and policy diffusion. For legal scholars, the focus on policies is of interest as it shows that the analysis can go beyond specific legal rules. However, in the policy literature, there are also variations as to the level of generality as it distinguishes, for example, between policy programmes, goals, and content, as well as policy ends and means (or policy aims and tools).[81] It may be the case

[74] Diego Eduardo López Medina, *Teoría impura del derecho. La transformación de la cultura jurídica latinoamericana* (Bogota: Legis, 2004). For legal universalism and its critics see also Chapter 6 at Section C 2 (b).

[75] Hirsch (n 43) 11–12.

[76] Thomas Wilhelmsson, *Free Movement of Legal Ideas: Towards a Dynamic Europeanisation of Private Law* (Oxford: Hart Publishing, 2024) 119–20 (calling it 'a matter of taste' whether it should be called a 'transplant').

[77] Andrew Harding, 'The Legal Transplants Debate: Getting Beyond the Impasse?' in Vito Breda (ed), *Legal Transplants in East Asia and Oceania* (Cambridge: CUP, 2019) 13, 20.

[78] Alejandro Nieto, 'El derecho comunitario europeo como derecho común vulgar' (2016) 200 *Revista de Administración Pública* 25, 31–4.

[79] In other words, they use a 'functional transplant', Doreen McBarnet, 'Transnational Transactions: Legal Work, Cross-border Commerce and Global Regulation' in Michael Likosky (ed), *Transnational Legal Processes: Globalisation and Power Disparities* (London: Butterworths, 2002) 98, 100.

[80] Christoph Engel and Keren Weinshall, 'Diffusion of Legal Innovations' (2022) 18 *Annual Review of Law and Social Science* 139, 146–7 (with further references). For a specific example see Gilles Cuniberti, 'Enhancing Judicial Reputation Through Legal Transplants—Estoppel Travels to France' (2012) 60 *American Journal of Comparative Law* 383.

[81] David Dolowitz and David Marsh, 'Learning from Abroad: The Role of Policy Transfer in Contemporary Policy-Making' (2000) 13 *Governance* 5, 12; Kidjie Saguin and Kritika Sha, 'Policy Transfer in Asia' in Osmany Porto de Oliveira (ed), *Handbook of Policy Transfer, Diffusion and Circulation* (Cheltenham: Edward Elgar, 2021) 317, 321. See also Kurt Weyland, *Bounded Rationality*

that researching policy transplants is more challenging in identifying a transplant than research on specific legal rules: thus, Daniel Ghezelbash suggests a four-stage procedure that (i) identifies a common policy problem, (ii) analyses law and policy in both source and receiving country, (iii) searches for evidence that transfer of information has occurred, and (iv) carries out interviews with agents of this process.[82]

As to the transfer of policies of one unit into legal rules of another unit, this is likely where the latter unit makes policy aims explicit in its legislation. In legislative drafting, it is discussed how far preambles and recitals should be used (as well as the status that they have) and how far policy objectives may be inserted in the actual provisions of a legislative act.[83] Thus, here, as the policy itself becomes part of the law, the transplant unit is also likely to be open about the use of this foreign policy transplant.

The *law in practice* plays a key role in the literature that refers to the limitations of legal transplants.[84] However, it is also widely acknowledged that the operation of courts, enforcement practices and compliance, legal education, and the legal profession themselves have been frequent objects of legal transplants. For example, there is extensive discussion in comparative law on the way forms of legal education and practice have spread across countries.[85] In two specific aspirational examples, it has been suggested that US instruments of corporate legal risk limitation may be used in the Nordic countries,[86] and that climate-change litigation can show the export of a successful litigation

and Policy Diffusion: Social Sector Reform in Latin America (Princeton, NJ: Princeton University Press, 2006) 17 ('model diffusion vs. principle diffusion').

[82] Daniel Ghezelbash, *Refugee Lost: Asylum Law in an Interdependent World* (Cambridge: CUP, 2018) 8; Daniel Ghezelbash, 'Legal Transfers of Migration Law: The Case for an Interdisciplinary Approach' (2023) 7 *International Journal of Migration and Border Studies* 182, 188.

[83] See eg Tadas Klimas and Jurate Vaiciukaite, 'The Law of Recitals in European Community Legislation' (2008) 15 *ILSA Journal of International & Comparative Law* 61; Kent Roach, 'The Uses and Audiences of Preambles in Legislation' (2001) 47 *McGill Law Journal* 129.

[84] See Chapter 5 at Section B 3.

[85] See eg Susan Bartie and David Sandomierski (eds), *American Legal Education Abroad: Critical Histories* (New York: NYU Press, 2021); Daniela Piana and Cristina Dallara, *Networking the Rule of Law: How Change Agents Reshape Judicial Governance in the EU* (London: Ashgate, 2015) 87–110; Sue Farran, 'The "Age of Empire": Again?' (2013) 47 *The Law Teacher* 345; Daniel Bonilla Maldonado (ed), *Los mandarines del derecho: Trasplantes jurídicos, análisis cultural del derecho y trabajo pro bono* (Bogota: Siglo del Hombre Editores, 2017); Arzu Oğuz, 'Hukuk Eğitimindeki Son Gelişmeler ve Karşılaştırmalı Hukukun Hukuk Eğitimindeki Rolü' (2003) 52 *Ankara Üniversitesi Hukuk Fakültesi Dergisi* 1.

[86] Ville Pönka, '#MeToo-liike ja yritysten oikeudellinen riskienhallinta—Miten yhdysvaltalaisten yritysten käyttämät vastuunrajoitusinstrumentit toimisivat oikeudellisina siirrännäisinä Pohjoismaissa?' (2019) 5 *Lakimies* 608.

strategy.[87] A transplantation of the 'law in practice' may also spread together with legal rules enacting certain enforcement institutions: here, examples are the spread of ADR and other informal forms of dispute resolution,[88] as well as the use 'problem-solving courts'.[89]

By its very nature, the law in practice is different from the law in the books. Yet, there can be cases where the transplant country enacts codified rules that aim to match the law in practice of other countries. The main example is the field of 'law and development': here, the typical advice given to countries of the developing world is to implement legal rules that can work as well *in practice* as in countries of the developing world. Thus, the argument is that simply enacting the same rules of the latter countries may not be sufficient as the former countries lack experience with such rules; rather, taking a socio-logical perspective, the aim is to have rules that effectively work in practice.[90]

Finally, *legal culture* may be seen as something difficult to transplant. It is, however, not impossible. Two modern examples are cases where—in combination with more specific legal transplants—countries have deliberately changed their legal family. As a former Belgian colony, Rwanda initially had a French-inspired law; however, in the early twenty-first century, it shifted closer to the common law, for example, by way of repealing many previous laws and changing to English as the main official language. Sudan presents a contrasting example: in the 1970s, the government attempted to implement a general shift from common law to French civil law, but this was reversed a few years later while retaining some civilian elements, also due to Egyptian influence.[91] Other types of examples concern cases where countries have changed to institutions typical for another legal family. For example, research by Carmine Guerriero has analysed cases where countries have shifted the power balance between legislator and courts.[92]

[87] Vibe Ulfbeck, 'Climate Change in Tort Law? The New Regulatory and External Effect of Suits Against Private Actors' in Anna Beckers and others (eds), *The Foundations of European Transnational Private Law* (Oxford: Hart Publishing, 2024) 345.

[88] Eg Naomi Creutzfeldt, *Ombudsmen and ADR: A Comparative Study of Informal Justice in Europe* (Cham: Palgrave Macmillan, 2018); Jairo Vladimir Llano Franco, 'Prácticas regulativas informales y acceso a la justicia en Latinoamérica' (2014) 11(1) *Revista Criterio Libre Jurídico* 85.

[89] James L Nolan, *Legal Accents, Legal Borrowing: The International Problem-Solving Court Movement* (Princeton, NJ: Princeton University Press, 2009).

[90] This was, for example, the rationale of the proposal by Reinier H Kraakman and Bernard S Black, 'A Self Enforcing Model of Corporate Law' (1996) 109 *Harvard Law Review* 1911.

[91] For both of these examples see Siems (n 12) 117–18.

[92] Carmine Guerriero, 'Endogenous Legal Traditions' (2016) 46 *International Review of Law and Economics* 49.

Going back further in history, it has been shown that legal cultures have spread due to the role of individuals and groups, such as colonisers, merchants, missionaries, activists, lobbyists, refugees, believers, etc.[93] Legal families have also diffused from certain origin countries in many directions with changes in legal culture being accompanied by more technical changes.[94] For example, in the nineteenth century, German lawyers travelled to Greece to give lectures and Greek lawyers travelled to Germany to study law,[95] while German legal doctrine also raised some interest in other civil law countries (eg, in Italy[96] and countries of Eastern Europe[97]) and even the common law world.[98] Finally, while these examples were about broad changes to domestic legal systems, transplants of legal culture have also happened where new systems of international or regional law have been created,[99] here too often leading to mixtures of different models.

To conclude, the objects and interactions displayed in Figure 3.1 are a first illustration of the variety of situations in which legal transplants occur. With respect to the typical cases, it is no coincidence that codified rules are often shown as typical cases in the transplant unit given that the design of transplants is likely to be more straight-forward for codified rules than other objects.[100] A limitation of this section has been that it simply presented the objects on both sides without explaining how the transplant is transmitted. In particular, it is likely that for many of the latter categories (eg, legal ideas, law in practice, and legal culture), the transplantation is not a one-off event but part of a longer process, possibly in combination with other transplants. Thus, referring to the importance of the transplant process sets the scene for its further analysis in this chapter and the following ones.[101]

[93] Twining (2004) (n 2) 17; specifically for 'reception based on theology': Bishal Khanal, *Legal Reform via Reception of Law* (Kathmandu: Bhrikuti Academic Publications, 2018) 55, 64–5.

[94] Silvia Ferreri and Larry A DiMatteo, 'Terminology Matters: Dangers of Superficial Transplantation' (2019) 37 *Boston University International Law Journal* 35, 54 calls this 'transplantation of legal tradition'.

[95] See Siems (n 12) 112.

[96] Pier Giuseppe Monateri, 'The Weak Law: Contaminations and Legal Cultures' (2003) 13 *Transnational Law and Contemporary Problems* 575 (for Italy being both French and German law influenced); Marta Infantino, 'The Italian Legal Recipe: Basic Ingredients and the Bustle of Time' (2013) 6 *European Journal of Comparative Law and Governance* 70 (emphasising also the importance of other 'legal formants').

[97] Tomasz Giaro, 'The Wave of Transfers: An East-European Chapter in the Civil Law Tradition' (2024) 14/2 *Comparative Law Review* 33.

[98] Ugo Mattei, 'Why the Wind Changed: Intellectual Leadership in Western Law' (1994) 42 *American Journal of Comparative Law* 195.

[99] For transplants as creating new legal regimes see generally Jutta Mues, *Rechtstransfer: Zur theoretisch-methodischen Komplexität der Interaktion normativer Ordnungen* (Frankfurt: Peter Lang, 2015) 49–50. For examples from international and regional law see Section C 2.

[100] For the design of transplants see Chapter 7.

[101] Notably, in Section C and then Chapters 4 and 5.

C. Relevant units

Most of the comparative law literature focusses on countries as the relevant units of legal transplants. However, other units, such as subnational, regional, and international laws, can also be relevant units. Indeed, it can be argued that legal transplants are typical in the regional and international sphere as such laws are often the result of deliberate design choices[102] based on ideas from other units. This section will therefore initially deal with countries as the conventional units but subsequently also such other units.

As in the previous section, the proposed taxonomy always distinguishes between origin and transplant unit. This is not to claim that transplants only occur in such a bilateral relationship, as transplants may also emerge as mixtures from multiple sources or be the outcome of a 'multi-player process'.[103] The focus on origin and transplant unit in this section also does not deny the role of third parties such as development organisations, advisors, lawyers, etc.[104]

1. Countries as conventional units

The literature traditionally writes about countries as the origin and transplant units of legal transplants. This leads to further distinctions as illustrated in Figure 3.2, namely between countries of civil and common law, core and periphery, and the Global North and South. In the following, the possible role of these divisions, as well as their evident limitations, are explained.[105]

Legal families are a key topic of comparative law. Figure 3.2 uses the civil and common law families as an illustration. It shows that, when countries

[102] See Tobias Lenz and Gary Marks, 'Regional Institutional Design' in Tanja A Börzel and Thomas Risse (eds), *The Oxford Handbook of Comparative Regionalism* (Oxford: OUP, 2016) 513.

[103] Twining (2004) (n 2) 17; Cohn (2010) (n 1) 601–2. See also Lorenzo Serafinelli, 'The Post-Westphalian Polyhedral Dimension of Legal Mutation—A Case Study: Party Autonomy in International Contracts in Latin America' (2022/2) *Isaidat Law Review* 43, 49 ('polyhedral' transplant from one state to another one through international law); Yseult Marique and Emmanuel Slautsky, 'Resistance to Transplants in the European Administrative Space' (2021) 14 *Review of European Administrative Law* 7 (analysing transplants 'channelled through European instruments'); Utkirbek Kholmirzaev and Manuchehr Kudratov 'Rethinking Legal Transfers: Epistemology, Power and Legitimacy' (2026) 39 *International Journal for the Semiotics of Law* 47 (on the relevance of intermediary models); Roman Uliasz, 'Rhizomatic Networks in Legal Transplants: Interconnected Interpretations of Legal Concepts Across Jurisdictions' (2025) 5 *Undecidabilities and Law: The Coimbra Journal for Legal Studies* 89 ('rhizome' as metaphor for non-linear influence).

[104] For those see eg Chapter 4 at Sections B 3 and C 3 (b).

[105] These factors also play a role in the subsequent chapter as it deals with the question of why certain transplants take place, see Chapter 4 at Section C.

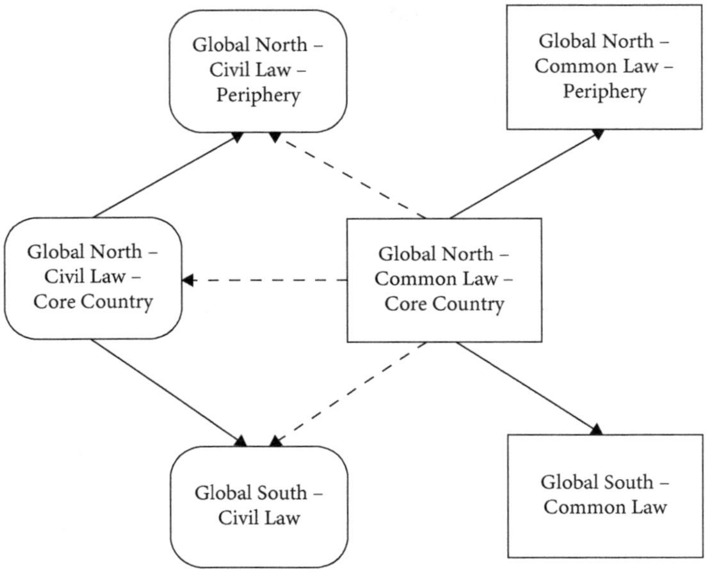

Figure 3.2 Typical cases of legal transplants in literature

consider adopting rules from abroad, they are likely to take rules from the same legal family as those may be relatively familiar to them and likely to be compatible with existing rules.[106] Thus, in this Figure, all the transplants of common law countries are directed towards other common law countries. In the wide understanding of the concept of transplants, this includes the use of case law from other common law jurisdictions, even if a court may merely aim to identify rules of the 'common law as a whole'.[107] For civil law countries, lines have been added that also indicate transplants to common law countries. The reason for this is that, since the mid-twentieth century, many countries of the world are said to have experienced a process of legal Americanisation, notably many civil law countries in Latin America, continental Europe, and East Asia.[108] This influence has extended to many areas

[106] See eg Holger Spamann, 'Contemporary Legal Transplants: Legal Families and the Diffusion of (Corporate) Law' (2009) *BYU Law Review* 1813.

[107] Peter de Cruz, *Comparative Law in a Changing World* (London: Routledge Cavendish, 3rd edn, 2007) 232–3. Similarly, the phrases of a 'single common law'—Thomas Allen and Bruce Anderson, 'The Use of Comparative Law by Common Law Judges' (1994) 23 *Anglo-American Law Review* 435, 455—or a 'unity of the common law'—KJ Keith, 'The Unity of the Common Law and the Ending of Appeals to the Privy Council' (2005) 54 *International and Comparative Law Quarterly* 197. For judicial dialogue within the common law see also Chapter 1 at Section B 2, as well as Section B in this chapter.

[108] David S Clark, *American Comparative Law* (Oxford: OUP, 2022) 349, 418–28; Jacques deLisle, 'Lex Americana: United States Legal Assistance, American Legal Models, and Legal Change in the

of law. For example, it can be seen in references to US law in contemporary constitutional debates.[109] Publications in many languages also cover the impact of US law on topics of corporate and commercial law,[110] and there is also some evidence that, in this field, UK law has been a global model for both common and civil law countries.[111]

However, beyond general critiques of the legal families divide,[112] the literature also acknowledges that transplants do not always neatly align with their origin country. To start with, it is possible to refer to findings that both English and US law themselves have been shaped strongly by continental European legal traditions.[113] Challenges to legal families are also a key topic in the discussion about mixed legal systems, notably referring to countries which combine elements of civil and common law traditions.[114] It has also been observed that countries may sometimes deliberately choose combinations of foreign models as most suitable, called a 'mixed legal transplant'.[115] Furthermore, some studies have explicitly aimed to show how US law is often an outlier and, thus, not a model that is globally adopted.[116]

Post-Communist World and Beyond' (1999) 20 *University of Pennsylvania Journal of International Economic Law* 179; Wolfgang Wiegand, 'The Reception of American Law in Europe' (1991) 39 *American Journal of Comparative Law* 229. For further literature see Chapter 4 at Sections B 3 and C 3 (c) and (d) and Chapter 5 at Section C 4 (b).

[109] Svitlana Chernykh and Zachary Elkins, 'How Constitutional Drafters Use Comparative Evidence' (2022) 24 *Journal of Comparative Policy Analysis* 529, 547.

[110] Eg, Véronique Magnier, 'Réception du droit américain dans l'organisation des sociétés commerciales' (2001) 45 *Archives de philosophie du droit* 213; Jan von Hein, *Die Rezeption US-amerikanischen Gesellschaftsrechts in Deutschland* (Tübingen: Mohr Siebeck, 2008); Pablo A Iannello, 'Eficiencia y recepción de los transplantes [sic] legales: el caso del cramdown power' (2008) 2 *Revista de Análisis Institucional* 289; Paolo Montalenti, 'Nuove clausole generali nel diritto commerciale tra civile law e common law' (2015) 4 *Osservatorio del diritto civile e commerciale* 133, 147–8; Marcin Łolik, *Współczesne prawo kontraktów—wybrane zagadnienia* (Warsaw: CH Beck, 2014) 3.

[111] Eg, Brian R Cheffins, 'Corporate Governance Reform: Britain as an Exporter' (2000) 8 *Hume Papers on Public Policy* 10; Dionysia Katelouzou and Mathias Siems, 'The Global Diffusion of Stewardship Codes' in Dionysia Katelouzou and Dan Puchniak (eds), *Global Shareholder Stewardship* (Cambridge: CUP, 2022) 631.

[112] See Siems (n 12) 73–80, 92–108.

[113] See eg H Patrick Glenn, *Legal Traditions of the World* (Oxford: OUP, 5th edn, 2014) 265, 268–71; Christophe Roda, 'L'influence des droits européens sur le droit américain' (2014) 3 *Recueil Dalloz* 157; Reimann (n 64). For the impact of EU law see Chapter 4 at Section C 3 (b).

[114] Jacques du Plessis, 'Comparative Law and the Study of Mixed Legal Systems' in Mathias Reimann and Reinhard Zimmermann (eds), *The Oxford Handbook of Comparative Law* (Oxford: OUP, 2nd edn, 2019) 474; Vernon Valentine Palmer (ed), *Mixed Jurisdictions Worldwide: The Third Legal Family* (Cambridge: CUP, 2nd edn, 2012).

[115] Kien Tran, Nam Ho Pham, and Quynh-Anh Lu Nguyen, 'Negotiating Legal Reform through Reception of Law: The Missing Role of Mixed Legal Transplants' (2019) 14 *Asian Journal of Comparative Law* 175 (for today's Vietnam).

[116] Eg, in corporate law: David Cabrelli and Mathias Siems, 'Convergence, Legal Origins and Transplants in Comparative Corporate Law: A Case-Based and Quantitative Analysis' (2015) 63 *American Journal of Comparative Law* 109. But for some US impact see Mathias Siems, 'Private Enforcement of Directors' Duties: Derivative Actions as a Global Phenomenon', in Stefan Wrbka,

The core/periphery and Global North/South categories partly overlap. As understood here, the core countries are the main origin countries of legal transplants of the Global North, notably England, the US, France, and Germany; periphery countries are other countries of the Global North (for example, other European countries but also Japan), as well as countries of the Global South.

These Global North/South and core/periphery categories derive from research in sociology, history, and development policy (including law and development).[117] They also feature, with these or other terms, prominently in the literature on legal transplants and policy diffusion as they may explain why there is often a unidirectional relationship between country pairs. For example, comparative law frequently emphasises the role of major jurisdictions, ie 'core countries', in presenting overviews of legal traditions across the world.[118] The Global South features in the literature as far as it notes that countries from developing countries are often influenced by legal and policy models of developed countries.[119]

Beyond general critiques of these typologies,[120] further nuances blur this general picture. In some cases, the relationship can be reciprocal; for example, this is said to be the case for judicial cross-citations between courts of (some) common law countries.[121] There is also a call, and some evidence, for transplants among countries of the Global South as part of 'South-South' development co-operation.[122] For example, in the late twentieth century, the

Steven Van Uytsel, and Mathias Siems (eds), *Collective Actions: Enhancing Access to Justice and Reconciling Multilayer Interests?* (Cambridge: CUP, 2012) 93.

[117] For previous research that uses these concepts in comparative law see Philipp Dann, Michael Riegner, and Maxim Bönnemann, 'The Southern Turn in Comparative Constitutional Law: An Introduction' in Philipp Dann, Michael Riegner, and Maxim Bönnemann (eds), *The Global South and Comparative Constitutional Law* (Oxford: OUP, 2020) 1; Jorge L Esquirol, *Ruling the Law: Legitimacy and Failure in Latin American Legal Systems* (Cambridge: CUP, 2019) 137.

[118] For example, René David, *Major Legal Systems in the World Today: An Introduction to the Comparative Study of Law* (London: Stevens, 3rd edn, 1985).

[119] Twining (2004) (n 2) 17; Hirsch (n 43) 3 (countries of the 'third world' need to catch up with civilisatory level of other countries); Stone and others (n 6) 2 (as part of the traditional assumptions). See also Vincent Hoppmann, 'Comparative Law and the Global South Gap: An Empirical Analysis of Comparative Legal Academia in Germany' (2025) 124 *Zeitschrift für vergleichende Rechtswissenschaft* 441 (main focus of German scholarship on transplants from the Global North).

[120] See eg Johanna Hoerning, 'Dividing the "World": Spatial Binaries in Global Perspective' in Dominik Bartmanski and others (eds), *Considering Space: A Critical Concept for the Social Sciences* (London: Routledge, 2024) 113; Nikita Sud and Diego Sánchez-Ancochea, 'Southern Discomfort: Interrogating the Category of the Global South' (2022) 53 *Development and Change* 1123.

[121] Kwai Hang Ng and Brynna Jacobson, 'How Global is the Common Law? A Comparative Study of Asian Common Law Systems—Hong Kong, Malaysia, and Singapore' (2017) 12 *Asian Journal of Comparative Law* 209.

[122] For the latter concept see eg Emma Mawdsley, Elsje Fourie, and Wiebe Nauta (eds), *Researching South-South Development Cooperation: The Politics of Knowledge Production* (London: Routledge, 2019); Peter Kragelund, *South-South Development* (London: Routledge, 2019). For Asia in particular: Matthew S Erie and Ching-Fu Lin (eds), *Inter-Asian Law* (Cambridge: CUP, 2026).

East Asian version of an active developmental state was seen as a model for other emerging economies;[123] Botswana, Costa Rica, and Singapore have often been regarded as role models for developing countries in Africa, Latin America, and Southeast Asia;[124] and, in the political science literature, it is suggested more generally that 'policy models produced in the South might be more effective in developing countries than those produced in the North, due to geographical, institutional, contextual demographic, and economic similarities'.[125]

In recent years, there have also been calls for 'reverse legal transplants' from the Global South to the Global North,[126] for example, that the transformative experience of the South African Constitution and its judicial commitment to substantive justice may now be a model for other countries,[127] and that the 'right of nature' in the laws of some Latin American countries should influence lawmakers in the Global North.[128] Prior literature has also explained how, already in the past, Western countries have shown interest in non-Western legal traditions. For example, it has been established that Greek and Roman law have been influenced by Hindu law, Egyptian law, and African legal traditions.[129] There has also been influence of Islamic law on Western laws: for example, Islamic educational institutions had an influence on European universities and the English Inns of Court[130] and the common law actions, the trial

[123] Kidjie Saguin and Kritika Sha, 'Policy Transfer in Asia' in Osmany Porto de Oliveira (ed), *Handbook of Policy Transfer, Diffusion and Circulation* (Cheltenham: Edward Elgar, 2021) 1. See also Ezra F Vogel, *Japan as Number One: Lessons for America* (Cambridge MA: Harvard University Press, 1979).

[124] See references in Siems (n 12) 408. This may also incorporate past laws from these countries, ie a 'diachronic legal transplant', see Chapter 4 at Section B 2.

[125] Porto de Oliveira (n 4) 10–11.

[126] Sital Kalantry, 'Reverse Legal Transplants' (2020) 99 *North Carolina Law Review* 49; Sabrina Ragone and Guido Smorto, *Comparative Law: A Very Short Introduction* (Oxford: OUP, 2023) 35–6; Kalypso Nicolaïdis and Richard Youngs, 'Reversing the Gaze: Can the EU Import Democracy from Others?' (2023) 61 *Journal of Common Market Studies* 1605.

[127] Michaela Hailbronner, 'Transformative Constitutionalism: Not Only in the Global South' (2017) 65 *American Journal of Comparative Law* 527.

[128] Jasper Mührel, *Rights of Nature in Liberal Legal Systems and International Law: Beyond Legal Anthropocentrism* (Cham: Springer, 2024) 343–4. More sceptical as they combine elements from the Global South and the Global North: Ralf Michaels, 'Rechte der Natur—ein erfolgreicher Reverse Legal Transplant?' (2024) *Zeitschrift für Umweltrecht* 643, 646; but see also Daniel Bonilla Maldonado, 'Global Legal Pluralism and the Rights of Nature' in Kevin E Davis and Mariana Pargendler (eds), *Legal Heterodoxy in the Global South* (Cambridge: CUP, 2025) 339, 363–9 (identifying various cross-fertilisations on this topic: peripheral North–South, South–South, and South–North).

[129] H Patrick Glenn, 'Are Legal Traditions Incommensurable' (2001) 49 *American Journal of Comparative Law* 133, 141; Pier Giuseppe Monateri, 'Black Gaius: A Quest for the Multicultural Origins of the "Western Legal Tradition"' (1999) 50 *Hastings Law Journal* 1.

[130] George Makdisi, *The Rise of Colleges: Institutions of Higher Learning in Islam and the West* (Edinburgh: Edinburgh University Press, 1981); George Makdisi, 'The Guilds of Law in Medieval Legal History: An Inquiry into the Origins of the Inns of Court' (1985–86) 34 *Cleveland State Law Review* 3.

by jury, and the trust also have Islamic origins.[131] For a more recent period, it has been found that, in the mid-nineteenth century, a British consul's interest in the Chinese system of public administration inspired British reforms in establishing a meritocratic civil service.[132]

2. Further units

The literature on both legal transplants and policy diffusion distinguishes between different levels of law. For example, Twining uses eight levels (global, international, regional, transnational, inter-communal, territorial state, sub-state, non-state), while Dolowitz and Marsh have three (international, national, local).[133] For the present purposes, Figure 3.3 uses a taxonomy of five levels. This framework will be used to identify transplants at the same level or at different levels (ie horizontal or vertical transplants), always taking a type of origin unit as a starting point.

Recent years have seen a growing field of research on 'comparative international law'.[134] One of its topics are horizontal transplants of international law. For example, this can happen between international rules that address the same topic but for different groups of countries,[135] or between rules of international law that apply to different parts of the world.[136] Horizontal transplants can also concern the governance structures, rule-making practices, and approaches to impact assessment of international organisations,[137] or the procedural rules, structures, and citation practices of international

[131] John A Makdisi, 'The Islamic Origins of the Common Law' (1999) 77 *North Carolina Law Review* 1635, 1696–717.

[132] Tim Legrand, *The Architecture of Policy Transfer: Ideas, Institutions and Networks in Transnational Policymaking* (London: Palgrave, 2021) xv and xvi (on the influence of Thomas Taylor Meadows on the Northcote-Trevelyan Report of 1854).

[133] William Twining, *Globalisation and Legal Theory* (Cambridge: CUP, 2001) 139; Dolowitz and Marsh (n 81) 12.

[134] Mathias Siems, 'Comparative International Law: State of the Art' in Robert Schütze and Mathias Siems (eds), *Comparative International Law: Foundations and Critique* (Oxford: Hart Publishing, 2026) 3, 5–6.

[135] Eg, Tomer Broude, Yoram Z Haftel, and Alexander Thompson, 'Who Cares About Regulatory Space in BITs? A Comparative International Approach' in Anthea Roberts and others (eds), *Comparative International Law* (Oxford: OUP, 2018) 527; Lorenzo Cotula, 'Expropriation Clauses and Environmental Regulation: Diffusion of Law in the Era of Investment Treaties' (2015) 24 *Review of European Community and International Environmental Law* 278.

[136] Eg, Simon Marsden, *Protecting the Third Pole: Transplanting International Law* (Cheltenham: Edward Elgar, 2019) 46–52.

[137] See eg OECD, *International Regulatory Co-operation: The Role of International Organisations in Fostering Better Rules of Globalisation* (Paris: OECD Publishing, 2016).

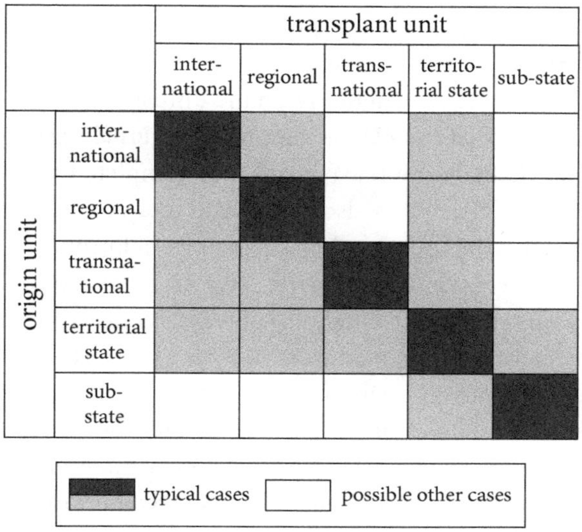

Figure 3.3 Categories of transplants based on the unit

courts and tribunals.[138] Vertical transplants can be about the 'upward diffusion' of domestic to international law—its general features but also specific rules and institutions.[139] A 'downward diffusion' from international to regional or domestic law is different from the situation where regions or countries simply comply with international rules. A clear example is a situation where a country is not bound by particular international rules but decides to transplant them. Yet, downward diffusion can, for example, also be about the way more general concepts of international law have impacted on a country's law,[140] or about the way international human rights have been selectively adopted by individual countries and regional bodies.[141]

[138] Caterina Milo, 'Tackling *Lacunae* in International Court and Tribunals' Procedure: The Role of External Precedent' (2022) 2 *The Italian Review of International and Comparative Law* 323; Erik Voeten, 'Borrowing and Nonborrowing among International Courts' (2010) 39 *The Journal of Legal Studies* 547.

[139] See eg Lucio Pegoraro, 'Derecho Nacional, Derecho Internacional, Derecho Europeo: La circulación horizontal y vertical entre formantes' (2013) 17 *Anuario Iberoamericano* 257; Mathilde Cohen, 'The Continuing Impact of French Legal Culture on the International Court of Justice' in Anthea Roberts and others (eds), *Comparative International Law* (Oxford: OUP, 2018) 181; Anna Dolidze, 'Bridging Comparative and International Law: Amicus Curiae Participation as a Vertical Legal Transplant' (2015) 26 *European Journal of International Law* 851, 853.

[140] See eg Rune Svarverud, *International Law as World Order in Late Imperial China: Translation, Reception and Discourse, 1847-1911* (Leiden: Brill, 2007).

[141] See eg Kevin L Cope, Cosette D Creamer, and Mila Versteeg, 'Empirical Studies of Human Rights Law' (2019) 15 *Annual Review of Law and Social Science* 155, 156–63 (on ratification of human rights

With respect to regional laws, the first chapter of this book already mentioned the example of EU-modelled regional courts in Latin America.[142] There is also a more general literature on the diffusion of regional organisations: here, it is said that the EU has supported regionalism in other parts of the world,[143] while there are few examples of complete transplants of particular regional models.[144] It is also possible to focus on more specific rules such as the impact of the (non-binding) Principles of European Contract Law (PECL) on similar rules in Latin America and Asia.[145] Vertical transplants of regional law can, on the one hand, go 'upward' towards international law. Regional agreements have moved from 'less to more institutionalisation',[146] also with the use of courts or tribunals. As similar trends happen at the international level, transplants from a regional organisation such as the EU to international organisations can be fruitful.[147] Other examples are that EU law has had an influence on the principle of 'mutual recognition' in international trade law,[148] and that the case law of the European Court of Human Rights has been considered by international investment tribunals.[149] For 'downward' transplants to territorial state law, reference can be made to research on the way both EU law and European human rights law have impacted on third countries.[150] For the member countries of a regional organisation, the use of

treaties); Magdalena Forowicz, *The Reception of International law in the European Court of Human Rights* (Oxford: OUP, 2010) (on how judges and Commission members endorsed but also rejected the relevance of certain international rules).

[142] Chapter 1 at Section B 2.

[143] Philippe De Lombaerde and Michael Schulz (eds), *The EU and World Regionalism: The Makability of Regions in the 21st Century* (Farnham: Ashgate, 2009).

[144] Thomas Risse, 'The Diffusion of Regionalism' in Tanja A Börzel and Thomas Risse (eds), *The Oxford Handbook of Comparative Regionalism* (Oxford: OUP, 2016) 87.

[145] Rodrigo Momberg and Stefan Vogenauer, 'The Principles of Latin American Contract Law: Text, Translation, and Introduction' (2018) 23 *Uniform Law Review* 144; Aleksander Grebieniow, 'Principles of Asian Contract Law at the Crossroads of Standardization and Legal Pluralism' (2023) 10 *Asian Journal of Law and Society* 306.

[146] Francesco Duina and Sonia Morano-Foadi, 'Introduction: The Institutionalisation of Regional Trade Agreements Worldwide: New Dynamics and Future Scenarios' (2011) 17 *European Law Journal* 561, 566.

[147] Considering the EU experience as a guide to the future of a global judicial regime: Charles H Koch, 'Envisioning a Global Legal Culture' (2003) 25 *Michigan Journal of International Law* 1, 10.

[148] Anne Margaret McNaughton, *The Reshaping of the Rules-based International Order: Case Studies in Action* (PhD thesis, ANU, 2024) 36, available at https://hdl.handle.net/1885/733723186 accessed 23 October 2025.

[149] Roberto Ruoppo, 'Common Features of the Right to Property and International Investments: Evidence from the Use of ECtHR Case-law in Investment Tribunals' (2022) 2 *The Italian Review of International and Comparative Law* 347.

[150] Eg, for the former: Anu Bradford, *The Brussels Effect: How the European Union Rules the World* (Oxford: OUP, 2020); Arie Reich and Hans-W Micklitz (eds), *The Impact of the European Court of Justice on Neighbouring Countries* (Oxford: OUP, 2020). For the latter: Francesco Duranti, 'La Commissione di Venezia e il diritto comparato' (2017) *Diritto pubblico comparato ed europeo* 243,

transplants is not the same as compliance with binding laws. However, often implementation is not straightforward, and thus it can sometimes be seen as a study of legal transplants to examine how, for example, regional rules are implemented in the language of domestic law and applied by domestic courts, but also how regional laws have wider implications on national legal cultures.[151]

The category of transnational law refers in its classical formulation to 'all law which regulates actions or events that transcend national frontiers';[152] yet, as distinguished from conventional international and regional law, it is usually focussed on laws that are created by non-state actors such as companies, NGOs, expert groups, arbitrators, and religious communities. Here, horizontal transplants can frequently happen as different sets of transnational law compete for attention but also influence each other, for example in the case of transnational rules on security rights by UNCITRAL and UNIDROIT,[153] or tools of green development in climate and biodiversity rules of transnational law.[154] Transnational laws can also lead to vertical legal transplants with respect to international, regional, and domestic laws. In this regard, the literature has identified the following two phenomena: first, that transnational law operates similarly to a model of a 'rough consensus and running code' where a rule is put forward followed by a process of consent and refinement,[155] and, second, that this process may lead to a 'creeping codification' of transnational rules.[156] For example, in the field of anti-money-laundering, transnational laws by the Financial Action Task Force and the Wolfsberg Group[157] have influenced international and EU laws on that matter.[158] The UNIDROIT

250–4; Öykü Didem Aydın, 'Ceza Hukuku'nun Çağdaş İlkeleri ve Avrupa Birliği Kriterleri Açısından Türk Ceza Kanunu' (2004) 53 *Türkiye Barolar Birliği Dergisi* 78, 91–123.

151 Eg, Uliasz (n 35); Virpi Koivu, *European Convention on Human Rights and Transition of the Legal Culture: Reception of the Argumentation of the European Court of Human Rights by the Finnish Supreme Jurisdictions* (Rovaniemi: Lapin Yliopisto, 2015); Diana Eunice Kawenda, *Legal Reception and Regional Economic Integration in Southern Africa* (Hamburg: Anchor Academic Publishing, 2017); Alejandro Nieto, 'El derecho comunitario europeo como derecho común vulgar' (2016) 200 *Revista de Administración Pública* 25.

152 Philip C Jessup, *Transnational Law* (New Haven, CT: Yale University Press, 1956) 2.

153 Theodora Kostoula, 'Security Rights in Crypto-assets: An Opportunity for Uniform Law?' (2023) 28 *Uniform Law Review* 434.

154 Jerneja Penca, 'Transnational Legal Transplants and Legitimacy: The Example of "Clean" and "Green" Development Mechanisms' (2016) 36 *Legal Studies* 706.

155 Gralf-Peter Calliess and Peer Zumbansen, *Rough Consensus and Running Code: A Theory of Transnational Private Law* (Oxford: Hart Publishing, 2010).

156 Klaus Peter Berger, *The Creeping Codification of the New Lex Mercatoria* (The Hague: Kluwer, 2nd edn, 2010).

157 See https://www.fatf-gafi.org/ and https://wolfsberg-group.org accessed 23 October 2025.

158 Simon NM Young, 'Money Laundering in International Law' (Oxford: Oxford Bibliographies, 2021), available at http://dx.doi.org/10.1093/obo/9780199796953-0233 accessed 23 October 2025.

Principles of International Commercial Contracts also had an impact on domestic reforms of contract and commercial law.[159]

Horizontal transplants between territorial states are still the main examples of legal transplants found in the literature today. However, such domestic rules may also be transplanted to the international, regional, transnational, or sub-state levels. Due to the growing institutionalisation of international and regional organisations, it is natural—though sometimes contentious[160]—to consider the domestic experience of lawmaking procedures and courts but also general legal principles and specific rules. Examples are transplants from domestic to global environmental law, the principles of reasonableness and proportionality in international investment law, the use of amicus curiae participation at the European Court of Human Rights, the impact of domestic climate litigation on a decision by this Court, and the migration of the 'constitutional idea' to the EU.[161] Transnational law is also likely to use domestic laws as a source of influence. Often, such use has the strategic advantage that its legitimacy can benefit from accepted domestic laws. For example, the G20/OECD Principles of Corporate Governance are, in its main parts, a common denominator of the legal norms of the OECD member countries.[162] A further example is the US concept of a uniform real security right which influenced model laws and guidances of organisations such as the EBRD, UNIDROIT, and UNCITRAL.[163] Finally, domestic law can also be transplanted to sub-state units. This may happen where, in a transplant country, central state powers are weak but regions, cities, or other units can step in, making use of ideas from a more centralised country. A prominent example is the establishment of 'special economic zones'[164] that apply English law within countries of other legal

[159] Alejandro M Garro and José A Moreno Rodríguez, 'The UNIDROIT Principles as a Common Frame of Reference for the Uniform Interpretation of National Laws' in Katharina Boele-Woelki, Diego P Fernández Arroyo, and Alexandre Senegacnik (eds), *General Reports of the XXth General Congress of the International Academy of Comparative Law* (Cham: Springer, 2020) 51.

[160] Due to the alleged autonomous nature of these laws, see Chapter 6 at Section C 4 (a).

[161] Jonathan B Wiener, 'Something Borrowed for Something Blue: Legal Transplants and the Evolution of Global Environmental Law' (2001) 27 *Ecology Law Quarterly* 1295; Valentina Vadi, *Proportionality, Reasonableness and Standards of Review in International Investment Law and Arbitration* (Cheltenham: Edward Elgar, 2018); Dolidze (n 139); Lorenzo Serafinelli, 'Dal caos all'ordine (e viceversa): l'impatto del trittico della Corte EDU sul contenzioso climatico europeo di diritto privato' (2024) 64.2 *DPCE Online* 1493; Neil Walker, 'The Migration of Constitutional Ideas and the Migration of the Constitutional Idea: The Case of the EU' in Sujit Choudhry (ed), *The Migration of Constitutional Ideas* (Cambridge: CUP, 2006) 316.

[162] Mathias Siems and Oscar Alvarez-Macotela, 'The G20/OECD Principles of Corporate Governance 2015: A Critical Assessment of their Operation and Impact' (2017) *Journal of Business Law* 310.

[163] Sjef van Erp, 'Personal and Real Security', in Jan M Smits and others (eds), *Elgar Encyclopedia of Comparative Law* (Cheltenham: Edward Elgar, 3rd edn, 2023) 171, 175.

[164] Ilias Bantekas, 'Wholesale Instant Transplants Through Transnational Legislative Dialogue?' (2023) 31 *European Review of Private Law* 497.

traditions. It is also possible to refer to another type of example, mentioned earlier in this chapter, namely, where contractual parties adopt codified rules from another country to facilitate cross-border business.[165]

Laws of sub-state units are not usually the focus of comparative law scholarship; yet, they can also be the origin units of legal transplants. The first chapter of this book already mentioned the example of the diffusion of anti-smoking policies between US cities and that this can lead to a snowball effect of local policy adoptions to the state level.[166] There is also a wealth of other studies from the US on legislative diffusion between its sub-units,[167] as well as some recent examples from Europe about the diffusion of policies and practices between cities.[168] Long before the current debate about legal transplants, Rheinstein too included cases where 'within the same country a legal phenomenon of one religious, racial, professional or social group is adopted as part of the law of another such group', referring to examples such as the 'adoption as the general law of the land of contractual and other institutions originally developed as the special law of the merchants'.[169]

This final example may also be seen as a form of influence which, conventionally, had not been included in comparative law, namely cases where different areas of law within the same legal system influence each other. However, this has recently been challenged: Matthew Dyson suggests that it can be 'comparative law' when a researcher compares, for example, how, within the same country, tort and criminal law deal with a particular behaviour.[170] Many considerations that apply to cross-jurisdictional transplants can also be applied to cross-subject transplants.[171] Accordingly, authors have, for example, discussed the use of transplants for the adoption of constitutional ideas in private law,[172] the diffusion is regulatory language between different administrative

[165] See n 35.

[166] See Chapter 1 at Section B 2.

[167] References in Engel and Weinshall (n 80) 141.

[168] Negar Noori, *Policy Transplantation for Smart City Initiatives* (PhD Thesis, Rotterdam, 2021); Negar Noori and others, 'Transplanting Good Practices in Smart City Development: A step-wise Approach' (2023) 40 *Government Information Quarterly* 101802; Eliška Vejchodská and Andreas Hendricks, 'Munich's Developer Obligations as a Legal Transplant to the Czech Institutional Context' (2023) 94 *Town Planning Review* 193.

[169] Rheinstein (n 8) 32.

[170] Matthew Dyson, 'Ligations Divide and Conquer: Using Legal Domains in Comparative Legal Studies' in Geneviève Helleringer and Kai Purnhagen (eds), *Towards a European Legal Culture* (Baden-Baden: Nomos, 2014) 115; Matthew Dyson (ed), *Comparing Tort and Crime: Learning from Across and Within Legal Systems* (Cambridge: CUP, 2015).

[171] Mathias Siems, 'The Power of Comparative Law: What Types of Units Can Comparative Law Compare?' (2019) 67 *American Journal of Comparative Law* 861, 873–4, 881.

[172] Francois du Bois, 'Constitutional Transplants in Private Law: From Liberal to Republican Legal Ordering' in Anat Scolnicov (ed), *Constitutional Transplantations: The Diffusion and Adoption of Constitutional Ideas* (Oxford: Hart Publishing, 2026).

agencies,[173] and the case of policymakers and courts borrowing ideas between groundwater and wind energy law.[174] A decision of the Court of Appeal of England and Wales has also used the term 'legal transplants' for the question of whether a procedural rule of discrimination legislation should be applied to a case of unfair dismissal (which it ultimately rejected).[175]

Overall, this subsection has shown that the interactions between the two units can lead to various horizontal and vertical transplants. It would be possible to add even more complexity by further considering the three categories mentioned earlier in this section (civil/common law, core/periphery, Global North/South) as those categories could again play a role at different scales (eg also at the regional or international level).

D. Transplantation

Having identified the object and units of transplants, the form and effect of the transplantation can again be divided into various categories. These categories are more briefly discussed here as they overlap with—but are not identical to—the topics of the subsequent two chapters. The form of transplantation (Section 1) is related to questions about the motivations and causal factors for legal transplants (Chapter 4); yet, the present focus is on the 'how' of the transplantation while the subsequent chapter deals with the 'why' (ie the precise mechanisms leading to a transplant). The effect of the transplantation (Section 2) is related to the question of whether legal transplants 'work' (Chapter 5); yet, in this section, the focus is on categorising different types of effect, while the latter chapter evaluates whether and how legal transplants really work in practice.

1. Form of transplantation

As in the previous sections of this chapter, Figure 3.4 distinguishes between the origin and the transplant unit and then displays various categories (which, different from Figures 3.1 and 3.3, are not symmetrical in this chart).

[173] Jennifer Nou and Julian Nyarko, 'Regulatory Diffusion' (2022) 74 Stanford Law Review 897.

[174] Vanessa Casado Pérez and Yael R Lifshitz, 'Natural Transplants' (2022) 97 *New York University Law Review* 933.

[175] *Kuzel v Roche Products Ltd* [2008] EWCA Civ 380 [48].

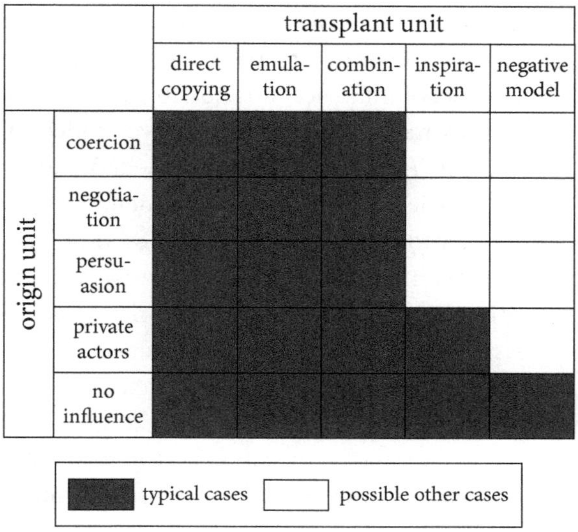

Figure 3.4 Categories of form of transplantation

The categories of the origin unit display how far this unit had an impact on the transplantation. This can also be read as displaying the inverse impact of the transplant unit: for example, if there was coercion, the transplant unit had no influence (ie it was an involuntary transplant), while if there was no influence by the origin unit, the transplant unit initiated the transplant (ie it was a voluntary transplant). These categories reflect common divisions in both the legal and the policy literature, though with some variations in detail.[176]

Conventional examples of 'coercion' are the colonial transplants,[177] but also other cases, such as, 'imposition by annexation',[178] contemporary cases of occupation,[179] as well as forms of (mere) 'external pressure'.[180] External pressure may sometimes be akin to forms of 'negotiation', ie the next category. In this regard, the ideal may be that countries (and similar for other units) are 'roughly equal in state capacity', while in practice legal transplants may often be an instrument of foreign policy.[181] By contrast, the category 'persuasion' would

[176] Cohn (2010) (n 1) 591–2; Bender (n 5) 11; Dolowitz and Marsh (n 81) 1.
[177] See Chapter 1 at Section B 2.
[178] Athanase C Papachristos, *La réception des droits privés étrangers comme phénomène de sociologie juridique* (Paris: LGDJ, 1975) 34.
[179] Khanal (n 93) 246 (referring to Iraq).
[180] Such as the changes of Japanese law due to US pressure after World War II, see Chapter 1 at Section B 2.
[181] Stone and others (n 6) 2–4 (for policy transfers).

leave the main decision to the transplant unit. The form of persuasion can vary. It may again relate to a country's foreign policy as a form of 'soft power'. As regards the precise channel of influence, it is possible to draw on insights from psychology on social learning, namely whether 'live models', 'verbal instructions', or 'symbolic models' (ie via fiction or other media) are used.[182]

The final two categories go beyond the influence of the origin unit. 'Private actors' are likely to play a role in many legal transplants, but in this category they are the main driving force of the transplant. In the literature, some authors mention the personal laws of migrants[183] and the role of missionaries[184] as possible examples. In some of the policy literature, we also find a strong emphasis on the role of actors (or agents), referring to persons of the origin and transplant units but also, for example, pressure groups, think tanks, and transnational corporations.[185] If this influence is negligible, we would lastly simply have 'no influence', ie a voluntary transplant of the transplant unit.

With respect to the role of the transplant unit, the distinction between direct copying, emulation, combination, inspiration, and negative model (Figure 3.4) refers to the extent to which this unit accepts or resists the transplant. To clarify, this is different from the topic discussed previously where the object of the transplant changes (see Section B, above): for example, in the latter case, we had examples such as the one in which a codified rule in the origin unit becomes case law in the transplant unit. However, even in such a case the content of the transplant may actually be identical (ie, it can potentially be 'direct copying'). It should also be noted that any of the objects identified in this prior section can fall under any of the different forms of transplantation discussed here: for example, a 'legal idea' may also be copied exactly or emulated, combined, etc.

In detail, 'direct copying' can be due to external pressure, but it may also occur in cases of voluntary transplants, for example when the transplant unit compares the costs and benefits of a quick transplant versus the costs of the

[182] Originally proposed by Albert Bandura and Walter Mischel, 'Modifications of Self-imposed Delay of Reward through Exposure to Live and Symbolic Models' (1965) 2 *Journal of Personality and Social Psychology* 698. See also John Braithwaite and Peter Drahos, *Global Business Regulation* (Cambridge: CUP, 2000) 578.

[183] Markus Müller-Chen, Christoph Müller, and Corinne Widmer Lüchinger, *Comparative Private Law* (Zurich: Dike, 2015) 105–6 call those 'factual transplants'. See also Chapter 4 at Section C 3 (a).

[184] Jedidiah J Kroncke, *The Futility of Law and Development: China and the Dangers of Exporting American Law* (Oxford: OUP, 2016) 29–35.

[185] Dolowitz and Marsh (n 81) 10. See also Chapter 4 at Section B 3.

time spent finding the best emulation.[186] Thus, in Figure 3.4, any of the options regarding the involvement of the origin unit may interact with 'direct copying'.

The option 'emulation' may often be the main choice of a transplant unit. It can also occur in cases of 'coercion' as the origin unit may accept reasonable adjustments to the transplant. The term 'emulation' is borrowed from the policy literature which refers to a situation where a 'particular programme elsewhere provides the best standard for designing legislation at home, albeit requiring adaptation to take different national circumstances into account'.[187] In a similar sense, Athanase Papachristos uses the term 'acclimation' to refer to the way foreign law should be adjusted in a manner that makes it acceptable for the transplant country.[188]

'Combination' goes further in mixing the new with the old law. How exactly the mixture occurs can differ, for example, whether the individual 'ingredients' are fully amalgamated or whether the different origins remain visible.[189] A prominent example is the mixture of Western and customary laws in many African countries. Here, the literature commonly distinguishes between different forms in which customary law is relevant today, namely living, textbook, codified, and judicial customary law. Details go beyond this chapter,[190] but it is interesting to see that the historically coercive nature of the transplanted Western law did not exclude a mixture with customary laws. Thus, in this category, combination can go also hand in hand with all variants of origin country influence.

The category 'inspiration' is from the policy literature,[191] but it can, with other terms, also be found in the legal literature. For example, according to Edward Rubin 'little can be borrowed, but much can be learned, from foreign law',[192] and Silvia Ferreri and Larry DiMatteo suggest the category of 'indirect transplantation (influence)' in which a foreign law is regarded as 'being advanced or modern'.[193] By their very nature, this category is most relevant when there is no influence of the origin unit. It can also occur when private actors are the main

[186] For a similar argument see Peter Grajzl and Valentina Dimitrova-Grajzl, 'The Choice in the Lawmaking Process: Legal Transplants vs. Indigenous Law' (2009) 5 *Review of Law and Economics* 615.

[187] Richard Rose, *Lesson-Drawing in Public Policy: A Guide to Learning across Time and Space* (Chatham, NJ: Chatham House, 1993) 21.

[188] Papachristos (n 178) 93–4.

[189] Esin Örücü, 'A General View of "Legal Families" and of "Mixing Systems"' in Esin Örücü and David Nelken (eds), *Comparative Law: A Handbook* (Oxford: Hart Publishing, 2007) 169, 180.

[190] For references see Siems (n 12) 122.

[191] Dolowitz and Marsh (n 81) 13.

[192] Edward Rubin, 'Administrative Law and the Complexity of Culture' in Anne Seidman, Robert Seidman, and Janice Payne (eds), *Legislative Drafting for Market Reform: Some Lessons from China* (Basingstoke: Macmillan, 2000) 88, 108.

[193] Ferreri and DiMatteo (n 94) 54.

driving force: for example, consider cases where students study law abroad and bring back knowledge and possible inspiration about the foreign legal system.[194]

Finally, the 'negative model' means that the transplanted law is used to understand what not to do. This is only sometimes discussed in the literature,[195] whereby quantitative research has found that explicit references to a foreign law are more likely to endorse it than to regard it as a counter-model.[196] Still, there are likely to be more situations where a unit initially considered a particular foreign law but then did not pursue it further as it failed to convince.

2. Effect of transplantation

This subsection is concerned with the time after the actual transplantation—be it of the same object or a different one, and be it transplanted in a precise or modified way.[197] Here, the main actor is the transplant unit. Thus, different from the previous text of this chapter, the following starts with the categories of the transplant unit and then addresses how far there is a remaining influence of the origin unit (see Figure 3.5).

The ultimate expectation may be that transplants have a 'full effect', ie that the effectiveness of the transplanted law is identical in the origin and the transplant country. It is, however, also conceivable that legal transplants are even more effective in the transplant than in the origin unit. This case of an 'overfit' was proposed by the author of this book a decade ago, and since then a number of further scholars have identified situations where this did happen or should have happened.[198]

[194] Wiegand (n 108) (referring to LLM students in the US); Gail J Hupper, 'The Academic Doctorate in Law: A Vehicle for Legal Transplants?' (2008) 58 *Journal of Legal Education* 413 (for foreigners doing SJDs in the US).

[195] Kim Lane Scheppele, 'Aspirational and Aversive Constitutionalism: The Case for Studying Cross-Constitutional Influence Through Negative Models' (2003) 1 *International Journal of Constitutional Law* 296; Intisar Rabb, 'Against Kadijustiz: On the Negative Citation of Foreign Law' (2015) 48 *Suffolk University Law Review* 343.

[196] Folker de Witte and others, 'Decoding Judicial Cross-Citations: How Do European Judges Engage with Foreign Case Law?' (2024) 72 *American Journal of Comparative Law* 292, 313–16; Chernykh and Elkins (n 109) 542.

[197] See Sections B and D 1.

[198] See Mathias Siems, 'The Curios Case of Overfitting Legal Transplants' in Maurice Adams and Dirk Heirbaut (eds), *The Method and Culture of Comparative Law* (Oxford: Hart Publishing, 2014) 133 and https://scholar.google.com/scholar?hl=en&as_sdt=0%2C5&q=%22Overfitting+Legal+Transplants%22&btnG= accessed 21 November 2025.

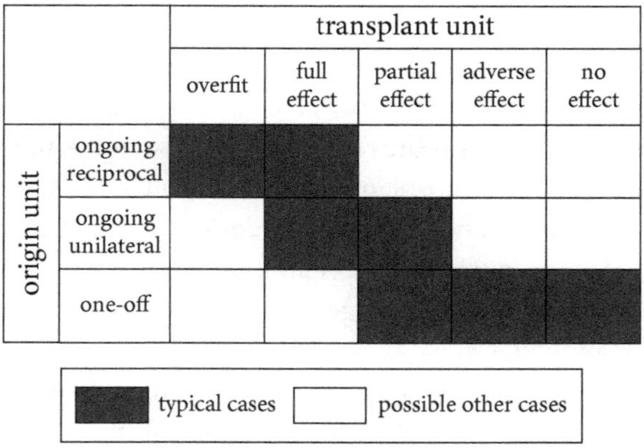

Figure 3.5 Categories of effect of transplantation

As we will see later in detail,[199] the literature on legal transplants often suggests that there is only a 'partial effect' of the transplant in the transplant unit. The intuitive reason is that circumstances that make the law work well in the origin unit are unlikely to be identical in the transplant unit. Within this category of a partial effect there can be further variations ranging from almost full convergence with the effect in the origin unit to cases of significant distortions with only limited effects.[200] There can also be variations in time as a limited initial effect may improve as the transplant unit becomes 'acculturated' to the new law.[201]

The category of 'adverse effect' may sometimes overlap with that of a partial effect. However, the difference is that, in this case, the effect is not just less than in the origin unit but mainly negative. Details of such a case are discussed later in this book; here, it is sufficient to refer to the normative debate in the field of 'law and development' as an example where some critics argue that the import of Western law to the non-Western world has been harmful as it mainly served the interests of foreign investors.[202]

The final category of 'no effect' is also a frequent theme in the debate about legal transplants. Suggesting such an outcome may sound surprising, but it is sometimes plausible, for example, if the transplantation has been very

[199] In particular in Chapter 5 at Section B 3.
[200] Cohn (2010) (n 1) 593.
[201] Papachristos (n 178) 109 (and 138 citing Roman law in Germany as 'perfect acculturation').
[202] See eg Ugo Mattei and Laura Nader, *Plunder: When the Rule of Law is Illegal* (Oxford: Wiley-Blackwell, 2008) 61, 69; Jedidiah J Kroncke, 'Law and Development as Anti-Comparative Law' (2012) 45 *Vanderbilt Journal of Transnational Law* 477, 524.

superficial,[203] or if there has been resistance against the received law due to religious, cultural, and practical reasons.[204]

Turning to the origin unit, in many cases it is typical that, at this stage, it has no further involvement on the effect of the transplant at the ground level. Thus, any influence on the transplantation is a 'one off'. This seems most likely in the case of voluntary transplants chosen entirely by the transplant unit. It is also possible that, even where the origin unit had some involvement in the transplantation, it does not want to get involved in the precise manner with which this law is applied.

In some cases, however, the origin country may want to influence the way the transplant is applied. Thus, the transplantation shifts from being a single event to a continuing process, possibly involving multiple types of transplant (say, a country initially adopts the codified rule from another country and subsequently also considers this country's case law).[205] This can be 'unidirectional' or 'reciprocal', depending on the question of whether the origin unit is also considering the experience in the transplant unit as feedback for its own law. Conventionally, the transplant literature has mainly focussed on cases of a 'one-way transfer', but in many situations reciprocal influence is also likely,[206] for example, where countries form a network in which there is a frequent exchange of information on legal matters (eg, the Commonwealth countries, member countries of a regional organisation).

As regards the relationship between the remaining influence of the origin unit and the effect of the transplantation in the transplant unit, Figure 3.5 aims to show that the effect of a transplant is likely to be stronger the closer the remaining link is with the origin country. For example, adverse or no effect are likely to be mainly prevalent where the transplant is just a one-off event, while a reciprocal and ongoing relationship is more likely to lead to full effect (or even an overfit).[207]

E. Conclusion

The anatomy of legal transplants in this chapter was based on the categories 'object', 'units', and 'transplantation', as well as interactions between the origin

[203] Ferreri and DiMatteo (n 94) 54 (referring to cases of mere 'adoption of foreign terminology').
[204] Papachristos (n 178) 83–93.
[205] Twining (2004) (n 2) 17. For examples see Spamann (n 106).
[206] Twining (2004) (n 2).
[207] See Chapter 5 at Section C 1.

and transplant unit. The interactions between the units meant to show that the analysis of legal transplants is most fruitful if we never lose sight of the origin and the transplant units. Thus, reflecting on criticisms that some of the literature is said to have either an 'exporter' or an 'importer bias',[208] giving due consideration to such interactions can avoid these biases.

This approach was then used to identify more or less typical cases of legal transplants for each of these interactions. In principle, it would be possible to examine further permutations across units, objects, and transplantations (eg, is a voluntary direct transplant of a codified rule of international law to a judicial rule of regional law more or less typical?); yet, this would eventually simply state that everything depends on the individual case, which would not be an interesting conclusion. In any case, the following chapters aim to remain attentive to the different contexts in which different types of legal transplants occur.

In substance, this chapter has presented the concept of legal transplants in a manner that captures a great variety of phenomena. Thus, this presentation is different from that which regards the term 'legal transplant' as narrowly referring to the copying of near-identical codified rules only.[209] The reason for doing so is, partly, the result of changes to the legal world which nowadays go beyond neatly defined laws of distinct nation states as can be seen, for example, in the rise of general discussions on soft law, transnational law, comparative international law, but also the growth of more specific literature on, for example, transnational judicial dialogue and global templates for contract drafting.[210]

Importantly, it is also seen here as a feature not a bug of this approach that the concept of legal transplants is treated as having a high degree of openness and flexibility. It is the aim of this book to bring together topics that are often discussed separately but share the commonality of incorporating foreign legal objects of different units, both widely understood. Thus, beyond aiming to discuss important topics covered by such a wide notion of legal transplants, the following chapters have the ambition to reach general findings about legal transplants.

208 See Chapter 1 at Section B 1.
209 ibid.
210 Similarly, Part III on 'Global Comparative Law' in Siems (n 12).

4

Why Do Legal Transplants Take Place?

A. Introduction

Laws can change for a variety of reasons, and, according to some voices, legal transplants are a rather unusual case. A standard narrative of the historical school of jurisprudence of the nineteenth century was that of a 'natural and unconscious development of law', which would thus be contradicted by, say, legal transplants of Western laws to Japan and Turkey.[1] It can also be suggested that socio-legal scholars and legal sociologists are likely to regard legal transplants with suspicion, given that there is often bound to be some mismatch with the local context of the transplant country.[2] Furthermore, it may be questioned how much truth there is in the claim that legal transplants really occur anywhere and everywhere.[3] For ordinary products such as food it may be the case that consumers happily mix products from any part of the world.[4] Yet, it seems often more likely that, for legal transplants, there is a mere 'receptivity' to a particular foreign law rather than 'an exhaustive evaluation of all possible alternatives'.[5]

The question of this chapter on 'why do legal transplants take place' therefore also implies dealing with the question of why, sometimes or even often, they do not take place. It is also part of this chapter's objective to explore 'from where' a

[1] Justine K Collins, *Tracing British West Indian Slavery Laws: A Comparative Analysis of Legal Transplants* (Abingdon: Routledge, 2021) 5. For the cases of Japan and Turkey see eg Chapter 1 at Section B 2 and Chapter 5 at Section C 3 (b).

[2] See Athanase C Papachristos, *La réception des droits privés étrangers comme phénomène de sociologie juridique* (Paris: LGDJ, 1975) 1 (exceptional phenomenon from a socio-legal perspective). See also Chapter 5 at Section B 3.

[3] As suggested by H Patrick Glenn, *Legal Traditions of the World* (Oxford: OUP, 5th edn, 2014) 42 ('nowadays all traditions are in constant contact with one or more of the other legal traditions').

[4] Cf David Harvey, 'Editorial: A Breakfast Vision' (1989) 3 *Geographical Review* 1 ('Consider, for example, where my breakfast comes from. The coffee was from Costa Rica, the flour that made up the bread probably from Canada, the oranges in marmalade came from Spain, those in the orange juice came from Morocco and the sugar came from Barbados. Then, I think of all the things that went into making the production of those things possible—the machinery that came from [West] Germany, the fertilizer from the United States, the oil from Saudi Arabia . . . ').

[5] George Mousourakis, *Traversing Legal Traditions: Perspectives on Comparative Law and Legal History* (Cham: Springer, 2nd edn, 2025) 322 (with reference to Watson).

Legal Transplants. Mathias Siems, Oxford University Press. © Mathias Siems 2026.
DOI: 10.1093/9780191991981.003.0004

legal transplant originates. In other words, this chapter aims to identify a wide range of possible reasons for legal transplants but then also scrutinise which of those reasons play a role in a particular scenario.

Following the general approach of this book, other disciplines feature prominently in this chapter. In the policy literature, it is suggested that the 'sources, inspiration, design, logic, and even funding [of public policies] often have origins elsewhere',[6] and that policy transfers are driven by a variety of reasons (coercion, competition, emulation, learning, etc). Research from international relations on transnationalism closely considers the state's 'complex interdependency' in the international system, which Tim Legrand recently incorporated into research on policy transfers.[7] Sociological research is also relevant as it is interested in a 'detailed examination of the pathways and processes' whereas legal scholarship is said to have a focus on large-scale transplants.[8] Similarly, historical scholarship is typically context-specific, while recently also showing a growing interest in the transfer of knowledge through 'entangled history'.[9]

The structure of this chapter is as follows: Section B discusses the literature on the motivations for legal transplants and how this research connects to the wider topic of why transplants take place. Section C then presents an analysis of the 'causes of causes' of legal transplants. The main idea is that merely listing a variety of factors is unsatisfactory given the complexity of causal chains, including a mix of necessary and sufficient conditions. Section D concludes that there is now a trend towards voluntary transplants which are often based on a reasonable evaluation of the advantages and disadvantages of the transplanted law.

B. The debate about motivations

The intuitive starting point to the question of why transplants take place is to ask who benefits from such a transplant (in other words: 'cui bono?'). This is indeed a main focus of the literature on this topic. This section discusses the

[6] Magdaléna Hadjiisky, Leslie A Pal, and Christopher Walker, 'Conclusion' in Magdaléna Hadjiisky, Leslie A Pal, and Christopher Walker (eds), *Public Policy Transfer: Micro-Dynamics and Macro-Effects* (Cheltenham: Edward Elgar, 2017) 271.

[7] Tim Legrand, *The Architecture of Policy Transfer: Ideas, Institutions and Networks in Transnational Policymaking* (London: Palgrave, 2021) 5 (with reference to Robert Keohane and Joseph Nye).

[8] William Twining, 'Diffusion of Law: A Global Perspective' (2004) 49 *The Journal of Legal Pluralism and Unofficial Law* 1, 9.

[9] Including the related concepts of 'cultural transfer' and 'transnational history', see references in Chapter 1 at Section C 2.

key findings of the literature on the motivations of the origin unit, the transplant unit, and agents. Doing so, it also demonstrates that the reasons for the occurrence of legal transplants often go beyond these motivations, thus setting the scene for the further analysis in Section C.

Within this book, the motivations of legal transplants relate to the topics of the subsequent three chapters as follows: Chapter 5 on whether transplants 'work' is relevant here as the motivations assume that transplants are, at least, somehow effective. Chapter 6 on whether it is generally desirable to transplant law will revisit the motivations as to whether transplants are legitimate from a normative perspective. Chapter 7 on the design of legal transplants analyses how the transplant unit can best fulfil the motivations of the transplant.

1. Motivations of the origin unit

In some of the categories of legal transplants, the origin unit may have little or no motivation about whether another unit transplants its law. For example, when a court borrows from another court's case law, the judges of the latter court may be personally pleased about it, but any such intrinsic motivation would not explain why this judicial transplant takes place.

However, in other cases, the motivations of the origin unit play a decisive role. Colonial transplants are sometimes seen as one of the typical cases of legal transplants.[10] Colonial expansion was motivated by the direct exploitation of the colonies which was facilitated by imposing colonial laws on the colonial territories, for example, by making it easier for colonial officials to rely on familiar laws. Of course, domination and coercion of other countries and people are not merely features of this period in time. 'Externally-dictated transplants'[11] have been part of neocolonial influence and other forms of imposition.[12] Beyond statute law, multi-national companies may impose their own contractual rules to business partners in global supply chains. Similarly, in

[10] See Chapter 1 at Section B 2.

[11] Jonathan M Miller, 'A Typology of Legal Transplants: Using Sociology, Legal History, and Argentine Examples to Explain the Transplant Process' (2003) 51 *American Journal of Comparative Law* 839, 847.

[12] See eg Gyula Eörsi, *Comparative Civil (Private) Law: Law Types, Law Groups, the Roads of Legal Development* (Budapest: Akadémiai Kiadó, 1979) 192–5 (capitalist expansion, unequal economic relationships, and neo-colonialism); Ugo Mattei and Laura Nader, *Plunder: When the Rule of Law is Illegal* (Oxford: Wiley-Blackwell, 2008) 142 (legal domination); Margit Cohn, 'Legal Transplant Chronicles: The Evolution of Unreasonableness and Proportionality Review of the Administration in the United Kingdom' (2010) 58 *American Journal of Comparative Law* 583, 591 (distinguishing between imposition, transnational commitment, and external pressure).

the literature on policy diffusion, 'coercion theorists' are said to refer to the way 'powerful nation-states, and international financial institutions [. . .] threaten sanctions or promise aid in return for fiscal conservatism, free trade, etc'.[13]

The benefits of making another unit adopt one's law can also be more indirect, which often occur through informal manners of influence. For example, a country may be interested in the prestige of having a legal system that has a global influence, possibly as it believes that its own law reflects universal values (eg, its human rights law or its religious law).[14] Having a legal system that is seen as prestigious may also have tangible benefits. For instance, foreigners may want to buy literature about this legal system or pay to study at its universities. In turn, the promotion of one's legal system through translations can be a soft means of influencing other legal systems. Other means of promoting one's law include setting up expert groups drafting model laws or other forms of international dialogue.[15] Considering the spread of legal traditions, influence is often also part of other forms of diffusion, for example, associations by way of language, religion, political alliances, or patterns of migration.[16] Thus, legal transplants happening along such forms of diffusion have indirect motivations from the perspective of the origin unit but they are also examples of the interconnected motivations of all units and agents involved in the process.[17]

Furthermore, the motivation of the origin unit may be linked to the interests and influence of private parties from this unit. For example, a country may indirectly benefit from its laws being transplanted, since a familiar legal system makes it easier for its firms to do business with firms from the transplant country. This assumes that, in this example, business interests 'win the day', which thus raises questions about the way lawmakers may sometimes respond to private interests.[18]

As regards the absence of motivations of the origin unit, there are few countries and cultures that explicitly want to keep their traditions (legal, cultural, etc) isolated with little interaction with other units.[19] Even in cases where a

[13] Frank Dobbin, Beth Simmons, and Geoffrey Garrett, 'The Global Diffusion of Public Policies: Social Construction, Coercion, Competition, or Learning?' (2007) 33 *Annual Review of Sociology* 449.

[14] For these two examples see eg Mathias Siems, *Comparative Law* (Cambridge: CUP, 3rd edn, 2022) 340–3; Fernanda Pirie, *The Anthropology of Law* (Oxford: OUP, 2013) 180–1. For the notion of 'universal law' more generally see Chapter 6 at Section C 2 (b).

[15] See eg Matthieu Burnay, *Chinese Perspectives on the International Rule of Law: Law and Politics in the One-Party State Book* (Cheltenham: Edward Elgar, 2018) 87 (as applied to legal transplants in China). See also the mapping of the role of the origin unit in Chapter 3 at Section D 1.

[16] William Twining, *General Jurisprudence: Understanding Law From a Global Perspective* (Cambridge: CUP, 2009) 16.

[17] For such cases see Section B 4.

[18] See Section B 3, as well as Section C.

[19] See n 184 in Chapter 6.

country (or other unit) engages with the outside world, it is, however, possible that it does not wish to transplant its laws. Matthew Erie and Ha Hai Do mention the example of today's China as a form of 'law and development minus legal transplants', suggesting that this may be due to factors such as the lack of prestige of the relatively recent PRC legal system, as well as linguistic hurdles and the valorisation of sovereignty.[20] Authors who use the term of legal transplants for China's influence agree that its Belt and Road Initiative does not aim to impose details of Chinese law on other countries.[21] However, even Erie and Do mention cases of Chinese legal influence in today's Vietnam,[22] and there is also a so-called 'China Index' that measures the influence of China across a number of domains, including its impact on the domestic politics of other countries.[23] Thus, the following section of this chapter will return to this topic within the general discussion about the global models that influence transplants today.[24]

2. Motivations of the transplant unit

In both the legal transplant and the policy diffusion literature, much writing has been devoted to the motivations of, what is called here, the transplant unit. Similar to the literature on the motivations of the origin unit, the benefits the transplant unit hopes to receive can be of a more or less tangible nature.

The most tangible reason is that the transplant provides a concrete benefit to the transplant unit and that this benefit is precisely what the transplant unit aspires to receive. For example, the transplant may be seen as a means to get legal rules that have already been successfully 'tested' abroad[25] in order to promote economic growth, fairness, clarity of law, or whatever the aim of the law may be, depending on the preferences of the transplant unit. Support for such

[20] Matthew Erie and Ha Hai Do, 'Law and Development Minus Legal Transplants: The Example of China in Vietnam' (2021) 8 *Asian Journal of Law and Society* 372, 389.

[21] Davide Zoppolato and Paolo Davide Farah, 'China's Path to Modernization and Legal Pluralism: Transplants and the Belt and Road Initiative' (2025) 12 *Asian Journal of Law and Society* 109 (noting 'voluntariness' and 'prioritizing policy over law').

[22] Erie and Do (n 20) 382. See now also Matthew S Erie, 'The Travels and Travails of Chinese Law in Inter-Asia' in Matthew S Erie and Ching-Fu Lin (eds), *Inter-Asian Law* (Cambridge: CUP, 2026) 169, 171 (examples on how Chinese law is 'slowly and hesitantly' moving 'to other jurisdictions'); Hang Duong, *Policy Transfer Under Authoritarianism: Meritocracy in Vietnam's Civil Service* (London: Palgrave Macmillan, 2023) 49–79 (models from China but also other countries).

[23] China Index, available at https://china-index.io, as well as https://china-index.io/domain/domestic-politics (though not measuring the impact of precise laws but factors such as visits of politicians to China) accessed 23 October 2025.

[24] See Section C 3 (b).

[25] Ralf Michaels, 'Make or Buy—A Public Market for Legal Transplants' in Horst Eidenmüller (ed), *Regulatory Competition in Contract Law and Dispute Resolution* (Munich: Beck, 2013) 27, 34.

learning from abroad was already made by some prominent voices from the nineteenth century: according to Alexis de Tocqueville, it was not only his 'legitimate curiosity' to travel to and examine America but 'to find there instruction by which we may ourselves profit',[26] and, according to Rudolph von Jhering, the 'reception of foreign legal institutions is not a matter of nationality, but of usefulness and need'.[27]

The contemporary literature on legal transplants, however, also discusses some issues which show that 'cost-saving transplants'[28] should not merely consider the quality of the transplanted law. Three of such factors consider counterfactuals. The first one is that the intended benefit of a legal transplant needs to be compared with the quality of the existing law.[29] Second, as there are costs associated with switching from one set of rules to another, the benefits of the transplant also need to exceed these costs.[30] Third, there is the counterfactual of a unit developing its home-made law; in other words, this refers to the choice of whether it is better to 'make' one's own law or to 'buy' it from elsewhere (ie use a transplant).[31] This final point is a frequent topic for law reforms of countries which, without delay, require new laws. In this sense, the French comparative lawyer René David justified his advice that Ethiopia should adopt a legal system based on French law with the words that 'Ethiopia cannot wait 300 or more years to construct in an empirical fashion a system of law which is unique to itself (. . .)'.[32] A similar argument has been made by other authors, for example, referring to the needs of transition economies and forms of transitional justice, also indicating that the model of the other unit may be taken from the past (ie as a diachronic legal transplant).[33]

[26] Alexis de Tocqueville, *Democracy in America, Volume I* (Cambridge, MA: Sever & Francis, 1864 [original from 1835]) 15.

[27] As translated from his 1873 book 'Geist des römischen Rechts'; see discussion and references in Chapter 6 at Section B 1.

[28] Miller (n 11) 845.

[29] Papachristos (n 2) 57.

[30] See Raffaele Caterina, 'Comparative Law and Economics' in Jan M Smits and others (eds), *Elgar Encyclopedia of Comparative Law* (Cheltenham: Edward Elgar, 3rd edn, 2023) 333, 333–5.

[31] For this analogy see Michaels (n 25). See also Peter Grajzl and Valentina Dimitrova-Grajzl, 'The Choice in the Lawmaking Process: Legal Transplants vs. Indigenous Law' (2009) 5 *Review of Law and Economics* 615 (uncertainty may be greater for imported than for home-made law).

[32] René David, 'A Civil Code for Ethiopia: Considerations on the Codification of the Civil Law in African Countries' (1963) 37 *Tulane Law Review* 187, 188–9. For a critical analysis of this process see Daniel Bonilla Maldonado, *Legal Barbarians: Identity, Modern Comparative Law and the Global South* (Cambridge: CUP, 2021) 117–26.

[33] Rainer Kulms, 'Optimistic Normativism after Two Decades of Legal Transplants and Autonomous Developments' in Christa Jessel-Holst, Rainer Kulms, and Alexander Trunk (eds), *Private Law in Eastern Europe: Autonomous Developments or Legal Transplants?* (Tübingen: Mohr Siebeck, 2010) 7; Peter Mankowski, *Rechtskultur* (Tübingen: Mohr Siebeck, 2016) 496; Bishal Khanal, *Legal Reform via Reception of Law* (Kathmandu: Bhrikuti Academic Publications, 2018) 143 (for transitional justice). For a conceptualisation that distinguishes 'legal transplants' from 'legal revivals': Rafał Mańko, 'Legal

These factors also point toward the role of context in understanding the motivations of transplants from the perspective of the transplant unit. Context matters for the question of how well transplants 'work' (and thus the topic of the next chapter). In the present chapter, context can show that a transplant may be beneficial as it enables the law to respond to changed societal circumstances.[34] It is also possible that law is used to change society in a particular way; thus, here the intended tangible benefit is something transformative the lawmaker aims to achieve (say, to make it a global financial hub or a carbon-neutral country).[35] Or, it may happen that both law and society are co-evolving parts of a general modernisation happening in a particular country or other unit with transplants being a part of this process.[36]

In the policy literature, the motivations akin to a search for the 'best law' (including its variants) appear in two categories: 'competition' and 'learning' (or 'lesson drawing').[37] Both share a view of diffusion based on frameworks of rationality and policy interests in order to identify the policies that the transplant unit wishes to adopt.[38] They are also connected to the role of private actors as those may often be the ones that push the transplant unit to enact competitive laws and/or to communicate about innovative foreign laws.[39]

Transplants with less tangible motivations have been called 'legitimacy-generating transplants'[40] or 'reception by admiration'.[41] For example, according

Transplants, Legal Survivals and Legal Revivals: Towards a Reconceptualisation of the Circulation of Legal Forms in Time and Space' (2024) 109 *Acta Universitatis Lodziensis. Folia Iuridica* 93.

[34] Eörsi (n 12) 564 (calling it 'adaptational reception').

[35] See Jutta Mues, *Rechtstransfer: Zur theoretisch-methodischen Komplexität der Interaktion normativer Ordnungen* (Frankfurt: Peter Lang, 2015) 104–10 (distinction between 'reactive' and 'active' use of legal transplants); Andrew Harding, 'The Legal Transplants Debate: Getting Beyond the Impasse?' in Vito Breda (ed), *Legal Transplants in East Asia and Oceania* (Cambridge: CUP, 2019) 13, 29 ('objective being to change society, not to reflect it'); David Nelken, 'Comparatists and Transferability' in Pierre Legrand and Roderick Munday (eds), *Comparative Legal Studies: Traditions and Transitions* (Cambridge: CUP, 2003) 437, 456 (for transplants 'geared to fitting an imagined future').

[36] See eg Stanisław Ehrlich, *Wstęp do nauki o państwie i prawie* (Warsaw: Państwowe Wydawnictwo Naukowe, 1971) 139–41 (reception never an isolated event but happens with the modernisation of socio-economic structure); John Armour and others, 'Law and Financial Development: What We are Learning from Time-Series Evidence' (2009) *BYU Law Review* 1435, 1449–53 (coevolution of legal, economic, and political systems). For the role of 'modernisation' see also Chapter 5 at Section C 2 b and 3 b (cases of Japan and Turkey) and Chapter 6 at Section B 1 (for the 'modernisation theory').

[37] See the overview of typologies in Johanna Kuhlmann, 'Mechanisms of Policy Transfer and Policy Diffusion' in Osmany Porto de Oliveira (ed), *Handbook of Policy Transfer, Diffusion and Circulation* (Cheltenham: Edward Elgar, 2021) 43, 50.

[38] See Kurt Weyland, *Bounded Rationality and Policy Diffusion: Social Sector Reform in Latin America* (Princeton, NJ: Princeton University Press, 2006) 30 (how domestic motivations claim forms of comprehensive or bounded rationality).

[39] See further Section B 3.

[40] Miller (n 11) 854.

[41] Khanal (n 33) 59.

to Alan Watson, it is 'a recognized pedigree' that makes a foreign law acceptable, and then, as 'acceptance implies respectability', such a law will also appeal to further countries.[42] It is thus said that Watson was sceptical about imitation occurring 'by rational weighing of advantages' but rather argued that it is the 'high reputation by which some codification is surrounded' with the analogy that adaptation of languages also 'evolve independently from economic growth, from political reversals, from segregation in social classes' etc.[43] In other words, certain models may be a priori more appealing because they are seen as more prestigious or signal a desired turn towards modernity.[44]

The policy literature mainly uses the term 'emulation' to refer to situations where the perceived appropriateness of policies is a driving force in the transplant unit.[45] Other terms that are sometimes used in a similar sense are 'imitation' and 'mimicry', referring for example, to the 'copying [of] foreign models in terms of symbolic or normative factors, rather than a technical or rational concern with functional efficiency'.[46] It is also said that mimetic processes are typical in cases of uncertainty, namely that institutions may use popular models 'when goals are ambiguous, or when the environment creates symbolic uncertainty'.[47] Finally, some authors use the term 'socialisation' in this context; yet, it has a somehow different connotation as it refers to a more unconscious process described as the 'internalization of the principles, beliefs, and norms of a foreign community'.[48]

The concept of 'mimesis' has also a long tradition in philosophy, literature, arts, sociology, and other fields.[49] It is a variant of the 'mimetic theory' which

[42] Alan Watson, 'The Birth of Legal Transplants' (2013) 41 *Georgia Journal of International and Comparative Law* 605, 607.

[43] Silvia Ferreri, 'The Unpredictable Path of Legal Transplants: Some Analogy with Language Evolution' (2022) 1 *Comparative Law and Language* 60, 67.

[44] See Michele Graziadei, 'Comparative Law as the Study of Transplants and Receptions' in Mathias Reimann and Reinhard Zimmermann (eds), *The Oxford Handbook of Comparative Law* (Oxford: OUP, 2nd edn, 2019) 442, 460; Rodolfo Sacco, 'Circolazione e mutazione dei modelli giuridici' (1988) *Digesto delle discipline privatistiche (sezione civile), vol. II* 365, 369. Discussing the similarity to Watson's position: Silvia Ferreri, 'Assonanze transoceaniche: Tendenze a confronto' (1993) 10 *Quadrimestre* 172, 192–4.

[45] Fabrizio Gilardi and Fabio Wasserfallen, 'The Politics of Policy Diffusion' (2019) 58 *European Journal of Political Research* 1245.

[46] David Marsh and JC Sharman, 'Policy Diffusion and Policy Transfer' (2009) 30 *Policy Studies* 269, 272 (for mimicry). See also Kuhlmann (n 37).

[47] Paul J DiMaggio and Walter W Powell, 'The Iron Cage Revisited: Institutional Isomorphism and Collective Rationality in Organizational Fields' (1983) 48 *American Sociological Review* 147, 151.

[48] Jean-Frédéric Morin and Edward Richard Gold, 'An Integrated Model of Legal Transplantation: The Diffusion of Intellectual Property Law in Developing Countries' (2014) 58 *International Studies Quarterly* 781, 783. See also Katja Bender, Sonja Keller, and Holger Willing, 'The Role of International Policy Transfer and Diffusion for Policy Change in Social Protection—A Review of the State of the Art' (IZNE Social Protection Working Paper 14/1, 2014) 15 (as a sub-category of emulation).

[49] For a recent interdisciplinary work see Nidesh Lawtoo, *Homo Mimeticus: A New Theory of Imitation* (Leuven: Leuven University Press, 2022).

has mainly been developed by René Girard. This theory emphasises the general importance of imitation for human behaviour and, in particular, how humans often follow the desires of others.[50] Applying such 'mimetic desire' to legal and policy transplants, the transplant unit may thus adopt new normative priorities[51] not in an autonomous and rational manner but rather through a gradual process that makes it desire what other units already prioritise.

Intangible motivations can be put on one end of a sliding scale with more tangible ones at the other. For example, the lawmaker of a democratic country may want to consider the perceptions of the general public about rules from particular foreign countries.[52] This may be due to the fact that those are well-tested ideas, but it may also reflect idiosyncratic preferences, or even misperceptions, of the general public. It may also be said that, while intangible motivations are not strictly utilitarian, the choice of a foreign model in such a case can be based on 'cognitive shortcuts' and thus be seen as an example of bounded rationality.[53] For example, the number of previous adopters of a law may not merely be an esteem indicator, but it can sometimes be evidence of the quality of this law (assuming that the previous adopters made rational decisions and that the context of the law is comparable in the transplant units).

Variables that aim to capture the motivations of the transplant unit also show that many of them can apply to both tangible and intangible motivations. For example, measures of similarities between units, such as whether they are from the same legal family, share the same language and culture, are members of the same regional organisation, or share a similar political or economic system, may be relevant for tangible motivations as they may determine whether a transplanted law works well in the transplant unit, but they are also relevant for intangible motivations given that the transplant unit may use them as a shortcut to evaluate the legitimacy of a transplant.[54] Another set of factors is about the transplant unit's lawmaking procedures, for example, whether the

[50] For overviews see eg https://violenceandreligion.com/mimetic-theory/ and https://www.imitatio.org/brief-intro accessed 23 October 2025 and, for more details, Wolfgang Palaver, *René Girard's Mimetic Theory* (East Lansing, MI: Michigan State University Press, 2013) 33–134.

[51] For transplants leading to changes in normative priorities see also Chapter 6 at Section C 2 and 5 and Chapter 7 at Section C 2 (a) and (b).

[52] See Katerina Linos, *The Democratic Foundations of Policy Diffusion: How Health, Family, and Employment Laws Spread Across Countries* (Oxford: OUP, 2013) 13–35 (in the sense that by 'pointing to models from abroad, politicians can persuade voters that their ideas are not radical, ill-thought out experiments, but mainstream, tried-and-true solutions').

[53] Cf Weyland (n 38) 30 (on bounded rationality and cognitive shortcuts).

[54] See eg Bender and others (n 38) 17–18 (referring to moderating variables such as proximity between countries); Martino Maggetti and Fabrizio Gilardi, 'Problems (and Solutions) in the Measurement of Policy Diffusion Mechanisms' (2016) 36 *Journal of Public Policy* 87, 97 (referring to indicators such as structural equivalence and geographic proximity).

persons involved have good comparative legal knowledge and are open to new ideas: this may be an indicator that helps lawmakers identify the most suitable laws, or it may simply mean that such lawmakers are attracted to the argument that drawing on foreign models fosters the legitimacy of a proposal.[55] Thus, these interconnections show that, while such motivations are important, it remains necessary to understand more fundamentally the complexity of any factors that can explain why transplants take place.[56]

3. Motivations of agents

A recent case study on legal transplants in Chinese law examined how multiple actors shaped this process in a complex manner that made the resulting law appear like an 'authorless product'.[57] This finding can also be read as supporting the recommendation to closely understand the role of the agents (or actors) behind the processes leading to a legal transplant.[58] In some situations, it can even be the case that the agents, and not the origin and transplant units, are the ones whose motivations really determine whether and how transplants take place. Miller calls these 'entrepreneurial transplants', referring to legal transplants initiated by groups 'who reap benefits from investing their energy in learning and encouraging local adoption of a foreign legal model'.[59]

In the legal literature, prominent agents of early legal transplants were said to be jurists and other legal elites but also colonists, missionaries, and merchants.[60] In modern times, in the cases of Japan and Turkey and then the transition economies of Central and Eastern Europe, both local politics and external advisors played a key role in the decision for legal transplants and their subsequent design.[61] Since the 1990s, joined work by Yves Dezalay

[55] See eg Albert Kocourek, 'Factors in the Reception of Law' (1935) 10 *Tulane Law Review* 209, 228 (referring to the important role of the 'political factor', such as 'nature of the sources of law, organization of courts, and the activity of the legislative power').

[56] See in particular Section C 3 (a).

[57] Jia Wang, 'Reflection on Legal Transplantation Theories: A Socio-legal Historical Study of the Formulation and Evolution of Chinese Marine Insurance Law' (2025) 21 *International Journal of Law in Context* 80.

[58] Michele Graziadei, 'Legal Transplants and the Frontiers of Legal Knowledge' (2009) 10 *Theoretical Inquiries in Law* 723 (arguing that 'legal transplants as social acts performed by individuals call for a study of the "micro" level of engagement with legal change by individuals').

[59] Miller (n 11) 849–50. See also Section B 3 (b).

[60] See eg Papachristos (n 2) 43 and 54; Twining (n 8) 22.

[61] See eg Gülnihal Bozkurt, 'Atatürk'ün Hukuk Alanında Getirdikleri' (1991) 8 *Atatürk Araştırma Merkezi Dergisi* 45; Gülnihal Bozkurt, 'Mahmut Esat Bozkurt'un Laik Hukuka Geçişe Katkıları' (1994) 2(4) *Çağdaş Türkiye Tarihi Araştırmaları Dergisi* 201; Paul-Christian Schenck, *Der deutsche Anteil an der Gestaltung des modernen japanischen Rechts- und Verfassungswesens: Deutsche Rechtsberater im Japan der Meiji-Zeit* (Stuttgart: Steiner, 1997); Lado Chanturia, 'Recht und Transformation.

and Bryant Garth explored the role of lawyers, arbitrators, and economists in the promotion of transnational commercial law in Latin America and Asia. In particular, they identified experts from Europe and North America but also 'double agents', such as Latin American lawyers trained at US law schools, as driving the export of institutions from the former regions to the latter ones.[62] More recently, Günter Frankenberg writes about '"small worlds" of elites, advisors, committees and commissions, social movements, and NGOs' as "merchants of transfer"',[63] and other research referred to the way international law firms, and international institutional investors stimulate the flow of ideas in company law.[64]

The role of agents can also matter in ways other than pushing lawmakers to enact a particular law. In some cases, the agents are themselves the transplant unit as the transplant concerns other objects than the positive law. For example, the literature has explored the globalisation of practices of the legal profession[65] and the role of transnational corporations in applying corporate social responsibility standards in response to international human rights law.[66] As far as legal thought can be the object of a transplant, legal scholars of different jurisdictions are themselves the respective origin and transplant units.[67] In other cases, agents matter despite not having their own motivations to make the transplant happen: for example, international networks of legal scholars and judges may be means of transmitting information about a foreign law to the lawmaking body.[68]

Rechtliche Zusammenarbeit aus der Sicht eines rezipierenden Landes' (2008) 72 *Rabels Zeitschrift für ausländisches und internationales Privatrecht* 114.

[62] Eg, Yves Dezalay and Bryant G Garth, *Dealing in Virtue: International Commercial Arbitration and the Construction of a Transnational Legal Order* (Chicago, IL: University of Chicago Press, 1996); Yves Dezalay and Bryant G Garth, *The Internationalization of Palace Wars: Lawyers, Economists, and the Contest to Transform Latin American States* (Chicago, IL: University of Chicago Press, 2002); Yves Dezalay and Bryant G Garth, 'The Import and Export of Law and Legal Institutions: International Strategies in National Palace Wars' in David Nelken and Johannes Feest (eds), *Adapting Legal Culture* (Oxford: Hart Publishing, 2001) 241; Yves Dezalay and Bryant G Garth, *Asian Legal Revivals: Lawyers in the Shadow of Empire* (Chicago, IL: University of Chicago Press, 2010).

[63] Günter Frankenberg, 'Legal Transfers' in Marie-Claire Foblets and others (eds), *The Oxford Handbook of Law and Anthropology* (Oxford: OUP, 2020) 333, 346.

[64] Mathias Siems, *Convergence in Shareholder Law* (Cambridge: CUP, 2008) 310–16.

[65] See eg the Harvard-based project on 'Globalization, Lawyers and Emerging Economies (GLEE)', https://clp.law.harvard.edu/research/pillars/globalization/ accessed 23 October 2025.

[66] Neli Frost, 'Transnational Corporations as Agents of Legal Change: The Role of Corporate Social Responsibility' (2016) 5 *Cambridge Journal of International and Comparative Law* 502. For further examples see Chapter 3 at Section B 2.

[67] This can also follow from 'legal scholarship' as one of the legal formants (in Sacco's terminology), see references in Chapter 5 at Section C 4 (a).

[68] For this point see Section C 3 (a).

In the policy and regulation literature, many publications emphasise the role of agency as opposed to 'structural explanations of policy mobility'.[69] Some of this literature classifies the agents and processes involved in this process. For example, David Dolowitz and David Marsh list 'elected officials, political parties, bureaucrats/civil servants, pressure groups, policy entrepreneurs and experts, transnational corporations, think tanks, supranational governmental and nongovernmental institutions and consultants'.[70] Others provide more conceptual distinctions. Thierry Delpeuch, for example, distinguishes between the role that agents play in the process of policy diffusion, differentiating between their involvement in the source, transfer, facilitation, and reception of the policy.[71] John Braithwaite and Peter Drahos use the terms 'missionaries', 'mercenaries', 'mongers', 'misers', and 'modernizers' to identify the motivations of those involved in the diffusion of regulatory models. Thus, these categories are, respectively, about cases where agents are convinced that the model is the best one, they benefit commercially, they use it to pursue a political agenda, they aim to save the costs of innovation, and they regard it as legitimate to modernise the law.[72]

These latter categories point towards the specific benefits which agents may aim to achieve, as well as the means they may use in order to push for a particular transplant. Doing so, it is possible to identify further details, for example, the tangible economic, social, political (etc) benefits agents seek but also their intrinsic motivation, the way migrants may influence the transplant legal system, and the importance of lobbying as an influence on lawmaking.[73]

4. Interconnected motivations of multiple units and agents

Legal transplants may be a result of more than one motivation: for example, it can happen that the motivations of the origin unit, the transplant unit, and agents all support the same transplant. However, there can also be cases where it is only through the interconnected motivations of multiple units and agents that it is possible to fully understand how these motivations matter.

[69] Legrand (n 7) 29 and 41.

[70] David Dolowitz and David Marsh, 'Learning from Abroad: The Role of Policy Transfer in Contemporary Policy-Making' (2000) 13 *Governance* 5, 10.

[71] Thierry Delpeuch, 'L'analyse des transferts internationaux de politiques publiques: un état de l'art' (CÉRIUM, Sciences Po, Questions de Recherche N° 27, 2008) 40, available at https://www.sciencespo.fr/ceri/sites/sciencespo.fr.ceri/files/qdr27.pdf with reference to Harold Wolman and Ed Page, 'Policy Transfer among Local Governments: An Information-Theory Approach' (2002) 15 *Governance* 477.

[72] John Braithwaite and Peter Drahos, *Global Business Regulation* (Cambridge: CUP, 2000) 585.

[73] See also Section C.

A first set of situations concerns cases where there is an interaction of two countries or other units. When two countries engage in regulatory competition, this may be a reason why one of them adopts the rules from the other unit,[74] with the possible further consequence that such a competitive market for the supply of law leads to 'convergence of legal systems as a movement towards efficiency'.[75] It can also be the case that the two countries collaborate in transplanting laws. For example, both may support a transplant (in whatever direction) in order to reduce transaction costs that arise from legal differences,[76] or they may have the idealistic aim of creating common rules with the aspiration of promoting a more peaceful world.[77] In other cases, the interaction may not be one of equals. For example, in the case of 'imposition by bargaining'[78] a developed country may make its aid conditional on a developing country adopting certain legal rules in order to foster the interests of foreign investors, possibly also with the aspiration that one or both countries may benefit economically.

Sometimes more than two units are involved. The transplant may be the result of international cooperation between multiple countries and/or other units.[79] In a recent monograph, Tim Legrand analyses this topic under the heading of 'transgovernmental policy network formation'. He distinguishes between the way 'politico-cultural propinquity', 'institutional-ideological networks', and 'agential articulation' matter.[80] Based on interviews with policymakers in the UK, the US, and Australia, these levels are then applied to the way policy transfers happen in the Anglosphere as like-minded countries with networks of cross-border learning and co-operation and as articulated in joined epistemic communities.[81]

[74] Daphne Barak-Erez, 'The Institutional Aspects of Comparative Law' (2009) 15 *Columbia Journal of European Law* 477, 483. The policy literature frequently also refers to competition as one of the categories of diffusion/transfer, see Kuhlmann (n 37).

[75] Raffaele Caterina, 'Comparative Law and Economics' in Jan M Smits and others (eds), *Elgar Encyclopedia of Comparative Law* (Cheltenham: Edward Elgar, 3rd edn, 2023) 333.

[76] For the role of transaction costs due to rule divergence see eg Katharina Pistor, 'The Standardization of Law and Its Effect on Developing Economies' (2002) 50 *American Journal of Comparative Law* 97. For a project on the economic effect of harmonisation: https://unidroitfoundation.org/economic-assessment-of-law/ accessed 23 October 2025.

[77] This is sometimes a general aspiration of comparative law: see eg Rahmatulla Khan and Sushil Kumar, 'Parts I and II' in Indian Law Institute (ed), *An Introduction to the Study of Comparative Law* (Bombay: NM Tripathi, 1971) 16–21; John Henry Wigmore, *A Panorama of the World's Legal Systems* (St Paul, MN: West Publishing, 1928) viii ('May this volume contribute to a better understanding of other peoples, and thus help toward greater intelligence and mutual toleration in world-affairs!').

[78] Ugo Mattei and Laura Nader, *Plunder: When the Rule of Law is Illegal* (Oxford: Wiley-Blackwell, 2008) 19; also Markus Müller-Chen, Christoph Müller, and Corinne Widmer Lüchinger, *Comparative Private Law* (Zurich: Dike, 2015) 103–5 (as 'semi-voluntary transplants').

[79] See the categories in Barak-Erez (n 74) 484–5.

[80] Legrand (n 7) 99.

[81] Legrand (n 7) 107–226.

Tim Legrand's book draws on earlier work by Mark Evans who suggested 'multi-level models of policy transfers' and distinguished between the interaction of global, international, and/or transnational, macro, meso, and micro explanations of policy transfers.[82] Reference can also be made to other publications from policy research that put emphasis on the importance of 'common kinship' and 'agreed culture',[83] that relate policy transfers to the interaction between 'expert epistemic communities and international organizations',[84] and that identify domestic judicial actors as well as networked and formal international actors as catalysts for the adoption and operation of specialised courts.[85]

In some cases, the motivations of multiple units and actors may be interconnected but it is difficult to identify any clear tangible benefits that any of them may receive. This is only sometimes discussed in the literature on legal transplants.[86] More often, it is a topic in the political science literature, referring to situations where structures leading to policy transfers transcend the acts of individuals.[87] Other terms may be used in a similar sense: for example, that there may be 'extra-logical' imitations,[88] unplanned cultural diffusion,[89] or forms of socialisation (referring to situations where a gradual consensus emerges on the social goals that countries pursue).[90] In comparative law, the transfer of legal ideas within the same legal family[91] may often be without the aim of clear tangible benefits. Similarly, if the initial spread of a particular legal

[82] Mark Evans, 'Understanding Policy Transfer' in Mark Evans (ed), *Policy Transfer in Global Perspective* (Aldershot: Ashgate, 2004) 10, 23 and Mark Evans, 'In Conclusion—Policy Transfer in Global Perspective' in ibid 211, 212.

[83] References in Evans (n 82) 14.

[84] Dobbin and others (n 13) 449 for 'constructivists' (as they argue that 'ideational factors' are key in understanding international relations and politics).

[85] J Michael Angstadt, 'Environmental Norm Diffusion and Domestic Legal Innovation: The Case of Specialized Environmental Courts and Tribunals' (2022) 31 *Review of European, Comparative & International Environmental Law* 222.

[86] For such 'unplanned legal transfer' see Jutta Mues, *Rechtstransfer: Zur theoretisch-methodischen Komplexität der Interaktion normativer Ordnungen* (Frankfurt: Peter Lang, 2015) 86–7.

[87] Marie-Laure Djelic, 'Institutional Perspectives—Working towards Coherence or Irreconcilable Diversity?' in Glenn Morgan and others (eds), *The Oxford Handbook of Comparative Institutional Analysis* (Oxford: OUP, 2010) 15, 29; Legrand (n 7) xiii. Similar also Martin de Jong and Virginie Mamadouh, 'Two Contrasting Perspectives on Institutional Transplantation' in Martin de Jong, Konstantinos Lalenis, and Virginie Mamadouh (eds), *The Theory and Practice of Institutional Transplantation: Experiences with the Transfer of Policy Institutions* (Deventer: Kluwer Academic Publishers, 2002) 19 (as contrast between a deliberate 'actors pulling in' and an evolutionary 'goodness of fit').

[88] Gabriel Tarde, *The Laws of Imitation* (New York: Henry Holt and Company, 1903) 83.

[89] Edward M Wise, 'The Transplant of Legal Patterns' (1990) 38 *American Journal of Comparative Law* (supplement) 1, 17.

[90] See eg Erin R Graham, Charles R Shipan, and Craig Volden, 'The Diffusion of Policy Diffusion Research in Political Science' (2013) 43 *British Journal of Political Science* 673, 692–3.

[91] See Chapter 3 at Section C 1.

tradition occurred together with general cultural influence (eg, Hindu legal influence in Southeast Asia, Chinese influence on Korea and Japan),[92] this may have happened in a gradual manner that makes it difficult to pinpoint precise motivations.

Overall, the discussion of this subsection shows that 'simply' searching for motivations comes with limitations in analysing the many complexities. To more fully understand as to why transplants take place, it is therefore necessary to analyse more deeply how the different causal elements related to legal transplants interact. This is the topic of the next section.

C. Understanding causes of causes

Legal transplants are not always clearly visible as 'the layering of domestic sources over foreign ones will eventually camouflage many distant origins'.[93] Another problem of identification concerns the question of causality, ie how to find out precisely why a particular transplant has occurred. Dealing with causal questions is said to be a core topic of large quantitative studies.[94] For the question of why transplants take place, such studies typically identify a list of variables that are classified under more general headings, such as the object (ie the transplant), relevant actors and environmental conditions,[95] diffusion mechanisms related to possible causes based on learning, emulation, and competition,[96] or variable clusters referring to topics such as geography, ideology, demographics, and politics.[97]

However, such large quantitative studies are not without limitations. If one follows theories that suggest that there can be different pathways to explain legal transplants, quantitative methods that simply test a series of variables may be less suitable than other research designs.[98] Moreover, quantitative studies which find that certain variables are 'significant' raise the question

[92] For references see Siems (n 14) 121.

[93] H Patrick Glenn, 'Are Legal Systems Incommensurable?' (2001) 49 *American Journal of Comparative Law* 133, 141.

[94] Osmany Porto de Oliveira, 'A Prelude to Policy Transfer Research' in Osmany Porto de Oliveira (ed), *Handbook of Policy Transfer, Diffusion and Circulation* (Cheltenham: Edward Elgar, 2021) 1, 3.

[95] Barbara Wejnert, 'Integrating Models of Diffusion of Innovations: A Conceptual Framework' (2002) 28 *Annual Review of Sociology* 297.

[96] Martino Maggetti and Fabrizio Gilardi, 'Problems (and Solutions) in the Measurement of Policy Diffusion Mechanisms' (2016) 36 *Journal of Public Policy* 87, 96–8.

[97] Daniel J Mallinson, 'Policy Diffusion Results: A New Database for Systematic Review and Meta-Analysis' (2020) 52 *State and Local Government Review* 18, 21.

[98] Such as 'qualitative comparative analysis' (QCA) which allows the analysis of different pathways. For its use in comparative law see Siems (n 14) 280–1.

as to why these factors mattered, which points towards the use of qualitative methods.[99] Given these challenges, this section cannot provide a conclusive answer to the question of why any specific legal transplant occurs. Rather, it will draw on research from diverse fields to identify general patterns of understanding the causes of causes of legal transplants. For this purpose, it starts with explaining the idea of 'causes of causes' (Section 1), followed by a presentation of categories and sub-categories of 'fully externally imposed transplants' and 'transplants adopted by the transplant unit' (Sections 2 and 3).

1. Idea and overview

The phenomenon of 'causes of causes' derives from the social science literature. How precisely this is conceptualised differs between authors; for example, some distinguish between surface and basic clauses, others between proximate and ultimate clauses.[100] A similar notion can be found in the literature on 'process tracing' which distinguishes between the causes and the causal mechanisms which this approach wishes to trace.[101]

This chapter will use flow charts to illustrate and explain how, in the case of legal transplants, chains of causal factors play a role. To be sure, implementing such research on causal complexity can face practical challenges. According to Jeremy Freese and Alex Kevern:

> 'The arrow salad: we have all seen examples before, and many of us have made them. One begins with the helpful convention of using boxes and arrows to specify consequential features of a system and the causal relations between them. But once one starts working theoretically—that is, trying to depict how we think some corner of human affairs might actually work—the boxes and arrows proliferate. Single-headed arrows turn into bidirectional ones as we

[99] Herbert Obinger, Carina Schmitt, and Peter Starke, 'Policy Diffusion and Policy Transfer in Comparative Welfare State Research' (2013) 47 *Social Policy & Administration* 111, 122 (on the limitations of quantitative methods: 'Why social policy is diffused, which actors are involved and why they are involved, are questions that cannot be answered in a fully satisfactory manner with these methods. Network analysis, as well as qualitative approaches, seems promising in this respect.').

[100] See, with references, Jeremy Freese and J Alex Kevern, 'Types of Causes' in Stephen L Morgan (ed), *Handbook of Causal Analysis for Social Research* (Dordrecht: Springer, 2013) 37–9.

[101] For an introduction see David Beach, 'Process Tracing Methods in the Social Sciences' in *Oxford Research Encyclopedia of Politics* (2017, updated 2022), available at https://doi.org/10.1093/acrefore/9780190228637.013.176 accessed 23 October 2025. Similar also in the policy literature: Kuhlmann (n 37) 43 ('Mechanism-based approaches stress that an explanation should disentangle the basic elements of a causal process—which more often than not remain black-boxed—that led to a certain outcome . . .').

> contemplate feedback effects. Boxes are drawn within boxes and arrows collide with other arrows in our efforts to represent dimensionality and synergy. The result is mess.'[102]

The following charts aim to avoid such a 'mess' by focussing only on the causal question 'why do transplants take place?', not others such as the question about the effects of legal transplants. It is also clear that any tracing of causes cannot go back ad infinitum in the sense that it would simply say that all started with the 'Big Bang' (or God's creation of the universe etc).[103] Thus, in the subsequent analysis, key institutional settings will be considered (eg, a country's legal family), but other background factors will be treated as given (eg, why there may be xenophilia or xenophobia in a particular country; why a particular law is drafted in a simple and transmissible manner).

Figure 4.1 provides a first illustration of the analysis of this section. It phrases the question about causes of causes as referring to a transplant T from unit A to unit B. Thus, this terminology leaves open whether the units are countries or other units, whether the transplant concerns a particular statutory provision or another object,[104] and how exactly the transplant is inserted in the transplant unit (eg whether it is merged with existing rules and how the implementation of the new law takes place).[105]

Furthermore, this figure, as well as the following ones, are parsimonious in the sense that they concentrate on the relationship between origin and transplant unit only. This is not meant to imply that there cannot be multiple sources of influence or other complexities such as reciprocal relations. If this is the case, these figures may be used separately for each of the elements (eg, different sources of influence). They may be extended to cover, say, two origin units that together influence the origin unit, and some of the figures also account for the possibility of more than two units (eg, the possible benefits of legal convergence in Figure 4.5 may be larger if more units are covered).

The two main answers ('fully externally imposed by A', 'enacted by B') of Figure 4.1 are followed by the two questions 'why did this happen?'. Thus, this 'why' question asks about the causes of causes as it aims to find out what has happened previously (note: this is thus different from a 'why' question that asks why a causal link happened, ie to ask about an intermediate step). On the

[102] Freese and Kevern (n 100) 27.

[103] Often phrased as the problem of 'infinite regress'. For a recent discussion see Ajay Verghese, 'The Problem of Infinite Regress: A Stopping Rules Approach' (2023) 41 *Sociological Theory* 27.

[104] See Chapter 3 at Sections B and C.

[105] See further Chapter 5 at Section C 2 (a) and 3 (a).

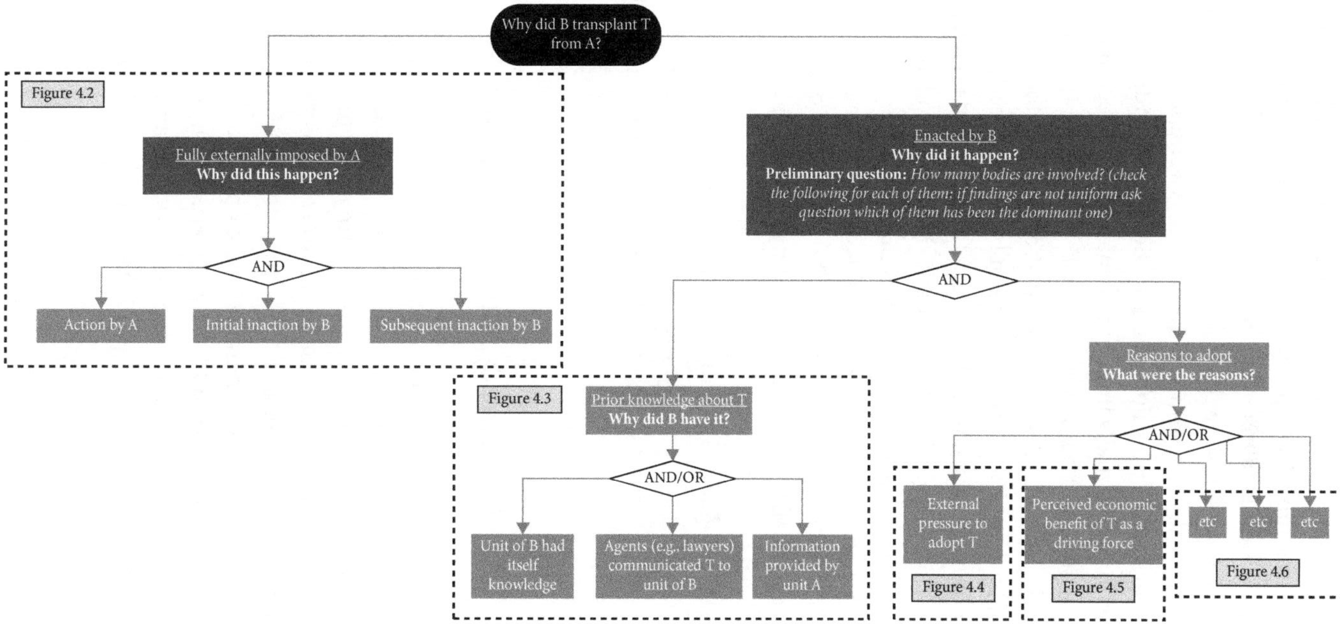

Figure 4.1 Overview of causes of causes of legal transplants

right-hand side, we find another 'why' question, here asking why B knew about T, as well as a 'what' question, asking about the reasons why B wanted to adopt the transplant. Thus, this latter question asks to elaborate on the various causal factors that are relevant for a transplant in this variant.

The forks of Figure 4.1 show how far the subsequent factors are related through 'or', 'and', or 'and/or' connections. If there is a simple fork, this means that there is an 'or' connection. For example, the first fork indicates that transplants are either fully externally imposed or enacted by B (technically: each of the conditions is sufficient but not necessary[106]). By contrast, the first fork on the left side includes an 'and' field, given that all three factors—action by A, initial inaction by B, and subsequent inaction by B—are needed for an externally imposed transplant (technically: each of the conditions is necessary but not sufficient). On the right-hand side of the chart, we also have some 'and/or' fields. For example, the transplant unit B may have received the information about T through various means—own research, information provided by agents, and/or information provided by unit A—and at least one of them needs to be present (technically: each of the conditions is not necessary and it may or may not be sufficient).

The flow chart of Figure 4.1 is only an extract of the causes of causes of legal transplants that will be discussed in the following sections. Due to the size of the full chart,[107] the further details will be displayed in five separate charts (Figures 4.2 to 4.6).

2. Fully externally imposed transplants

Both the origin and transplant unit usually have some involvement in the process leading to a legal transplant. In some cases, however, the origin unit is the one that fully imposes the transplant on the origin unit. This case is discussed in this section, while cases which include at least some degree of involvement of the transplant unit are discussed in the subsequent one.

The first requirement is an action by the origin unit. Figure 4.2 distinguishes between occupation, coercion, and binding international rules. The cases of colonial occupations were already mentioned previously, and the literature has also discussed other examples, such as the impact of Napoleon's occupation

[106] For a discussion of these terms see eg Freese and Kevern (n 100) 32–4.

[107] The full chart can be found at https://drive.google.com/file/d/1fZSnY3wYjzDyH04QlZEv33N2iL7x9jg7/ accessed 23 October 2025.

Figure 4.2 Factors determining fully externally imposed transplants

on the reception of the French Civil Code in Germany.[108] It was also already mentioned that the category 'coercion' is frequently used in the literature.[109] It is meant to refer to cases of military or economic coercion that make it justified to speak of a fully externally imposed transplant (and not simply a negotiation where the origin unit puts pressure on the transplant unit).[110] A further category is that of imposition through binding international rules if the origin but not the transplant unit had a key influence on these international rules.[111] Finally, in this part, Figure 4.2 displays the motivations of the origin unit, drawing on the literature of the previous section.[112]

The second requirement is that the transplant unit remained inactive when the external imposition of the transplant happened. Figure 4.2 displays three reasons why this can be the case. In some situations, it can simply be impossible for B to oppose it, for example, to fight a country's occupation. There can also be reasons that are due to the internal structures of the transplant unit: for example, lack of resistance may be due to the fact that it does not have the state capacity to oppose external pressure or because civil society groups are weak. The category 'trade-off' is about cases where the transplant unit reluctantly accepts the transplant given that resistance would be too costly (ie this case is different from situations where the two units are in a co-operative relationship).[113]

The third requirement is the subsequent inaction of the transplant unit, ie the fact that the transplant still exists today, even if in a modified form. This may be due to the continued influence of the origin unit, for example, its coercive influence. It can also be because the transplant unit has subsequently accepted the transplanted law, say, because it is perceived to work well or because the switching costs would be too high. It may also be due to weak adaptability of the law in the transplant unit, for example, where it would be better to revoke or adjust the transplanted law, but this does not happen.[114] Often, these

[108] For the former see Chapter 1 at Section B 2 and Chapter 3 at Section D 1. For the example see TT Arvind and Lindsay Stirton, 'Explaining the Reception of the Code Napoleon in Germany: A Fuzzy-Set Qualitative Comparative Analysis' (2010) 30 *Legal Studies* 1.

[109] See Section B 1.

[110] This can also be seen in the categories of Braithwaite and Drahos (n 72) 532–3 ('military coercion', 'economic coercion', 'systems of reward', 'modelling', 'reciprocal adjustment', 'non-reciprocal coordination, 'capacity building').

[111] Thus, this is different from the mere implementation of international or regional norms (see eg for the EU: https://single-market-scoreboard.ec.europa.eu/ accessed 23 October 2025) which does not fall under the concept of a legal transplant.

[112] See Section B 1.

[113] For the latter see Section C 3 (b).

[114] For legal adaptability see also Section C 3 (a).

factors may also play a combined role, for example, for the retention of colonial transplants in today's world.

These fully externally imposed transplants have contributed to the evolution of the law in many countries and other units. However, overall, forms of transplantation that include a decision by the transplant unit are said to have been even more relevant.[115] These will be discussed in the following section.

3. Transplants adopted by the transplant unit

Figure 4.1 already displayed the initial questions that need to be answered as to why transplants are adopted by the transplant unit. It also referred to the preliminary question 'How many bodies are involved? (check the following for each of them; if findings are not uniform ask question which of them has been the dominant one)'. An example where this question is relevant are legislative acts that need to be proposed by the government, then approved by one or more parliamentary chambers, and finally signed by the president or monarch. Here, for example, the government may propose a law that draws on the experiences of a number of other countries, one of the chambers of the parliament insists that the model should mainly be from one of these countries and then discussions with the other bodies eventually lead to some resolution.

Focussing on one of these bodies, Figure 4.1 then displays the requirements that this body needs to have knowledge about the transplant (ie the legal phenomenon that becomes the transplant) and has one or more reasons to adopt it. The following discusses, first, the question about knowledge (a), followed by the reasons to adopt the transplant due to external pressure (b), perceived economic quality (c), and/or perceived other qualities (d).

(a) Knowledge about transplant

The spread of knowledge is a prominent topic in historical research as it explores how human beings but also skills, texts, and instruments have circulated across continents and communities.[116] In the present case, this dissemination depends on how and when the information underlying the transplant has become known to the transplant unit. At a general level, a distinction can be made between scenarios where the transplant unit itself had knowledge about

[115] Braithwaite and Drahos (n 72) 539.

[116] For an example (and references) see Kapil Raj, *Relocating Modern Science: Circulation and the Construction of Knowledge in South Asia and Europe, 1650–1900* (New York: Palgrave MacMillan, 2007). See also the topic 'entangled history', Chapter 1 at Section C 2.

it, where it was communicated to it by agents, and where it derived from the origin unit.

Figure 4.3 indicates in the first branch that the transplant unit itself may have had knowledge about the transplant due to a variety of different reasons. The reason 'high legal adaptability' refers to the situation where the transplant unit constantly tries to update and improve its laws[117] and, doing so, also considers experiences from other units in order to find innovative solutions.[118] It is also possible that the transplant unit has particularly good comparative skills. For example, the historical case of legal transplants in late nineteenth century Japan is a well-known example of a lawmaker conducting a detailed comparative analysis prior to a law reform.[119] As a follow-up question, it can then be asked in which situations the transplant unit is likely to be highly knowledgeable about foreign models. Here, research from policy diffusion among US states refers to the role of a unit's size, economic wealth, and professionalism;[120] yet, in the international sphere, there are also cases of small jurisdictions being particularly adaptable and keen on benefitting from comparative insights.[121]

Another variant is that the transplant unit has particular familiarity with the law of the origin unit. For this reason (and possibly others),[122] some studies find that transplants typically happen within the same legal families. For example, quantitative research of comparative constitutional law confirms that legal origin is one of the significant variables explaining constitutional transplants.[123] More specifically, the exchange of legal ideas is said to be frequent between France, Belgium, and Luxembourg.[124] Common law countries too share a close bond as their courts tend to closely follow each other's case law.[125]

[117] Mathias Siems, 'Legal Adaptability in Elbonia' (2006) 2 *International Journal of Law in Context* 393.

[118] This link between transplants (or diffusion) and innovative law could already be found in the classical study by Jack L Walker, 'The Diffusion of Innovations among the American States' (1969) 63 *The American Political Science Review* 880.

[119] See Chapter 1 at Section B 2.

[120] Daniel J Mallinson, 'Growth and Gaps: A Meta-review of Policy Diffusion Studies in the American States' (2021) 49 *Policy & Politics* 369, 378; Charles R Shipan and Craig Volden, 'The Mechanisms of Policy Diffusion' (2008) 52 *American Journal of Political Science* 840 (for antismoking policies).

[121] For examples from financial law see Christopher M Bruner, *Re-Imagining Offshore Finance: Market-Dominant Small Jurisdictions in a Globalizing Financial World* (Oxford: OUP, 2016).

[122] Such as a better 'fit' with the existing law, see Chapter 5 at Section C 2 (a).

[123] Benedikt Goderis and Mila Versteeg, 'The Diffusion of Constitutional Rights' (2014) 39 *International Review of Law and Economics* 1. But see also Tom Ginsburg and Mila Versteeg, 'Why Do Countries Adopt Constitutional Review?' (2014) 30 *Journal of Law, Economics, and Organization* 587 (right to constitutional review mainly driven by domestic electoral politics).

[124] Safia Bouabdallah, 'La réception réciproque de la jurisprudence et de la doctrine dans les systèmes belge, français et luxembourgeois' (2019) 60 *Les Cahiers de droit* 95; Safia Bouabdallah, *La réception du modèle français en droit civil belge: exemple d'un transfert de droit* (PhD thesis, Université Jean Monnet Saint-Etienne, 2007).

[125] In this regard, we may therefore speak of the 'common law as a whole', a 'unity of the common law', and a 'single common law'. See n 107 in Chapter 3 at Section C 1.

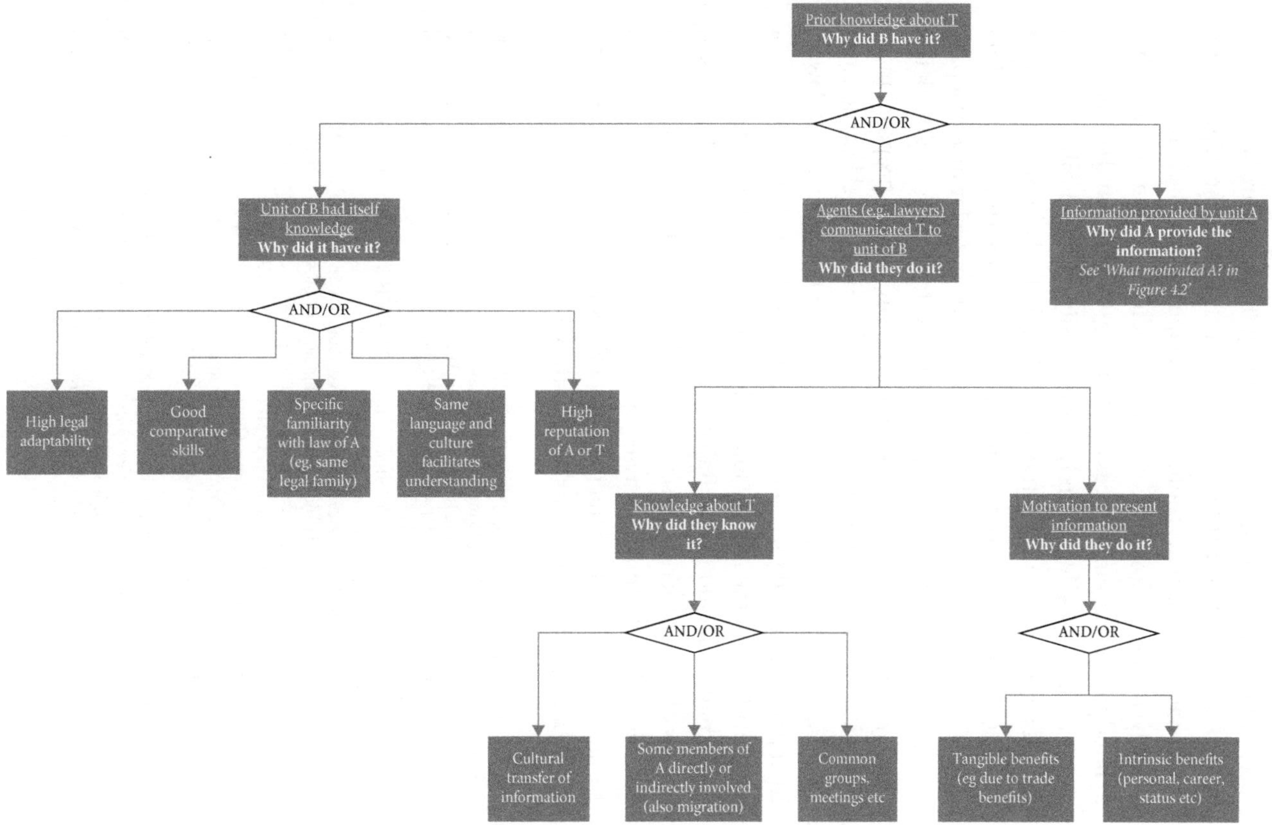

Figure 4.3 How knowledge about transplant may be attained

For example, a quantitative study on courts from Hong Kong, Malaysia, and Singapore found that they cite non-domestic common-law case law in more than 60 per cent of reported opinions, concluding that these are 'as common as domestic citations'.[126] A recent English decision also notes the 'high regard' that the court has for judicial decisions from Singapore given that their judges 'go about analysing points and then expressing their reasoning in a way that makes their judgments extremely accessible to English lawyers and scholars'.[127]

However, in other cases, legal family ties play only a limited role. For judicial transplants in Europe, quantitative research only finds some evidence of many citations among courts from common law countries while other factors are generally found to be more relevant.[128] As regards the relevance of a path dependent use of transplants, while it is clear that 'history matters',[129] such ties can weaken over time. For example, in Poland, a law reform proposal mentioned the importance of German law as the conventional model but then also the plan to consider French, Austrian, Swiss, and, to a lesser extent, US law.[130] For Japan, it has been found that, since the 1990s, the lawmaker has shown 'a greater curiosity towards the study of foreign legal systems that previously were virtually unexplored, including the Italian legal system'.[131] Last but not least, the private law of Latin America presents interesting case studies of lawmakers that have made deliberate choices between various European civil law models (eg, for social conceptions of contract law), as well as some use of common law models and some use of 'local donors' such as the Chilean Civil Code.[132]

[126] Kwai Hang Ng and Brynna Jacobson, 'How Global is the Common Law? A Comparative Study of Asian Common Law Systems—Hong Kong, Malaysia, and Singapore' (2017) 12 *Asian Journal of Comparative Law* 209. For the high use of UK precedents in Hong Kong see also Nuno Garoupa and Weijia Rao, 'Foreign Judges and Foreign Case Citations: A Study of the Hong Kong Court of Final Appeal' (2025) 13 *Journal of Law and Courts* 547.

[127] *Glas SAS (London Branch) v European Topsoho SARL* [2024] EWHC 83 (Comm) [135]. For judicial transplants more generally see Chapter 3 at Section B 2.

[128] Mathias Siems, 'A Network Analysis of Judicial Cross-Citations in Europe' (2023) 48 *Law & Social Inquiry* 881; Martin Gelter and Mathias Siems, 'Language, Legal Origins, and Culture before the Courts: Cross-Citations between Supreme Courts in Europe' (2013) 21 *Supreme Court Economic Review* 215. For the underlying data see also Sabrina D'Andrea and others, 'Asymmetric Cross-Citations in Private Law: An Empirical Study of 28 Supreme Courts in the EU' (2021) 28 *Maastricht Journal of European and Comparative Law* 498 and Martin Gelter and Mathias Siems, 'Citations to Foreign Courts—Illegitimate and Superfluous, or Unavoidable? Evidence from Europe' (2014) 62 *American Journal of Comparative Law* 35.

[129] Alba Fondrieschi, 'Uniformazione del diritto ed esportabilità dei modelli giuridici: il caso del Giappone' (2015) 3(1) *Osservatorio del diritto civile e commerciale, Rivista semestrale* 153, 175–6. For an introduction to the notion of legal path dependency see also Siems (n 14) 129–30.

[130] Założenia reformy prawa spółek handlowych (z prac Komisji Kodyfikacyjnej Prawa Cywilnego) Warszawa, 25 lutego 1997, (1997) 4 *Monitor Prawniczy* 142.

[131] Andrea Ortolani, 'The Italian Legal Model Outside of Europe: Japan' (2014) 3(1) *Osservatorio del diritto civile e commerciale* 177, 177.

[132] Gerardo Caffera, Rodrigo Momberg, and María Elisa Morales, 'Legal Transplants: A Case Study of Private Law in Its Historical Context' in Mathias Siems and Po Jen Yap (eds), *The Cambridge Handbook of Comparative Law* (Cambridge: CUP, 2024) 453.

Beyond legal similarities, it can matter that units have the same (or a similar) language and culture. Such similarity can facilitate communication and reduce the risk of misunderstandings and make it more likely that the transplant unit knows about the law of the origin one. For example, this can be seen in the aforementioned studies of constitutional transplants as they identify a shared language between countries, shared colonial ties and commonalities in religion as among the significant variables.[133] In the quantitative research on cross-citations between courts in Europe, the main finding is that both native languages and language skills are key determinants; cultural variables are also sometimes found to be significant as is a variable on whether populations 'feel European'.[134] Likewise, there is some evidence that, for the flow of academic legal ideas, it matters in which language a particular piece is published (at least as far as comparative law is concerned; less so for international law).[135]

Finally, in the first branch of Figure 4.3, the high reputation of the origin unit or the transplant itself can mean that knowledge about it is available in the transplant unit. Thus, in the words of Alan Watson, in such situations there may be a 'transplant bias'.[136] For example, US law has sometimes been seen as being an attractive model to stimulate investment,[137] while the French Code Civil was historically a code frequently borrowed by other countries.[138] In the quantitative research on cross-citations, it is usually found that larger jurisdictions are cited more frequently,[139] which can be seen as an (imperfect) proxy for the reputation of a country.

The information about the transplant can also be transmitted by agents of the transplant and/or the origin unit. This raises the questions of why the agents knew about the possible transplant and what motivated them to present it to the lawmakers (and possibly also lobby for it, to be discussed later in this section).

As there can be a large variety of agents, there can be many different reasons why they had this information. The first category of this branch of Figure 4.3 refers to the general cultural transfer of information. For example, lawyers,

[133] See n 123.
[134] See n 128.
[135] For the former see Basil Markesinis and Jörg Fedtke, *Engaging with Foreign Law* (Oxford: Hart Publishing, 2009) 77–120. For the latter see Anthea Roberts, *Is International Law International?* (Oxford: OUP, 2017) 169–70.
[136] Alan Watson, 'Comparative Law and Legal Change' (1978) 37 *Cambridge Law Journal* 313, 326–7.
[137] For example, as part of the law and development discourse, as well as the law and finance research, see references in Siems (n 14) 379–82 and 249–50.
[138] Namely, due to its 'systematic, de-contextualized and a-historical' nature: Horatia Muir Watt, 'Globalization and Comparative Law' in Mathias Reimann and Reinhard Zimmermann (eds), *The Oxford Handbook of Comparative Law* (Oxford: OUP, 2nd edn, 2019) 599, 609.
[139] See n 128.

journalists, or other constituents of the transplant unit may have gained knowledge about a foreign law by studying abroad,[140] by reading publications on foreign law,[141] or by simply consulting information available online. Specifically, some of the literature on the use of foreign case law in courts has discussed the importance of the role of lawyers and the availability of assistants.[142] There is also literature on the way national legal writing may impact not only legal scholarship but also foster the transplantation of ideas by courts and legislators,[143] which then also raises the question of whether interest in foreign law (and/or comparative law) has become more pronounced in legal scholarship and education.[144]

Second, agents from the origin unit may, directly or indirectly, be involved in the knowledge that is provided to the transplant unit. For example, they may publish in the language of the transplant unit or be invited by its lawmaking body to provide information about their home jurisdiction.[145] Furthermore, the literature discusses the role of migration for legal transplants. The historical case is that of migrants taking their laws with them, for example in the colonial empires (and sometimes later confirmed by a 'reception statute' that accepted these elements of the former colonial law).[146] There is some debate about whether such cases should be called 'transplantation' or whether the participants did not really regard it as a transplant but an 'expanding area of

[140] For historical examples see Albert Kocourek, 'Factors in the Reception of Law' (1935) 10 *Tulane Law Review* 209, 218 (reception of Roman law due to education of German jurists at Italian universities); Khanal (n 33) 77, 78, and 202 (for Nepal: Buddhist and Hindu influence; Nepali scholars having studied in India).

[141] Kocourek (n 140) 218 (also referring to the 'spread of textbooks dealing with Roman law').

[142] See eg Elaine Mak, *Judicial Decision-Making in a Globalised World* (Oxford: Hart Publishing, 2013) 114–24; Folker de Witte and others, 'Decoding Judicial Cross-Citations: How Do European Judges Engage with Foreign Case Law?' (2024) 72 *American Journal of Comparative Law* 292, 297, 300–1.

[143] Jan M Smits, 'Comparative Law and Its Influence on National Legal Systems' in Mathias Reimann and Reinhard Zimmermann (eds), *The Oxford Handbook of Comparative Law* (Oxford: OUP, 2nd edn, 2019) 502, 506 (the 'most common way in which foreign law permeates national law is through national legal writing'). This may even be the case where the actual law is very different: Jan Kleinheisterkamp, 'Development of Comparative Law in Latin America' in Mathias Reimann and Reinhard Zimmermann (eds), *The Oxford Handbook of Comparative Law* (Oxford: OUP, 2nd edn, 2019) 252, 283–4 (for the use of foreign legal doctrine in Latin America).

[144] See Christophe Jamin and William Van Caenegem (eds), *The Internationalisation of Legal Education* (Berlin: Springer, 2016) but also Siems (n 14) 214–15 (for decline of terms referring to foreign scholarship in US law journals).

[145] For example, German scholars in nineteenth century Japan (see Schenck (n 61)), Indian and UK legal experts in post-WW II Nepal (see Khanal (n 33) 83), and Western experts after the fall of communism in Central and Eastern Europe (see Catherine Dupré, *Importing the Law in Post-Communist Transitions: The Hungarian Constitutional Court and the Right to Human Dignity* (Oxford: Hart Publishing, 2003) 42).

[146] See eg Khanal (n 33) 58, 88–9.

influence'.[147] In more recent years, the reverse case has also become a prominent topic, namely how far migrants to Europe transplant their own informal laws,[148] whereby it may also matter that, according to some studies, migrants usually keep prior cultural attitudes in the new environment.[149]

Third, the divide between agents of the origin and the transplant unit breaks down as far as both are part of a joined group or meeting. In cases where the transplant unit is a regional or international organisation, this may be due to the fact that the persons of this organisation come from different legal traditions.[150] It can also be the result of joined educational institutions (eg, judicial training programmes), participation in judicial networks and personal contacts of judges,[151] as well as more informal varieties of transnational dialogue of civil society actors.[152] Such interactions may happen within the same legal family,[153] but there are also examples of groupings that deliberately foster the flow of ideas across such divides.[154]

The motivation of agents to present this knowledge to the transplant unit depends again on many details of the type of agents and how they relate to the transplant.[155] Some benefits can be of a tangible nature. For example, firms

[147] H Patrick Glenn, 'On the Use of Biological Metaphors in Law: The Case of Legal Transplants' (2006) 1 *The Journal of Comparative Law* 358, 363. Different: Rheinstein (n 8) 34 (using the term transplantation, as distinguished from reception, explicitly for the 'situation in which a group of migrants takes with it its old law from its former to its new surroundings'); following this view: Papachristos (n 2) 8–9; Khanal (n 33) 62.

[148] See eg Pablo Lerner, 'La discusión sobre trasplantes legales: recapitulación y análisis' (2023) 34 *Revista General de Derecho Público Comparado* 232, 268–70 (as a form of understanding transplants in light of multiculturalism); Prakash Shah, 'Globalisation and the Challenge of Asian Legal Transplants in Europe' (2005) *Singapore Journal of Legal Studies* 348 (also noting at 355 that positivist European legal thinking often does not regard such transplanted norms 'as being properly "legal" phenomena').

[149] Garett Jones, *The Culture Transplant: How Migrants Make the Economies They Move To a Lot Like the Ones They Left* (Stanford, CA: Stanford Business Books, 2022), referring eg to Louis Putterman and David N Weil, 'Post-1500 Population Flows and The Long-Run Determinants of Economic Growth and Inequality' (2010) 125 *The Quarterly Journal of Economics* 1627.

[150] For example, the current procedural rules indicating that appointments to the International Court of Justice should represent 'the principal legal systems of the world', ICJ Statute, art 9.

[151] See eg Mak (n 142) 83–98; Brian Flanagan and Sinéad Ahern, 'Judicial Decision-Making and Transnational Law: A Survey of Common-Law Supreme Court Judges' (2011) 60 *International and Comparative Law Quarterly* 1.

[152] Evgeny Postnikov and Ida Bastiaens, 'Does Dialogue Work? The Effectiveness of Labor Standards in EU Preferential Trade Agreements' (2014) 21 *Journal of European Public Policy* 923 (as found for EU trade partners implementing labour provisions of PTAs). See also Kuhlmann (n 37) 43 (example of diffusion by learning).

[153] Be it among common law countries (eg, the Commonwealth Network, https://www.commonwealthofnations.org/?sectors=business/legal/ accessed 23 October 2025), civil law countries (eg, the International Union of Notaries, https://uinl.org/mission/members/ accessed 23 October 2025), or mixed legal systems (eg, the World Society of Mixed Jurists, https://www.wsmjj.org/ accessed 23 October 2025).

[154] Eg, the various bilateral lawyer associations such as the ones between the UK and Germany (https://bgja.org.uk/ accessed 23 October 2025), France and the UK (https://ajfb-fbls.org/ accessed 23 October 2025), the UK and Italy (http://www.bila.biz/ accessed 23 October 2025), and Germany and the United States (https://www.dajv.de/ accessed 23 October 2025).

[155] See Section B 3.

may communicate foreign rules to lawmakers that increase their profit, say, because these rules are well-designed to promote economic trade, or because having internationally converging rules has such an effect (and thus international lobbies may also push for transplants). Lawyers trained in the jurisdiction of the origin unit also gain directly from the transplant as it increases their client base. There can also be intrinsic benefits that make agents communicate their insights to the transplant unit. For example, legal scholars usually appreciate it when their work has some impact—which then can also have tangible benefits, for instance if this helps their career prospects.[156]

The final branch of Figure 4.3 refers to knowledge provided by the origin to the transplant unit. The reasons why the origin unit may do so are akin to those of externally imposed transplants.[157] The information about its law may be provided by the origin unit directly or through other means. For example, many countries have development aid agencies[158] which provide advice on law reform, but such transmission can also occur more indirectly through co-operations between bar associations, law schools, or government-sponsored translations of domestic laws (including case law).[159]

In the literature, the role of neighbouring units is sometimes also discussed as a variable for legal transplants and/or policy diffusion. For example, this has been examined in quantitative studies on the diffusion of policies between US states,[160] as well as internationally for topics such as the diffusion of democratic innovations and dual citizenship policies.[161] However, this criterion is likely to be a reflection of other more precise factors, such as those discussed in this subsection: for example, the variable of neighbouring units is typically positively correlated with other similarities between these units (eg, belonging to the same legal family or cultural similarity); it is also more likely that agents know about the law of a neighbouring unit, or that the origin unit may benefit

[156] In countries such as Australia and the UK impact beyond academia is explicitly rewarded, see https://dataportal.arc.gov.au/EI/Web/Impact/ImpactStudies accessed 23 October 2025 and https://results2021.ref.ac.uk/impact accessed 23 October 2025.

[157] See Section B 2.

[158] See list at https://ngobase.org/agencies/t/ida accessed 23 October 2025.

[159] For the latter see eg https://www.gesetze-im-internet.de/ accessed 23 October 2025 and https://www.bundesverfassungsgericht.de/EN/Homepage/home_node.html accessed 23 October 2025.

[160] Mallinson (n 120) 378 (as part of a meta-analysis).

[161] References in Gilles Pradeau, 'The Diffusion of Democratic Innovations' in Osmany Porto de Oliveira (ed), *Handbook of Policy Transfer, Diffusion and Circulation* (Cheltenham: Edward Elgar, 2021) 365, 375; Maarten Vink and others, 'The International Diffusion of Expatriate Dual Citizenship' (2019) 7 *Migration Studies* 362. Further references to 'geographical clustering' in Weyland (n 38) 19. But for a different finding see Gerrit Faber and Michiel Gerritse, 'Does Institutional Change Spread Across Countries? Explaining Spatial Patterns in Human Rights' (2017) 40 *The World Economy* 906 ('neighbouring countries seem to have little effect on domestic human rights records').

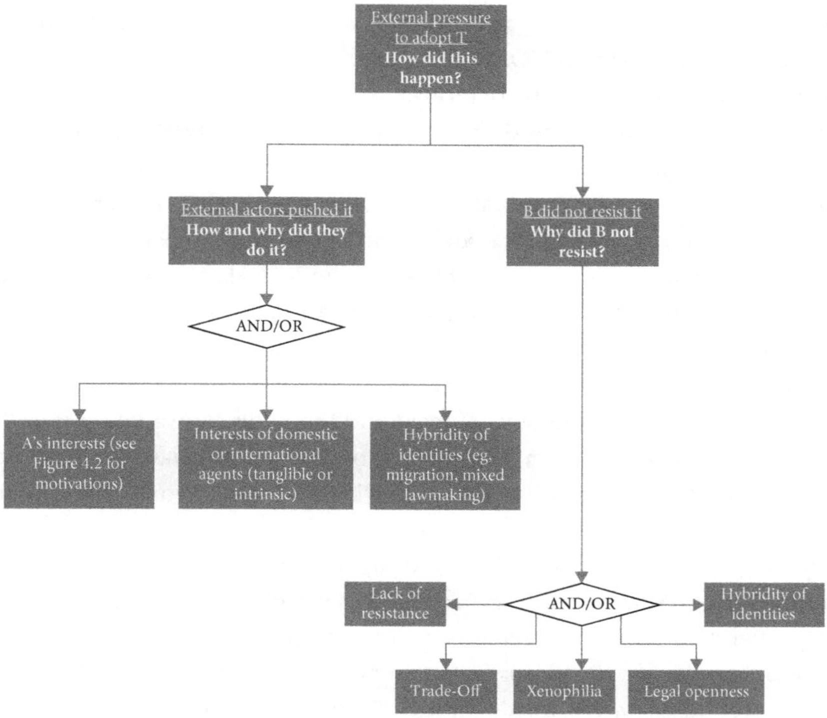

Figure 4.4 Reasons to adopt transplant due to external pressure

from communicating such information (eg, as it may foster cross-border trade or other forms of co-operation).

(b) External pressure to adopt transplant

Figure 4.4 displays the details of the first reason (see Figure 4.1) that can make the transplant unit adopt a transplant: 'external pressure', which is here widely understood.

The first question about transplants through external pressure is how and why external actors push for such a transplant. Figure 4.4 shows three cases. The first one is about situations where the origin unit directly or indirectly benefits from the transplant and thus uses its influence to make the transplant happen. This is akin to the situation of fully externally imposed transplants,[162] but in the current variant the pressure can be less pronounced. For example, it

[162] See Section B 2.

can derive from conditionality requirements to join international and regional organisations such as the WTO, OECD, and EU. It can also be the result of economic pressure, such as the use of tariffs.

As to the precise origin units that can and do use such pressure, much depends on shifts in geopolitical, economic, and cultural power structures. For example, some observers refer to the way China's growing soft-power may lead to Chinese-inspired transplants elsewhere in the world.[163] Specifically, two recent empirical studies trace how China uses trade deals to export its model of digital surveillance to other countries, in particular in the Global South.[164] This observation about Chinese influence is made against the backdrop of the global impact of Western legal systems. The previous chapter already referred to the literature on law and development and the Americanisation of laws.[165] Pressure may also derive from the extraterritorial effect of US law: for example, as US authorities imposed financial penalties on non-US companies, other countries have started to adopt similar penalty rules to reclaim the control over their companies and to benefit from the payment of such penalties.[166] Recent studies have also examined the impact of EU law in other continents. From the perspective of international relations, a monograph by Tobias Lenz shows how active engagement by the EU impacts on other regional organisations that, like the EU, rest on an 'open-ended contract'.[167] Empirical legal research has, for example, identified a global impact of EU competition law as 'the European Union actively promotes its model through preferential trade agreements and has an administrative template that is easy to emulate'.[168] In other cases, the impact of EU law is said to be less a question of political pressure but about

[163] Daniel Pascoe, 'Hong Kong's National Security Law: A Socialist Legal Transplant?' (2022) 28 *The Chinese Journal of Comparative Law* 28, 53. See also Matthew S Erie and Thomas Streinz, 'The Beijing Effect: China's "Digital Silk Road" as Transnational Data Governance' (2021) 54 *New York University Journal of International Law and Politics* 1.

[164] Chibuzo Achinivu, 'The Supply of Digital Authoritarianism to Africa: an Empirical Study' (2024) 51 *The African Review* 525 (using as data the FBIC index, available at https://korbel.du.edu/fbic accessed 23 October 2025); Martin Beraja and others, 'Exporting the Surveillance State via Trade in AI' (NBER Working Paper No. 31676, 2023), available at https://www.nber.org/papers/w31676 accessed 23 October 2025. See also Gorden Moyo (ed), *An Anatomy of AI Surveillance in Africa: The Contradictions of Digital Technologies* (Cham: Springer, 2025).

[165] Chapter 3 at Section C 1. See also Chapter 5 at Section C 4 (b).

[166] Cornelia Woll, *Corporate Crime and Punishment: The Politics of Negotiated Justice in Global Markets* (Princeton, NJ: Princeton University Press, 2023) 9.

[167] Tobias Lenz, *Interorganizational Diffusion in International Relations: Regional Institutions and the Role of the European Union* (Oxford: OUP, 2021).

[168] Anu Bradford and others, 'The Global Dominance of European Competition Law Over American Antitrust Law' (2019) 16 *Journal of Empirical Legal Studies* 731. For the underlying data see http://comparativecompetitionlaw.org/ accessed 23 October 2025 and Anu Bradford and Adam Chilton, 'Competition Law Around the World from 1889 to 2010: The Competition Law Index' (2018) 14 *Journal of Competition Law and Economics* 393.

non-European companies adjusting their behaviour to EU regulations;[169] yet, here too, this may go hand in hand with negotiations between the EU and other countries.[170]

Second, the pressure can derive from domestic and international agents as they push for tangible (economic, political, etc) or intrinsic interests. These can be private agents at different levels (national, international, etc), and here the motivations to act as lobbies are akin to those presented in the previous section (ie the motivations to present legal transplants to lawmakers). It is also possible that international and regional organisations exert forms of pressure to adopt models of other units (ie not merely the models of these organisations). At the international level, a prominent example concerns the way the World Bank influences domestic laws by promoting 'best practices and policy innovations' from both states and other international organisations,[171] through means of its funding conditions[172] but also the use of rankings.[173] In other cases, international organisations, states, and private firms may act together in order to campaign for certain standards.[174] With respect to regional organisations, their influence is often said to be mainly driven by the interests of their member countries[175] and, thus, possibly also their legal models.

Third, the category 'hybridity of identities' refers to situations similar to the categories which the previous section discussed for the knowledge about the transplant (Figure 4.3, above), namely 'some members of A directly or

[169] Anu Bradford, *The Brussels Effect: How the European Union Rules the World* (Oxford: OUP, 2020).

[170] Paul M Schwartz, 'Global Data Privacy: The EU Way' (2019) 94 *New York University Law Review* 771 (for the GDPR's adequacy requirement).

[171] Porto de Oliveira (n 94) 13. For another example see Kim Lane Scheppele, 'The Migration of Anti-constitutional Ideas: The Post-9/11 Globalization of Public Law and the International State of Emergency' in Sujit Choudhry (ed), *The Migration of Constitutional Ideas* (Cambridge: CUP, 2006) 352 (how 'international law enters our subject and alters it').

[172] See https://ieg.worldbankgroup.org/topic/development-policy-financing-dpf accessed 23 October 2025 and http://documents.worldbank.org/curated/en/361051468339909585/Reports-on-the-Observance-of-Standards-and-Codes-ROSCs accessed 23 October 2025.

[173] Marta Infantino, *Numera et impera. Gli indicatori giuridici globali e il diritto comparato* (Milan: FrancoAngeli, 2019) 302. See also Daniele D'Alvia and Matteo Nicolini, *Global Legal Indicators and Comparative Law: The Factory of Indexes* (Abingdon: Routledge, 2026) 56–121.

[174] See eg JC Sharman, 'Power and Discourse in Policy Diffusion: Anti-Money Laundering in Developing States' (2008) 52 *International Studies Quarterly* 635 ('discursively mediated exercises of power' rather than rational learning).

[175] Notably, such 'intergovernmentalism' has been discussed for the EU, see eg Ernest A Young, 'The European Union: A Comparative Perspective' in Robert Schütze and Takis Tridimas (eds), *Oxford Principles of European Union Law: Volume 1: The European Union Legal Order* (Oxford: OUP, 2018) 142, 157–71. See also Sören Stapel, *Regional Organizations and Democracy, Human Rights, and the Rule of Law: The African Union, Organization of American States, and the Diffusion of Institutions* (Basingstoke: Palgrave Macmillan, 2022) 12 (interplay of both member states and other organisations for diffusion processes); Tobias Lenz, 'Spurred Emulation: The EU and Regional Integration in Mercosur and SADC' (2011) 35 *West European Politics* 155, 170 (for role of domestic politics in emulating EU model).

indirectly involved (also migration)' and 'common groups, meetings etc'. In other words, in such cases, it is not only likely that some persons of the transplant unit know about the to-be-transplanted law but also push for it.

The second question displayed in Figure 4.4 is why the transplant unit did not resist the pressure of the external actor. The first two reasons—lack of resistance and trade-off—are similar but not identical as in the case of fully externally imposed transplants (Figure 4.2, above). In the present case, given the lower level of pressure, even some resistance (say, by civil society groups) can make a difference. Trade-offs may be forms of bargaining, for example, in the case where countries follow US demands for increased IP protection in exchange for development aid.[176] It is also possible that the traded benefit is illegal (or, at least, unethical), for example, when lawmakers receive a side payment from agents of the origin unit to act on its behalf.

While some authors emphasise the way nationalism or xenophobia may resist legal transplants,[177] it is also possible that xenophilia makes lawmakers willing to adopt a foreign model due to external pressure. According to historical research by Benedict Beckeld, elites in Western countries may actually be inclined to oikophobia, ie fear of one's home culture, which may go hand-in-hand with a general appreciation of foreign ideas.[178] An experimental study from the US also found that US citizens appreciate legislative proposals more if they are told that other countries already follow similar rules.[179] A similar result has been reached in a survey from five European countries (Bulgaria, England, Norway, Poland, and Ukraine).[180]

The category of legal openness can sometimes be connected to xenophilia, but it is not the same. Such legal openness is typical, for example, in the way courts in common law countries consider case law from other common law countries given their shared legal tradition. Openness may also be tied to following the 'leader' of a particular legal matter with the adopters wishing to be perceived as modern.[181]

[176] Morin and Gold (n 48) 785.

[177] See generally Papachristos (n 2) 69 and, for an example, Arvind and Stirton (n 108) ('nativism among the governing elites and popular anti-French sentiment' as relevant conditions against adopting the French Civil Code in German states in the early nineteenth century).

[178] Benedict Beckeld, *Western Self-Contempt: Oikophobia in the Decline of Civilizations* (Ithaka, NY: Cornell University Press, 2022) 9. Further support may derive from the concept of 'mimetic desire', see Section B 2.

[179] Linos (n 52) 36–66. For a different result: Brett Curry and Banks Miller, 'Looking for Law in All the Wrong Places? Foreign Law and Support for the U.S. Supreme Court' (2008) 36 *Politics & Policy* 1094.

[180] Åse B Grødeland and William L Miller, *European Legal Cultures in Transition* (Cambridge: CUP, 2015).

[181] This latter point is particularly discussed in the literature on innovation and policies; see Weyland (n 38) 2 and the literature on innovation cited in the following subsection.

Finally, as far as there is the aforementioned hybridity of identities, the decisive question is about the extent to which the hybrid origin-transplant members can effectively make the transplant happen in the transplant unit. This can depend on a variety of further factors: for example, if there is a common body of lawmakers, it depends on the power dynamics within the body and the skills of the respective members to influence the outcome.

(c) Perceived economic quality

The aim to transplant laws for economic benefit has long been seen as one of the main paradigms of legal transplants.[182] In this regard, the term 'economic' can refer to a variety of criteria, not only GDP (or GDP per capita) but also indicators such as the employment rate, consumer confidence, or foreign trade.[183] Moreover, it is possible that economic quality is not the only motivation of the transplant unit, and thus this category can occur together with perceived other qualities, discussed in the subsequent subsection (see the 'and/or' in Figure 4.1, above).

As shown in Figure 4.5, this category of transplants requires that the transplant is perceived to have this economic benefit and that the relevant unit cares about it. The first requirement involves an evaluation that the transplant is expected to have an economic benefit compared to the perceived quality of the status quo. The latter comparison can raise several further questions about the status quo, notably why the current law is perceived to be deficient and whether this perception is accurate. It can also happen that the existing law was initially well suited but that changing circumstances have made it economically deficient (in other words, the transplant is more modern than the current law). Another frequent case is that of a country not having a law on a particular subject matter. Such cases have been discussed frequently for countries in transition,[184] with quantitative research aiming to identify the foreign models which countries have most frequently adopted over time.[185]

[182] See generally Section B 1, and eg Papachristos (n 2) 30, 52.

[183] For illustration see also https://tradingeconomics.com/indicators accessed 23 October 2025.

[184] From the large literature see eg Thomas W Waelde and James L Gunderson, 'Legislative Reform in Transition Economies: Western Transplants: A Short-Cut to Social Market Economy Status?' (1994) 43 *The International and Comparative Law Quarterly* 347; DM Davis, 'Constitutional Borrowing: The Influence of Legal Culture and Local History in the Reconstitution of Comparative Influence: The South African Experience' (2003) 1 *International Journal of Constitutional Law* 181; John Jupp, 'Legal Transplants as Solutions for Criminal Law Reform in Post-Intervention States: Afghanistan's Interim Criminal Procedure Code 2004' (2013) 61 *American Journal of Comparative Law* 51.

[185] For an example from company law see Siems (n 14) 218–19 (finding that since 1990 countries of CEE were initially similar to German law but subsequently also adopted provisions from English, French, and US law).

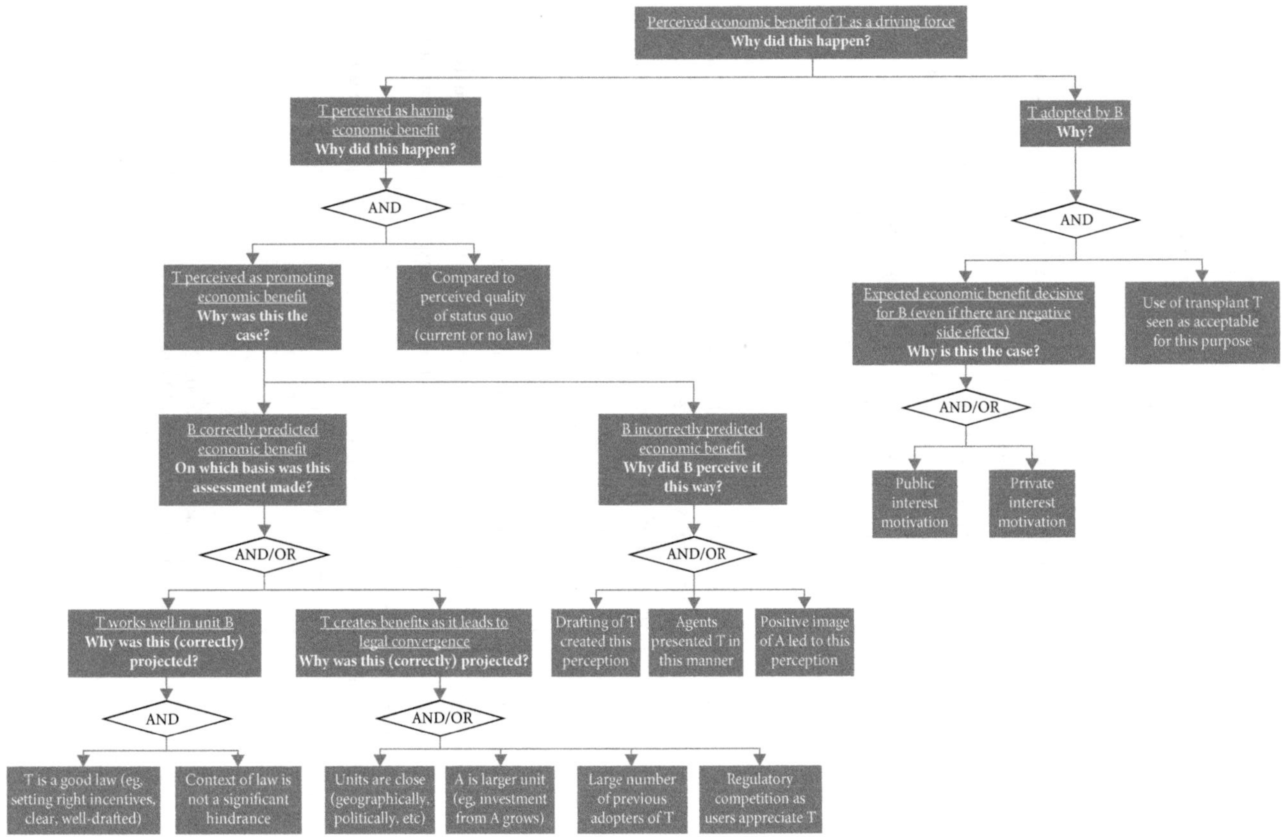

Figure 4.5 Reason to adopt transplant due to perceived economic quality

Continuing with the options of Figure 4.5, there is the variant that the transplant unit correctly predicted the economic benefit. On the one hand, this can be the case because the transplant does indeed work well; in other words, the law is economically beneficial. How the law matters specifically depends on the law in question, whereby not only the substance of the law may play a role but also that it is drafted in a clear and consistent manner. In addition, the transplant needs to work well in the context of the transplant unit. In some cases, there is no mismatch in context as societies face the same problem (say, the emergence of a new technology) and the origin unit had simply been faster to design rules on this topic.[186] In other cases, differences in context raise more complex questions which are addressed in detail in the following chapters.[187] For example, factors can play a role, such as the character of the law (eg, whether it is codified in a manner making it easily transplantable), the prior experience of the transplant unit with such law (eg, the belonging to the same legal family can be a relevant factor), and the way the transplant is inserted in the transplant unit (eg, whether adjustments are made to avoid a rejection of the transplant).[188]

On the other hand, the fact that a transplant fosters legal convergence can create an economic benefit for the transplant unit due to the reduction of transaction costs.[189] In principle, such a benefit may occur between any unit, but it is also possible to identify some cases where this is particularly likely (Figure 4.5). First, if the two units are 'close', it is likely that there is both a push for and a benefit of common rules. For example, this can be seen in studies that have shown that variables such as geographic proximity, joint membership in an international or regional organisation, and existing trade flows are criteria that explain policy diffusion.[190] Second, it can be an economic advantage for the transplant unit to align its rules with that of a larger unit. Prominent examples are the global impact of US, EU, and Chinese law, which may also involve forms of external pressure, as discussed in the previous subsection.[191] There is also the interesting case of Switzerland which, beyond the treaties with the EU, has the policy of autonomously adapting EU law ('*autonomer*

[186] For this variant see already Section B 2.
[187] See Chapters 5 to 7.
[188] For details on these points see in particular Chapter 5 at Section C.
[189] For transaction costs as a reason for common rules see already Section B 4.
[190] See the meta-analysis by Maggetti and Gilardi (n 96) 97. Beyond economic quality, such factors are also found to matter for cross-citations between courts: see eg de Witte and others (n 142) 317–29 (for the role of EU and international law).
[191] See Chapter 4 at Section C 3 (b), as well as Chapter 3 at Section C 1.

Nachvollzug'), which some authors have conceptualised as a form of legal transplants.[192] Third, it can matter that a transplant has seen a large number of previous adopters. This literature mainly derives from outside legal scholarship given that much of the research on transplants is interested in specific cases, not general patterns.[193] As regards such patterns, following the literature on imitation and innovation,[194] there is now a large body of research that has found that diffusion patterns of policies often follow the 'leader', with the popularity of a policy gradually increasing until it reaches a plateau.[195]

There can be cases where all of these three factors point in the same direction. For example, it has been found that the international diffusion of EU competition law is widespread but particularly prominent in non-EU countries of the Global North. Thus, geographic vicinity seems to play a role but also the large size of the EU and its leading function in this area of law.[196] The fourth category, 'regulatory competition' can also overlap with the other categories. Yet, it is distinct as it follows the preferences of users impacting on the decision of the transplant unit. The literature on both policy diffusion and legal transplants includes many examples: market-friendly policies to attract international investment,[197] the privatisation of telecommunications, postal, and railway providers,[198] the protection of intellectual property,[199] and migration policies.[200] The most well-known example comes from the field of corporate law. In the US context, the successful model of Delaware's corporate law is both based on experiences from other US states and has led

[192] Andreas Heinemann, 'Rechtliche Transplantate zwischen Europäischer Union und der Schweiz' in Lukas Fahrländer and Reto A Heizmann (eds), *Europäisierung der schweizerischen Rechtsordnung* (Zurich: Dike, 2013) 3, 21–4.

[193] Michal Shur-Ofry, Gadi Fibich, and Shira Green, 'The Diffusion of Legal Innovation—Insights from Mathematical Modeling' (2019) 52 *Cornell International Law Journal* 313, 319.

[194] Going back to Tarde (n 88) and Everett M Rogers, *Diffusion of Innovations* (New York: Free Press of Glencoe, 1962; 5th edn, 2003). Notably, it presents diffusion as a 'slight incline, a relatively sharp rise, and then a fresh modification of the slope until the plateau is reached' (Tarde (n 88) 127), subsequently called 's-curve' (Rogers).

[195] See eg James W Dearing and Jeffrey G Cox, 'Diffusion Of Innovations Theory, Principles, And Practice' (2018) 37 *Health Affairs* 183, 187 (referring to the seminal study by Walker (n 118) and then 'hundreds of diffusion studies about policies concerning education, health, civil rights, and lotteries', also showing the s-curve in some of these studies); Shur-Ofry and others (n 193) (examined for US laws on licensing requirements and reforms of corporate and tort law).

[196] Anu Bradford, Adam Chilton, and Katerina Linos, 'Dynamic Diffusion' (2024) 27 *Journal of International Economic Law* 538; Anu Bradford, Adam Chilton, and Katerina Linos, 'The Gravity of Legal Diffusion' (2023) 2 *University of Chicago Legal Forum*, available at https://chicagounbound.uchicago.edu/uclf/vol2023/iss1/2 accessed 23 October 2025.

[197] Dobbin and others (n 13) 457–60.

[198] Kuhlmann (n 37) 43.

[199] Morin and Gold (n 48) 788.

[200] Daniel Ghezelbash, 'Legal Transfers of Migration Law: The Case for an Interdisciplinary Approach' (2023) 7 *International Journal of Migration and Border Studies* 182.

to some changes in other states.[201] A recent article also discusses the impact of Delaware corporate law in Israel, through legislation and case law but also M&A agreements.[202] In the EU, the main story is that companies—supported by incorporation agents—have pushed lawmakers for lower costs of incorporation (eg, reductions of minimum share capital), with some lawmakers having transplanted such rules and ideas from other Member States.[203]

The other variant in the first branch of Figure 4.5 is that the transplant unit incorrectly predicted an economic benefit. It is not surprising that the evaluation of the effect of a law can be mistaken. Indeed, it can be argued that lawmakers are typically operating under a process of bounded-rational learning, which can also mean that the likelihood of adopting a good foreign model may differ between areas of law.[204]

More specifically, three reasons can contribute to such an incorrect perception. First, it may be due to the transplant itself. Examples can be about topics that may be classified as 'fads and fashions' at a particular point in time. For example, in company law, the requirement of independent directors was a frequent case of legal transplants in recent decades; yet, empirical research has not found that these rules actually benefitted financial performance and economic growth.[205] However, there can also be cases where certain perceptions about good rules subsequently have a self-fulfilling prophecy: for example, a recent study found that the perception of a country's strength of shareholder protection is more significant than actual shareholder protection for investment decisions.[206] Second, it is possible that agents present the to-be-transplanted law in a manner that it only appears to have a positive economic effect. We have seen in the previous sections that agents (including the origin unit itself) have various means of influencing the transplant process, as well as the motivations

[201] See eg Marco Ventoruzzo, 'The Role of Comparative Law in Shaping Corporate Statutory Reforms' (2014) 52 *Duquesne Law Review* 151, 154–62; Michael P Dooley and Michael D Goldman, 'Some Comparisons Between the Model Business Corporation Act and the Delaware General Corporation Law' (2001) 56 *The Business Lawyer* 737.

[202] Ido Baum and Dov Solomon, 'Delaware's Copycat: Can Delaware Corporate Law Be Emulated?' (2022) 22 *Theoretical Inquiries in Law* 1.

[203] Martin Gelter, 'Minimum Capital and Cross-Border Firm Formation in Europe' (2023) 8 *Journal of Law, Finance and Accounting* 165.

[204] Weyland (n 38) (finding diffusion of privatisation of pensions but not reforms in the healthcare sector in Latin America).

[205] Eg Wolf-Georg Ringe, 'Independent Directors: After the Crisis' (2013) 14 *European Business Organization Law Review* 401. See also Carsten Gerner-Beuerle, 'Diffusion of Regulatory Innovations: The Case of Corporate Governance Codes' (2017) 13 *Journal of Institutional Economics* 271 (on soft-law codes following benchmarks such as board independence).

[206] Gerhard Schnyder and others, 'Legal Perception and Finance: The Case of IPO Firm Value' (2022) 33 *British Journal of Management* 88.

to do so. Thus, alone or in combination with pressure, it is possible that they present the transplant in a way that is, deliberately or negligently, incorrect in its expected consequences. Third, the mistake may happen on the side of the transplant unit as it incorrectly draws on the positive image of the origin unit in order to project the economic consequences of the transplant. Some of the reasons why this can happen are similar to the ones discussed previously, for example, the reputation of the law of the origin unit or xenophilia on the side of the transplant unit.[207] There is also the common belief that the EU is seen as a good model to adopt in other parts of the world.[208] Moreover, reference can be made to studies that have examined how, at the subnational level, some cities became global models for successful policies, sometimes regardless of differences in local context.[209]

Figure 4.5 then shows the second main requirement, namely that the transplant unit adopted the transplant which is expected to create an economic benefit. This requires, first, that the transplant unit cared about this economic benefit. Moreover, it includes a balancing with other consequences the law may have. Possible examples are laws that would benefit the economy but have detrimental effects in other fields (nature, equality, justice, etc). This issue thus connects to the topic of the following subsection which discusses the (real or perceived) other qualities transplants may have.

To answer the question of why the transplant unit cared about the expected economic benefits, Figure 4.5 provides a simplified divide between public interest and private interest motivations. This distinction is based on the main theories of regulation studies. Public interest theories are said to attribute to lawmakers a desire 'to promote the general welfare of the community'.[210] By contrast, private interest theories (including the 'public choice theory')

[207] Section C 3 (a) and (b). See also the measurement of the global reputation of countries in the Global Soft Power Index, https://brandirectory.com/softpower/ accessed 23 October 2025 (with subindices such as familiarity, reputation, and influence).

[208] For the model role of the EU see eg Philippe Lombaerde and Michael Schulz (eds), *The EU and World Regionalism: The Makability of Regions in the 21st Century* (Farnham: Ashgate, 2009) but also Thomas Risse, 'The Diffusion of Regionalism' in Tanja A Börzel and Thomas Risse (eds), *The Oxford Handbook of Comparative Regionalism* (Oxford: OUP, 2016) 87 (some emulation of ideas but few complete transplants of particular regional models); Tobias Lenz and Kalypso Nicolaïdis, 'EU-topia? A Critique of the European Union as a Model' (2019) 4 *Culture, Practice and Europeanization* 78 (applying a constructive critique).

[209] See eg Jennifer Robinson, 'Policy Mobilities as Comparison: Urbanization Processes, Repeated Instances, Topologies' in Osmany Porto de Oliveira (ed), *Handbook of Policy Transfer, Diffusion and Circulation* (Cheltenham: Edward Elgar, 2021) 100; Eugene McCann and Kevin Ward (eds), *Mobile Urbanism: Cities and Policymaking in the Global Age* (Minneapolis: University of Minnesota Press, 2011).

[210] Karen Yeung and Sofia Ranchordás, *An Introduction to Law and Regulation: Text and Materials* (Cambridge: CUP, 2nd edn, 2024) 120.

suggest that the content and direction of regulation are determined by the self-interested conduct of voters, parties, politicians, and bureaucrats.[211] Further institutional theories emphasise how institutional factors influence regulation.[212] In the present case, Figure 4.5 presents public and private interests as 'and/or', ie it accepts that both sets of theories may have some truth to them. In this regard, institutional factors can also play a role: for example, effective forms of public accountability may lead to closer alignment with the common good, and the possibility of public participation may lead to closer alignment with private interests.

Specifically with respect to the expected economic benefits of a transplant, a public interest argument means that the economic benefit is perceived as being beneficial to all citizens (or constituents, members, etc) of the unit. In some cases, it may depend on the ideology of the representatives (or citizens etc) of the unit whether the economic benefit is really considered relevant; thus, for this reason, it is (again) likely that transplants often happen between ideologically similar units.[213] The importance of private interests can also mean that economic benefits support such a transplant as lawmakers (as well as political parties etc) may politically benefit from such rules ('It's the economy, stupid'[214]). Furthermore, it can matter how far citizens (or firms, NGOs, etc) are able to evaluate the likely economic effects of the law, which again may depend on a number of further factors (strength and independence of economics profession, role of business media, etc).

The final criterion displayed in Figure 4.5 is that the use of the transplant is seen as acceptable for this economic purpose. In other words, this raises the question of whether a law which is expected to have a desired economic benefit may still be rejected because it is a transplant. For example, nationalism, parochialism, and xenophobia may be possible factors, as there may be a sense of (legal) uniqueness.[215] It is also possible that, due to historical, ideological, or other reasons, the objection is against a transplant from a specific origin country. This latter objection therefore again relates to the point mentioned previously that lawmakers often look for legal models within networks of units (including legal families).[216]

[211] Yeung and Ranchordás (n 210).

[212] Yeung and Ranchordás (n 210) and eg Robert Baldwin Martin Cave and Martin Lodge, *Understanding Regulation: Theory, Strategy, and Practice* (Oxford: OUP, 2nd edn, 2011) 40–67.

[213] Mallinson (n 120) 378 (as part of a meta-analysis).

[214] For the origins of this slogan see https://politicaldictionary.com/words/its-the-economy-stupid/ accessed 23 October 2025.

[215] For the former see Section C 3 (b). The latter topic is frequently discussed in the comparative law literature for a possible 'American exceptionalism', see Siems (n 14) 74–7.

[216] See Section B 4.

(d) Perceived other qualities
Figure 4.6 displays three general reasons other than external pressure and perceived economic benefits that may lead to the adoption of a transplant by the transplant unit. Depending on the type of transplant, it may also be possible to identify further reasons and/or subcategories.

The reason that a transplant is perceived as promoting fairness or other non-economic aims often leads to similar questions as the one about the economic benefits of a transplant, discussed in the previous subsection. This similarity is not surprising given that economic indicators may also reflect non-economic aims (eg, the Gini coefficient and distributive justice). Specifically, similar to economic benefits, the aim to promote fairness or other non-economic aims may involve the question of whether the benefits are correctly or incorrectly assessed (as well as the reasons for an incorrect assessment), the consideration of the context of the transplanted law, and motivations based on public and/or private interests.

How frequently are transplants intended to promote non-economic aims? A study on the evolution of shareholder, creditor, and labour protection found that shareholder protection is strongly driven by international trends (notably, the push to increase protection but also the popularity of specific tools) while labour protection is more often driven by domestic politics (notably

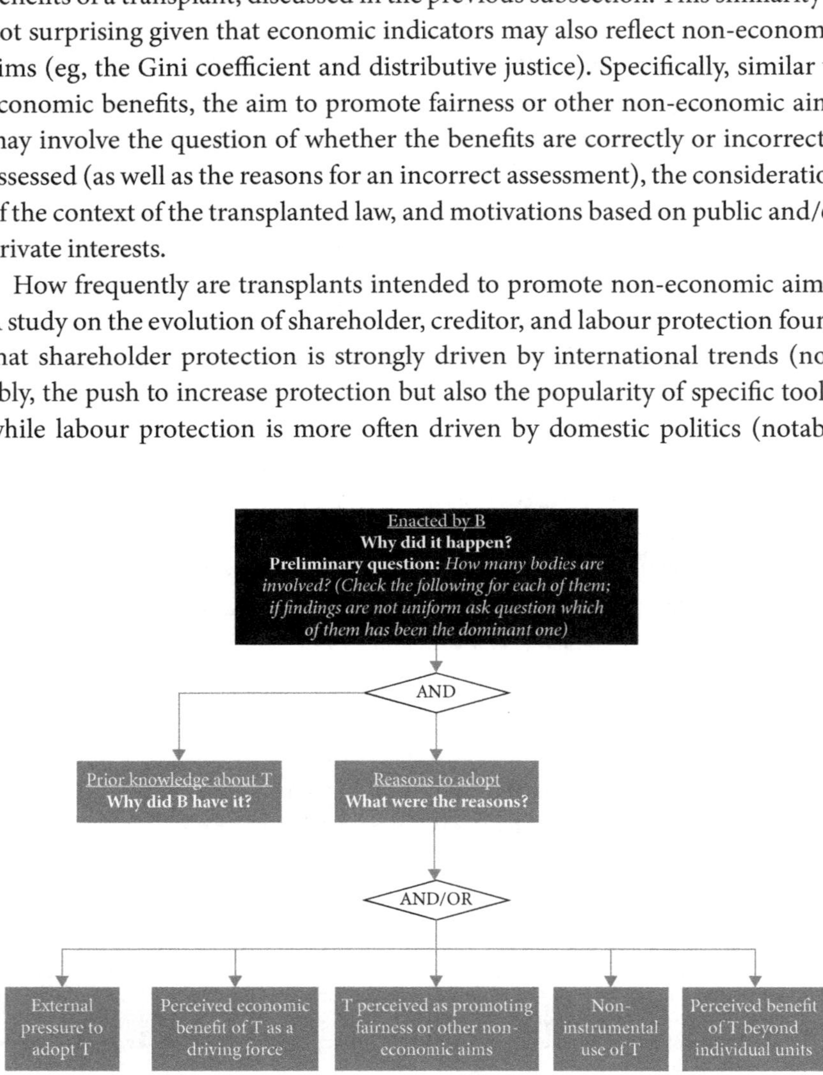

Figure 4.6 Reason to adopt transplant due to other qualities

changes between left and right-wing governments).[217] In the Polish literature, two publications also argue that transplants are likely in contract law due to its common values across countries, while in constitutional law the specificity of historical and political conditions often speaks against them.[218] However, even in matters of private law, lawmakers may hold 'different values or worldviews' that may limit the use of legal transplants.[219] On the other hand, today, there is considerable literature on cases of legal transplants from any area of law.[220] Specifically, there are many examples of transplants in areas of law that are mainly concerned with non-economic aims, such as constitutional and human rights law, family law, and religious legal norms.[221] In other words, to quote a book on the import of law in post-communist transitions, such transplants challenge the (old) 'assumption that public law and, in particular constitutional rules, can only be the result of national inventiveness and that, as a result, they are not subject to foreign influences, or are subject to them to a lesser extent than private law'.[222]

Still, the likelihood of certain topics to travel can vary between areas of law. For example, it has been found that innovations in lawmaking and governance procedures from the US have influenced other countries; yet, less so for parliamentary procedures.[223] The US influence on questions of criminal procedure[224] also offers useful lessons on the 'other qualities' that such transplants

[217] John Armour and others, 'How Do Legal Rules Evolve? Evidence from a Cross-Country Comparison of Shareholder, Creditor and Worker Protection' (2009) 57 *American Journal of Comparative Law* 579.

[218] Michał Romanowski, *Życie umowy konsumenckiej po uznaniu jej postanowienia za nieuczciwe na tle orzecznictwa* (Warsaw: CH Beck, 2017) 24; Jerzy Parchomiuk, *Nadużycie prawa w prawie administracyjnym* (Warsaw: CH Beck, 2018) 185–91.

[219] Kevin E Davis and Mariana Pargendler, 'Legal Heterodoxy in the Global South: Adapting Private Laws to Local Contexts' in Kevin E Davis and Mariana Pargendler (eds), *Legal Heterodoxy in the Global South* (Cambridge: CUP, 2025) 1, 6.

[220] See generally Dominik Dworniczak and others, 'The Notion of Legal Transplants Beyond the Anglosphere: Decentring the Debate' (2025) 16 *Transnational Legal Theory* 357, 372–74.

[221] See eg Matteo Nicolini and Silvia Bagni, *Comparative Constitutional Justice* (The Hague: Eleven, 2021) 55–100; Günter Frankenberg (ed), *Order from Transfer: Comparative Constitutional Design and Legal Culture* (Cheltenham: Edward Elgar, 2013); Sujit Choudhry (ed), *The Migration of Constitutional Ideas* (Cambridge: CUP, 2006); Delia Ferri, 'L'accomodamento ragionevole per le persone con disabilità in Europa: dal Transatlantic Borrowing alla Cross-Fertilization' (2017) *Diritto pubblico comparato ed europeo* 381; Pascale Fournier, *Muslim Marriage in Western Courts: Lost in Transplantation* (Abington: Routledge, 2010); Mahmood Kooria, *Islamic law in Circulation: Shāfiʿī Texts Across the Indian Ocean and the Mediterranean* (Cambridge: CUP, 2022). From the policy literature see also Obinger and others (n 99).

[222] Dupré (n 145) 42.

[223] Fabrizio De Francesco, 'The Diffusion of Regulatory Governance Innovations: A Research Synthesis' in Osmany Porto de Oliveira (ed), *Handbook of Policy Transfer, Diffusion and Circulation* (Cheltenham: Edward Elgar, 2021) 443.

[224] Besides the work by Grande, cited in the following footnote, see eg, Valerie P Hans, 'Trial by Jury: Story of a Legal Transplant' (2017) 51 *Law and Society Review* 471; Józef Gurgul, 'Proces kosztowny, przewlekły, poznawczo niewydolny' (2016) (1) *Prokuratura i Prawo* 5; Máximo Langer,

may offer. In several publications, Elisabetta Grande has explored the substance and motivations of these transplants. In her interpretation, they did not happen for reasons of efficiency or doctrinal quality (as identified for transplants in other areas of law and/or for transplants from other countries); rather, they were based on temporary trends of popularity or even the deliberate use of a shallow transplant to immunise the domestic law against meaningful changes.[225] This also points towards the need to consider 'other qualities' that go beyond simply aiming for specific economic or non-economic qualities.

The next category is, accordingly, the non-instrumental use of a legal transplant. Such use can be related to Alan Watson's position which argues that transplants are mainly used by legal experts in order to improve laws from a positivistic perspective.[226] Yet, the non-instrumental use of a transplant can also overlap with instrumental benefits. Mauricio García-Villegas distinguishes between law as a 'system of instrumental controls' and a 'cultural system of meaning'. For the latter, he argues that symbolic uses of law communicate 'images of justice, equity, security, and other values' for strategic reasons.[227] Thus, a non-instrumental transplant may indirectly also have instrumental aims. Yet, the deeper reason for such a transplant is that, in the social world (including law), cultural diffusion, cross-border learning, and the flow of ideas are akin to natural phenomena.[228] This is similar to but not the same as a situation where there is 'just' convergence but not an identifiable legal transplant.

'From Legal Transplants to Legal Translations: The Globalization of Plea Bargaining and the Americanization Thesis in Criminal Procedure' (2004) 45 *Harvard International Law Journal* 1, revisited in Máximo Langer, 'Quince años después: traducciones legales, globalización del plea bargaining y americanización del proceso penal' (2018) 21(1) *Revista Discusiones* 213.

[225] Elisabetta Grande, *Imitazione e diritto: ipotesi sulla circolazione dei modelli* (Turin: Giappichelli, 2000); Elisabetta Grande, 'Italian Criminal Justice: Borrowing and Resistance' (2000) 48 *American Journal of Comparative Law* 227; Elisabetta Grande, 'Legal Transplants and the Inoculation Effect: How American Criminal Procedure Has Affected Continental Europe' (2016) 64 *American Journal of Comparative Law* 583; Elisabetta Grande, 'Comparative Approaches to Criminal Procedure: Transplants, Translations, and Adversarial-Model Reforms in European Criminal Process' in Darryl K Brown, Jenia Iontcheva Turner, and Bettina Weisser (eds), *The Oxford Handbook of Criminal Process* (Oxford: OUP, 2019) 67. See also Chapter 5 at Section C 2 (b) and 4 (b) for possible differences between areas of law in the way transplants 'work'.

[226] See Chapter 5 at Section B 1.

[227] Mauricio García-Villegas, *The Powers of Law: A Comparative Analysis of Sociopolitical Legal Studies* (Cambridge: CUP, 2018) 19–20.

[228] For selective literature on these three topics see E Anthon Eff, 'Does Mr. Galton Still Have a Problem? Autocorrelation in the Standard Cross-Cultural Sample' (2004) 15 *World Cultures* 153 (empirical paper finding that cultures in nearby locations and with related languages are more similar); Braithwaite and Drahos (n 72) 25 and 532–3 ('modelling' defined as a form of legal globalisation by learning); Trisha Greenhalgh and others, *Diffusion of Innovations in Health Service Organisations: A Systematic Literature Review* (Malden, MA: Blackwell, 2005).

A corresponding distinction can be found in the political science literature as it observes that forms of 'clustered decision making' may be due to policy diffusion but also forms of co-ordination or 'just' similar responses to similar conditions.[229]

Specifically, the flow of (mere) legal ideas may often be of a non-instrumental nature.[230] It also seems likely that transplants between courts are often non-instrumental as they support the argumentation of the court but do not pursue the explicit aim of achieving economic or non-economic benefits.[231] Rather the main reasons may often be that countries share the same language and can easily access the sources and texts of the other legal system,[232] and that the law of the origin unit has a form of legitimacy within the argumentative field of the transplant unit.[233] In a similar sense, Edward Wise draws a parallel between cultural diffusion and legal borrowing, suggesting the common conditions of transmissibility, accessibility (eg, due to geographic or linguistic vicinity), and receptivity (eg, due to the perception that borrowed elements are superior to the status quo).[234] For research on legal transplants, it can sometimes be difficult to identify transplants which are akin to cultural diffusion: for example, in the aforementioned cases of judicial transplants, many courts in civil law countries have a general reluctance to explicitly cite foreign case law, while inspiration from other jurisdictions may still happen behind the scenes.[235]

Sometimes transplants pursue the main aim to have laws that are drafted in a better manner than the existing ones (clearer, more concise, more consistent, etc). Such an advantage may indirectly have economic or non-economic benefits. But considering, for example, the adoption of major codes, it is often mainly a technical exercise to draft a clear, consistent, and consistent text. For example, the French Civil Code has been described as an example of a code that is 'systematic, de-contextualized and a-historical' and, therefore, relatively easy to

[229] Zachary Elkins and Beth Simmons, 'On Waves, Clusters, and Diffusion: A Conceptual Framework' (2005) 598 *The Annals of the American Academy of Political and Social Science* 33, 35.

[230] For legal ideas see generally Chapter 3 at Section B. Of course, in some cases, ideas may also be linked to economic policies; eg, see Mariana Mota Prado, 'Diffusion, Reception and Transplantation' in Peter Cane and others (eds), *The Oxford Handbook of Comparative Administrative Law* (Oxford: OUP, 2020) 258 (for the transplantation of regulatory agencies driven by 'neoliberal theories of economic growth').

[231] See the empirical study by de Witte and others (n 142) 311–13 (presenting data on how far courts are interested in the result or the reasoning of foreign case law).

[232] For example, between England and Scotland, see Alexandra Braun, 'The Value of Communication Practices for Comparative Law: Exploring the Relationship Between Scotland and England' (2019) 72 *Current Legal Problems* 315. For the role of languages for cross-citations between courts see also Section C 3 (a).

[233] For such legitimacy-generating transplants see Section B 2.

[234] Wise (n 89) 17.

[235] For 'judicial style' and its relation to cross-citations see Siems (n 14) 209–10, 211–12.

transplant.[236] Yet, some lawmakers have chosen to mix different codes in order to achieve the 'best of all worlds'. For example, apart from French law, German legislative models played a role in Italy, Spain, and Portugal.[237] In Greece, some of the nineteenth-century codes followed either French or German models, while the civil law remained initially 'Greek' (being based on the Byzantine Hexabiblos) and was only replaced by a German-inspired civil code in 1946.[238]

For the details of whether and when there is a non-instrumental use of a transplant, it is also possible to consider the criteria identified for perceived economic quality, as discussed in the previous subsection. For example, in both cases, lawmakers would compare the transplanted law with the status quo, they would consider the context of the law (be it the extra-legal context or, here, the existing laws), the benefits of international convergence (eg, here in terms legal certainty), the role of agents in promoting and exporting certain models, and then also why the transplant unit cared about the respective aim.

The final category of other qualities concerns the case where the perceived benefits of a transplant go beyond those of individual units. In the previous (sub-)sections, the possible benefits of common rules were mentioned for cases where the origin unit imposed or pressurised the adoption of the transplant and where the transplant unit adopts it to gain a benefit from it.[239] By contrast, in the present case, the ultimate aim is likely to be broader, say, the wish that common rules can lead to a more peaceful world, address the world's environmental problems, or enhance global social welfare.

Examples of such common-good aims can concern any type of legal transplant. As in the previous category, it may sometimes be difficult to identify such an aim as law may converge more gradually towards transnational policy concerns. A visible example concerns again the case of judicial references to foreign case law. For supreme courts in Europe, it has been found that cases which include elements of international or EU law often make domestic courts consider the experience of other domestic courts.[240] Similarly, Indian courts are said to rely on judgments from other common law courts in the interpretation of international treaties in areas such as human rights and the environment.[241]

Figure 4.6 displays the five reasons as 'and/or'. This raises the question of what happens if these reasons pull the transplant unit in different directions.

[236] Muir Watt (n 138) 609.

[237] Zweigert and Kötz (n 25) 104–9.

[238] Tomasz Giaro, 'Westen im Osten—Modernisierung Osteuropäischer Rechte bis zum Zweiten Weltkrieg' (2003) *Rechtsgeschichte* 123, 129.

[239] See Section C 2 and 3 (b).

[240] See the empirical study by de Witte and others (n 142) 317–21.

[241] Library of Congress, 'The Impact of Foreign Law on Domestic Judgments' (2010) 2, available at https://www.loc.gov/item/2013417620/ accessed 23 October 2025.

In such a case, it can matter how a particular issue is framed, for example, whether the need for a new law is presented as an economic issue or as one providing a technically clearer law. For this framing, it is also possible that foreign influence plays a role. This latter point has been examined in a study on policy diffusion between smoking restrictions of US states, finding that 'frames regarding the policy's concrete implications are predicted by prior adoptions in other states, whereas frames regarding its normative justifications are not'.[242]

With respect to further details, it depends on the specific circumstances whether the overall result will be a mixture of rules motivated by different reasons or the prevalence of one of them. In an ideal situation, the transplant unit would make use of the experience of various places to get closer to the aim of domestic and/or global common welfare.[243] Yet, in practice, it can happen that legal transplants are more one-sided—in other words, the transplant unit cherry picks laws that support a particular policy it aims to implement.[244] Moreover, it can matter that the different bodies involved in the law-making process push and pull the law in different directions (eg, consider a case of a minority government whose proposal is then challenged by the parliamentary majority).[245]

D. Conclusion

Inspired by the literature on 'causes of causes' and 'process tracing',[246] it was the main idea of this chapter to analyse the complexity of determinants of transplants, making use of various flow charts. The full flow chart is available online,[247] and it may thus be used by other scholars to guide research on why and how in specific circumstances legal transplants have occurred.

While the answer to the question 'why do legal transplants take place?' thus depends on the specific circumstances shown in these charts (and, thus also to the object and units in question, as identified in the previous chapter) some general conclusions can be drawn. This chapter acknowledged the existence of

[242] Fabrizio Gilardi, Charles R Shipan, and Bruno Wüest, 'Policy Diffusion: The Issue-Definition Stage' (2021) 56 *American Journal of Political Science* 21.

[243] See further Chapter 6, Section C 2.

[244] For example, see the contentious statement by US Chief Justice John Roberts: 'if you don't find it in the decisions of France or Italy, it's in the decisions of Somalia or Japan or Indonesia, or wherever' (confirmation hearings, 13 September 2005, see https://opiniojuris.org/2005/09/13/judge-roberts-hearing-use-of-foreign-law-in-constitutional-cases/ accessed 23 October 2025).

[245] For the role of the variable 'divided government' in a meta-analysis: Mallinson (n 120) 378.

[246] See Section C 1.

[247] See n 107.

fully externally imposed transplants. Yet, in today's world, the transplant unit is typically the main driving force for transplants. The precise reasons can then be complex as the interaction of its own preferences and external influences determines whether or not a transplant happens. This interaction of various causes in the individual case is also relevant for the question about the normative stance reflected in this decision (eg, economic or non-economic aims, including the non-instrumental use of a transplant). Throughout this chapter, we also saw that the role of agents is often important,[248] drawing on literature from political science and regulation studies.

Sometimes, the transplant unit may misjudge the intended effect of the transplanted law.[249] However, given that transplants are so widespread today, this is not the typical case. It also helps that there are multiple means by which information about the to-be-transplanted law can be obtained.[250] Some of it can derive from self-interested parties. There is also the view that, in today's world, it has become considerably easier to gather such information independently as one may 'simply use a web search engine to consult a collectively produced online database'.[251] While there can still be problems of finding and understanding foreign law, there is no denying that online sources, translation tools, and AI have made information gathering much easier than in the past. Thus, it can be said that, today, there is indeed often a reasonable evaluation of the advantages and disadvantages of the transplanted law.

Despite this broadly positive assessment,[252] it is clear that the present mapping of causes of causes did not find a perfect 'marketplace of ideas'[253] in the sense that lawmakers are effortlessly able to learn about and evaluate any laws that exist on a particular topic. Rather we have seen that the occurrence of a transplant is also influenced by factors such as similarities of cultures and languages, common groups or meetings, attraction of the law of larger units, etc. The importance of such structural reasons thus also confirmed the decision of this chapter not to merely follow the motivations of the origin and transplant units,[254] but to unpack the causes of causes that are likely to play a role in many situations.

[248] Likewise in the subsequent Chapter 5 for the way transplants 'work'.
[249] See Section C 3 (c).
[250] See Section C 3 (a).
[251] Annelise Riles, 'From Comparison to Collaboration: Experiments With a New Scholarly and Political Form' (2015) 78 *Law and Contemporary Problems* 147, 155.
[252] A more detailed normative evaluation follows in Chapter 6.
[253] In a similar sense: Matthew Dyson, 'Comparative Legal History: Methodology for Morphology' in Olivier Moréteau, Aniceto Masferrer, and Kjell A Modéer (eds), *Comparative Legal History* (Cheltenham: Edward Elgar, 2019) 110 (comparative law and legal history can work together to challenge the view that legal rules are 'adopted solely on its merits in the marketplace of ideas').
[254] See Section B.

5

Do Legal Transplants 'Work'?

A. Introduction

How law is meant to 'work' is a regular theme in socio-legal research. Lawrence Friedman phrases this question as one of 'law's impact', for example referring to the 'difference between formal law and the law in action' and the way 'culture, tradition, and personality' determine the impact of law.[1] There is also a line of empirical literature, however, that shows that one should not overestimate the importance of law in society.[2] Moreover, as also suggested in the quote by Friedman, countries and cultures differ in their assessment of the character and importance of law in society.[3]

In the case of legal transplants, the key question is whether the foreign element creates additional problems—or, possibly, also certain advantages as far as a particular law has been successfully tested in the origin unit. Thus, asking the question 'do' legal transplants work also includes the questions how legal transplants work and when legal transplants fail. As to the use of the term 'work', the assessment of these questions in this chapter will consider three different variants, namely whether law is known and understood, whether it is complied with and/or enforced, and whether it has the desired influence on society.[4]

Friedman indicates that the way law affects behaviour is a cross-disciplinary topic that should draw on research in political science, sociology, economics, criminology, law, and psychology.[5] As for the impact of legal transplants, insights from other academic fields also play a key role. According to David Dolowitz and David Marsh, one of the questions in the policy transfer

[1] Lawrence M Friedman, *Impact: How Law Affects Behavior* (Cambridge, MA: Harvard University Press, 2016) 2, 6.

[2] The classical work is Stewart Macaulay, 'Non-Contractual Relations in Business: A Preliminary Study' (1963) 28 *American Sociological Review* 55.

[3] Thus, in this book, this relates to the question whether transplants should happen: see Chapter 6 at Section C 1 (a), 2 (a), and 3 (a).

[4] See Section C.

[5] Friedman (n 1) 251–2.

DOI: 10.1093/9780191991981.003.0005

literature is the link between policy transfers and policy outcomes.[6] According to William Twining, it is mainly research by economists and other non-lawyers that tries to develop performance measures of the way transplants work.[7] Indeed, research in many fields can contribute to understanding the way transplants 'work': for example, anthropology, geography, and sociology can examine the way transplanted legal rules operate in practice; linguistics and translation studies can help to understand how the meaning of legal terms changes in different places; and historical research can help in the evaluation of whether doubts about the way transplants work are justified by historical examples.

The structure of this chapter is as follows: Section B presents a critical overview of the general positions in the literature by 'optimists', 'pessimists', and 'realists'. Section C scrutinises whether studies have shown to what extent we can be optimistic about their use. On this basis, Section D concludes that transplants can indeed often be said to work, at least in the long term.

B. General positions in the literature

As we will see throughout this chapter, most authors discuss the way legal transplants work by way of differentiating between different cases. However, it is also worth considering the more one-sided views which argue that transplants either (simply) work or are (completely) irrelevant. These positions have shaped the debate on this topic. They also relate to the general question of whether 'law' is closely connected to its socio-legal context or whether it is a relatively independent field.[8] Thus, while this section discusses diverse positions as to the societal effects of the law, it also considers the corresponding question whether and how societal factors shape the content of the law.[9]

[6] David Dolowitz and David Marsh, 'Learning from Abroad: The Role of Policy Transfer in Contemporary Policy-Making' (2000) 13 *Governance* 5, 8.

[7] William Twining, 'Diffusion of Law: A Global Perspective' (2004) 49 *The Journal of Legal Pluralism and Unofficial Law* 1, 32.

[8] Similarly, Mathias Reimann, 'Comparative Law, An Overview of the Discipline' in Konrad Zweigert and Ulrich Drobnig (eds), *International Encyclopedia of Comparative Law, Volume II: Chapter 4* (Leiden: Brill, 2020) para 350.

[9] For this latter aspect see also Chapter 4 on why legal transplants take place.

1. Optimists: they work

Alan Watson was not the first person to write about legal transplants; yet, Watson most prominently took the view that legal transplants were fairly 'easy', in particular that they could work regardless of differences in the social, political, and economic conditions between the origin and the transplant country.[10] This finding was reached on the basis of research that found that the private law of many countries was significantly based on the reception of Roman law. According to William Ewald, these transplants are said to lead to the belief that 'a law student of the time of Justinian, transported to the twentieth century, would find little to wonder at in the civil codes of modern Europe'.[11] Thus, as said by Watson, laws 'can survive without any close connection to any particular people, any particular period of time or any particular place'.[12] In a later book, he related this view to the position that 'law is out of context much of the time' as 'one independent state accepts much of the law and legal structure of another despite differences', notably due to the way judges, jurists, or law professors often 'find legal authority by borrowing'.[13] Thus, given this insulation of law from society, it can be followed that 'when a rule moves from one legal system to another it remains itself identical'.[14] In other words, according to this legalistic position, transplants (simply) work as lawyers apply these transplanted rules.

However, it is also possible to be an optimist and accept some relationship between law and society. In some cases, the transplanted law is deliberately not in line with the society of the transplant country but aims to change society in a particular manner.[15] Thus, here, the optimist is confident in the way legal transplants can be used as a form of legal engineering. Another variant can be that society features at both sides of the causal relationship as transplants are an example of an efficient 'marketplace of ideas';[16] in other words,

[10] See Chapter 2 at Section B 1.

[11] William Ewald, 'The Jurisprudential Approach to Comparative Law: A Field Guide to "Rats"' (1998) 46 *American Journal of Comparative Law* 701, 703 (paraphrasing Watson's view).

[12] Alan Watson, 'Legal Transplants and Law Reform' (1976) 92 *Law Quarterly Review* 79, 81.

[13] Alan Watson, *Law Out of Context* (Athens, GA: University of Georgia Press, 2000) xi, 163–4.

[14] AA Saparova, 'Legal Transplants: Nature and Structure of Content' (2015) 10 *The Journal of Comparative Law* 101. See also William Ewald, 'Comparative Jurisprudence (II): The Logic of Legal Transplants' (1995) 43 *American Journal of Comparative Law* 489, 509 (as the 'strong version' of Watson's argument in the sense of a 'strong insulation thesis').

[15] See Chapter 4 at Section B 2. See also eg Kurt Lipstein, 'Conclusion' (1957) 9 *International Social Science Bulletin* 70, 76 (for Turkey: 'the law as initially introduced by the Government in 1926 was a deliberate measure of policy with the purpose of changing existing customs').

[16] See Chapter 4 at Section D, and Chapter 6 at Section B 1.

the argument is here that societal forces make a unit adopt those foreign rules that can be expected to work as well in the transplant as in the origin unit.

With respect to these latter arguments, such an optimistic view of the way transplants work is likely to go hand-in-hand with the view that transplants should also be supported. Thus, it connects to the normative question of whether it is desirable to use legal transplants, to be discussed in the subsequent Chapter 6.

2. Pessimists: they are irrelevant

Pierre Legrand can be seen as the main 'pessimistic' challenger to Watson's position. In one of his publications, he states that his disagreement with Watson is due to the latter's 'most impoverished explanation of interactions across legal systems—the result of a particularly crude apprehension of what law is and of what a rule is'.[17] Specifically, Legrand rejects the view that law is only about the words that can be found in legal texts. Rather, he suggests that 'meaning is a function of the application of the rule by its interpreter',[18] and thus 'as the understanding of a rule changes, the meaning of the rule changes', and 'as the meaning of the rule changes, the rule itself changes'.[19] It therefore also follows that any interpretation of the law is subjective and shaped by the larger cognitive framework of a particular country, in particular its culture and mentality.[20]

Terminologically, Legrand phrases these objections as 'the impossibility of legal transplants'. However, it does not seem to be the case that he denies that lawmakers occasionally draw on foreign legal ideas. Rather, as he writes that 'the addition of a litre of green paint to four litres of yellow does not give us the same colour as the addition of a litre of red paint to four litres of yellow',[21] the argument is that the use of these foreign ideas does not lead to legal uniformity across different units; rather every legal system remains 'singular'.[22] Specifically, when Watson claims that there have been transplants from Roman law to modern civil laws, Legrand regards these similarities as entirely meaningless.[23]

[17] Pierre Legrand, 'The Impossibility of Legal Transplants' (1997) 4 *Maastricht Journal of European and Comparative Law* 111, 113.
[18] Pierre Legrand, 'What "Legal Transplants?"' in David Nelken and Johannes Feest (eds), *Adapting Legal Culture* (Oxford: Hart Publishing, 2001) 55, 57.
[19] ibid 61.
[20] ibid 59.
[21] Legrand (n 17) 117.
[22] Pierre Legrand, *Negative Comparative Law: A Strong Programme for Weak Thought* (Cambridge: CUP, 2022) 301–2.
[23] Legrand (n 18) 63–4.

Legrand's view draws on the general idea, prominently expressed by Bruno Latour, that there can be no transportation (of information) without transformation.[24] It also connects to positions by Stanley Fish and other literary theorists that readers (re-)make the text that they read.[25] From other scholarship on legal transplants, reference can be made to a statement by Ernst Hirsch that 'identical legislation does not imply identical law'.[26] In recent years, an article by Julio Carvalho also expresses a view similar to Legrand in stating that legal transplants are misleading in the 'assumption that two different legal cultures share a common concept of law and common epistemological accounts of what is meant by law'.[27] In detail, Carvalho draws on a wide range of authors from different academic fields ('Wittgenstein's pragmatic philosophy of language, Geertz's cultural anthropology, Eco's semiology, Harris' integrational epistemology, and Rosen's cultural theory of law'[28]) to show how the meanings incorporated in the language of the law fundamentally change if a law is inserted in a different cultural context.

As regards the relationship between law and society, it has been argued that Legrand's pessimistic view of legal transplants is close to the 'mirror theory',[29] ie that law is a reflection of a particular society and thus essential to maintain social order in this context.[30] However, Legrand does not use such a terminology. Indeed, arguments that refer to the empirical link between law and its socio-economic context can rather be found in the writings of other authors. For example, Katharina Pistor states that 'experience suggests that importing laws and legal standards rarely works well',[31] and Silvia Ferreri and Larry DiMatteo write about 'superficial transplantations' that only sow 'misunderstanding and

[24] Bruno Latour, *Aramis or the Love of Technology* (Cambridge: CUP, 1996) 118–19.

[25] See references in Pierre Legrand, 'What is That, to Read Foreign Law' (2019) 14 *The Journal of Comparative Law* 290.

[26] Ernst Hirsch, *Rezeption als sozialer Prozeß: erläutert am Beispiel der Türkei* (Berlin: Duncker & Humblot, 1981) 134 ('Einheitliches Gesetz erzwingt nicht einheitliches Recht').

[27] Julio Carvalho, 'Law, Language, and Knowledge: Legal Transplants From a Cultural Perspective' (2019) 20 *German Law Journal* 21, 21.

[28] Carvalho (n 27).

[29] John Gillespie, 'Towards a Discursive Analysis of Legal Transfers into Developing East Asia' (2008) 40 *New York University Journal of International Law and Politics* 657, 674 ('Legrand is conceptually closest to mirror theory, which links law with "felt social needs," while Kahn-Freund and especially Watson lean toward legal autonomy').

[30] Brian Z Tamanaha, *A General Jurisprudence of Law and Society* (Oxford: OUP, 2001) 1–3. For the question of whether this refers to the history of a society or current conditions see Mathias Siems, *Comparative Law* (Cambridge: CUP, 3rd edn, 2022) 177–8.

[31] Katharina Pistor, 'The Limits of Legal Imperialism' (*Project Syndicate*, 20 December 2000), available at https://www.project-syndicate.org/commentary/the-limits-of-legal-imperialism-2000-12 accessed 23 October 2025.

confusion in the adopting country's legal system'.[32] Conceptually, such a pessimistic view may take the following position about the extent to which society and law interact: first, the society of a particular place uniquely shapes the law of that place. Second, legal changes that come from inside this society are believed to have an effect on this society, and, thus, in line with the 'mirror theory', there is indeed a mutual relationship.[33] Third, it is not seen as realistic that external legal models can have an effective impact on society given the unbridgeable gap between law and society in such a case.

3. Realists: it depends on the society of the transplant unit

The realist position is located between the optimists and the pessimists as it asks us to consider the society of the transplant unit in order to assess whether or not a legal transplant works. For example, this may conclude that legal transplants are often not a clear success or failure, but rather that the picture is a mixed one,[34] or that 'imported laws function less well than internally developed laws'.[35]

Regarding the role of the transplant unit, it is said, for example, that the process of legal reform may be more important than the substance of transplanted rules.[36] It is also observed that the result of a transplant may often be a mix of old and new elements, ranging from complete amalgamation to a situation where domestic and foreign elements remain clearly visible.[37] This latter point also connects to the question about the way the new official law interacts with pre-existing informal laws: for instance, it may have the result of creating a pluralist legal order,[38] or the new laws may be used to challenge the previous ones.[39]

32 Silvia Ferreri and Larry A DiMatteo, 'Terminology Matters: Dangers of Superficial Transplantation' (2019) 37 *Boston University International Law Journal* 35, 45 (but note that they do not claim that these are the only types of transplants).

33 In this sense: Gunther Teubner, 'Legal Irritants: Good Faith in British Law or How Unifying Law Ends Up in New Divergences' (1998) 61 *Modern Law Review* 11, 16–17 ('in his polemic against contextualising he [Watson] overgeneralises . . . [and] seems obsessed with the somewhat sterile alternative of cultural dependency versus legal insulation, of social context versus legal autonomy').

34 David Nelken, 'Towards a Sociology of Legal Adaptation' in David Nelken and Johannes Feest (eds), *Adapting Legal Culture* (Oxford: Hart Publishing, 2001) 7, 19.

35 Jan Torpman and Fredrik Jörgensen, 'Legal Effectiveness: Theoretical Developments Concerning Legal Transplants' (2005) 91 *Archiv für Rechts- und Sozialphilosophie* 515.

36 Randall Peerenboom, 'Toward a Methodology for Successful Legal Transplants' (2013) 1 *The Chinese Journal of Comparative Law* 4.

37 See eg Esin Örücü, 'A General View of "Legal Families"' in Esin Örücü and David Nelken (eds), *Comparative Law: A Handbook* (Oxford: Hart Publishing, 2007) 169, 180 (drawing the analogy to different types of salad bowls or plates).

38 See Siems (n 30) 145–8 and Section C 2 (a).

39 See Tamanaha (n 30) 120.

To support the answer that 'it depends', research from other disciplines is often seen as valuable. For example, Michele Graziadei cites psychological research, according to which higher mental functions incorporate new information into previous material whereby legal transplants are seen an example of such a process.[40] By contrast, a publication by Antara Haldar on 'legal emotions' starts with a rather sceptical position given that transplants such as the 'mentally individualistic' Western rule of law are said to clash with character traits in other parts of the world; yet, as she also refers to the need 'to engage with agents at either the cognitive (including affective) or the cultural levels', this may mean that, if this is done properly, transplants may be more effective.[41]

The literature has also explored how far the domestic reception of legal transplants can be seen as an example of cross-border cultural borrowings. Thus, such research is based on the insight that 'cultural awareness' is key to the understanding of legal transplants.[42] Specifically, it is said that cultural borrowings show that the transfer of cultural elements often requires creative forms of assimilation and modification,[43] and that we observe a process of hybridisation in situations of cultural contact.[44] Some of the literature also draws on law as a form of communication. David Nelken suggests that such a view enables us to see a transplant as 'an opportunity for society authoritatively to reinterpret the principles it stands for, rather than merely as an instrument used for the purpose of achieving regulatory goals'; thus, in his words, the transfer of law may have 'more in common with the spread of fashion or other aspects of culture' than (simple) policy transfers.[45] Similarly, John Gillespie refers to systems theory to suggest that transplants 'shape contingent practices, assumptions, goals, and categories of thought in recipient countries', which he also regards as a way to overcome the extreme views that regard law as being either

[40] Michele Graziadei, 'Legal Transplants and the Frontiers of Legal Knowledge' (2009) 10 *Theoretical Inquiries in Law* 723, 736–7.

[41] Antara Haldar, 'Legal Emotions: Why Affect Matters for Law' in Sanjit Chakraborty (ed), *Human Minds and Cultures* (Cham: Springer, 2024), 123, 129–30. For research from anthropology and psychology on whether there are these broad differences see Siems (n 30) 431–43.

[42] Alexandra Mercescu, 'What Kind of Critique for Central and Eastern European Legal Studies? Comparison as One of the Answers' (2019) 89 *Acta Universitatis Lodziensisfolia Iuridica* 45, 50. See also Alexander Graser and Martin Löhnig, 'Rechts(rezeptions)vergleichung als Kulturwissenschaft' (2018) 6 *Rechtskultur* 1 (as distinguished from a functional perspective).

[43] Edward M Wise, 'The Transplant of Legal Patterns' (1990) 38 *American Journal of Comparative Law* (supplement) 1, 17.

[44] Matteo Solinas, 'The Nature of Legal Transplants—Inspirations from Postcolonial Scholarship' (2017) 22 *NZACL Yearbook* 179 (with reference to postcolonial scholarship). This question has also been explored in a project at the Max Planck Institute in Frankfurt on 'Legal Transfer in the Common Law World', see https://www.lhlt.mpg.de/research-field/legal-transfer-in-the-common-law-world accessed 23 October 2025.

[45] Nelken (n 34) 14, 22 (presented as debate between 'evolutionists' and 'diffusionists').

simply reflecting society or completely autonomous.[46] In addition, Gillespie uses discourse analysis as a way of showing that human agency plays a key role in the way transplants are received. Specifically, it asks us to see laws as the way 'people interpret them from particular sets of beliefs, practices, and goals', which can also apply to laws originating from legal transplants.[47] In this sense, Jan Torpman and Fredrik Jörgensen also challenge the frequent focus on the compliance of the transplanted rules and point towards law as a system of communication.[48]

Last but not least, scholarship has referred to the connection with languages in the way the legal transplant is received. Marc Galanter suggests that laws are like languages, being able to absorb foreign influences while also 'preserving a distinctive structure and flavour'.[49] Others focus on the role of the language of the law. For example, as linguists distinguish between the precise elements of the language which are borrowed (lexical, grammatical, meanings, semantics, phonemes, etc),[50] research on legal transplants can examine how far the legal languages of countries are similar according to these elements. Another perspective is to consider parallels between the evolution of languages and legal transplants. For example, as comparative linguistics has identified how languages interact in more or less complex ways,[51] it can be explored how far language trees find their parallel in tree-like structures of legal traditions.[52] And, as linguists observe that some people have abandoned their prior mother tongue and adopted a foreign language, by analogy, legal transplants may sometimes fully replace the prior law.[53]

These positions are called 'realist' here as they ask us to be attentive to the precise way law operates in the transplant unit. However, they are not fully satisfactory as far as they seem to say that it all depends on the way we understand

[46] Gillespie (n 29) 681 and 679. See also Loet Leydesdorff, 'Luhmann, Habermas, and the Theory of Communication' (2000) 17 *Systems Research and Behavioral Science* 273.

[47] Gillespie (n 29) 685.

[48] Torpman and Jörgensen (n 35) (with reference to Luhmann).

[49] Marc Galanter, 'Predators and Parasites: Lawyer-Bashing and Civil Justice' (1994) 28 *Georgia Law Review* 633, 680.

[50] Alexandra Y Aikhenvald, 'Language Contact and Areal Linguistics' in Carol Genetti (ed), *How Languages Work: An Introduction to Language and Linguistics* (Cambridge: CUP, 2nd edn, 2019) 314, 317–19.

[51] William Labov, 'Transmission and Diffusion' (2007) 83 *Language* 344. See also Heikki ES Mattila, *Comparative Legal Linguistics* (Farnham: Ashgate, 2nd edn, 2013) 17, 147–51, 357–9 (on interaction between legal languages); Silvia Ferreri, 'The Unpredictable Path of Legal Transplants: Some Analogy with Language Evolution' (2022) 1 *Comparative Law and Language* 60.

[52] Örücü (n 37) 173.

[53] Thomas Lundmark, *Charting the Divide Between Common and Civil Law* (Oxford: OUP, 2012) 32 (referring to the United States).

law in general terms. The following section therefore addresses how we can develop a nuanced but also realistic perspective on this topic.

C. Framework and differentiations

What exactly does it mean to say that a legal transplant 'works'? The following starts with presenting a framework of analysis that identifies the different, though interconnected, ways this term can be understood (Section 1). On this basis, it is analysed whether transplants work in the sense that the transplanted law is known and understood (Section 2), that it is complied with and/or enforced (Section 3), and that it has the desired influence on society (Section 4).

1. Framework of analysis

When the literature writes about the way transplants 'works', this is often followed by a clarification that this phrase concerns different types of questions. For example, Maximilian Wörner-Schönecker refers to the societal expectation of the lawmaker of the transplant unit but also the congruence with the legal reality between the origin and the transplant unit;[54] Barbara Dufková distinguishes between the fit of a legal transplant and its success in terms of aspects such as its promulgation, change in behaviour, and benefit to society;[55] Ulf Larsson-Olaison uses four categories, namely transplant as label, content, practice, and outcome;[56] and Mathias Reimann lists a variety of questions that can matter for the question of whether a transplant is a success.[57]

This section distinguishes between three categories: (i) that the transplanted law is known and understood, (ii) that it is complied with and/or enforced, and (iii) that it has the desired influence on society. The third category may often be the most important one; however, it also shows further complexities as laws can have diverse socio-economic effects. For example, consider a

[54] Maximilian Wörner-Schönecker, *Rechtstransfers: Eine Analyse anhand von Typologien* (Tübingen: Mohr Siebeck, 2022) 214–15.

[55] Barbara Dufková, *Success in Legal Transplanting* (Prague: Charles University, 2022) 29–52.

[56] Ulf Larsson-Olaison, 'Convergence of Corporate Governance Systems: A Legal Transplant Perspective' (2020) 24 *Competition & Change* 450.

[57] Reimann (n 8) para 4-349 ('If the transplant firmly establishes itself in the recipient system—regardless of its positive or negative impact? If it fulfils the expectations of the receiving or of the donor system—whatever these expectations may be? If the transplanted law works for the recipient as it did for the donor? If it functions at all, albeit in a modified fashion? If it has unplanned but still beneficial effects?').

situation in which the transplanted law leads to economic growth but increases inequality. In the literature, it is sometimes said that the benchmark may be whether the law meets the policy goal that the lawmaker was aiming to achieve, or that it may be evaluated according to whether the public in the transplant unit regards the reform as a success.[58] In this manner, some of the literature also notes that different countries may have culturally determined variations in what is meant by success.[59] For the analysis in this book, it should be noted that this question about different objectives of the law is connected to the subsequent Chapters 6 and 7 as they deal with the questions of whether and how transplants should be used.[60]

As regards the relationship between categories, Larsson-Olaison suggests that there is a 'transplant staircase' from 'label' to 'content' to 'practice' and to 'outcome'.[61] Thus, this assumes that, for example, transplants can only lead to a positive outcome if their content is well implemented and applied in the transplant unit. Often, this is a plausible assumption. However, other variants are also conceivable. For example, it may happen that a transplant does not 'fit' well in the sense that, for the first two categories used here, there is a deterioration in the knowledge and enforcement of the law; yet, let us further assume that this is deliberate as the transplanted law has the eventual aim—and then does so successfully—to influence the social reality of the transplant country.[62] Another possibility is that, again, at the first stages the transplant seems deficient but it may lead to a positive effect on society as a 'legal placebo'. For example, assume that a transplanted law unsuccessfully aims to increase the protection of investors; yet, foreign investors believe in its positive effect and therefore increase investment in the transplant country.[63]

Another critical question is the time dimension in which any positive effect of a transplant may be expected. To illustrate these and other complexities this

[58] Ghezelbash (n 70) 190–1.

[59] James L Nolan, *Legal Accents, Legal Borrowing: The International Problem-Solving Court Movement* (Princeton, NJ: Princeton University Press, 2009) 5 (referring to the example 'where a therapeutic idiom is more dominant, the notion of what constitutes success may not match up with such conventional criminal justice measurements as reduced recidivism rates').

[60] In particular, see Chapter 6 at Section C 1 (a), 2, and 3 (a) on the legitimate (and sometimes non-legitimate) aims that transplants may pursue.

[61] Larsson-Olaison (n 56).

[62] Similarly, Nolan (n 59) 38 ('Therefore, we wish not only to make sense of the manner in which law is adapted to fit its new context, but also to understand (if only in a preliminary manner) how the imported legal program might influence the new social context.'). For transplants being motivated to change or even disrupt society see also Chapter 4 at Section B 2, and Chapter 6 at Section C 3 (b).

[63] For similar arguments see Gerhard Schnyder and others, 'Legal Perception and Finance: The Case of IPO Firm Value' (2022) 33 *British Journal of Management* 88; Amitai Aviram, 'The Placebo Effect of Law: Law's Role in Manipulating Perceptions' (2006) 75 *George Washington Law Review* 54.

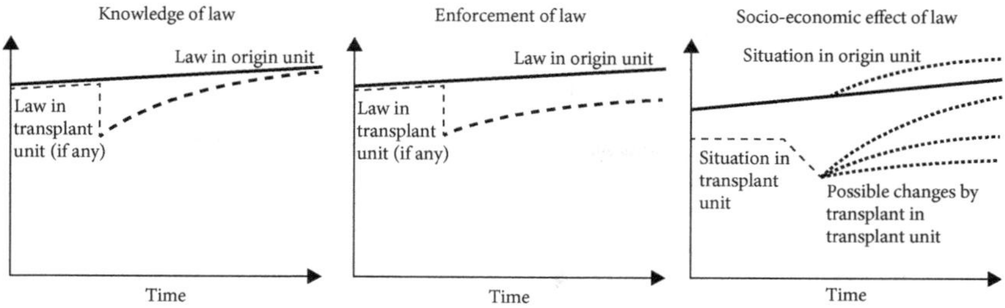

Figure 5.1 Possible effect of transplant on different elements of quality of law

section uses charts showing the possible evolution in the origin and the transplant unit.[64] In this subsection, these charts are deliberately kept abstract in order to then evaluate in the following subsections how far reality may confirm any expectations about the effect of a legal transplant. The analysis will also show that sometimes the answer may be that it depends, for example, on the time horizon and the types of effect a transplant may have.

Figure 5.1 displays how the effect of a transplant may differ according to the three categories across time. In the main scenario presented here, the knowledge and enforcement of the law were initially at the same level in the origin and the transplant unit. Following the transplant, both decline in the transplant unit but then the knowledge of the law gradually recovers while the enforcement of law still lags behind the level in the origin unit (eg, this may be due to incompatibility with other law-related issues in the transplant unit). As regards the socio-economic effect of the law, the immediate negative impact of the transplant is more gradual, while it is then conceivable (though not certain) that the situation improves in a way that it exceeds the pre-transplant socio-economic situation in the transplant unit.

The panels of first two categories of Figure 5.1 indicate that it can also happen that there is no prior law (for that reason, the initial lines are displayed in fainter lines). Thus, here, the question of knowledge and enforcement may only be benchmarked against the law of the origin unit or the expectations that the transplant unit had. With respect to the third category, the previous socio-economic situation in the transplant unit can, in any case, be used to assess whether the transplant may be seen as successful, while the socio-economic benchmark may also be the expectation of the transplant unit in the effect of the new law. Finally, the panel on the socio-economic effect also includes the

[64] Similar solutions would also apply to transplants that derive from multiple sources, see Chapter 3 at Section C and Chapter 4 at Section B 4.

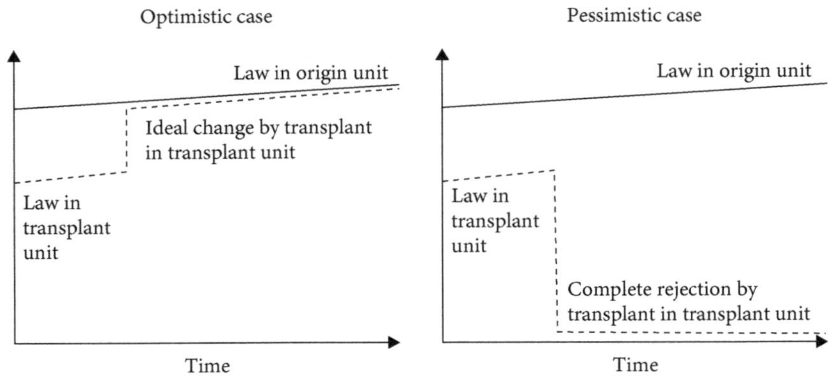

Figure 5.2 Possible optimistic and pessimistic cases of effect of transplant on quality of law

possibility that the situation in the origin unit improves with the transplant; for example, this may happen if a transplant is imposed on the transplant unit in the interest of the origin unit or if it reduces the transaction costs for the benefit of both units.[65]

Such abstract charts can also be used to illustrate the (strongly) optimistic and pessimistic positions of the previous section. Figure 5.2 shows these possible narratives, whereby the y-axis refers to any possible quality of the law (ie any of the three categories). The two variants of this chart have in common that the origin unit had a better law than the transplant unit at the beginning, which motivated the use of a transplant. However, the optimist then simply assumes that the transplant changes the law akin to that of the origin unit,[66] while the pessimist assumes that there is an immediate and permanent change for the worse.

Sometimes the 'fit' of a transplant is presented as being a key feature for its success.[67] A good fit can indeed be relevant for the moment a transplant takes place. This is shown in the two panels of Figure 5.3 (being again open as to the precise quality of the law). However, they also indicate that subsequent developments may mean that, in either case, the initial positive fit may then turn to

[65] See Chapter 4 at Sections B 1 and C 2, and Chapter 6 at Section C 2 (b).

[66] Similarly, for one of the benchmarks for a transplant's success or failure: Reimann (n 57).

[67] Already in Jeremy Bentham, 'Of the Influence of Time and Place in Matters of Legislation' in John Bowring, *The Works of Jeremy Bentham, Volume i* (Edinburgh: William Tate, 1838–1843) 169, 185; also eg World Bank, 'Legal Culture and Judicial Reform' (27 April 2012), available at https://moj.gov.vn/en/Pages/Talking-Laws.aspx?ItemID=14 accessed 23 October 2025.

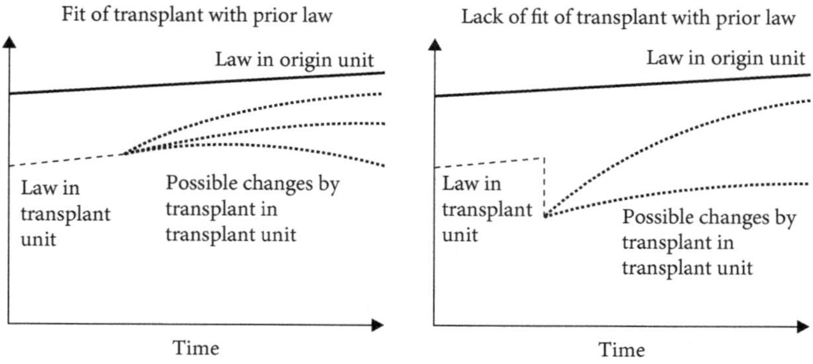

Figure 5.3 Possible effect of transplant on quality of law distinguished by fit

a negative outcome, or the initial lack of fit may then turn to a positive one. It also means that, depending on the point in time, a different evaluation may be made about the way a transplant 'works' and, thus, for example, invite an analysis of both the short-term and long-term effects.

Figure 5.4 illustrates possible further variants of the way legal transplants can work. For example, a transplant which is inferior to the current situation of the transplant unit may happen by mistake or because it is externally imposed (while it is also conceivable that it 'works well' later in the sense that, over time, it operates similarly to the origin unit). The other extreme may be a situation where the transplanted law in the transplant unit gradually exceeds the quality of its operation in the origin unit (ie the case of an 'overfitting legal transplant').[68]

As regards the reasons why any of the variants displayed in Figures 5.1 to 5.4 may happen, it is likely that the object (ie the transplant), as well as the identity of both the origin and the transplant units play a key role. Often, assuming (largely) voluntary legal transplants,[69] the focus will be on the transplant unit, such as its existing institutional structures and its compatibility with the to-be-transplanted law. Contextual issues are also likely to be relevant to the question of whether the transplant survives in the transplant unit. For example, it may, for whatever reason, be challenged in courts,[70] face resistance by special interest groups, or not survive politically because it is not well-received by the

[68] See already Chapter 3 at Section D 2.

[69] As the typical case today, see Chapter 4.

[70] Daniel Ghezelbash, 'Legal Transfers of Migration Law: The Case for an Interdisciplinary Approach' (2023) 7 *International Journal of Migration and Border Studies* 182, 190–1 (as 'legal success').

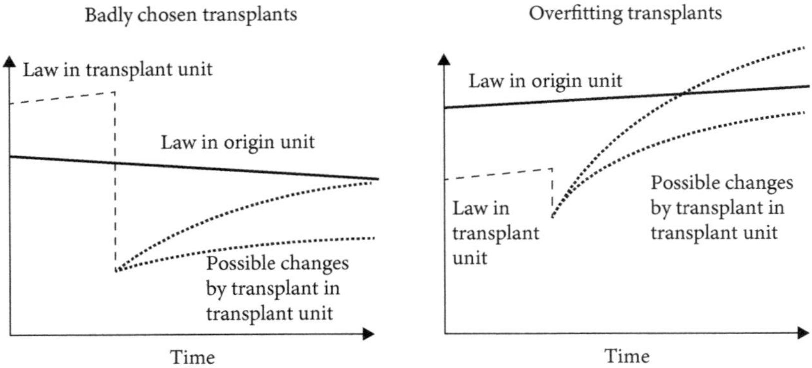

Figure 5.4 Illustrations of badly chosen and overfitting legal transplants

public.[71] Moreover, it is possible that the transplant unit reacts in other ways to make the transplant work better (eg, consider a situation where the initial transplant had been entirely focussed on the positive law but, later on, some means of law enforcement were also transplanted).

To conclude, there are a variety of dimensions that need to be considered in order to assess whether transplants work. It is therefore unrealistic to expect simple answers that would hold in all circumstances. Still, the following aims to uncover with the help of case studies how far, in the three categories of Figure 5.1, we are more or less likely to see transplants that usually do or do not work.

2. Law known and understood

The category that the transplanted law is known and understood is unlikely to lead to the conclusion that either everyone or no-one knows and understands the transplanted law. Indeed, as a similar conclusion may be drawn for most domestic laws, the point of reference here is the knowledge and understanding of domestic laws. This will be analysed in three steps: to set the scene, the first

[71] Ghezelbash (n 70) ('as political success'). Similarly, John Jupp, 'Legal Transplants as Tools for Post-Conflict Criminal Law Reform: Justification and Evaluation' (2014) 3 *Cambridge Journal of International and Comparative Law* 381, 403 (transplant needs to be 'accepted by the local population' and achieve 'the objectives for which it was enacted'); Martino Maggetti and Fabrizio Gilardi, 'Problems (and Solutions) in the Measurement of Policy Diffusion Mechanisms' (2016) 36 *Journal of Public Policy* 87, 90 (distinction between goals, implementation, and political support of diffused policy).

subsection presents general factors discussed in the literature, followed by representative examples and a conclusion.

(a) General factors discussed in literature

The transplanted positive law on a particular topic is likely to be related to the legal context in which this specific law is embedded. This is meant to refer to the systematic legal context in which a transplanted law is inserted,[72] but also more general questions related to the role and nature of law in a particular society.[73] For example, it is said that a developed legal culture may have the capabilities to successfully absorb a legal transplant.[74] Another author explains that, often, the positive law is transplanted but not the underlying legal theories and scholarship needed to make the transplant 'work'.[75]

In particular, it is frequently suggested that legal families not only play a role in the occurrence of legal transplants,[76] but also the way they 'work', in the sense that intrasystemic transplants will be more easily known and understood in the transplant unit than extrasystemic ones.[77] Thus, it may be that legal families share a particular 'interpretive community'[78] that facilitates the common reading of particular legal text. This emphasis on the importance of legal families may be based on the view that (major) legal traditions each have distinct features which have emerged over history. For example, Patrick Glenn notes that the continuation of differences between major legal traditions is due to the fact that these traditions have been able to reconcile diversity and contradictions, while nonetheless maintaining some form of coherence.[79] This insight about the success of legal traditions can also be linked to other research that has explored the survival of legal rules and traditions. Some of it has discussed the

[72] Referring to it as one of the *canones* of interpretation: Reinhard Zimmermann, 'Legal Methodology in Germany' (2022) 26 *Edinburgh Law Review* 153, 169–71.

[73] See eg Fernanda Pirie, *The Anthropology of Law* (Oxford: OUP, 2013); Werner Menski, *Comparative Law in a Global Context* (Cambridge: CUP, 2nd edn, 2006) 129–90.

[74] Ugo Mattei, Teemu Ruskola, and Antonio Gidi, *Schlesinger's Comparative Law* (New York: Foundation Press, 7th edn, 2009) 227–9.

[75] Adriaan Bedner, 'Indonesian Legal Scholarship and Jurisprudence as an Obstacle for Transplanting Legal Institutions' (2013) 5 *Hague Journal on the Rule of Law* 253. See also Chapter 3 at Section A 1 (for the objects of legal transplants).

[76] See Chapter 4 at Section C 3 (a).

[77] Ugo Mattei, 'Three Patterns of Law: Taxonomy and Change in the World's Legal Systems' (1997) 45 *American Journal of Comparative Law* 5, 6.

[78] For this term see Stanley E Fish, 'Interpreting the Variorum' (1976) 2 *Critical Inquiry* 465. See also Section B 2.

[79] H Patrick Glenn, *Legal Traditions of the World* (Oxford: OUP, 5th edn, 2014) 361, 366–7, 374. Similarly, George Mousourakis, *Traversing Legal Traditions: Perspectives on Comparative Law and Legal History* (Cham: Springer, 2nd edn, 2025) 2 (long-standing legal traditions as having a foundational core).

notion of a 'survival of the fittest' akin to evolutionary theories,[80] while others refer to 'path dependencies' in explaining both the relevance of insights from the past on legal traditions and ongoing linkages within countries of the same tradition due to factors such as academic collaborations, judicial dialogue, and student migration.[81]

However, legal transplants are often also examples of mixtures of laws. In an early article on the reception of law, Albert Kocourek notes that new and old laws may be in accord, conflict, or they may create a new legal institution.[82] Athanase Papachristos' book discusses the notion of 'juridical dualism' as far as the old law is still considered by some groups while others already follow the new law.[83] Other authors refer to the phenomenon of legal pluralism as a typical result of legal transplants.[84] Reference can also be made to the notion of 'legal formants', frequent in the Italian literature[85] but also in some Spanish language publications;[86] here, the argument of a mixture is that the transplant may be successful in communicating a change in one of the formants (legislation, court decisions, legal scholarship) but not the other two. Research from other disciplines also contributes to the notion of mixtures. For example, according to the French sociologist Gabriel Tarde, when law reform incorporates foreign elements, 'old rites' such as ceremonial legal forms often remain.[87] Matteo Solinas connects the notion of legal transplants to the literature on 'cultural hybridity' as a means to understand the 'in-betweenness of

[80] For details see Liam McHugh-Russell, *Limits of Legal Evolution: Knowledge and Normativity in Theories of Legal Change* (PhD thesis, EUI, 2019); Jan M Smits, 'Is Law a Parasite? An Evolutionary Explanation of Differences Among Legal Traditions' (2011) 7 *Review of Law and Economics* 791. See also Alessandro Somma, 'Tanto per cambiare . . . Mutazione del diritto e mondializzazione nella riflessione comparatistica' (2006) 116 *Boletín mexicano de derecho comparado* 535, 536–40 (challenging both evolutionary and diffusionist views of transplants).

[81] See eg Holger Spamann, 'Contemporary Legal Transplants: Legal Families and the Diffusion of (Corporate) Law' (2009) *BYU Law Review* 1813, 1845, 1850.

[82] Albert Kocourek, 'Factors in the Reception of Law' (1935) 10 *Tulane Law Review* 209 (also noting the further possibility of a 'lacunae in the domestic law supplied by the imposed law').

[83] Athanase C Papachristos, *La réception des droits privés étrangers comme phénomène de sociologie juridique* (Paris: LGDJ, 1975) 108, 111–19; also 141 (reception is a transitional phenomenon as it transforms the existing system).

[84] Michele Graziadei, 'Frontiere, legal transplants, comparazioni: le vie del diritto e l'incontro con il pluralismo' (2023) 134 *Quaderni fiorentini per la storia del pensiero giuridico moderno* 23; Guido Smorto, 'Diritto comparato e pluralismo giuridico' in Pietro Cerami and Mario Serio (eds), *Scritti di comparazione e storia giuridica, vol 2* (Turin: Giappichelli, 2013) 105; Mireille Delmas-Marty, 'Le pluralisme ordonné et les interactions entre ensembles juridiques' (2006) 14 *Recueil Dalloz* 951.

[85] Following Rodolfo Sacco, *Introduzione al diritto comparator* (Turin: Giappichelli, 4th edn, 1990) 47–74; Rodolfo Sacco, 'Legal Formants: A Dynamic Approach to Comparative Law' (1991) 39 *American Journal of Comparative Law* 1 and 343.

[86] Alfredo Ferrante, 'Trasplante y formante: hermanos, pero no gemelos. Hacia una mejor comprensión de la metodología en la comparación jurídica' (2021) 14 *Actualidad Jurídica Iberoamericana* 168; Renzo Saavedra Velazco, 'Sobre formantes, transplantes e irritaciones: apuntes acerca de las teorías del cambio jurídico y la comparación jurídica' (2010) 40 *Ius et Veritas* 70.

[87] Gabriel Tarde, *The Laws of Imitation* (New York: Henry Holt and Company, 1903) 201.

people and their actions', including the notion of a 'third space between colonial and indigenous cultures'.[88] Further literature in the interconnected fields of policy transfer and comparative institutional analysis discusses pluralism and bricolage as describing the way transfers rearrange old and new norms and policies.[89]

As to the precise way law is known and understood, a monograph by Beata Kviatek provides several criteria that can matter for the ease with which a transplant is incorporated in the host legal system. Particularly, she refers to the positive conditions that the transplanted law has a concise scope, that it has well-defined objectives and means to achieve those, and that it is flexible enough to be suitable outside its home jurisdiction.[90] The language of the law is another factor related to the object often discussed in the literature. For example, as far as the transplanted law has been translated, it is noted that a translated term will often not mean the same in both languages,[91] and that any interaction between legal systems may need to be perceived as a process of 'cultural translation'.[92] In a recent article by Roman Uliasz, it is elaborated that—regardless of whether both units share the same language—a distorted reception of the legal concepts may be due to the way the transplanted law is drafted, implemented, and interpreted;[93] yet, Uliasz then also notes that minor shifts in meaning should actually be appreciated as a means to embed the legal concept in the different cultural and legal context.[94]

[88] Matteo Solinas, 'The Nature of Legal Transplants—Inspirations from Postcolonial Scholarship' (2017) 22 *NZACL Yearbook* 179, 195–6 (with reference to Homi K Bhabha), also 208 ('pure transferable forms and transparent knowledge is largely an illusion').

[89] Fabien Terpan, 'A Legal Approach to Norm Transfer', in Laure Delcour and Elsa Tulmets (eds), *Policy Transfer and Norm Circulation: Towards an Interdisciplinary and Comparative Approach* (London: Routledge, 2019) 19, 20; John L Campbell, 'Institutional Reproduction and Change' in Glenn Morgan and others (eds), *The Oxford Handbook of Comparative Institutional Analysis* (Oxford: OUP, 2010) 87, 98–9.

[90] Beata Kviatek, *Explaining Legal Transplants: Transplantation of EU Law Into Central Eastern Europe* (Nijmegen: Wolf Legal Publishers, 2015) 120–2.

[91] Michele Graziadei, 'Comparative Law as the Study of Transplants and Receptions' in Mathias Reimann and Reinhard Zimmermann (eds), *The Oxford Handbook of Comparative Law* (Oxford: OUP, 2nd edn, 2019) 442, 456–7.

[92] Lena Foljanty, 'Legal Transfers as Processes of Cultural Translation: On the Consequences of a Metaphor' in Noorhaidi Hasan and Irene Schneider (eds), *International Law between Translation and Pluralism* (Wiesbaden: Harrassowitz, 2022) 23. The notion of 'translation' is also used in the policy transfer literature: Patrick Hassenteufel and Ulrike Zeigermann, 'Translation and Translators in Policy Transfer Processes' in Osmany Porto de Oliveira (ed), *Handbook of Policy Transfer, Diffusion and Circulation* (Cheltenham: Edward Elgar, 2021) 58.

[93] Roman Uliasz, 'The Transplantation of Legal Concepts by Means of Language: A Private Law Perspective' (2023) 12 *Cambridge International Law Journal* 266. See also Roman Uliasz, 'Rhizomatic Networks in Legal Transplants: Interconnected Interpretations of Legal Concepts Across Jurisdictions' (2025) 5 *Undecidabilities and Law: The Coimbra Journal for Legal Studies* 89.

[94] Uliasz, 'The Transplantation of Legal Concepts' (n 93) 285.

With respect to the role of transplant agents,[95] Kviatek mentions that it facilitates the adoption of a transplant if there are prior experience, preparedness, and support in the transplant unit.[96] Others suggest that their contribution may go beyond facilitation. Noting that transplants often lead to plural legal orders, Masaji Chiba and Daniel Bonilla Maldonado observe that this may provide agents with a degree of choice and empowerment.[97] Extensively, a book by John Gillespie and collaborators addresses the question of 'how do recipients interpret and at times reclaim and deploy legal transfers?' using case studies from different countries.[98] In a theoretical chapter of this book, Gillespie also challenges the view that the transplantation of 'global legal scripts' is simply like a 'conduit' that can easily transfer knowledge across geographic and cultural boundaries. Rather, he suggests that we should focus on the 'habits and patterns of thought' in the transplant unit in order to understand how the received knowledge is socially (re-)constructured.[99]

(b) Representative examples

How far does experience show that transplanted law is known and understood? The examples of this subsection discuss cases that are presented in the literature as negative, intermediate, and positive (Figure 5.5 illustrates these examples). Of course, considering the diverse factors discussed in the previous subsection, it is unlikely that these examples will lead to an entirely positive or negative conclusion; yet, discussing them, this subsection aims to show how far, overall, cases typically point in either of the two directions.

A first set of negative examples is about situations where colonial transplants are said to not have become properly known or understood given the persistence of pre-colonial norms and traditions. For example, some of the general comparative law literature suggests that 'one must ask how much effect less than a century of colonial domination could have had on many peoples of Africa'[100] and that it would be 'wholly erroneous' to assume that 'in the areas of Africa which were previously under British rule most legal relations today

[95] Broadly understood, see Chapter 4 at Section B 3. See also Section C 3 (a).

[96] Kviatek (n 90) 122–3.

[97] Masaji Chiba, 'Other Phases of Legal Pluralism in the Contemporary World' (1998) 11 *Ratio Juris* 228, 239, 242; Daniel Bonilla Maldonado, *Legal Barbarians: Identity, Modern Comparative Law and the Global South* (Cambridge: CUP, 2021) 160.

[98] John Gillespie and Pip Nicholson (eds), *Law and Development and the Global Discourses of Legal Transfers* (Cambridge: CUP, 2012).

[99] John Gillespie, 'Relocating Global Legal Scripts in Local Networks of Meaning' in John Gillespie and Pip Nicholson (eds), *Law and Development and the Global Discourses of Legal Transfers* (Cambridge: CUP, 2012) 29.

[100] Menski (n 73) 462.

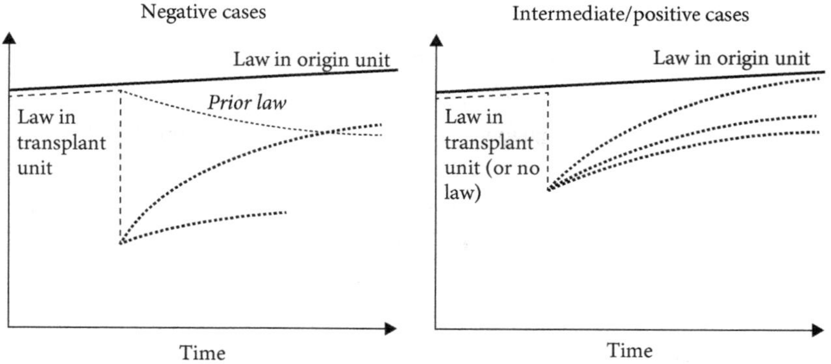

Figure 5.5 Effect of transplant on knowledge and understanding of law

are governed by the rules of English Common Law'.[101] The latter quote can also be related to the well-known difference between English and French colonial strategies, namely that only England relied on an explicit 'indirect rule', not insisting on the universal application of English law (while, in practice, even with the French 'direct rule' many local customs persisted).[102] Specifically for the common law, some specialised publications challenge the view that India is 'simply' a common law country. According to MP Singh and Niraj Kumar, there are multiple legal traditions in India: it includes elements from the common law but others 'closely resemble other legal families, such as the codes and general impetus to codify (as in the case in the civil law system), customary legal systems based on Hindu and Islamic law, and the presence of state-acknowledged systems of tribal law'.[103] Werner Menski's historical research also identified a customary legal system in classical Hindu society,[104] which has partly survived until today.[105] The colonial influence can then be portrayed as a process through which these traditional laws have continued as modified personal laws, while legal transplants from English law only happened in a piecemeal manner.[106]

[101] Konrad Zweigert and Hein Kötz, *An Introduction to Comparative Law* (Oxford: Clarendon, 3rd edn, 1998) 230.

[102] See eg Wolfgang J Mommsen and JA de Moor (eds), *European Expansion and Law* (Oxford: Berg, 1992); Christian Burset, *An Empire of Laws: Legal Pluralism in British Colonial Policy* (New Haven, CT: Yale University Press, 2023) 159–62 (as a form of legal pluralism).

[103] MP Singh and Niraj Kumar, *Indian Legal System: An Enquiry* (New Delhi: OUP, 2019) xxix–xxx.

[104] Werner F Menski, *Hindu Law. Beyond Tradition and Modernity* (New Delhi: OUP, 2003) 121–30.

[105] Menski (n 73) 203.

[106] Jean-Louis Halpérin, 'Western Legal Transplants and India' (2010) 2 *Jindal Global Law Review* 14, 29–32; Ronald J Daniels, Michael J Trebilcock, and Lindsey D Carson, 'The Legacy of

Interpreting this development graphically, Figure 5.5 (left panel) shows the variant that the former law has remained somehow relevant, though with declining intensity. Thus, as already contemplated in the previous subsection, the result is a form of mixed legal system/legal pluralism. How far this should then be seen as a negative case may, however, be less clear: such initial mixture could be regarded as relatively common for many legal transplants, and it may then depend on the time frame whether the level of knowledge and understanding eventually reaches the level of the prior laws and/or the origin unit.

The second example is the law of Afghanistan after 2001 and prior to the retaking of power by the Taliban in 2021. Here, a representative statement of the attempted legal transplants may that this period was 'a case study in how many things can go wrong in post-conflict state-building'.[107] Specifically, as to the enactment of a new criminal procedure code based on an Italian model, it has been said, for instance, that the limited Afghan involvement led to an imposition of law and probable resistance by Islamic religious scholars,[108] and that judges and prosecutors were ignorant of many rules of the code and often decided cases 'on nothing more than their own personal intuition'.[109] Thus, here, we may have had a situation of transplanted rules not (merely) having been underenforced (ie the category of the next section) but not even having been known and understood by many lawyers and citizens.

In Figure 5.5 (left panel), it is illustrated that this transplant then simply stopped at some point, namely with the retaking of power by the Taliban. Thus, it is at least conceivable that, in a longer time frame, the transplanted rules of criminal procedure, perhaps after further modifications, would have been assessed in a more positive light. Drawing another parallel to the first example, it has also been argued that Afghanistan during this period was a 'divided legal system' where different legal traditions remained in continual contestation.[110] Thus, it is possible that we had an unexceptional example of a more mixed

Empire: The Common Law Inheritance and Commitments to Legality in Former British Colonies' (2011) 59 *American Journal of Comparative Law* 111, 134–5.

[107] Geoffrey Swenson, 'Why U.S. Efforts to Promote the Rule of Law in Afghanistan Failed' (2017) 42 *International Security* 114, 151.

[108] Faiz Ahmed, 'Judicial Reform in Afghanistan: A Case Study in the New Criminal Code' (2005) 29 *Hastings International and Comparative Law Review* 93.

[109] John Jupp, 'Legal Transplants as Solutions for Criminal Law Reform in Post-Intervention States: Afghanistan's Interim Criminal Procedure Code 2004' (2013) 61 *American Journal of Comparative Law* 51, 69.

[110] M Bashir Mobasher and Haroun Rahimi, 'Divided Legal Systems: Understanding Legal Systems in Conflict-Prone Societies' in Mathias Siems and Po Jen Yap (eds), *The Cambridge Handbook of Comparative Law* (Cambridge: CUP, 2024) 525.

picture of legal plurality in which the interaction between the different elements may have worked better in the long run.

The following intermediate examples share the attribute that the legal effect of transplants is said to be modified in the transplant unit. The first one is Gunther Teubner's influential article on good faith in English law as a 'legal irritant' transplanted from the civil law tradition through EU harmonisation.[111] Specifically, Teubner rejects the dichotomy between repulsion or interaction in emphasising that common lawyers understand 'good faith' in a different way than, for example, Germans understand '*Treu und Glauben*', and that the corresponding EU harmonisation thus did not lead to functional convergence between English and German law. To support this argument, Teubner also uses Luhmann's theory of autopoiesis, namely that legal systems are normatively closed but cognitively open to their environment, which means here that laws are cognitively open to foreign influence but that the way this happens is through the self-referential nature of the domestic legal system.[112]

Akin to this study by Teubner, some of the literature also discusses the diverse effect of unification efforts as cases of legal transplants not leading to full legal convergence. TT Arvind, for instance, writes about the divergent judicial interpretations of harmonised international commercial laws due to the way prior legal doctrine and legal culture shape the interpretation of the new law.[113] Similarly, Adam Dyrda and Tomasz Gizbert-Studnicki find that in international commercial arbitration, concepts such as 'ownership', 'contract', and 'negligence' often 'travel badly' across different legal cultures due to the way they are embedded in many related concepts of the respective domestic legal systems.[114] Other research makes a similar point but in a broader sense. For example, Lasse Schuldt presents the topic of corporate criminal liability in Thailand as a form of legal irritation. Specifically, he refers to the understanding of the transplanted English law by the Supreme Court of Thailand, leading him to the conclusion that irritation does not happen automatically but rather depends on the preferences and actions of domestic actors.[115] Margit

[111] Teubner (n 33).

[112] See David Nelken, 'Beyond the Metaphor of Legal Transplants?: Consequences of Autopoietic Theory for the Study of Cross-Cultural Legal Adaption' in Jiří Přibáň and David Nelken (eds), *Law's New Boundaries: The Consequences of Legal Autopoiesis* (Dartmouth: Ashgate, 2001) 265.

[113] TT Arvind, 'The "Transplant Effect" in Harmonization' (2010) 59 *International & Comparative Law Quarterly* 65.

[114] Adam Dyrda and Tomasz Gizbert-Studnicki, 'Do Legal Concepts Travel?' in Anne Lise Kjær and Joanna Lam (eds), *Language and Legal Interpretation in International Law* (Oxford: OUP, 2022) 50.

[115] Lasse Schuldt, 'Driving Irritation: Thailand's Supreme Court and the English Roots of Corporate Criminal Liability' (2024) 19 *Asian Journal of Comparative Law* 142.

Cohn's notion of 'warped transplants' may also be seen as a form of irritation as she discusses the transplant of the principle of 'margin of appreciation' from a regional setting (granting some flexibility to member countries) to domestic laws in Canada and Israel.[116]

As a result, Figure 5.5 (right panel), contains a number of variants illustrating that it often depends on the specific details whether it can be said that the transplanted law is known and understood. It should also be said that taking the benchmark of the origin unit would, in any case, not be fair as any new law will take time to be known and understood, even if modified in the transplant unit.

The time dimension is also crucial for the positive examples that follow. The first one is the use of legal transplants in Japanese law, already mentioned as an example in the introductory chapter of this book.[117] This classification as a positive example may not be uncontroversial as some authors suggest that there is only a 'façade of Western law' in Japan,[118] and that the US-influenced postwar constitution has often been misinterpreted.[119] However, it is more plausible to agree with others who see Japan as an example of successful legal transplants.[120] To understand this argument, first, it is worth considering the period of the late nineteenth century in which the initial sets of Western-influenced codes were drafted. At this point in time, Japan embarked on a general cultural modernisation of its society and, therefore, had a practical motivation to enact new laws that would be known, understood, and applied.[121] The drafting process of the laws was also taken seriously in terms of consulting with foreign experts: for example, the German jurist Hermann Roesler spent, on invitation by the Japanese government, fifteen years in Japan, advising on the reforms of Japanese law.[122] Second, the subsequent period also saw close connections between Japanese and foreign legal scholarship. Notably, this led

[116] Margit Cohn, 'Legal Transplants: A Theoretical Framework and a Case Study from Public Law' in Mathias Siems and Po Jen Yap (eds), *The Cambridge Handbook of Comparative Law* (Cambridge: CUP, 2024) 426, 441–51.

[117] See Chapter 1 at Section B 2.

[118] Henry W Ehrmann, *Comparative Legal Cultures* (Englewood Cliffs, NJ: Prentice Hall, 1976) 47.

[119] Kyoko Inoue, *MacArthur's Japanese Constitution* (Chicago, IL: University of Chicago Press, 1991); Kyoko Inoue, 'From Individual Dignity to Respect for Jinkaku: Continuity and Change in the Concept of the Individual in Modern Japan' in Michael Likosky (ed), *Transnational Legal Processes: Globalisation and Power Disparities* (London: Butterworths, 2002) 295.

[120] Explicitly: C Alexander Evans and J Mark Ramseyer, 'What Makes Private Law Transitions Succeed: Lessons from Japan and from Around the World' (2023) 33 *Journal of Transnational Law & Policy* 1.

[121] Luke Nottage, 'Development of Comparative Law in Japan' in Mathias Reimann and Reinhard Zimmermann (eds), *The Oxford Handbook of Comparative Law* (Oxford: OUP, 2nd edn, 2019) 201, 203; Lan Cao, *Culture in Law and Development: Nurturing Positive Change* (New York: OUP, 2016) 323–50.

[122] See Paul-Christian Schenck, *Der deutsche Anteil an der Gestaltung des modernen japanischen Rechts- und Verfassungswesens: Deutsche Rechtsberater im Japan der Meiji-Zeit* (Stuttgart: Steiner, 1997).

to a process of theory reception, namely that Japanese private law was strongly influenced by German legal doctrines, in particular in the early period.[123] After the Second World War, many Japanese lawyers also studied in the US, while legal scholarship still maintained close links with continental Europe.[124]

As a result, it is clear that contemporary Japanese law is not merely a 'façade'. Of course, it is in many fields a mixture of different origins with further modifications,[125] while it still remains possible to identify many (long) legal transplants, notably from German and US law.[126] There has been some discussion about the effectiveness these laws have in the Japanese context,[127] but at the level that laws are known and understood, Japan is, in any case, a positive example.

The second example is of a more general nature, namely the spread of legal traditions over long time periods. The argument that such transplanted law is at least known and understood can partly be based on Watson's research in showing that Roman law has spread to many places which today regard it as a natural part of their own legal system.[128] It can also be seen in the literature on legal traditions. For example, Patrick Glenn explains that legal traditions have a 'universalising' tendency as they aim to extend geographically, absorbing other influences but ultimately having some form of coherence that is accepted in any of the countries that today belong to this tradition.[129] It may then also happen that the foreign origins of a tradition have gradually been forgotten, which has been argued for some of the origins of both Roman and Islamic law.[130] But it is also possible that, within the same legal family, an ongoing influence due to legal co-operation and education leads to new legal transplants, reinforcing the ties between origin and transplant units.[131]

With respect to the history of Islamic law in particular, we can note that, as it spread to different parts of the world and mixed with other laws, it has become

[123] The classical work on this topic is Zentaro Kitagawa, *Rezeption und Fortbildung des europäischen Zivilrechts in Japan* (Frankfurt: Metzner, 1970), summarised in English in Zentaro Kitagawa, 'Theory Reception: One Aspect of the Development of Japanese Civil Law Science' (1970) 4 *Law in Japan* 1. More recently, Christoph Sokolowski, '100 Jahre juristischer Austausch mit Japan' (2009) 28 *Zeitschrift für Japanisches Recht* 53.

[124] Nottage (n 121) 204.

[125] See eg Ko Hasegawa, 'Normative Translation in the Heterogeneity of Law' (2015) 6 *Transnational Legal Theory* 501; J Mark Ramseyer, 'Mixing-and-Matching Across (Legal) Family Lines' (2009) *BYU Law Review* 1701.

[126] Sean McGinty, 'Long Legal Transplants' (Working Paper, 2021), available at https://ssrn.com/abstract=3916055 accessed 23 October 2025.

[127] See references in Siems (n 30) 188–90.

[128] See Section B 1.

[129] Glenn (n 79) 49–53.

[130] See Chapter 2 at Section A.

[131] Spamann (n 81).

known and understood in all of the Muslim-majority countries in which it applies today. The initial spread of Islam went hand in hand with the spread of different schools of Islamic law present today in different parts of the Muslim world.[132] Legal diffusion of Islamic law also continued in modern times, for example, in the field of Islamic finance but also with the spread of conservative traditions within the Islamic world.[133] Mixtures with laws from Western countries occurred in various stages with variations across areas of law,[134] and—as in Japan—this also included 'legal theory, doctrinal literature, comparative law, and case law, all pertaining to European law and all transportable to the Arab world'.[135]

It can therefore be said that, over a long time period, legal traditions tend to spread in a way that knowledge and understanding of the law are not negatively impaired by foreign elements (see the upper line in Figure 5.5, right panel). This positive finding can also happen when the initial transplant was involuntary,[136] and when changes and mixtures have occurred with other traditions. Thus, the finding that legal traditions are a positive example does not imply that there is identity of the transplanted law across all units (including the origin one);[137] rather, the argument is that, whatever the law says, the affiliation of a country with a particular legal tradition eventually means that laws of this tradition are widely known and understood.

(c) Conclusion

What can be followed from the negative, intermediate, and positive examples presented and discussed in this section? In all of them, we have seen that the time dimension can make a difference. Notably, even in the (more) negative examples, it is conceivable that, after amendments, a foreign-inspired law

[132] Glenn (n 79) 207. See also Mahmood Kooria, *Islamic Law in Circulation: Shāfiʿī Texts Across the Indian Ocean and the Mediterranean* (Cambridge: CUP, 2022) 19 ('. . . we need to provincialise and disaggregate Islamic law as a monolithic, inflexible and timeless phenomenon as much as to identify its value as conceived and perceived by jurists in their specific contexts . . .').

[133] See references in Siems (n 30) 124–5.

[134] ibid. See also Jan Michiel Otto (ed), *Sharia Incorporated: A Comparative Overview of the Legal Systems of Twelve Muslim Countries in Past and Present* (Leiden: Leiden University Press, 2010).

[135] Leonard Wood, *Islamic Legal Revival: Reception of European Law and Transformations in Islamic Legal Thought in Egypt, 1875–1952* (Oxford: OUP, 2016) 3.

[136] Of course, from a normative perspective, this can be criticised: see Charles Manga Fombad, 'Africanisation of Legal Education Programmes: The Need for Comparative Legal Studies' in Salvatore Mancuso and Charles M Fombad (eds), *Comparative Law in Africa: Methodologies and Concepts* (Cape Town: Juta, 2015) 1.

[137] In other words, outcomes can differ according to the relevant circumstances, see also Chapter 3 at Section D 2.

is eventually known and understood. Thus, this confirms that, in principle, cross-cultural learning is possible in the legal field.

With respect to variations, it was contemplated in the first subsection that differences in legal context matter. Indeed, a mismatch between new and old law can prolong the process in which the law is widely known and understood in the transplant unit. However, as the many examples of mixtures show (or, indeed as it may be argued that all legal traditions are mixed[138]), there is often sufficient plasticity in the law to adjust to different legal systems. Moreover, it seems likely that the proliferation of such mixtures in today's world further increases the receptiveness towards foreign influence, thus creating a virtuous circle of being able to successfully incorporate transplants into one's legal systems.

Finally, the examples have shown that transplants happen for various types of legal phenomena. This confirms the words of TT Arvind that 'no legal system is entirely a prisoner of its own past traditions' given that 'informal institutions can be changed, or new ones developed, to conform to those traditions that exist in the country of origin of the transplanted law, or the countries on whose jurisprudence a harmonised law was based'.[139] Considering these different phenomena can also help in understanding which actors drive the knowledge and understanding of the transplant. For example, there may be cases where lawyers have expertise in the foreign law, but the general public is unaware of these rules; or, there can be situations where rules are widely known in some part of the country (say, in bigger cities) but not elsewhere.

3. Law complied with and/or enforced

This section analyses the 'law in practice' of legal transplants, as distinguished from both the law in the books and the wider implications of the law on society (see the previous and subsequent sections). The reference to compliance and enforcement employs the 'and/or' connection in order to cover the variety of laws (hard law, soft law, other legal phenomena) which can fall under the heading of legal transplants.[140] As in the previous section, the following discusses general factors and representative examples in order to assess whether transplants can usually be said to 'work' according to this category.

[138] See Siems (n 30) 99–102.
[139] Arvind (n 113) 81.
[140] See Chapter 3 at Section B 1.

(a) General factors discussed in literature

The notion of 'legal culture' is often defined as referring to two elements: 'internal legal culture', which includes, for example, the attitudes of judges and practising lawyers, and 'external legal culture', which refers to the behaviours and views of the general public.[141] Both elements are said to be relevant for the compliance and enforcement of legal transplants.[142] Within internal legal culture, further distinctions may be made, for example when some, but not all, enforcement authorities of the transplant unit apply the transplanted law in an authentic manner.[143] As for external legal culture, an analogy can be drawn to the use of the term 'reception' in Catholic thought, whereby a canonical doctrine is only regarded as fully received if it is accepted by the believing community.[144] Of course, here too, this leaves open the possibility that different segments of the public may accept a new law to varying degrees.

In the institutional and policy literature, we also find many statements that ask us to explore how transplants are received. For example, Martin de Jong and Virginie Mamadouh mention the need to understand the 'operational level' of transplants.[145] Giulia Romano refers to the role of culture in general but also the way 'local elites, interest groups, institutional settings, organizational mindsets, administrative arrangements, habits, beliefs, customary practices, needs, etc' impact on the way policies arrive in the transplant unit.[146] The role of agents is also emphasised in further literature in this field. For example, the literature highlights the role of elites in shaping the design and application of policy transfers in domestic and international

[141] Lawrence M Friedman, *The Legal System: A Social Science Perspective* (New York: Russell Sage Foundation, 1975).

[142] Nelken (n 34) 10, 14, 27.

[143] For an example see Jasminka Pecotić Kaufman, 'Judicial Interpretation and Competition Law Enforcement: Authoritarian Legal Culture, Semantic Dissonance and Skewed Agencification in Post-Socialist Croatia' (2023) 48 *Review of Central and East European Law* 275 (comparing courts and competition authority in Croatia).

[144] Bishal Khanal, *Legal Reform Via Reception of Law* (Kathmandu: Bhrikuti Academic Publications, 2018) 19–26 with reference to James A Coriden, 'The Canonical Doctrine of Reception' (1990) 50 *The Jurist* 58.

[145] Martin de Jong and Virginie Mamadouh, 'Two Contrasting Perspectives on Institutional Transplantation' in Martin de Jong, Konstantinos Lalenis, and Virginie Mamadouh (eds), *The Theory and Practice of Institutional Transplantation: Experiences with the Transfer of Policy Institutions* (Deventer: Kluwer Academic Publishers, 2002) 19, 22.

[146] Giulia C Romano, 'Understanding the Role of Culture in Policy Transfers' in Osmany Porto de Oliveira (ed), *Handbook of Policy Transfer, Diffusion and Circulation* (Cheltenham: Edward Elgar, 2021) 258. Similarly, Hang Duong, 'Culture and Policy Transfer: From Insight to Impact' (2023) 21 *Political Studies Review* 306.

institutions,[147] as well as the transnational reach of private consultants and policy advisory organisations.[148]

Legal geographers ask us to consider 'the concrete realities of the social and environmental landscape' where a transplant is implemented.[149] These local conditions are likely to be narrower than that of a jurisdiction; yet, as legal geographers also identify 'law as a mode of spatial production',[150] transplants may also shape the way space is perceived. Furthermore, geographers studying policy mobilities have a natural interest in the way policies operate in different places. This includes understanding the role of private and public actors at various scales while also emphasising the complexities of policy mobilities referring, for instance, to notions such as fluidity and deterritorialisation. Specifically, the term 'policy assemblages' is used to refer to the way models mutate as they move, which may lead to 'a combination of everyday local practice and global connection'.[151] Thus, in the present context, this line of research tells us that questions about the 'law in practice' of transplants can be time-dependent, challenging simple conclusions that they either work or do not work.[152]

Some legal scholarship also closely draws on insights from other disciplines. Michele Graziadei regards legal transplants as a tool that may trigger a 'mediated action'.[153] This notion is based on psychological research which aims to understand the features of the environment as indirectly being incorporated in human behaviour. In other words, the argument here is that this research can help us in understanding how far the transplanted text of the law really shapes its application in the transplant unit. Günter Frankenberg, criticising the metaphor of legal transplants, suggests that Edward Said's 'traveling

[147] Osmany Porto de Oliveira, 'A Prelude to Policy Transfer Research' in Osmany Porto de Oliveira (ed), *Handbook of Policy Transfer, Diffusion and Circulation* (Cheltenham: Edward Elgar, 2021) 1, 5 with reference to the research by Dezalay and Garth, discussed in Chapter 4 at Section B 3.

[148] Diane Stone, Leslie A Pal, and Osmany Porto de Oliveira, 'Private Consultants and Policy Advisory Organizations: A Blind Spot on Policy Transfer Research' in Osmany Porto de Oliveira (ed), *Handbook of Policy Transfer, Diffusion and Circulation* (Cheltenham: Edward Elgar, 2021) 173.

[149] Liesel Spencer, 'Comparative Legal Geography: Context and Place in "Legal Transplants"' in Tayanah O'Donnell, Daniel F Robinson, and Josephine Gillespie (eds), *Legal Geography: Perspectives and Methods* (London: Routledge, 2020) 149, 162.

[150] Matteo Nicolini, *Legal Geography: Comparative Law and the Production of Space* (Cham: Springer, 2022) 130–6.

[151] Eugene McCann and Kevin Ward, 'A Multi-disciplinary Approach to Policy Transfer Research: Geographies, Assemblages, Mobilities and Mutations' (2013) 34 *Policy Studies* 2, 14 (as well as 8 and 9). See also Eugene McCann and Kevin Ward (eds), *Mobile Urbanism: Cities and Policymaking in the Global Age* (Minneapolis, MN: University of Minnesota Press, 2011).

[152] In this sense also Jessica Viven-Wilksch, 'How Long Is Too Long to Determine the Success of a Legal Transplant? International Doctrines and Contract Law in Oceania' in Vito Breda (ed), *Legal Transplants in East Asia and Oceania* (Cambridge: CUP, 2019) 132.

[153] Graziadei (n 40) 736–7. See also Section B 3.

theory'[154] may be more fitting. According to this theory, ideas are said to travel in four stages, whereby the final stage is about the 'recontextualization at the receiving end that involves bricolage and yields a variety of outcomes'.[155] This position directly relates to the compliance and enforcement of the transplanted law as those depend on the way they are 'put to use (. . .) by the new epistemic community—courts, governmental agencies, legal scholars, social movements, legal consultants, and more'.[156]

In further legal scholarship, Katharina Pistor emphasises the importance of the 'perceptions of both users and law enforcers' for compliance and enforcement, notably the role of voluntary compliance.[157] Athanase Papachristos' book on legal reception as a phenomenon of legal sociology also contains several statements that refer to this theme at a general level. For example, he writes that the transplanted law goes through a process of 'acclimation' by legislation, courts, and scholarship, and that this would ideally need to be researched using socio-legal methods such as surveys and statistics in order to compare the legal reality across countries.[158] He and other legal authors also mention cases where certain groups have been opposed to the transplanted law and thus obstruct its practical application.[159]

(b) Representative examples

The following examples of negative, intermediate, and positive cases (illustrations in Figure 5.6) have been chosen as they are often discussed in the literature; yet, we will also see that for many of these examples their classification is not straightforward.

First, the literature sometimes presents the recent transplantation of Western laws in China, mainly in areas of private and commercial law, as an example of a transplant for which the judicial application and enforcement of these new laws are said to be weak.[160] Specifically for the Chinese Civil Code of 2020,

[154] Edward Said, *The World, the Text, and the Critic* (New York: Vintage, 1983) 226–47.

[155] Günter Frankenberg, 'Legal Transfers' in Marie-Claire Fobletsand others (eds), *The Oxford Handbook of Law and Anthropology* (Oxford: OUP, 2020) 333, 337 (the previous stages are the initial circumstances, the decontextualisation of the information, and its subsequent inclusion in a global space). See also Chapter 7 at Section B 1.

[156] Frankenberg (n 155) 340. Restated in Fernanda Nicola and Günter Frankenberg, *Comparative Law: Introduction to a Critical Practice* (Cheltenham: Edward Elgar, 2024) 36–8.

[157] Pistor (n 31). Similarly, Amber Darr, 'The Legitimacy Gap in Borrowed Laws: A Case Study of Competition Law Transplants in South Asia' (2025) 45 *Legal Studies* 469.

[158] Papachristos (n 83) 93–108.

[159] Papachristos (n 83) 83–93; Wörner-Schönecker (n 54) 77; Yseult Marique and Emmanuel Slautsky, 'Resistance to Transplants in the European Administrative Space' (2021) 14 *Review of European Administrative Law* 7.

[160] Wang Jingen and Larry A DiMatteo, 'Chinese Reception and Transplantation of Western Contract Law' (2016) 34 *Berkeley Journal of International Law* 44. See also Tianshu Zhou and Mathias Siems,

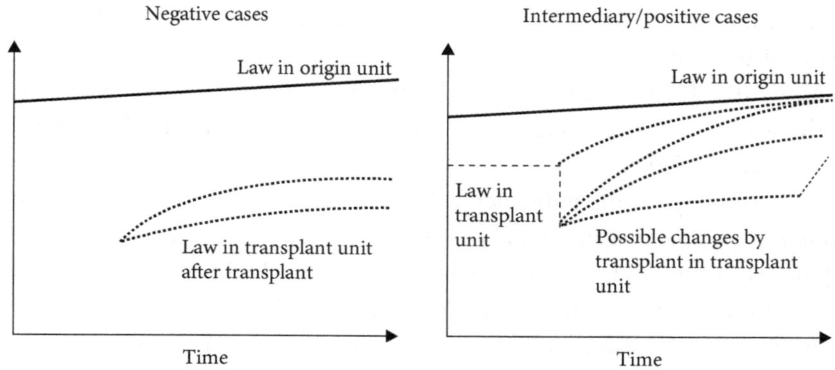

Figure 5.6 Effect of transplant on compliance and enforcement of law

it has been said that the Code 'has already been decodified shortly after the promulgation of this civil code' due to the many judicial interpretations and guiding opinions of Chinese courts that went contrary to its Western models.[161] Similarly, to refer to another area of law, the introduction of international anti-money laundering rules in China is called an example of a weak implementation of global regulatory standards due to discretionary enforcement.[162]

However, it is important to distinguish between two issues. On the one hand, it is unsurprising that the transplanted rules are at least somehow applied differently in China than in the Western origin countries. Moreover, this deviation may actually be helpful for compliance and enforcement as, without any adjustment, the rules may clash with China's existing legal culture. On the other hand, there is some evidence that the role of law, including legal compliance and law enforcement, has been changing in China, in particular in private law. For example, an interview-based study found that, while there is (still) some scepticism about the role of formal contracts and judicial enforcement, today's picture is often more mixed with growing trust in the objectivity of courts and more control of judicial independence, at least outside the political sphere.[163]

'Contentious Modes of Understanding Chinese Commercial Law' (2015) 6 *George Mason Journal of International Commercial Law* 177.

[161] Lihong Zhang, 'A Brief Analysis of Cryptotypes in the Chinese Civil Code: Legalism and Confucianism' in Michele Graziadei and Lihong Zhang (eds), *The Making of the Civil Codes: A Twenty-First Century Perspective* (Singapore: Springer, 2023) 365, 382 (as well as its incompatibility with Legalism and Confucianism).

[162] Sebastian Heilmann and Nicole Schulte-Kulkmann, 'The Limits of Policy Diffusion: Introducing International Norms of Anti-Money Laundering into China's Legal System' (2011) 24 *Governance* 639.

[163] Ding Chen and others, 'Law, Trust and Institutional Change in China: Evidence from Qualitative Fieldwork' (2017) 17 *Journal of Corporate Law Studies* 257. See also Mary M Shirley and Lixin Colin

A second example is the case of the Andean Tribunal of Justice as a transplant of the European Court of Justice (ECJ). In general, the literature argues that the EU has been a model for regional organisations in many parts of the world.[164] A monograph by Karen Alter and Laurence Helfer zooms in on the Andean Tribunal of Justice (ATJ), noting that the Andean Community did indeed copy the main distinct features of the ECJ design.[165] However, the book then argues that the actual case law of the two courts has been very different: while the ATJ has copied some ideas from the ECJ, it 'has not replicated the ECJ's role as an engine of legal integration'.[166] Thus, in the interpretation by Alter and Helfer, the ATJ is more closely concerned with the interests of the member countries of the Andean Community, while the ECJ primarily has a concern for supranational interests.

Both (relatively) negative examples therefore have in common that the role of law and courts is different in the origin and the transplant unit. While it is possible that sometimes the transplanted law is enforced more strongly in the transplant than in the origin unit,[167] in these examples, as illustrated in the left panel of Figure 5.6, compliance and enforcement can be seen as weaker compared to the origin unit. For the Chinese case in particular, it may, however, also be said that the application of the transplanted laws may simply be different from that of its origin countries. Moreover, as shown in Figure 5.6, if there is no prior law, the benchmark of the law of the origin unit may not be decisive from a policy perspective if the influence on society—discussed in the next section—is positive.

The first intermediate example is the transplanted law of Turkey, following the introduction of mainly Swiss and German-inspired law after the establishment of the Turkish Republic in 1922.[168] The drafting process of these laws has been criticised due its hastiness, translation errors and lack of wide public

Xu, 'Formal and Informal Institutions Explaining China's Modern Economic Development: Their Historical Roots and Recent Evolution' in Claude Ménard and Mary M Shirley (eds), *Handbook of New Institutional Economics* (Cham, Springer, 2nd edn, 2025) 927, 938–42.

[164] See references in Chapter 1, n 45.

[165] Karen J Alter and Laurence R Helfer, *Transplanting International Courts: The Law and Politics of the Andean Tribunal of Justice* (Oxford: OUP, 2017) 31 (namely: directly applicable community legal rules, preliminary ruling mechanism, possibility to challenge use validity of supranational decisions, noncompliance procedures by nonstate actors).

[166] Alter and Helfer (n 165) 109–10.

[167] See Figure 5.4 in Section C 1.

[168] See eg Gülnihal Bozkurt, *Batı Hukukunun Türkiye'de Benimsenmesi, Osmanlı Devletinden Türkiye Cumhuriyetine Resepsiyon Süreci 1839–1939* (Ankara: Türk Tarih Kurumu, 1996); Esin Örücü, 'A Synthetic and Hyphenated Legal System: The Turkish Experience' (2006) 1 *The Journal of Comparative Law* 261; Hirsch (n 26); Yeşim M Atamer, 'Rezeption und Weiterentwicklung des schweizerischen Zivilgesetzbuches in der Türkei' (2008) 72 *Rabels Zeitschrift für ausländisches und internationales Privatrecht* 723.

participation.[169] Yet, subsequently, efforts were undertaken to improve the reception of the new laws, for example, through special programmes for the training of judges,[170] exchange with European academics, as well as juridical influence, with the result that the transplanted law was gradually not regarded as 'foreign' any more.[171] Still, an ethnographic study from the 1970s found that in rural Turkey matters of family law were typically solved without court involvement.[172] The same study also mentioned, however, some use of judicial dispute resolution, which is likely to have increased in subsequent decades. Moreover, comparative quantitative empirical data show that the number of judges and lawyers and the clearance rate of cases put Turkey in the middle of rankings of European countries.[173] Other indicators may point to a more negative direction, for example Turkey's low rule of law ranking which includes topics of civil and criminal justice.[174] Yet, regarding this latter data, it may also be argued that these indicators are not specifically about transplanted rules but the enforcement of any laws in Turkey, including those not based on foreign legal models.

Second, contractual rules and soft laws applicable to companies are often based on models from economically powerful countries of the West, but the application of these rules may be somehow different in the transplant units. For example, a study on corporate acquisition contracts found that, while Japanese lawyers used provisions modelled on American-style contracts, courts then (mis-)interpreted these contracts based on Japanese principles of contract interpretation.[175] We can also observe the globalisation of voluntary rules of corporate conduct; yet, in some countries, these rules are not very relevant in practice. For example, while the idea of firms following a voluntary corporate

[169] Erhan Taş, 'Kabul Sürecinde Türk Medeni Kanunu'na Yönelik Bazı Eleştiriler' (2018) 9 *Bingöl Üniversitesi Sosyal Bilimler Enstitüsü Dergisi* 1.

[170] Şafak Uğurlu, 'Türk Hukuk Devrimi ve Bu Devrimde Ankara Hukuk Mektebi'nin Yeri ve Önemi' (2009) 85 *Turkiye Barolar Birligi Dergisi* 414.

[171] Hirsch (n 26) 18 (for the role of foreign academics and translations of commentaries) and 21 (distinguished from prior receptions where the transplanted law remained foreign); Erdem Büyüksagis, 'What Europeans Can Learn from an Untold Story of Transjudicial Communication: The Swiss/Turkish Experience' in Mads Andenas and Duncan Fairgrieve (eds), *Courts and Comparative Law* (Oxford: OUP, 2015) 680.

[172] June Starr, *Dispute and Settlement in Rural Turkey: An Ethnography of Law* (Leiden: EJ Brill, 1978). For a mixed more recent assessment, also with a focus on family structures, see Zeynep Özlem Üskül Engin, 'Medeni Kanun ve Toplumsal Dönüşüm' in Fethi Gedikli (ed), *I. Turk Hukuk Tarihi Kongresi Bildirileri* (Istanbul: XII Levha Yayinlari, 2014) 31, 36–42.

[173] CEPEJ (European Commission for the Efficiency of Justice), *European judicial systems—CEPEJ Evaluation report—2024 Evaluation cycle (2022 data)*, available at https://www.coe.int/en/web/cepej/cepej-work/evaluation-of-judicial-systems accessed 23 October 2025 at pp 42, 82, and 118.

[174] See https://worldjusticeproject.org/rule-of-law-index/country/2025/T%C3%BCrkiye/ accessed 30 December 2025.

[175] Akio Hoshi, 'Interpretation of Corporate Acquisition Contracts in Japan: A Legal Transplant through Contract Drafting' (2021) 16 *Asian Journal of Comparative Law* 106.

governance code has spread from the UK and the OECD to other parts of the world, these codes are not treated as equally important by firms everywhere in the world.[176] In a further example, a quantitative study of codes of conduct of MNEs to protect worker standards found that adherence to such standards depends on a multitude of factors related to the country where the factory is located (eg, its domestic labour law and the level of pressure by consumers).[177]

On the right panel of Figure 5.6, the responses related to these intermediate examples are displayed with multiple lines. For example, soft laws (or contractual rules) may 'fit' the conditions of a country well and therefore be applied immediately in some places while in others their application is limited—though it may rise over time. In this sense, Turkey can also be seen as an example where the transplanted rules have over time been more often complied with and/or enforced,[178] while the extent of this rise may be a matter of debate. Moreover, for both sets of intermediate examples, differences from the level of compliance in the origin unit may be connected to variations of the actual law, and thus we may lack a precise counterfactual to the situation in the origin unit.

The following two positive examples are specifically about the way agents facilitate the compliance and enforcement of the law. They are presented here as showing that transplants can 'work'; yet they also imply that, without such agents, the result would have been different (and thus they overlap with the intermediate examples, see also Figure 5.6 with the possibility that agents only later make a transplant work better).

First, literature on the British colonial empire examines how agents ensured that, within the spheres that applied the common law,[179] this law was also complied with and enforced. The political economist Valentin Seidler has examined the role of colonial officers in the British empire in detail, amongst others making use of empirical historical records. Specifically, his research shows how well-trained British and local officers played a key role in colonial administration, the success of transplants, and their persistence today.[180] There

[176] Eg William E Daniel, 'Corporate Governance in Indonesian Listed Companies—A Problem of Legal Transplant' (2003) 15 *Bond Law Review* 345. A previous website also tracked the application of such codes, see https://web.archive.org/web/20170822221337/http://www.ecgcn.org:80/Monitoring-Reports.aspx accessed 23 October 2025.

[177] Michael W Toffel, Jodi L Short, and Melissa Ouellet, 'Codes in Context: How States, Markets, and Civil Society Shape Adherence to Global Labor Standards' (2015) 9 *Regulation and Governance* 205. See also Jodi L Short, 'Transplanting Law in a Globalized World: Private Transnational Regulation and the Legal Transplant Paradigm' in Francesca Bignami and David Zaring (eds), *Comparative Law and Regulation: Understanding the Global Regulatory Process* (Cheltenham: Edward Elgar, 2016) 430.

[178] Cf also Hirsch (n 26) 128 (the term 'reception' referring to a process of long duration).

[179] See Section C 2 (b), for the continuing role of indigenous rules.

[180] Valentin Seidler, 'Colonial Bureaucrats, Institutional Transplants, and Development in the 20th Century' (2016) 1 *Administory* 237; Valentin Seidler, 'Institutional Copying in the 20th Century: The Role of 14,000 British Colonial Officers' (2017) 137 *Journal of Contextual Economics* 93.

is also a large literature on British colonial history, including its use of laws (eg, in India),[181] with frequent references to the importance of different types of agents: for example, the establishment of English courts in the early colonial period to hear disputes between English citizens,[182] the subsequent integration of British and local court systems, as well as the use of local personnel to create 'strong judicial institutions with deep ties to the local populace, well-equipped to respond effectively to shifts in citizen demands',[183] and the ongoing links among judges and courts from common law countries.[184]

Second, it has been noted that in some situations the transplantation of human rights law has worked well in terms of compliance and enforcement. In a study by Sally Merry, the emphasis was on the way transplanted rules can be made 'vernacular'. Specifically, based on qualitative empirical work, Merry explains how, in the context of gender violence, social movements by human rights lawyers, feminist activists, and social workers translate human rights norms locally, for example, launching gender training programs and counselling centres but also raising the legal consciousness of the general population.[185] Further support for the working of transplanted human rights can come from the role of courts. For example, it has been suggested that the highest courts of South Africa and India apply human rights in an expansive manner;[186] there is also some evidence of judicial dialogue in human rights law with some suggesting an emerging '*ius commune* of human rights' based on comparative reasoning.[187]

To be sure, such positive cases of transplanting human rights are not universal. For example, a monograph on German legal transplants in the constitution of Thailand finds that the Constitutional Court of Thailand has been unwilling to monitor the respect for human rights.[188] This is explained with reference to the underlying politics of the court as it closely follows the interests

[181] See Chapter 1 at Section B 2.
[182] Halpérin (n 106) 19.
[183] Daniels and others (n 106) 131, 147.
[184] See Chapter 4 at Section C 3 (a).
[185] Sally E Merry, *Human Rights and Gender Violence: Translating International Law into Local Justice* (Chicago, IL: University of Chicago Press Merry, 2006) 134–78.
[186] See eg Daniel Bonilla Maldonado (ed), *Constitutionalism of the Global South: The Activist Tribunals of India, South Africa and Colombia* (Cambridge: CUP, 2013); Neha Jain, 'The Democratizing Force of International Law: Human Rights Adjudication by the Indian Supreme Court' in Anthea Roberts and others (eds), *Comparative International Law* (Oxford: OUP, 2018) 319.
[187] Andrew J Harding and Peter Leyland, 'Comparative Law in Constitutional Context' in Esin Örücü and David Nelken (eds), *Comparative Law: A Handbook* (Oxford: Hart Publishing, 2007) 313, 328. For further references to this literature see Siems (n 30) 114.
[188] Poonthep Sirinupong, *Same Same But Different: Grundgesetzimport und Verfassungsmutation in Thailand* (Baden-Baden: Nomos, 2022) 214.

of the government and the king. However, sometimes, politics can change. For example, a study of six Asian countries (China, India, Japan, Korea, Malaysia, and Taiwan) in the second part of the twentieth century notes that transplants in many areas of law were initially rarely enforced; however, since the 1980s, this improved in some of these countries due to political support for stronger enforcement.[189]

As already indicated in Merry's notion of 'vernacularisation', the finding that transplanted rules work in practice does not mean that they work exactly in the way as in the origin unit. The qualitative empirical work by Sapna Reheem Shaila points in a similar direction. She examines the transfer of rule of law reforms in East Timor, focussing on the way the dynamics between different groups influenced the localisation of the reform. Thus, it is crucial how non-domestic norms 'settle' at the local level.[190] Overall, her research thus cautions against binary views of success or failures but rather emphasises how reforms can lead to 'the gradual shift in normative standards and attitudes'.[191]

(c) Conclusion

The conclusion of the previous section emphasised the time dimension of a transplant, ie that often only after some time a transplant may really be known and understood. In this section too, many of the examples show that it can be premature to claim that transplants do not work because they are not immediately widely complied with and enforced. Rather experience shows that, over time, many transplants can become the 'law in practice' of the transplant unit. In other words, the internal and external legal culture of a country (or other unit) can change and thus accommodate the operation of the transplanted law.

Another striking feature of many of the examples has been the role of agents in shaping the compliance and enforcement of law. This insight further implies that the way transplants work in practice depends on changing the way individuals and groups (including lawyers, judges, etc) think and operate. The feasibility of such changes can, of course, not be taken for granted; yet, many of the examples show that transplants can eventually work, even if they come from another legal family or culture. As far as there are problems in

[189] Katharina Pistor and Philip A Wellons, *The Role of Law and Legal Institutions in Asian Economic Development, 1960–1995* (New York: OUP, 1999) 4.

[190] For this notion, developed in the context of transnational legal orders, see Terence C Halliday and Gregory Shaffer, 'Transnational Legal Orders' in Terence C Halliday and Gregory Shaffer (eds), *Transnational Legal Orders* (Cambridge: CUP, 2015) 3, 5.

[191] Sapna Reheem Shaila, *A 'Good enough' Rule-of-law transfer and Adaptation? A Case Study of Transnational Rule-of-law Promotion in East Timor* (PhD thesis, King's College London, 2022); Sapna Reheem Shaila, 'A Translocal Compromise: Adoption of Anti-corruption Reforms in East Timor' (2025) 50 *Law & Social Inquiry* 406.

enforcement or compliance, this should also not lead to the plain conclusion of a failed transplant: as no laws are 'totally effective, totally obeyed, without dissent or noncompliance or nonuse',[192] legal transplants may often at least be partially successful, similar to many home-grown laws.

Moreover, we have seen that the law in practice will often be different in the origin and the transplant unit. This should also not come as a surprise, at least for those who do not believe that law and its context are fully independent of each other.[193] Indeed, as we will see later in this book, from a policy perspective, it would be inappropriate to insist that a transplant needs to function in exactly the same way in both of the units.[194]

4. Law has desired influence on society

Roger Cotterrell suggests that someone who regards 'law as culture' will call a transplant successful when the law is consistent with the environment of the transplant unit, and someone who regards 'law as an instrument' will do so when the law has the intended effect.[195] The instrumental variant is clearly about the societal influence that the transplant unit desires from adopting the transplant. However, the cultural variant can also be subsumed under this heading as a cultural fit is an aspiration that goes beyond the transplanted law simply being understood and applied, as discussed in the previous sections. Thus, beyond rare cases—say, a judicial transplant that only has the aim to improve a particular doctrinal construction—most transplants aim for some societal influence.

The structure of this section mirrors the previous two in that it discusses general factors and representative examples of research that have evaluated the effect of transplanted law on any aspects of society. Here, as already mentioned, the application of this evaluation also needs to consider that the same law may have diverse impacts on different parts of society.[196]

(a) General factors discussed in literature

Comparative law often examines the situation in which different laws from different countries function in a way that their societal effect is similar.[197] It has

[192] Friedman (n 1) 251.
[193] See discussion in Section B.
[194] See Chapter 7 at Section C 3.
[195] Roger Cotterrell, 'Is There a Logic of Legal Transplants?' in David Nelken and Johannes Feest (eds), *Adapting Legal Culture* (Oxford: Hart Publishing, 2001) 71, 79.
[196] See Section C 1.
[197] For an overview of such functional comparative law see Siems (n 30) 15–49.

been suggested that transplants may therefore be thought of as a form of 'inverted comparative law', namely that the situation here is that the law is, due to the transplant, similar in both units but the societal context is different.[198] For this latter situation, we have already seen that the 'realist' literature discusses whether and how the transplanted law may work differently in the transplant and origin units.[199] Thus, it can matter whether units are similar to each other, in terms of existing laws but also socio-culturally. For example, in the institutional literature, it is suggested that new 'foreign-introduced exogenous institutions' are likely to be more effective if they align with 'indigenously introduced endogenous institutions'.[200] Yet, such a similarity requirement should not be applied in a schematic way. For example, a study on transplants from the Soviet Union to Socialist Vietnam mentions their shared political ideology but then also the permutations of the transplants in Vietnam.[201] In the policy literature, we also find the statement that 'at times policy institutions taken from very different legal or cultural backgrounds happen to work out' while 'transplants coming from the very same "family of nations" occasionally fail'.[202]

Two of the classical books on transplants, by Papachristos and Hirsch, refer to the concept of 'acculturation' as a process to overcome the gap between law and context in the transplant unit.[203] Acculturation is also frequently used in (other) French writings on legal transplants, but also occasionally in other languages.[204] Papachristos discusses details on how this process can operate. He starts by referring to the general definition of acculturation as cases where

[198] Alexander Graser, 'Rechtsrezeptionsforschung als invertierte Rechtsvergleichung' in Nada Bodiroga-Vukobrat, Siniša Rodin, and Gerald G Sander (eds), *Globalisation and Legal Culture* (Berlin: Logos, 2013) 21.

[199] See Section B 3.

[200] Peter J Boettke, Christopher J Coyne, and Peter T Leeson, 'Institutional Stickiness and the New Development Economics' (2008) 67 *American Journal of Economics and Sociology* 331 (as a form of 'regression theorem').

[201] Penelope (Pip) Nicholson, *Borrowing Court Systems: The Experience of Socialist Vietnam* (Leiden: Martinus Nijhoff, 2007). See also Matthew Erie and Ha Hai Do, 'Law and Development Minus Legal Transplants: The Example of China in Vietnam' (2021) 8 *Asian Journal of Law and Society* 372.

[202] Konstantinos Lalenis, Martin de Jong, and Virginie Mamadouh, 'Families of Nations and Institutional Transplantation' in Martin de Jong, Konstantinos Lalenis, and Virginie Mamadouh (eds), *The Theory and Practice of Institutional Transplantation: Experiences with the Transfer of Policy Institutions* (Deventer: Kluwer Academic Publishers, 2002) 33, 45.

[203] Papachristos (n 70) 109; Hirsch (n 26) 26, 136.

[204] For the former see references in Dominik Dworniczak and others, 'The Notion of Legal Transplants Beyond the Anglosphere: Decentring the Debate' (2025) 16 *Transnational Legal Theory* 357, 367–8. For the latter see eg Jorge A Sánchez Cordero, 'The Process of Legal Acculturation—A Mexican Perspective' (Paper for International Congress of Comparative Law, Washington/DC 2010), available at https://archivos.juridicas.unam.mx/www/bjv/libros/7/3194/3.pdf accessed 2 December 2025; Alba Fondrieschi, 'Uniformazione del diritto ed esportabilità dei modelli giuridici: il caso del Giappone' (2015) 1 *Osservatorio del diritto civile e commerciale, Rivista semestrale* 153, 154 (with reference to Rodolfo Sacco's book on 'Antropologia giuridica').

the contact of individuals from different cultural groups leads to changes in cultural patterns of at least one of the groups.[205] He then shows that this has occurred in various instances due to legal transplants, such as in economic transformations and changes to family structures and concepts of property and contract.[206] He also indicates that the effect of acculturation on individuals and, thus, the mechanisms through which the transplanted law influences society should be a topic for interdisciplinary research, such as sociology of law.[207] Moreover, as in the previous categories, agents are likely to play a key role in making the foreign elements acceptable to the local context.

The gap between law and context in the transplant unit has also invited the response that it can be the aim of the transplant unit to change the context—and that this may succeed if government and courts are sufficiently attentive to the domestic social reality.[208] Others are more sceptical of the potential of legal transplants as a tool of legal engineering. For example, Jaakko Husa writes about the way 'deeply embedded belief systems' can pose limits to the ambitions to transform social reality through legal transplants.[209] From the perspective of institutional research, Martin de Jong recognises that lawmakers often hope that changes in the law would trigger the desired changes in cultural practices;[210] yet, he suggests that formal institutions not in line with informal ones (such as cultural practices) often remain dysfunctional.[211] It may also be the case that, in some areas of law, transplants are more problematic due to the likelihood of a cultural mismatch, akin to the view that the use of transplants differs across areas of law.[212]

As in the previous categories, it is possible that the social effect of a transplant may only occur after some time. In this sense, Tarde explains the delay in imitating others by saying that any imitation needs to overcome resistance based on prior influence.[213] In other words, there is path dependence at the individual as well as the societal level. This does not mean that society is always an impediment to transplants: as societies modernise, obstacles to transplants

[205] Referring to Robert Redfield, Ralph Linton, and Melville J Herskovits, 'Memorandum for the Study of Acculturation' (1936) 38 *American Anthropologist* 149.

[206] Papachristos (n 70) 119–30.

[207] Papachristos (n 70) 130–1.

[208] Lipstein (n 15) 81.

[209] Jaakko Husa, 'Developing Legal System, Legal Transplants, and Path Dependence: Reflections on the Rule of Law' (2018) 6 *The Chinese Journal of Comparative Law* 129, 149.

[210] De Jong and Mamadouh (n 145) 22.

[211] Martin de Jong and Suzan Stoter, 'Institutional Transplantation and the Rule of Law: How this Interdisciplinary Method Can Enhance the Legitimacy of International Organisations' (2009) 2 *Erasmus Law Review* 311, 319.

[212] See Chapter 4 at Section C 3 (d).

[213] Tarde (n 87) 166–67.

are likely to become smaller.[214] Even more fundamentally, it can be the case that societal factors have already changed and that the existing law of the transplant unit lags behind these changes. In many cases, this sequence may indeed be likely as social, political, and economic circumstances often change more rapidly than legal norms.[215] Thus, in such a situation, these societal factors are not a hurdle but the main driving forces for a legal transplant given that the origin unit had simply been faster to enact rules on this topic.[216]

(b) Representative examples

The following examples are again structured according to negative, intermediate, and positive cases (overview in Figure 5.7). In the present category, a key tool to evaluate the examples is that of counterfactual thinking. In other words, the aim is to compare whether the relevant societal variable would have been different with or without the respective transplant.

A first negative example is the mistaken use of Western laws in the developing world. This is meant to refer to the large number of critics of the field of 'law and development' as the latter often includes the use of legal transplants. For example, Frank Upham criticises the way Western countries and development organisations have pushed for the enactment of formal property laws as a means to stimulate economic growth, disregarding the role of pre-existing property structures.[217] Paul Carrington criticises exports of US law as cases of unsuccessful legal transplants due to a lack of sensitivity of the American exporters but also their personal and political interests.[218] Considering the situation in specific transplant units, a number of publications from Latin America criticise various transplants in Columbia, Mexico, and Peru as having been insensitive to the local context.[219] In another work, the export of Western law to

[214] Already noted by Otto Kahn-Freund, 'On Uses and Misuses of Comparative Law' (1974) 37 *Modern Law Review* 1, 9.

[215] See generally Chapter 4 at Section C 3.

[216] See already Chapter 4 at Sections B 2 and C 3 (c).

[217] Frank K Upham, *The Great Property Fallacy: Theory, Reality, and Growth in Developing Countries* (Cambridge: CUP, 2018).

[218] Paul D Carrington, *Spreading America's Word: Stories of Its Lawyer-Missionaries* (New York: Twelve Tables, 2005). For details see also Jedidiah J Kroncke, *The Futility of Law and Development: China and the Dangers of Exporting American Law* (Oxford: OUP, 2016).

[219] José Manuel Castro Arango, 'La capitalización encubierta en la Reforma Tributaria de 2012: ¿trasplante legal o engendro legal?' (2014) 31 *Revista Derecho del Estado* 161; Laura Roldán Castellanos, 'Problemas en la regulación del programa de beneficios por colaboración en Colombia y posibles soluciones al respecto' (2017) 13(13) *Revista de derecho de la competencia CEDEC* 253; Juan Sebastian Palacios Parra, 'La Reincidencia Criminal Como un Trasplante Juridico Resiliente en el Ordenamiento Legal de Colombia y Mexico' (2018) 53 *Revista Jurídica Universidad Interamericana de Puerto Rico* 203; Guido César Águila Grados, 'Trasplante legal y jurisprudencial: patologías del derecho peruano en general y el procesal en particular' in Carina Gómez Fröde and Marco Ernesto Briseño

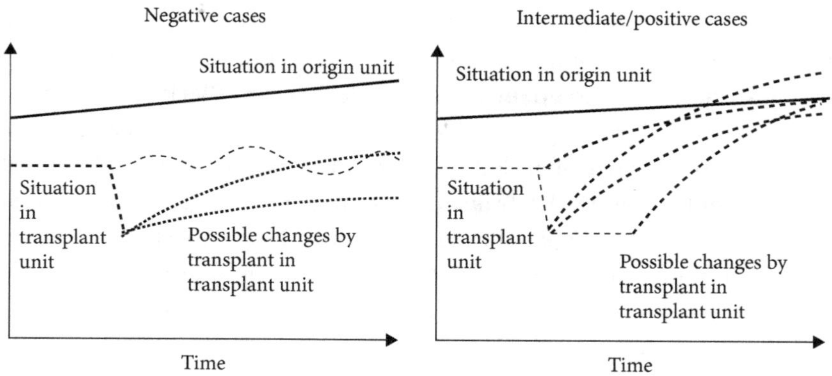

Figure 5.7 Socio-economic effect of transplant

Niger is presented in a negative light as it led to social unrest due to the disregard of existing traditions.[220] Further negative examples concern case studies of modern law reforms in Ghana, Senegal, and Micronesia.[221]

Second, the literature has discussed the failures of transplants in post-communist countries of Central and Eastern Europe. For example, according to Wade Channell, the transplanted laws did not lead to the desired effect as they were often drafted without the involvement of local stakeholders and did not address the systemic problems of many of these countries.[222] Others have referred to failed attempts of 'neoliberal' market reforms[223] and widespread problems of corruption.[224] More specifically, for example, authors from Poland criticise the unreflective transplantations of laws from US

García Carrillo (eds), *Nuevos Paradigmas del derecho procesal* (Mexico City: Universidad Nacional Autónoma de México, 2016) 821; León Hilario Leysser, *Derecho Privado. Parte general. Negocios, actos y hechos jurídicos* (Lima: Fondo Editorial PUCP, 2019) 15, 36.

220 Thomas A Kelley, 'Exporting Western Law to the Developing World: The Troubling Case of Niger' (2007) 7/3 *Global Jurist* article 8.

221 Robert C Pozen, 'Public Corporations in Ghana: A Case Study in Legal Importation' (1972) 3 *Wisconsin Law Review* 802; Julie Paquin, *Legal Reform and Business Contracts in Developing Economies: Trust, Culture, and Law in Dakar* (Abingdon: Routledge, 2012); Brian Z Tamanaha, *Understanding Law in Micronesia: An Interpretive Approach to Transplanted Law* (Leiden: Brill, 1993).

222 Wade Channell, 'Lessons Not Learned: Problems with Western Aid for Law Reform in Post-Communist Countries' (2006) 1 *The Journal of Comparative Law* 321, 322.

223 Ioannis Glinavos, *Neoliberalism and the Law in Post Communist Transition: The Evolving Role of Law in Russia's Transition to Capitalism* (Abingdon: Routledge, 2010).

224 Marina Kurkchiyan, 'The Impact of the Transition on the Role of Law in Russia' in Fred Bruinsma and David Nelken (eds), Explorations in Legal Culture, *Recht der Werkelijkheid* (special issue 2007) 75; Kathryn Hendley, '"Telephone Law" and the "Rule of Law": The Russian Case' (2009) 1 *Hague Journal on the Rule of Law* 241.

antitrust and German corporate law,[225] and Croatian authors observe that the transplant of EU competition law has faced both cultural and institutional obstacles.[226] In a frequently cited article, Bernard Black and colleagues write about the failures of privatisation and corporate governance in Russia, namely that the former often led to self-dealing by managers and controlling shareholders while the transplanted corporate rules remained ineffective.[227] The latter point can be supported by other research showing that transplanting rules of corporate law to countries with different shareholder ownership structures than in the origin country does not produce the same beneficial social outcomes.[228]

In the left chart of Figure 5.7, these negative examples are mainly about situations where a particular socio-economic variable (eg, GDP per capita) is said to drop with the introduction of the transplant. However, as the figure then also shows, it is possible that, after a while, the law shows a more positive effect. It may also be said that, in the two situations discussed here, there are also more positive examples: notably, many countries of the developing world and the former communist block have seen a rise in GDP per capita over time.[229] Furthermore, as illustrated by the curved line in the chart, socio-economic variables may change in an uneven manner due to multiple factors, with only some related to the transplanted law. Thus, in order to evaluate the socio-economic effect of transplants more robustly, we would need to have counterfactuals that can tell us, for example, how countries of the developing world or the former communist block would have evolved without any legal transplants. Such a desire to show a robust causal effect can be difficult to apply;[230] yet, the following examples will draw on some empirical work that aims to consider such counterfactual thinking.

[225] Rajmund Molski, 'Dysfunkcje prawa antymonopolowego' in Marian Zdyb, Emil Kruk, and Grzegorz Lubeńczuk (eds), *Dysfunkcje publicznego prawa gospodarczego* (Warsaw: CH Beck, 2018) 257; Paweł Błaszczyk, 'Pojęcie interesu grupy spółek jako kategoria wyjściowa dla polskiego prawa holdingowego' (2011) (19) *Monitor Prawniczy* 1029.

[226] Jasminka Pecotić Kaufman and Ružica Šimić Banović, 'The Role of (In)formal Governance and Culture in a National Competition System: A Case of a Post-Socialist Economy' (2021) 44 *World Competition* 81; Jasminka Pecotić Kaufman, 'On the Development of (Not So) New Competition Systems—Findings from an Empirical Study on Croatia' (2022) 10 *Journal of Antitrust Enforcement* 326.

[227] Bernard S Black, Reinier H Kraakman, and Anna Tarassova, 'Russian Privatization and Corporate Governance: What Went Wrong?' (2000) 52 *Stanford Law Review* 1731.

[228] Larsson-Olaison (n 56) 456; Katharina Pistor, 'The Standardization of Law and Its Effect on Developing Economies' (2002) 50 *American Journal of Comparative Law* 97, 127; Dan W Puchniak, 'The False Hope of Stewardship in the Context of Controlling Shareholders: Making Sense Out of the Global Transplant of a Legal Misfit' (2024) 72 *American Journal of Comparative Law* 109.

[229] For data see eg https://ourworldindata.org/economic-growth accessed 23 October 2025.

[230] For further discussion see Chapter 6 at Section C 3 (a).

The two intermediate examples are quantitative studies that have found that in some but not all units the effect is positive. The first one is a historical study by Giampaolo Lecce and Laura Ogliari on the effect of French law in nineteenth-century Prussia.[231] It makes use of the different extent to which French law played a role in different counties, measuring changes in economic performance based on wage data. Using other variables, notably religion as a proxy for cultural proximity with France, it finds that the transplanted laws had a positive effect on long-term economic performance in the counties that were culturally similar to France. In terms of econometric technique, the paper presents its findings as a 'quasi-natural experiment' given that the French impact was exogenous (and using the quasi-experimental method of a difference-in-difference analysis). However, in a critical comment, it has been noted that the non-randomness of the reforms—notably, with French law being more prevalent in Western Prussia—may be a challenge to the findings.[232]

The second example is a more general study by Daniel Berkowitz and colleagues that evaluated the different effects of 'receptive' and 'unreceptive' legal transplants.[233] They define 'receptiveness' in the way that the transplant country either had a baseline of similarity with the origin country as both belonged to the same legal family or that it adapted the transplant to the conditions of the transplant country. Data on this information was collected for forty-nine countries from 1800 to 2000. Subsequently, Berkowitz and colleagues established that having a receptive transplant is related to higher levels of legality (measured by variables, such as rule of law and absence of corruption) and that higher levels of legality are a determinant of better economic development. This study therefore provides the plausible finding that transplant units should not naively copy a model from anywhere in the world without adjustments to the local conditions.[234]

The answer from these studies that 'it depends' (see also Figure 5.7, right panel) is also in line with further quantitative research. For example, studies

[231] Giampaolo Lecce and Laura Ogliari, 'Institutional Transplant and Cultural Proximity: Evidence from Nineteenth-Century Prussia' (2019) 79 *Journal of Economic History* 1060.

[232] Jeremy Edwards, 'Can Institutional Transplants Work? A Reassessment of the Evidence from Nineteenth-Century Prussia' (CESifo Working Paper No 9333, 2021), available at https://ssrn.com/abstract=3938646 accessed 23 October 2025.

[233] Daniel Berkowitz, Katharina Pistor, and Jean-François Richard, 'The Transplant Effect' (2003) 51 *American Journal of Comparative Law* 163; Daniel Berkowitz, Katharina Pistor, and Jean-François Richard, 'Economic Development, Legality, and the Transplant Effect' (2003) 47 *European Economic Review* 165. Applying the same data: Tay-Cheng Ma, 'Legal Transplant, Legal Origin, and Antitrust Effectiveness' (2013) 9 *Journal of Competition Law & Economics* 65.

[234] For the design of transplants see also Chapter 7.

on the transplantation of international human rights laws on 'de facto' measurements of human rights[235] have led to mixed results: some found a positive result but also variations according to the political system, economic development, and the time passed after the enactment of the right.[236] The general challenge of any of the studies presented here as intermediate cases is whether they are really able to show that certain rules have causally led to a particular outcome. One response may be that causal identification is a general challenge for social sciences (including empirical legal studies),[237] not limited to the evaluation of the effect of legal transplants. Another response is that case studies could be preferable as means to show the precise effect of a law, which thus leads us to the following examples.

The first example of a positive case is the law of Singapore as a transplant from English law. For example, a book by the economic historian Niall Ferguson refers to the 'downloading' of Western ideas, such as strong protection of property rights, as one of the reasons for Singapore's economic wealth.[238] Others doubt how true Singaporean law is to its original English legacy. For example, it has been suggested that the 'Singapore model of law and development' is different from the English model as it relies more on an interventionist state as a means of promoting development; in other words, 'the transplant grew into something substantially different from its domestic root'.[239] From a different perspective, UK policymakers are now advised to learn from Singapore's more flexible and innovation-friendly laws.[240] Yet, despite any such differences, there is also evidence that some elements of Singapore's law which are closely tied to the English model are indeed part of its success story. In international commerce, Singaporean law is a popular choice of contract law,[241] and Singapore is one of the main centres for institutional arbitration.[242] Singapore also ranks

[235] Usually, based on the CIRI Human Rights Data, www.humanrightsdata.com accessed 23 October 2025.

[236] For these studies see eg Adam S Chilton and Mila Versteeg, *How Constitutional Rights Matter* (Oxford: OUP, 2020) 70–7; Kevin L Cope, Cosette D Creamer, and Mila Versteeg, 'Empirical Studies of Human Rights Law' (2019) 15 *Annual Review of Law and Social Science* 155.

[237] See Chapter 6 at Section C 3 (a).

[238] Niall Ferguson, *Civilization: The West and the Rest* (New York: Penguin Press, 2011) 306.

[239] Connie Carter, *Eyes on the Prize: Law and Economic Development in Singapore* (The Hague: Kluwer Law International, 2002) 60. See also Andrew J Harding and Connie Carter, 'The Singapore Model of Law and Development: Cutting Through Complexity' in John Hatchard and Amanda Perry-Kessaris (eds), *Law and Development: Facing Complexity in the 21st Century* (London: Cavendish, 2003) 191.

[240] 'The UK has a lot to learn from speedy Singapore' (*Financial Times*, 18 June 2025); 'UK financial regulators should copy Singapore model, say peers' (*Financial Times*, 13 June 2025).

[241] Gilles Cuniberti, 'The Laws of Asian International Business Transactions' (2016) 25 *Washington International Law Journal* 35.

[242] See eg https://www.globalarbitrationnews.com/2025/09/25/arbitration-statistics-2024-arbitration-is-the-preferred-method-of-dispute-resolution-for-large-disputes/ accessed 30 December 2025.

highly in measures of the rule of law[243] and global competitiveness.[244] Thus, a fair assessment seems that at least some elements of English law are among the determinants of Singapore's economic success.

Second, modern technical transplants can be positive examples that (simply) work well. Detailed road traffic rules, for instance, only emerged with the rise of automobiles in the 1920s, and many of these rules were then transplanted across countries. Specifically, European countries initially provided different rules on whether cars should drive on the left or the right, and some countries even had different driving directions in different parts of the country.[245] For the latter countries, it seems obvious that it was a good decision to eventually choose one of the two main models. Moreover, Sweden shifted from driving on the left to driving on the right in 1967. At that point in time, most Swedish cars already had the wheel on the left-hand side (which makes it safer to drive on the right) and the neighbouring countries were also driving on the right, and thus the change led indeed to the expected reduction of traffic accidents.[246] To provide a further example, we can consider the transplantation of a system of criminal sanctions that distinguishes between the income of the offender. Such a 'day fine system' has been transplanted from Scandinavian to other European countries,[247] and the success of this transplant is simply that the application of these rules led to the desired fairness in distinguishing between high- and low-income offenders.

These specific examples may raise the critical comment that the positive societal impact of the transplant can only be affirmed for these specific cases. In other words, the external validity of these examples may be limited. For example, Singapore seems to benefit from certain legal rules as a small jurisdiction with a distinct specialisation,[248] possibly even in a way that these rules work 'better' than in the origin country (see also Figure 5.7, right panel); yet, this may not be generalisable. Also, regarding technical transplants, there may also be examples where differences in the environment change their societal

[243] https://worldjusticeproject.org/rule-of-law-index/country/2025/Singapore accessed 30 December 2025 (notably 'absence of corruption', 'order and security', 'regulatory enforcement', and 'civil justice').

[244] https://worldcompetitiveness.imd.org/ accessed 23 October 2025.

[245] For an illustration see https://brilliantmaps.com/driving-side-of-the-road-in-europe-in-1922/ accessed 2 December 2025.

[246] https://www.bbc.com/worklife/article/20180417-a-thrilling-mission-to-get-the-swedish-to-change-overnight accessed 23 October 2025. See also Felix Roesel, 'The Causal Effect of Wrong-hand Drive Vehicles on Road Safety' (2017) 11–12 *Economics of Transportation* 15.

[247] Thomas Weigend, 'Criminal Law and Criminal Procedure' in Jan M Smits and others (eds), *Elgar Encyclopedia of Comparative Law* (Cheltenham: Edward Elgar, 3rd edn, 2023) 483, 484–5.

[248] See generally Christopher M Bruner, *Re-Imagining Offshore Finance: Market-Dominant Small Jurisdictions in a Globalizing Financial World* (Oxford: OUP, 2016).

effect.[249] However, beyond such scepticism, it can be noted that quantitative empirical research found that there is typically a positive effect of the rule of law and property rights (both widely understood) on economic prosperity;[250] thus, the findings from the positive examples are, at least, in line with the general suitability of certain laws to pursue certain aims.

(c) Conclusion

Of the three categories discussed in this section, the societal effect of the transplanted law is the most complex one. It relates to the general debate about the interaction between law and society. It is also connected to the general question of whether we can really be sure how exactly law impacts on society, and what kind of empirical methods are best suited to research it. For legal transplants in particular, it is likely to be a challenge that they are often included in a law reform that combines them with other changes to the law. Moreover, the transplant may be modified from the version of the origin country or else go through a process of acculturation that makes it difficult to say precisely whether and how the transplant 'worked'.

Still, the examples discussed here show that often it can be said that transplants have a desired influence on society. This may even happen for transplants between units that are relatively different, for example in terms of belonging to different cultures and legal families. Thus, law often seems to be quite adaptable to the different context of the transplant unit. Naturally, this does not always happen automatically and immediately but requires adjustments of the transplant. Notably, it will often be relevant that, to refer to the previous categories, transplants are properly understood and applied in the transplant unit in order to increase the likelihood that they have a positive societal effect.

A deliberate limitation of this section has been that it did not address the actual normative question of whether the 'desired influence on society' is something lawmakers should pursue. This will be the topic of the subsequent Chapter 6. In this next chapter, it will also be discussed how far, in today's interconnected world, it really makes sense to think about the effect of the law at the level of individual units, or whether we need to (also) address how law operates across societies, be it in a positive or negative manner.

249 See eg Mariana Mota Prado, 'Diffusion, Reception and Transplantation' in Peter Cane and others (eds), *The Oxford Handbook of Comparative Administrative Law* (Oxford: OUP, 2020) 258, 259 (for transplants of independent regulatory agencies).

250 See references and discussion in Chapter 6 at Section C 3 (a).

D. Conclusion

Do legal transplants 'work'? This chapter started with a presentation of three general positions of the literature. Yet, each of them has its shortcomings: Watson's 'optimist' view is problematic as it does not consider the importance of the socio-economic context of the law; the 'pessimist' view is inconsistent with the many examples of transplants successfully happening throughout history; and some versions of the 'realist' view are too schematic in claiming that it all depends on the 'fit' with the society of the transplant unit as there have also been cases of successful transplants in different socio-economic contexts.

Such general positions also fail to consider that transplants can work at different levels. This chapter presented three ways transplants may or may not work, namely according to the categories 'knowledge and understanding of the law', 'compliance and enforcement', and 'desired societal influence'. It found that it is typically the case that a positive response in the category knowledge and understanding of the law is more straightforward than compliance and enforcement, and that both are more straightforward than achieving the desired influence on society. However, this chapter has also shown that transplants often do manage to have a positive societal influence as lawmakers want transplants to be meaningful and thus choose and design them in a manner so that they can have such an effect.[251]

To be sure, measuring precisely how transplants work is challenging due to the three categories necessitating the use of different methods. Thus, beyond the cautiously positive assessment of whether transplants 'do' work, the findings of this chapter have also contributed to the question of the circumstances which determine 'how' transplants work. For example, it discussed the possible roles of legal families, areas of law, and contextual differences. Specifically, this chapter has found that, in many of the examples, transplants are adjusted to their new host environment, often with the contribution of agents. This should not lead us to say that we cannot call this influence a legal transplant; rather, these adjustments are often necessary to ensure that the transplant can work as intended. In particular, this means that there is a benefit of transplants being based on a rational design, though this does not exclude the use of certain shortcuts such as legal families.[252]

[251] Thus, this finding also reflects the fact that, today, we typically have voluntary legal transplants, see Chapter 4.

[252] For further details see Chapter 7 at Section C.

Another finding has been that, while a short time horizon may lead to a negative conclusion, over the long run many transplants become indigenised in the sense that they can work similarly to other laws. The subsequent chapter will answer the question how far the time dimension is a relevant consideration in assessing whether a transplant should be used.[253] There is also a natural link to the next chapter as this chapter has found that, at least, transplants are not irrelevant and, thus, it is a valid question to ask whether their use should be supported from a normative perspective.

[253] Chapter 6 at Section C 3 (c).

6

Is it Desirable to Use Legal Transplants?

A. Introduction

The previous two chapters have touched on some topics that are related to an assessment of the desirability of legal transplants. For example, the insight of Chapter 4, that today many transplants are voluntary, and the finding of Chapter 5, that transplants typically work, may both speak in favour of transplanted laws. However, the ultimate normative question of whether a transplant should happen is not fully determined by such empirical information; in other words, 'is' and 'ought' may not always be aligned.[1]

This chapter asks whether it is desirable to use legal transplants. This general question may often lead to the response that it depends on the circumstances of a particular case (ie the respective units and the object) whether a particular transplant should be supported. In this chapter, a key objective is therefore to develop normative criteria that should guide this decision. In addition, it will discuss how some authors express general tendencies on whether or not transplants should be used. These views have a heuristic value. Moreover, the differentiated view presented here also aims to explore whether it is typically the case that transplants should be supported.

As in the previous chapters of this book, this chapter also draws on research from outside legal scholarship. The two main types of such research are, on the one hand, studies from ethics and political theory that have explored when it can be said that a particular rule is 'good law'. On the other hand, the answer to this question may depend on empirically proven determinants for such laws and, thus, the following also considers research in fields such as applied economics and political science.

The structure of this chapter is as follows. Section B starts with a review of the literature that has expressed general tendencies of whether or not transplants should be used. These publications point towards certain arguments that are explored in detail in Section C, suggesting a differentiated view. Specifically,

[1] For details see Section C 1.

Legal Transplants. Mathias Siems, Oxford University Press. © Mathias Siems 2026.
DOI: 10.1093/9780191991981.003.0006

this section addresses the relevance of the 'is/ought' relationship, followed by criteria on the acceptability of legal transplants. Section D concludes that law-makers should be open to the use of legal transplants.

B. Views of literature expressing general tendencies

Is it helpful to express general views about the desirability of legal transplants? Athanase Papachristos is sceptical as he writes that it is difficult to condemn reception as a legislative method as a whole, and that research of legal sociology cannot be simply for or against legal transplants but should rather provide suggestions for their adjustments.[2] Indeed, it can be said that all legal systems of the world have experienced some influence from other systems, while they also have certain features which are unique to them. Thus, it may seem to create strawmen to argue fully in favour or against legal transplants.

However, in the literature, we do find some general supporters and opponents of legal transplants. These authors have strongly shaped the normative debate about legal transplants—together with the equally antagonistic, and sometimes overlapping, positions on the way transplants work.[3] In addition, this literature provides some historical context to the controversies surrounding questions about the desirability of legal transplants.

1. General supporters

Jeremy Bentham's work can be seen as the first prominent publication that generally supported legal transplants. For example, he wrote that 'laws need not be of the wild and spontaneous growth of the country to which they are given' and that a non-prejudicial lawmaker would be able 'to make laws for one country as for another'.[4] The test case for his analysis was the transplantation of English law to Bengal which, in his own words, was a place 'as different as can be'.[5] Here, however, another of Bentham's positions also becomes apparent, namely that he regarded elements of English law as problematic: thus, his actual suggestion

[2] Athanase C Papachristos, *La réception des droits privés étrangers comme phénomène de sociologie juridique* (Paris: LGDJ, 1975) 4 and 143.

[3] See Chapter 5 at Section B.

[4] Jeremy Bentham, 'Of the Influence of Time and Place in Matters of Legislation' in John Bowring, *The Works of Jeremy Bentham, Volume i* (Edinburgh: William Tate, 1838–1843) 169, 180.

[5] Bentham (n 4) 172.

was that a new system 'might be devised, which, while it would be better for Bengal, would also be better even for England'.[6] This type of advice is tied to his more general idea of a global utilitarian law called Pannomion, consisting of codified law and being, in principle, suitable for any country.[7]

Rudolf von Jhering has been compared with Bentham due to his utilitarian leanings.[8] This can also be seen in his fairly general support for legal transplants. A translated quote in Zweigert and Kötz from Jhering's book on Roman law is frequently cited in the literature, namely that the 'reception of foreign legal institutions is not a matter of nationality, but of usefulness and need. No one bothers to fetch a thing from afar when he has one as good or better at home, but only a fool would refuse quinine just because it didn't grow in his back garden.'[9] In the original version of Jhering's book, we also find some further statements worth quoting: in the context of the aforementioned quote, Jhering mentions the parallel to other phenomena that cross borders ('as if we mind to import foreign wine because we didn't press it'); for law in particular, he praises the fact that, in the past, Roman law fostered communication about legal thought across European countries ('What an uplifting feeling this community had, and how enviable the state of jurisprudence at the time!').[10]

In modern times, Basil Markesinis has been one the scholars most aligned with a general support for legal transplants. He regarded it as a key task of comparative law to 'increase intellectual interaction and borrowings'[11] and expressed the view that it is 'deeply rooted in human nature, to look around and borrow, where possible, good and tested ideas'.[12] From legal practice, the former US Justice Breyer justified his support for foreign case citations with

[6] Bentham (n 4) 185.

[7] Jeremy Bentham, 'Of Nomography' in John Bowring, *The Works of Jeremy Bentham, Volume iii* (Edinburgh: William Tate, 1838–1843) 231–96; but see also Bentham (n 4) 180 (lawmakers should be 'informed of the local situation'). See also Juan Pablo Couyoumdjian, 'Are Institutional Transplants Viable? An Examination in Light of the Proposals by Jeremy Bentham' (2012) 8 *Journal of Institutional Economics* 489.

[8] See the prefaces by Jospeph H Drake and WM Geldart in Rudolf von Ihering, *Law As A Means To An End* (Boston: The Boston Book Company, 1913) [published in German as 'Der Zweck im Recht' in 1877], notably Drake at xvii ('To American lawyers Ihering is known as the German Bentham') but then also xix (Jhering more concerned with the interest of society than the interest of the individual).

[9] Konrad Zweigert and Hein Kötz, *An Introduction to Comparative Law* (Oxford: Clarendon, 3rd edn, 1998) 17.

[10] Rudolph von Jhering, *Geist des römischen Rechts auf den verschiedenen Stufen seiner Entwicklung, Erster Theil* (Leipzig: Breitkopf & Härtel, 3rd edn, 1873) 8 and 9 (own translations).

[11] Basil Markesinis, 'Our Debt to Europe: Past, Present and Future' in Basil Markesinis (ed), *The Coming Together of the Common Law and the Civil Law* (Oxford: Hart Publishing, 2000) 37, 49. See also Basil Markesinis, 'Comparative Law: A Subject in Search of an Audience' (1990) 53 *Modern Law Review* 1; Basil Markesinis, *Comparative Law in the Courtroom and Classroom: The Story of the Last Thirty-Five Years* (Oxford: Hart Publishing, 2003).

[12] Markesinis (2000) (n 11) 61.

the words: 'It is not the cosmopolitanism of some jurists that seeks this kind of engagement but the nature of the world itself that demands it.'[13] Beyond such general statements, some authors have attempted to show more fundamentally why comparative arguments should matter. For example, this can refer to the persuasive authority of foreign law, natural law principles, or other forms of legal universality.[14] The challenge is, however, that such universalist views have their own historical contingency. For example, they have often been tied to Aristotelian views, Christianity, or the Enlightenment,[15] while the belief in universal laws could also be based on Hindu and Islamic rules and values.[16]

Another reason in support of transplants is to regard law from an 'instrumentalist' and 'technological' perspective and argue that legal transplants are needed in order to solve social and economic problems, while dismissing opposition as 'parochialism'.[17] The historical context of such a view is found in the interconnected notions of 'modernisation theory' and 'law and development', ie that, after the Second World War, countries were advised to 'modernise' in order to stimulate their development, in particular their legal institutions, including courts and legal education.[18] In substance, this view argues that there are certain empirically-proven features of the law, such as secure property rights and an effective judicial system, that any country can implement in order to stimulate their development.[19] Moreover, the benefit of lowering economic transaction costs can be seen as a reason why transplants contribute to the evolution of efficient legal institutions.[20] Such a position is also supported

[13] Stephen Breyer, *The Court and the World: American Law and the New Global Realities* (New York: Knopf, 2015) 245. See also Stephen Breyer, 'Keynote Address: The Supreme Court And The New International Law' (2003) 97 *American Society of International Law Proceedings* 265, 267 ('cross-country results resemble each other more and more, exhibiting common, if not universal, principles in a variety of legal areas' and reflect 'a near universal desire for judicial institutions that, through guarantees of fair treatment, help to provide the security necessary for investment and, in turn, economic prosperity').

[14] See the discussion in Thomas Coendet, 'Legal Reasoning: Arguments from Comparison' (2016) 102 *Archiv für Rechts- und Sozialphilosophie* 476, 477–8; Thomas Coendet, *Rechtsvergleichende Argumentation: Phänomenologie der Veränderung im rechtlichen Diskurs* (Tübingen: Mohr Siebeck, 2012) 12–16; Papachristos (n 2) 5 (citing Giorgio del Vecchio). See also Section C 2 (b).

[15] See eg James Gordley, 'The Universalist Heritage' in Pierre Legrand and Roderick Munday (eds), *Comparative Legal Studies: Traditions and Transitions* (Cambridge: CUP, 2003) 31; Mathias Siems, *Comparative Law* (Cambridge: CUP, 3rd edn, 2022) 35–6.

[16] Bishal Khanal, *Legal Reform Via Reception of Law* (Kathmandu: Bhrikuti Academic Publications, 2018) 122, 132–3.

[17] Edgardo Buscaglia and William Ratliff, *Law and Economics in Developing Countries* (Stanford, CA: Hoover Institution Press, 2000) 31.

[18] Overview in Frank H Stephen, *Law and Development: An Institutional Critique* (Cheltenham: Edward Elgar, 2018) 3–9.

[19] For references see Section C 3 (a).

[20] Michele Graziadei, 'Comparative Law as the Study of Transplants and Receptions' in Mathias Reimann and Reinhard Zimmermann (eds), *The Oxford Handbook of Comparative Law* (Oxford: OUP, 2nd edn, 2019) 442, 461.

by some international development organisations, notably the World Bank and the IMF, which use their financial influence and soft power to make countries adopt certain rules seen by them as necessary for the structural improvements of their legal systems.[21]

2. General opponents

Parallel to the previous subsection, it is tempting to present two 'classical' authors as general opponents of legal transplants: Montesquieu and Savigny. According to Montesquieu's *The Spirit of Laws*, laws should reflect the climate, geography, culture, and character of a nation, and thus it is very unlikely that the laws of one nation suit another.[22] Specifically, the book elaborates on the way different climates are said to explain different behaviours of peoples,[23] while subsequent authors have criticised Montesquieu for stereotyping people on that basis.[24] Savigny is most well-known for his historical analysis of Roman law. Yet, his book *Of the Vocation of Our Age for Legislation and Jurisprudence* has a more political dimension as he argued against proposals to enact Codes in Germany (as happened in France) since, in his view, this would break the link between the law and the people. Specifically, he writes that 'the law, as well as the language, exists in the consciousness of the people' and that there is an 'organic connection of law with the being and character of the people'.[25] Thus, this mirrors the statements by Montesquieu.[26]

In the writings by both Montesquieu and Savigny, we thus see a preference for historically home-grown law, but it may not be entirely clear how far, time-travelling to today's world, they would really be general opponents of legal transplants. Montesquieu's statement about deep differences between national cultures (due to climate etc) can be read as implying that, as far as there are

[21] See Chapter 4 at Section C 3 (b).

[22] Charles de Secondat Montesquieu, *The Spirit of Laws* (London: G Bell & Sons, 1914 [original from 1748]), Book I, Chapter III.

[23] Montesquieu (n 22) in Books XIV to XVIII.

[24] See the discussion in Ralf Michaels, 'Climate's Empire in Comparative Law' (2023) 28 *Tilburg Law Review* 1. For some confirmation by psychological research see Evert Van de Vliert, Brett Pelham, and Joseph A Vandello, 'East-West Beliefs Challenged by North-South Evidence about Collectivism versus Individualism' (2025) 101 *Journal of Environmental Psychology* 102498.

[25] Frederick Charles von Savigny, *The Vocation of Our Age for Legislation and Jurisprudence* (London: Littlewood, 1831 [original from 1814]) 25 and 27. See also Andreas Rahmatian, 'Friedrich Carl von Savigny's Beruf and Volksgeistlehre' (2007) 28 *The Journal of Legal History* 1.

[26] Cf also Michele Graziadei, 'Legal Transplants and the Frontiers of Legal Knowledge' (2009) 10 *Theoretical Inquiries in Law* 723, 726 fn 4 ('The influence of Montesquieu on Savigny is obvious'). Yet, Savigny's book only contains two short citations of Montesquieu.

no such differences, he may be willing to accept transplants. With respect to Savigny, it has been noted that interpreting his connection between the people and law as a complete rejection of any foreign legal influence does not align with his endorsement of Roman law in Germany.[27] Thus, it may also be said that Montesquieu and Savigny 'merely' emphasised the role of the context that any decision about a transplant needs to consider. In this regard, their views may thus be similar to modern authors who suggest that there are often complementarities between the law, society, culture, and politics of a particular country, as well as complementarities between different legal topics. We have already seen in the previous chapter that this emphasis on context leads some authors to conclude that certain transplants often 'do not work'. Within the present chapter, the context of the law will feature in the discussion about the suitability of a transplant.[28]

Another line of objections starts with the more positivistic stance that 'law is the expression of the will of the state',[29] or, more generally, that each country, or other unit, has its own source of legitimacy and that it should not 'outsource' this task to 'a global marketplace'.[30] Extending such an argument to the importance of democratic legitimation, it has also been suggested that Watson's insight that 'lawyer-elites' are the main driving force for legal transplants may actually be an argument against their use.[31] On the specific topic of foreign case law, some conservative voices from the US are also close to this position. For example, the late Justice Scalia stated that 'this Court . . . should not impose foreign moods, fads, or fashions on Americans',[32] and, according to Richard Posner, if there are useful legal ideas developed abroad, it is only for the legislator to consider adopting such rules.[33] In this US context, such a position can be linked to the contentious notion of 'originalism' (ie that the US Constitution should be interpreted in its original meaning),[34] as well as a more

[27] Stefan Kirchner, 'Limits of Legal Transplants' (2021) 7 *International Comparative Jurisprudence* 126, 129–30; FP Walton, 'The Historical School of Jurisprudence and Transplantations of Law' (1927) 9 *Journal of Comparative Legislation and International Law* 183, 187 (most German law 'did not grow out of the consciousness of the German people' but 'bears the stamp of the Roman mind').

[28] See Section C 3.

[29] Graziadei (n 20) 465.

[30] Upendra Baxi, '"Ordering" Constitutional Transfers: A View from India' in Günter Frankenberg (ed), *Order from Transfer: Comparative Constitutional Design and Legal Culture* (Cheltenham: Edward Elgar, 2013) 189, 194.

[31] Pier Giuseppe Monateri, 'The Weak Law: Contaminations and Legal Cultures' (2003) 13 *Transnational Law and Contemporary Problems* 575, 581. For Watson see generally Chapter 5 at Section B 1.

[32] *Lawrence v Texas* 123 Ct 2472, 2495 (2003) (Scalia J).

[33] Richard A Posner, 'Foreword: A Political Court' (2005) 199 *Harvard Law Review* 32.

[34] For the problems of defining this term see Lawrence B Solum, 'What is Originalism? The Evolution of Contemporary Originalist Theory' in Grant Huscroft and Bradley W Miller (eds), *The Challenge of Originalism: Theories of Constitutional Interpretation* (Cambridge: CUP, 2011) 12.

general belief in US legal exceptionalism.[35] However, there are also examples from other countries where courts have opposed the incorporation of norms and ideas from other legal systems into their domestic law,[36] for instance, as a turn against the liberal model of a 'global constitutionalism'.[37]

Criticism of legal transplants also comes from the political left. A version of identity politics argues that one's group identity is so essential that persons from other groups should not act as if they are of this group.[38] Applying such a strong view of 'cultural appropriation' to law[39] may mean that legal systems, like cultures, should be kept relatively separate and that each should follow its own path of development. Thus, rather than using transplants, differences between legal systems should remain as we should 'celebrate plurality', acknowledge that 'difference often drives creativity' and reject any 'suppression of local knowledge'.[40] This view can also be connected to a stance that is sceptical about the use of comparative law for policy recommendations: according to Pierre Legrand, '[t]here cannot be a "better" law. The very notion is fallacious. Who could finally and definitively say what it is?'[41] Thus, this position rejects the aforementioned view of law as an instrument for solving problems.

Another general left-wing critique is that the choice between different models is seen as inherently favouring those of rich and powerful countries, international organisations, and private interests. To support this position, reference may be made to dark elements of the history of legal transplants. In the words of Katharina Pistor: 'Transplanting law from the core to the periphery has its origins in colonialism and has always been closely associated with further commerce, trade and investment for the entrepreneurs from the core, or for coding their private wealth'.[42] From such a perspective, it is

[35] See discussion in Siems (n 15) 74–7.

[36] See Christopher Roberts, *Foreign Law? Congress v. the Supreme Court* (El Paso: LFB Scholarly Publishing LLC, 2014) 146.

[37] Alessandra Di Martino, 'Circolazione delle soluzioni giuridiche e delle idee costituzionali. Questioni di metodo comparativo e prassi tra culture costituzionali e spazi globali' (2022) 50 *DPCE Online* 812, 863.

[38] For cases where such behaviour has been associated with cultural appropriation see Mathias Siems, 'The Law and Ethics of "Cultural Appropriation"' (2019) 15 *International Journal of Law in Context* 408, 408–9; Patti Tamara Lenard and Peter Balint, 'What is (the Wrong of) Cultural Appropriation?' (2020) 20 *Ethnicities* 331, 332.

[39] Cf Sally E Merry, 'Law, Culture and Cultural Appropriation' (1998) 10 *Yale Journal of Law* 101.

[40] For these quotes see Christopher McCrudden, 'Judicial Comparativism and Human Rights' in Esin Örücü and David Nelken (eds), *Comparative Law: A Handbook* (Oxford: Hart Publishing, 2007) 371, 373–4; Nora V Demleitner, 'Combating Legal Ethnocentrism: Comparative Law Sets Boundaries' (1999) 31 *Arizona State Law Journal* 737, 746; Geoffrey Samuel, *An Introduction to Comparative Law Theory and Method* (Oxford: Hart Publishing, 2014) 42.

[41] Pierre Legrand, 'Comparative Legal Studies and the Matter of Authenticity' (2006) 1 *The Journal of Comparative Law* 365, 448.

[42] Katharina Pistor, 'Coding Capital: On the Power and Limits of (Private) Law: A Rejoinder' (2021) 30 *Social & Legal Studies* 317, 322. See also Katharina Pistor, *The Law of Capitalism and How*

therefore argued that, rather than relying on further transplants, a decolonised African law should engage in a 'rediscovery of the African pre-colonial legal tradition and philosophy of law'.[43] Some critics of law and development[44] further claim that the postcolonial world is (still) dominated by countries of the Global North, including their power over international organisations, such as the World Bank, and large corporations. Thus, their argument is that, due to the enduring hegemony of the Global North, legal transplants are simply a continuation of forms of 'neo-imperialism',[45] while also overlooking the necessary context-specificity of the law, in particular by economists using standardised performance measures of law reform.[46] Such arguments have also been phrased as transplants typically following a 'neoliberal' agenda, not only in the development context but also, for example, in the European Union.[47]

3. Preliminary assessment

The beginning of this section started with the statement that any general support or rejection of legal transplants may be challenged by the fact that all legal

to Transform it (New Haven, CT: Yale University Press, 2025) 7 ('In the post-colonial setting, conquest and the imposition of foreign law by force was no longer an option, but this did not stop the transplantation of law from the core to the periphery of the increasingly global capitalist system.').

[43] Justin Monsenepwo, 'Decolonial Comparative Law and Legal Transplants in Africa' (2022) 121 *Zeitschrift für Vergleichende Rechtswissenschaft* 167, 172. Similarly, Pilisano Masake and Eugene L Libebe, 'Decolonial Theory: A Critical Analysis of the Ways in Which Legal Transplant Manifests Coloniality—A Comparative Study of Southern African and Southern Asian States' in Samuel Kwesi Amoo, Tapiwa Victor Warikandwa, and Kennedy Kariseb (eds), *Comparative Law and Jurisprudence in Namibia: Functions, Methods and Perspectives from Selected Jurisdictions* (Windhoek: University of Nairobi Press, 2024) 337; Williams C Iheme, 'Anglophone Africa, Colonial Legacy and the Limits of Legal Transplantation: Should the One-legged Walk on Two Feet?' (2025) 13 *Comparative Legal History* 63; Williams C Iheme, 'The Overdependence of African Courts and Businesses on English Law and Forum: The Negative Repercussions on the Development of African Legal and Economic Systems' (2024) 15 *Pravni Zapisi* 151.

[44] See already Chapter 5 at Section C 4 (b).

[45] Martijn W Hesselink, 'Reconstituting the Code of Capital: Could a Progressive European Code of Private Law Help us Reduce Inequality and Regain Democratic Control?' (2022) 1 *European Law Open* 316, 340–1. See also James A Gardner, *Legal Imperialism: American Lawyers and Foreign Aid in Latin America* (Madison, WI: University of Wisconsin Press, 1980).

[46] Ugo Mattei and Laura Nader, *Plunder: When the Rule of Law is Illegal* (Oxford: Wiley-Blackwell, 2008) 47, 89; Magdaléna Hadjiisky, 'International Organizations as Complex Agents in Policy Transfer Processes' in Osmany Porto de Oliveira (ed), *Handbook of Policy Transfer, Diffusion and Circulation* (Cheltenham: Edward Elgar, 2021) 121, 134–8.

[47] Alessandro Somma, 'Il mercato delle riforme e la circolazione imposta di modelli' in Michele Graziadei and Alessandro Somma (eds), *Esperienze giuridiche in dialogo. Il ruolo della comparazione* (Rome: Sapienza Università Editrice, 2024) 111; Alessandro Somma, 'Scienza giuridica, politica ed economia nell'uniformazione del diritto privato' (2021/1) *Osservatorio sulle fonti* 277; Alessandro Somma, *Comparative Law: A Critical Introduction* (London: Routledge, 2026) 147–203.

systems have experienced some influence from other systems, while they also have certain features which are unique to them. The literature cited in the previous two subsections confirmed this point as both supporters and opponents tend to emphasise particular cases for which they hold their respective positions—for instance, as they write about particular countries, voluntary or involuntary transplants, the role of courts, or other lawmaking bodies. Still, reflecting on these general views is helpful as they highlight a number of points that play a role in the differentiated view that will be presented in the remainder of this chapter.

First, some authors draw on theoretical views about the nature of the law, such as utilitarianism, universalism, originalism, positivism, etc. In order to understand transplants from a normative perspective, it is indeed imperative to engage with views that have tried to explore what may be seen as 'good law'. This importance of theoretical priors is also evident if we consider that comparative legal scholarship usually accepts that comparative insights can contribute to policy recommendations, but that it is then often uncertain how exactly this should proceed (eg, choosing the preferred law of the majority of countries, a common denominator, the clearest law, the most impartial one?).[48]

Second, the link to specific topics and examples shows that the normative question about the desirability of transplants is closely connected to empirical facts about the use of transplants. In other words, there seems to be the implicit assumption that 'is' and 'ought' questions are not as separate as it is sometimes claimed (and as discussed in the following section). Thus, this makes it necessary to analyse how 'is' and 'ought' are connected for any criteria or arguments that speak in favour or against the use of legal transplants. This analysis also includes awareness of the way contemporary transplants are likely to be different from those used in previous times.

Third, political positions seem to play a role in many of the arguments made by general supporters and opponents of transplants. However, legal transplants are neither inherently left-wing nor right-wing. If there are good left-wing ideas in another legal system, it is clear that left-wing politics is more inclined to adopt them than right-wing politics—and vice versa for good right-wing ideas. By contrast, as far there is opposition towards transplants, there is always the temptation to 'blame others',[49] whether it is done by persons on the political

[48] See Siems (n 15) 26–7.

[49] For this general notion see eg Neal A Tognazzini and D Justin Coates (eds), *Blame: Its Nature and Norms* (Oxford: OUP, 2013); Thomas M Scanlon, *Moral Dimensions: Permissibility, Meaning, Blame* (Cambridge, MA: Belknap, 2008).

left or right. As far as such opposition draws on concepts of 'identity', this may also reflect either left-wing or right-wing versions of identity politics.[50]

Fourth, the question of whether to use a transplant is connected to the question of how transplants should be designed, analysed in Chapter 7. For example, if it is seen as feasible to design transplants in a way that makes them operate smoothly across borders and cultures (eg, similar to IKEA furniture[51]), this would also have an impact on their desirability. There is also a link between the 'if' and the 'how' question as it will be proposed here that both should, as far as possible, follow an evidence-based approach.

C. Differentiated view

This chapter suggests a differentiated view of whether it is desirable to use legal transplants. Section 1 introduces the general considerations and line of reasoning of this position. The subsequent sections discuss the normative criteria applied here, namely for the transplant to follow a legitimate interest (Section 2), to be suitable to fulfil this interest (Section 3), to overcome principled objections against the transplant (Section 4), and, on balance, to be worth supporting considering all possible interests and objections (Section 5).

1. General considerations and line of reasoning

The question of what lawmakers *should* do raises general questions about the diverse normative approaches to law and how they relate to more positive aspects of the law (ie the relationship between 'ought' and 'is'). These topics are discussed in this section, which then also outlines the argumentative framework used to assess the desirability of the use of legal transplants.

(a) Diverse normative approaches to law

Questions of ethics and their role in normative approaches to law have filled entire libraries. As in one of my previous publications,[52] it is possible to, first,

[50] See generally Mathias Siems, 'Identity Politics and Comparative Law' (2023) 30 *Maastricht Journal of European and Comparative Law* 719, as well as Hani Sayed, 'La globalización de la teoría del derecho: malinterpretación y resistencia' in Daniel Bonilla Maldonado (ed), *Teoría del derecho y trasplantes jurídicos* (Bogota: Siglo del Hombre Editores, 2009) 119, 155–60 (how emphasising the local may also be a form of nationalism).

[51] See Chapter 7 at Section B 1.

[52] For the following see Mathias Siems, 'The Law and Ethics of "Cultural Appropriation"' (2019) 15 *International Journal of Law in Context* 408, 414, 419.

distinguish between ethical positions that take either a consequentialist or a deontological perspective.[53] From a consequentialist perspective, 'the moral rightness of an act is determined by the act's consequences', while this position can also incorporate multiple forms of consequences.[54] From a deontological perspective, it is the act itself which is either right or wrong; for example, using Kant's Categorical Imperative, the ethical rule is that you are 'to act only in accordance with that maxim through which you can at the same time will that it become a universal law'.[55] The second question is whether any such ethical position should have legal relevance. In countries of the West, works on law's legitimate scope often start with John Stuart Mill's 'harm principle' and then discuss how far legal intervention may sometimes also be justified on other grounds.[56] Furthermore, it can also be seen as a typical 'Western' position that morality and law are treated as substitutes: thus, if there are strong moral norms, it is argued that the repressive force of law is not needed.[57] By contrast, non-Western legal traditions, notably religious laws, are often less hesitant to extend the law to moral questions in many areas of life.[58]

Other authors refer to views of political philosophy to map directly what kind of theories support the use and content of law. In particular, this is typical for Western theories of justice. For example, Michael Sandel's book on justice contains chapters on topics such as utilitarianism, libertarianism, Kant's freedom as autonomy, Rawls' justice as fairness, distributive justice, and Aristotle's justice and virtue;[59] a book edited by Johanna Ohlsson and Stephen Przybylinski distinguishes between liberal, libertarian, cosmopolitan, feminist, radical, indigenous, and capabilities-oriented theories of justice;[60] and Martijn Hesselink distinguishes between utilitarianism, liberal-egalitarianism,

[53] For these and other ethical perspectives see also Copp David (ed), *The Oxford Handbook of Ethical Theory* (Oxford: OUP, 2006).

[54] Martin Peterson, *The Dimensions of Consequentialism: Ethics, Equality and Risk* (Cambridge: CUP, 2013).

[55] Immanuel Kant, *Groundwork of the Metaphysic of Morals* (Oxford: OUP, 2003 [original from 1785]) 4:421; in another formulation, it says that you should 'act in such a way that you treat humanity, whether in your own person or in any other person, always at the same time as an end, never merely as a means' (4:429).

[56] Overview in John Stanton-Ife, 'The limits of law' in *Stanford Encyclopedia of Philosophy* (2006), available at https://plato.stanford.edu/entries/law-limits/ accessed 23 October 2025.

[57] Mark Osiel, *The Right to Do Wrong: Morality and the Limits of Law* (Cambridge, MA: Harvard University Press, 2019).

[58] Siems (n 15) 180–3. For an overview of legal traditions see H Patrick Glenn, *Legal Traditions of the World* (Oxford: OUP, 5th edn, 2014).

[59] Michael J Sandel (ed), *Justice: A Reader* (New York: OUP, 2007).

[60] Johanna Ohlsson and Stephen Przybylinski (eds), *Theorising Justice: A Primer for Social Scientists* (Bristol: Bristol University Press, 2023).

libertarianism, communitarianism, civic republicanism, and discourse theory in order to analyse the normative foundations of European contract law.[61]

A comment on Hesselink's book noted that its combined analysis of various theories may be read as suggesting that EU law is not dominated by 'a narrow set of values and normative commitments', but rather that it is an example of normative pluralism.[62] For an analysis of law in a global context—as in the present book—it is even more evident that there cannot be a single 'correct' normative position that can apply to all legal transplants anywhere in the world. Thus, it is the aim of this chapter to assess at a general level how units should use legal transplants given any legitimate interest (analysed further in Section 2) that they pursue. The variety of normative approaches to law also remains relevant for the other elements of the normative evaluation of legal transplants. As we saw in the review of the literature on general tendencies towards transplants, some normative approaches tend to be used as either supporting or opposing legal transplants. For example, utilitarianism may often be keen on having a transplant that works well (analysed further in Section 3), while communitarian counterarguments, such as a particular country's history and culture, may be a principled objection against a transplant (analysed further in Section 4). There can also be the situation that, through a legal transplant, the transplant unit shifts to a different normative approach. For example, consider the situation that a lawmaker who was initially mainly interested in economic growth now shifts to a focus on inequality, or vice versa. Thus, in many cases, multiple normative approaches will be relevant as the use of the transplant needs to balance all possible interests and objections (analysed further in Section 5).

(b) Relationship to positive aspects of legal transplants

The previous chapters of this book were mainly concerned with positive questions, such as, what types of transplants exist, why they take place, and how they work. The normative question of this chapter is a different one; yet, it is suggested here that the positive aspects of legal transplants can also play a role for their normative assessment.

An objection to such a claim may refer to the is-ought divide, namely that it is said that one cannot derive an 'ought' from an 'is'. This statement has been associated with David Hume (though it is a matter of debate how far it

[61] Martijn W Hesselink, *Justifying Contract in Europe: Political Philosophies of European Contract Law* (Oxford: OUP, 2021) 24–54.

[62] Giacomo Tagiuri, 'Pluralism as Inability to Choose: Celebrating the Normative Diversity of EU Contract Law' (2022) 51 *Netherlands Journal of Legal Philosophy* 18. See also Section C 5.

really follows from his writings).[63] It is also aligned with concepts proposed by GE Moore (notably, the 'naturalistic fallacy' and the 'open-question argument'),[64] as well as the more general epistemological distinction between fact and value.[65] However, there is also a large literature that has challenged this distinction—or at least blurred its absoluteness. Some authors have provided examples where 'is' and 'ought' are connected,[66] but it is also possible to start more fundamentally with the question:

> 'If "ought" cannot be derived from "is'" just what can "ought" be derived from? [. . .] The most compelling answer is this: ethics must be somehow based on an appreciation of human nature—on a sense of what a human being is or might be like, and on what a human being might want to have or want to be. If that is naturalism, then naturalism is no fallacy. No one could seriously deny that ethics is responsive to such facts about human nature'.[67]

This line of thought opens the discussion to positions that reconsider the, allegedly, distinct nature of 'ought' statements. For example, moral (or ethical) realism argues that moral obligations are at least potentially explainable by 'moral facts'.[68] Forms of moral (or ethical) naturalism go further and suggest that it is possible to scientifically study the moral behaviour of the human brain.[69] This latter position can also blur the line between facts and values in showing that facts are not simply 'objective' but based on certain values and beliefs.[70] Philosophical pragmatism also challenges both sides of the fact-value divide: in the words of Hilary Putnam, 'factual description and valuation can

[63] David Hume, *A Treatise of Human Nature* (London: John Noon, 1739) 335 and eg Rachel Cohon, 'Hume's Moral Philosophy' in *The Stanford Encyclopedia of Philosophy* (2018), available at https://plato.stanford.edu/entries/hume-moral/ accessed 23 October 2025.

[64] George Edward Moore, *Principia Ethica* (Cambridge: CUP, 1903) § 10 para 3 and § 13.

[65] See eg Philip S Gorski, 'Beyond the Fact/Value Distinction: Ethical Naturalism and the Social Sciences' (2013) 50 *Society* 543, 544–8.

[66] Notably, John R Searle, 'How to Derive "Ought" From "Is"' (1964) 73 *The Philosophical Review* 43.

[67] Daniel C Dennett, *Darwin's Dangerous Idea: Evolution and the Meanings of Life* (New York: Simon and Schuster, 1995) 467–8.

[68] Geoff Sayre-McCord, 'Moral Realism' in *The Stanford Encyclopedia of Philosophy* (2023), available at https://plato.stanford.edu/entries/moral-realism/ accessed 23 October 2025. In a similar sense, from the perspective of Chinese philosophy: Xiangyang Qian, 'On Truth as the Source of Good: An Is/Ought Reinterpretation' (2009) 10 *Filosofi a Unisinos* 233.

[69] Matthew Lutz, 'Moral Naturalism' in *The Stanford Encyclopedia of Philosophy* (2024), available at https://plato.stanford.edu/entries/naturalism-moral/ accessed 23 October 2025. In *Britannica*, available at https://www.britannica.com/topic/ethical-naturalism accessed 23 October 2025 it is presented as a form of moral realism.

[70] Sam Harris, *The Moral Landscape: How Science Can Determine Human Values* (New York: Free Press, 2010) 11 (referring to values such as logical consistency and reliance on evidence, and pointing to the finding that 'beliefs about facts and beliefs about values seem to arise from similar processes at the level of the brain').

and must be entangled' given that science itself is based on certain normative judgments, but also given that ethical questions are not outside the scope of rational and scientific investigation.[71]

In the present case, there are further reasons why applying a strict is-ought (or fact-value) divide is not helpful. To start with, typical 'ought' questions of the aforementioned literature are about the moral behaviour of individuals,[72] while, in the present case, the question is what laws should be enacted, in particular the possible use of foreign legal models.[73] This latter question can incorporate moral considerations, but there are clearly also other aspects that matter—say, the 'is' question of whether there is compliance with procedural rules of the respective lawmaking body. Moreover, we have seen in the previous subsection that there are many diverse normative approaches to law. Some of them are based on empirical aspirations (eg, utilitarianism). But even for normative approaches closer to a strict is-ought divide (eg, deontological legal theory), we may need to consider, for example, empirical research from moral and cross-cultural psychology[74] in order to evaluate how far a legal transplant is likely to be regarded as acceptable due to similar notions of justice in the origin and transplant units.

Thus, it is suggested here that the normative question about legal transplants has to concede that there is at least an entanglement between facts and values. In a previous paper, co-authored with Martin Gelter, a similar approach was undertaken for the specific question of citations of foreign courts.[75] The framework and findings of this paper are displayed in Table 6.1.

[71] Hilary Putnam, *The Collapse of the Fact/Value Dichotomy and Other Essays* (Cambridge, MA: Harvard University Press, 2002) 27 as well as 28–45. See also Catherine Legg and Christopher Hookway, 'Pragmatism' in *The Stanford Encyclopedia of Philosophy* (2021), available at https://plato.stanford.edu/entries/pragmatism/ accessed 23 October 2025 (under 5.2 discussing how far Putnam was a 'pragmatist').

[72] Ed Gibney, 'Bridging the Is Ought Divide' (2014), available at https://www.evphil.com/blog/bridging-the-is-ought-divide accessed 23 October 2025 (using the examples: 'You ought to keep the Sabbath holy. You ought to honor your ancestors. You ought to kill your daughter if she's dishonored your family. You ought to treat others as you would wish to be treated yourself. You ought to hold the door open for strangers. You ought to listen to your gut. You ought to cut down on your intake of saturated fats. You ought to act "only according to that maxim whereby you can, at the same time, will that it should become a universal law." ').

[73] Thus, this is different from scholarship that refers to the way factual practices ('is') may be transformed into legal rules ('oughts'): see eg Nicoletta Bersier Ladavac, Christoph Bezemek, and Frederick Schauer (eds), *The Normative Force of the Factual: Legal Philosophy Between Is and Ought* (Cham: Springer, 2019), referring to the notion coined by Georg Jellinek, *Allgemeine Staatslehre* (Berlin: O Häring, 3rd edn, 1914) 338.

[74] See eg Benjamin G Voyer and Tor Tarantola (eds), *Moral Psychology: A Multidisciplinary Guide* (Cham: Springer, 2017); John W Berry and others, *Cross-Cultural Psychology: Research and Applications* (Cambridge: CUP, 3rd edn, 2011).

[75] Martin Gelter and Mathias Siems, 'Citations to Foreign Courts—Illegitimate and Superfluous, or Unavoidable? Evidence from Europe' (2014) 62 *American Journal of Comparative Law* 35.

Table 6.1 Patterns of argument in citations of foreign courts

	A. Character of law	B. Quality of decision	C. Procedural reasons
1. Pro	*common core* (+) as far as relevance of international / EU law and legal families	*useful information* (+/−) often superficial citations but smaller jurisdictions benefit from larger ones	*transparency* (+) non-transparent style of some courts harmful for fruitful dialogue
2. Contra	*national character* (+/−) no uniqueness but other legal systems may be more or less remote	*'cherry picking' and misapplications* (−) data do not show random 'cherry picking' or desire to evade domestic laws	*costs and lack of benefits* (+/−) problems of accessibility of foreign case law; but also positive examples
3. Reply	*foreign case law not authoritative* (+) yes, persuasive or even rhetorical	*develop criteria for using foreign case law* (−) none of the courts has developed such criteria	*make foreign case law more easily accessible* (+/−) some efforts to improve availability of foreign case law

The nine arguments of Table 6.1 are divided into three types of arguments and then always three arguments of pro/contra/reply. The text underneath each argument displays the findings of an analysis of cross-citations between supreme courts of ten European countries. For example, it shows how far the empirical analysis of this study confirmed that these courts use cross-citations in order to create a common core of European rules, how far they do so to gather useful information, how far they cherry-pick certain countries as models, and how far they use objective criteria to guide their decisions.[76]

This previous study can be seen as a proof of concept for an approach that provides a normative assessment but also considers positive aspects of legal transplants. Concretely, it would in principle be possible to extend the argumentative field of Table 6.1 to any legal transplants.[77] However, the present

[76] For details see Gelter and Siems (n 75) 82–5.
[77] See Siems (n 15) 301.

research found that Table 6.1, while useful, is somehow limited in identifying the arguments that may matter for all possible types of legal transplants. Thus, the subsequent subsection introduces a modified framework.

(c) Overview of argumentative framework

The topics shown in Table 6.2 are those that will be analysed in detail in the subsequent four sections. The table also indicates how far 'is' and 'ought' questions are likely to be relevant for each topic. This shows some variations, namely that the question about legitimate interests is mainly an 'ought' topic, the suitability of the transplant is mainly an 'is' one, and for the topics 'principled objections' and 'balancing' both 'ought' and 'is' play a key role.

For the overall assessment of a legal transplant based on the factors shown in Table 6.2, the comparison is between a transplant (including mixtures of foreign and domestic laws[78]) and the counterfactual of a fully home-grown law of the transplant unit. This can be 'no law' or the original law on a particular topic that exists in the transplant unit at the moment of the transplant. For the subsequent period, it is conceivable that the transplant unit may have enacted its own new law: thus, if this is likely, the comparison is between the legal transplant and the transplant unit's own hypothetical new law,[79] also considering that this law may have only been enacted after some delay (see also the field on 'temporary delay' in this table).

A related point concerns questions of burden of proof and likelihood/risk. For example, an assessment of the alleged positive effects of the new law may be more uncertain than the effect of the current law and, thus, a sceptic of a transplant may argue that the burden of proof should be on those who support it. However, in some situations, the opposite can be the case. For example, a transplant may be based on empirically proven rules from another jurisdiction, while the effect of a new home-grown law (or even the existing law, or non-law, of the origin unit in changed circumstances) may be less certain. Thus, it is preferable not to apply a general burden of proof, but rather to consider the likelihoods and risks associated with any of the relevant factors of Table 6.2 in each individual case.

This framework can apply to all possible transplants from all possible units.[80] As it is applied, it is then possible that certain transplants, say, transplants in

[78] See Chapter 5 at Section C 2 (a).
[79] For this choice see already Chapter 4 at Section B 2.
[80] See generally Chapter 3.

Table 6.2 Evaluating the 'is-ought' framework for transplants

Topic	Possible relevance of 'ought'	Possible relevance of 'is'
Legitimate interest		
Domestic interest?	*Legitimate aims following deontological ethics (eg, good or malicious transplants)*	*Mapping of interests transplant unit generally pursues* *Facts underlying ethical questions*
International interest?	*Idealist view of comparative law, including role of natural law and universalism*	*Measurable benefits of lower transaction costs and mutual learning etc* *Costs of exploitation etc*
Suitability of transplant		
Transplant can achieve interest?	*Laws which pursue intrinsic normative interests*	*Empirical effect of law*
Can it work in transplant unit?	*Normative interests sometimes regarded as universal*	*Role of legal and extralegal context* *Adjustments often inevitable; use of evidence-based lawmaking*
Temporary delay and costs acceptable?	*Long-term horizon of aims*	*Distinction between different time horizons* *Experience from origin unit and prior transplant units*
Principled objections		
Character of law objection?	*Communitarian views based on national, cultural or religious identities*	*Possible relevance due to unit's legal and cultural history*
Procedural objection?	*Procedural normative positions (eg, civic republicanism)*	*Identifying degree of reflection and voluntariness* *Measuring public opinion*
Balancing	*Various normative positions*	*Possible to examine different types of effects*

certain areas of law or by certain origin units are typically more desirable. However, again, the following will not start with any a priori assumptions given that the relevance of all of factors of Table 6.2 may well mean that a transplant which is desirable in one context is debatable in another context. Throughout this analysis, reference will also be made to examples, some from the previous chapters but also new ones.

2. Legitimate interest

The following distinguishes between two types of legitimate interests: domestic—referring to the transplant unit, whether it is a country or another unit—and international. To some extent, this is related to the discussion in Chapter 4 about the motivations for the occurrence of a transplant. However, at this stage, the question is of a normative nature, namely which interests can be regarded as legitimate. Different from Chapter 4, the interests of the origin unit play a secondary role as they will only feature as part of international legitimate interests (as well as in the context of procedural considerations).[81]

(a) Domestic interests

As there are diverse normative approaches to law,[82] the transplant unit may pursue diverse aims, many of which may, in principle, be regarded as legitimate. For example, it may use a legal transplant to stimulate economic growth, fight poverty, reduce crime, or promote culture since, in many of these and other cases, at least one of the normative approaches would justify legal rules. Beyond such specific aims (and thus also beyond a narrow instrumental use of law), transplanting laws can be justified by broader interests, for instance, to improve the clarity of the law, incorporate an innovative legal idea, or align with the case law of a jurisdiction from the same legal family.

This openness towards diverse aims does not exclude disagreements about the underlying values laws may pursue. For example, in Singapore, the post-independence government may have had no hesitation in 'interfering in the private lives' of citizens,[83] and the same may be said about the Chinese Social Credit System today; yet, while transplanting such rules may be in line with a form of virtue ethics,[84] liberal normative approaches to law would typically be opposed to it.[85] Another example may be that of a country that, in order to stimulate foreign investment, lowers the costs of doing business benefitting economic interests but potentially harming others (eg, social interests, the fiscal capacity of the state).[86] In the context of this chapter, such normative

[81] See Section C 2 (b) and 4 (b).

[82] See Section B 1.

[83] Lee Kuan Yew on 'interfering' in the private lives of Singaporeans (1986), available at https://www.youtube.com/watch?v=FkYEFeHUGPw accessed 23 October 2025.

[84] For this possible connection see Wessel Reijers, 'Technology and Civic Virtue' (2023) 36 *Philosophy & Technology* 71.

[85] Daithí Mac Síthigh and Mathias Siems, 'The Chinese Social Credit System: A Model for Other Countries?' (2019) 82 *Modern Law Review* 1034.

[86] For this example, see Charles R Shipan and Craig Volden, *Why Bad Policies Spread (and Good Ones Don't)* (Cambridge: CUP, 2021) 13.

disagreements are addressed at the stages of the suitability of the transplant for a particular context and, if this is confirmed, the balancing of various interests.[87]

Another problem is that the interests that lawmakers claim to pursue cannot always be taken at face value. Alvin Cheung introduces the term 'legal gaslighting' for situations where the transplant unit conveys to the public that the transplanted rules will work in the same manner as in the origin country, while in reality they facilitate 'authoritarian practices, such as the arrogation of executive power'.[88] This is akin to the research by Rosalind Dixon and David Landau on cases of 'abusive constitutional borrowing', defined as 'the use of designs, concepts, and principles taken from core aspects of liberal democratic constitutionalism, but which are turned into attacks on the minimum core of electoral democracy'.[89] Thus, their argument is that, in certain cases, the problem is not the transplant as such but the actual operation of the transplant due to 'sham', 'selective', 'acontextual', or 'anti-purposive' borrowing.[90] For the categories proposed here, in some cases, it may indeed be said that there is no legitimate interest, namely where the only possible explanation for a transplant is a power grab by the executive.[91] In other cases, the assessment may be more ambiguous. For example, consider a situation where, due to a transplant, a country switches from a parliamentary to a presidential democracy,[92] which may have selfish motivations but could also be regarded as an acceptable choice. Thus, here, a legitimate interest may be acknowledged, but the actual evaluation of the transplant may still be negative due to unsuitability, principled objections, or balancing, ie the stages of the next three sections.

The policy transfer literature discusses more generally whether certain motivations indicate the spread of 'bad policies'. An article by Fabrizio Gilardi and Fabio Wasserfallen contemplates this point given that lawmakers may often focus less on the actual policy consequences than their political effects in terms of electoral consequences and the advancement of certain ideological

[87] Section C 3 (b) and 5.
[88] Alvin YH Cheung, 'Legal Gaslighting' (2022) 72 *University of Toronto Law Journal* 50.
[89] Rosalind Dixon and David Landau, *Abusive Constitutional Borrowing: Legal Globalization and the Subversion of Liberal Democracy* (Oxford: OUP, 2021) 36.
[90] Dixon and Landau (n 89) 42.
[91] Dixon and Landau (n 89) 134 mentions, for example, cases of a 'strong form of abusive judicial review' where courts in Latin America eradicated presidential term limits.
[92] For this example see Muhammet Derviş Mete, 'Turkey's Experience of Legal Transplantation and Turkish-Style Presidential System' (2022) 30 *Selçuk Law Review* 1159 (1171 noting that only over time it will become apparent 'whether Turkey's recent transplant attempt is considered a successful, failed, or even malicious transplant').

positions.[93] Charles Shipan and Craig Volden's book on *Why Bad Policies Spread* goes even further in suggesting that bad policy transfer is typically the result of competition, imitation, or coercion, while good policies spread only if they are based on a form of learning.[94] However, these statements go too far as they would imply that, for example, any motivations based on electoral consequences or the wish to compete globally would, as such, make transplants unacceptable; rather, it is possible that, for example, even selfish political motivations may lead to transplants that benefit the common public. Thus, here too, any problems that may be associated with such a transplant are better solved through the subsequent stages of examination.

One of my own writings presented the case of 'malicious legal transplants'[95] as a scenario where transplants should not happen. This type of transplant was defined as having a negative objective element ('harm'), for example, where one group of society imposes its social norms on another one without need, as well as the subjective element that at least one actor of the transplant process recognises that it can use the transplant in such a manner. In this regard, this article argued that, while societies require some common rules, it is not justifiable to intervene in religious, sexual, and other practices that do not pose any harm to other groups of society.[96] As paradigmatic examples, the article referred to the way Nazi race laws influenced the laws of Mussolini's Italy, how discriminatory elements of Islamic law took hold in countries such as the Maldives, and how British colonial influence led to the criminalisation of homosexual acts in India.[97] In other research, scholars have explored possible links between American race policies and Nazi law,[98] and between both of those and the South African apartheid regime.[99] Reference can also be made to a special journal issue on the misappropriation of human rights law where its editors refer to factors such as the exclusionary and repressive effect of law,

[93] Fabrizio Gilardi and Fabio Wasserfallen, 'The Politics of Policy Diffusion' (2019) 58 *European Journal of Political Research* 1245, 1252–3.

[94] Shipan and Volden (n 86). For the reasons usually discussed in the policy transfer literature see also Chapter 4 at Sections A, B 1, and 2.

[95] Mathias Siems, 'Malicious Legal Transplants' (2018) 38 *Legal Studies* 103.

[96] Based on Martha C Nussbaum, '"Equal Respect for Conscience": Roger Williams on the Moral Basis of Civil Peace' (2007) 15 *Harvard Review of Philosophy* 4, 14 (with reference to Locke).

[97] Siems (n 95) 105–7.

[98] James Q Whitman, *Hitler's American Model—The United States and the Making of Nazi Race Law* (Princeton, NJ: Princeton University Press, 2017); Bill Ezzell, 'Laws of Racial Identification and Racial Purity in Nazi Germany and the United States: Did Jim Crow Write the Laws That Spawned the Holocaust?' (2002) 30 *Southern University Law Review* 1; Stefan Kühl, *The Nazi Connection: Eugenics, American Racism, and German National Socialism* (Oxford: OUP, 1994).

[99] Hermann Giliomee, 'The Making of the Apartheid Plan, 1929–1948' (2003) 29 *Journal of Southern African Studies* 373; Werner Schellack, 'The Afrikaners' Nazi Links Revisited' (1992) 27 *South African Historical Journal* 173.

deliberate polarisation, and the scapegoating of certain groups,[100] while another publication explored when transplants can said to have harmful effects on constitutional democracy.[101]

As a result, there can be some cases where legal transplants cannot be justified by a legitimate domestic interest. But how frequent are they? The answer to this question is tied to the general interests that lawmakers of any possible unit may pursue, which is ultimately dependent on many details that may defy a general assessment. However, the examples of this book show that we rarely have the extreme situations where a transplant is entirely used for false reasons ('gaslighting') or morally unacceptable ones ('malicious').

Assessing this topic from 'ought' or 'is' perspectives,[102] the initial question about legitimate domestic interests belongs the remit of 'ought' in that it seeks to identify acceptable reasons or malicious ones. However, 'is' perspectives also feature in a number of respects. Empirical information is needed to explore the interests that a lawmaker pursues in transplanting a law, which may also draw on information of the interests that a particular transplant unit generally pursues. Furthermore, such information can be used to say whether a transplant is objectively malicious, creating harm to a particular group. Finally, it is in the remit of 'is' to consider that the denial of legitimate domestic interests is in practice the exception to the rule.

(b) International interests

Some may argue that the domestic character of law speaks against the relevance of international interests to support a legal transplant. As a similar objection may be raised against transplants more generally, this point will be addressed separately, in the category of 'principled objections'.[103] The present subsection thus (merely) aims to outline how international interests cover a variety of considerations, some potentially less and some more contentious.

Legal transplants can target a problem that only the origin and the transplant units can solve together. This can be something relatively narrow, for example, that certain legal norms would reduce the transaction costs for businesses operating in both units.[104] Such economic advantage can also go beyond the two

[100] Gráinne de Búrca and Katharine G Young, 'The (Mis)appropriation of Human Rights by the New Global Right: An Introduction to the Symposium' (2023) 21 *International Journal of Constitutional Law* 205, 213.

[101] Jan Petrov, 'How to Detect Abusive Constitutional Practices' (2024) 20 *European Constitutional Law Review* 191.

[102] See Table 6.3.

[103] See Section C 4 (a).

[104] See Chapter 4 at Section B 4.

units, for instance, by having similar accounting rules globally.[105] Thus, the reasoning is that, if many units transplant laws on a particular topic, this is likely—though not guaranteed—to lead to the convergence of legal systems.[106] The advantage of uniform rules can also be of a non-economic nature. For example, it is possible that common rules are needed to address the world's environmental problems and to enhance global social welfare.[107] Following on from findings that increased economic and social interdependence reduces the risks of military conflicts,[108] it may also be argued that any growing convergence of legal rules can generally promote a more peaceful world.[109]

In some of these instances, the normative justification may also be derived from the indirect domestic benefits that the pursuit of such international interests entails for the transplant unit. However, even without a domestic advantage, or where this is unclear, normative arguments are usually available that can justify the pursuit of addressing such common problems. From a utilitarian perspective, Peter Singer and others have argued that, for the ethical assessment of behaviour, the well-being of human beings anywhere in the world should matter.[110] In the recent variant of 'effective altruism', such a position also suggests that this should take a long-term view, notably that it should also consider future generations.[111] The notion of altruism is also present in many religious traditions.[112] Moreover, there are a variety of deontological approaches that justify moral obligations beyond one's country (or other units): notably, some authors have drawn on Kantian ideas[113] but

[105] For this example of a legal transplant see Zehra G Kavame Eroglu, 'Global Adoption of IFRS as an Example of International Financial Law Making' (2021) 53 *George Washington International Law Review* 239, 295.

[106] See Siems (n 15) 290–1. Similar for policy diffusion: John L Campbell, 'Institutional Reproduction and Change' in Glenn Morgan and others (eds), *The Oxford Handbook of Comparative Institutional Analysis* (Oxford: OUP, 2010) 87, 95–7.

[107] See Chapter 4 at Section B 4.

[108] See eg Edward D Mansfield, 'International Trade and Conflict' in Jon CW Pevehouse and Leonard Seabrooke (eds), *The Oxford Handbook of International Political Economy* (Oxford: OUP, 2025) 660; Lilach Gilady, 'Triangle or "Trilemma": Rousseau and the "Kantian Peace"' (2017) 20 *Journal of International Relations and Development* 135.

[109] For references see n 77 in Chapter 4.

[110] Peter Singer, *One World Now: The Ethics of Globalization* (New Haven, CT: Yale University Press, 2016), and the following footnotes.

[111] Peter Singer, *The Most Good You Can Do: How Effective Altruism Is Changing Ideas About Living Ethically* (New Haven, CT: Yale University Press, 2015) and eg Hilary Greaves, William MacAskill, and Elliott Thornley, 'The Moral Case for Long-Term Thinking' in Natalie Cargill and Tyler M John (eds), *The Long View: Essays on Policy, Philanthropy, and the Long-term Future* (London: FIRST, 2021) 19; Hilary Greaves, Jacob Barrett, and David Thorstad, *Essays on Longtermism: Present Action for the Distant Future* (Oxford: OUP, 2025).

[112] See eg Jacob Neusner and Bruce D Chilton (eds), *Altruism in World Religions* (Washington, DC: Georgetown University Press, 2005).

[113] Notably, by Stanley I Benn, *A Theory of Freedom* (Cambridge: CUP, 1988); Onora O'Neill, *Faces of Hunger: An Essay on Poverty, Development and Justice* (London: Allen & Unwin, 1986).

also suggestions for international distributive justice applying an extended version of Rawls' theory of justice.[114]

Referring to reasons that justify the relevance of non-domestic interests is not the same as claiming that there are certain natural laws universal to all human beings. While some authors address both topics together,[115] others use parallels with other fields to suggest that there may be at least some legal universals. For example, Vivian Grosswald Curran refers to Johann Wolfgang von Goethe's search for universal principles, which he called 'Urphänomene';[116] John Mikhail draws on an analogy with Noam Chomsky's idea of a universal grammar as a possible support for universal moral and legal judgements;[117] and Jeremy Waldron indicates that his idea of 'laws common to all mankind' finds an analogy in the gradual emergence of scientific consensus.[118] To be sure, any search for legal universals is usually made with many caveats, indicating that they may not necessarily be prevalent everywhere in the world,[119] and that there is often considerable variation even if some form of universality is accepted.[120] Specifically for legal transplants, it has been suggested that they (only) create a pluralist transnational space, distinct from national legal systems,[121] and thus not a universal legal regime. There is also a prominent line of research from Latin America that the influence of European legal theories should (merely) be regarded as creating forms of 'transnational legal theories' which differ between 'reception sites'.[122] Accordingly, recommending legal

[114] Charles R Beitz, *Political Theory and International Relations* (Princeton, NJ: Princeton University Press, 1979). For subsequent debates see Darrel Moellendorf, 'Real-World Global Egalitarianism' in Chris Brown and Robyn Eckersley (eds), *The Oxford Handbook of International Political Theory* (Oxford: OUP, 2018) 118.

[115] Singer (n 110) 122–73 (eg, referring to universal prohibition on genocide, ethnic cleansing, war crimes, and crimes against humanity).

[116] Vivian Grosswald Curran, 'Cultural Immersion, Difference and Categories in U.S. Comparative Law' (1998) 46 *American Journal of Comparative Law* 43, 72.

[117] John Mikhail, *Elements of Moral Cognition: Rawls' Linguistic Analogy and the Cognitive Science of Moral and Legal Judgment* (Cambridge: CUP, 2011).

[118] Jeremy Waldron, *Partly Laws Common to Mankind: Foreign Law in American Courts* (New Haven, CT: Yale University Press, 2012) 100–8 (as a form of positive law).

[119] Waldron (n 118) 187 ('a consensus of less than 100 percent'). For an example from the debate about human rights: Albert HY Chen, 'Conclusion: Comparative Reflections on Human Rights in Asia' in Randall Peerenboom, Carole J Petersen, and Albert HY Chen (eds), *Human Rights in Asia* (London: Routledge, 2006) 487–516 (human rights as feature of modern societies). For the concept of '*praesumptio similitudinis*' limited to developed nations: Zweigert and Kötz (n 9) 40.

[120] Waldron (n 118) 5; also eg Russell Wilcox, 'Natural Law as the Basis of Cultural and Legal Diversity' (2013) 8 *The Journal of Comparative Law* 45; David Goldman, *Globalisation and the Western Legal Tradition: Recurring Patterns of Law and Authority* (Cambridge: CUP, 2007) 213–40 (for human rights law).

[121] Jennifer Hendry, 'Legal Pluralism and Normative Transfer' in Günter Frankenberg (ed), *Order from Transfer: Comparative Constitutional Design and Legal Culture* (Cheltenham: Edward Elgar, 2013) 153.

[122] Diego Eduardo López Medina, *Teoría impura del derecho. La transformación de la cultura jurídica latinoamericana* (Bogota: Legis, 2004). For more references see Chapter 3 at Section B 2.

transplants based on general claims of legal universality is likely to be weaker than arguments on the substantive benefits of any specific uniform rules.

Another international line of argumentation is that allowing transplants is seen as beneficial as it creates a market for the best laws in all of the units. The general background of this reasoning are arguments that the free flow and exchange of ideas is advantageous as, for example, seen in notions such as the 'marketplace of ideas', 'collective intelligence', and 'wisdom of crowds'.[123] Yet, there are also examples from many fields (history, culture, politics, economics, etc) where authors have shown how mistaken, or even malicious, ideas have won the day.[124] Applied to legal rules, a prominent reference point is that, according to Friedrich Hayek, spontaneous orders are said to be better able to adapt to unknown facts.[125] Thus, some legal scholars argue that, using transplants, a 'process of competition may determine the survival of the most efficient legal doctrine',[126] that courts should at least consider foreign case where it contains valuable information,[127] and that there can be a 'marketplace for legal ideas' which, in parallel to the notion of 'regulatory competition', may push lawmakers 'to experiment and try to find the best legal rules' (ie a 'race to the top').[128] However, these and other authors also mention various limitations to the effective operation of such market forces such as, for example, a lack of knowledge of foreign laws, legal parochialism, the prevalence of hegemonic jurisdictions,[129] as well as non-market-based

[123] See eg Stanley Ingber, 'The Marketplace of Ideas: A Legitimizing Myth' (1984) 1 *Duke Law Journal* 1; James Surowiecki, *The Wisdom of Crowds* (New York: Doubleday, 2004); Thomas W Malone and Michael S Bernstein (eds), *Handbook of Collective Intelligence* (Cambridge, MA: MIT Press, 2015).

[124] GV Scammell, 'Essay and Reflection: On the Discovery of the Americas and the Spread of Intolerance, Absolutism, and Racism in Early Modern Europe' (1991) 13 *The International History Review* 502; Ruth Mayer, *Serial Fu Manchu: The Chinese Supervillain and the Spread of Yellow Peril Ideology* (Philadelphia, PA: Temple University Press, 2013); Raymond Boudon, *L'idéologie ou L'origine des idées reçues* (Paris: Fayard, 1986); John Quiggin, *Zombie Economics: How Dead Ideas Still Walk Among Us* (Princeton, NJ: Princeton University Press, 2010).

[125] Friedrich A Hayek, *Law, Legislation and Liberty, Volume 1: Rules and Order* (Chicago, IL: University of Chicago Press, 1978) 36–8.

[126] Ugo Mattei, 'Efficiency in Legal Transplants: An Essay in Comparative Law and Economics' (1994) 14 *International Review of Law and Economics* 3, 8.

[127] Steven G Calabresi and Bradley G Silverman, 'Hayek and the Citation of Foreign Law: A Response to Professor Jeremy Waldron' (2015) 5 *Michigan State Law Review* 1.

[128] Filomena Chirico and Pierre Larouche, 'Conceptual Divergence, Functionalism, and the Economics of Convergence' in Sacha Prechal and Bert van Roermund (eds), *The Coherence of EU Law: The Search for Unity in Divergent Concepts* (Oxford: OUP, 2008) 463, 488.

[129] Chirico and Larouche (n 128); Mattei (n 126) 16; Ugo Mattei, 'A Theory of Imperial Law: A Study on U.S. Hegemony and the Latin Resistance' (2003) 10 *Indiana Journal of Global Legal Studies* 383; Nuno Garoupa and Anthony Ogus, 'A Strategic Interpretation of Legal Transplants' (2006) 35 *Journal of Legal Studies* 339. Similarly, referring to shortcomings of automatically choosing the orthodox international model: Kevin E Davis and Mariana Pargendler, 'Legal Heterodoxy in the Global South: Adapting Private Laws to Local Contexts' in Kevin E Davis and Mariana Pargendler (eds), *Legal Heterodoxy in the Global South* (Cambridge: CUP, 2025) 1, 12–13.

forms of legal evolution.[130] Thus, while it is possible that legal transplants stimulate a market for good legal ideas (and thus the design of transplants is important, see Chapter 7), it cannot be assumed that this is automatically the case whenever transplants are considered.

As a result, there are, in principle, a variety of international interests that can justify the use of legal transplants, though their precise justification can be a matter of debate. As far as such international arguments make use of 'ought' arguments, this can face the aforementioned criticisms against universalism and natural law. Moreover, it may be argued that, from a normative perspective, the widespread occurrence of legal transplants speaks against such universal arguments: as transplants demonstrate the constant flow of legal ideas and concepts between legal systems, it may be difficult to claim that there are uniform eternal features shared by all of them.[131]

Regarding international 'is' arguments, it is more straightforward to argue that legal transplants lower transaction costs or create other mutual benefits. Likewise, Chapter 4 on 'why transplants take place' has shown that these arguments matter for the use of transplants, and that the identification of a suitable transplant is increasingly facilitated by the availability of foreign legal materials.[132] To be sure, transplants driven by international interests can sometimes be problematic as those interests may go against domestic ones. For example, this previous chapter mentioned cases where international businesses and investors push for common rules in their interest which, in some cases, may cause detriment to local concerns.[133] In the context of this chapter, this possible counterargument will be considered in the subsequent analysis, notably within the context of procedural considerations (Section 4) and balancing (Section 5).

(c) Conclusion

Table 6.3 summarises the findings of this section. It can be seen that both 'ought' and 'is' topics play a role in arguments that refer to domestic or international interests. As the third column shows, it can mainly be affirmed that a legal transplant can be based on a legitimate interest. Of course, this does not

[130] See n 80 in Chapter 5.

[131] Judith Schacherreiter, 'Das Verhängnis von Ethnozentrismus und Kulturrelativismus in der Rechtsvergleichung' (2013) 77 *Rabels Zeitschrift für ausländisches und internationales Privatrecht* 272, 295.

[132] See Chapter 4 at Sections B 4 and C 3 (a).

[133] See Chapter 4 at Section C 3 (b).

Table 6.3 Evaluating the legitimate interests in using a transplant

Sub-topic	Possible relevance of 'ought' and 'is'		Does experience show likely support for transplants?
Domestic interests?	'ought'	Legitimate aims following deontological ethics (eg, good or malicious transplants)	Yes: most of those interests reflect legitimate purposes
	'is'	Mapping of interests transplant unit generally pursues Facts underlying ethical questions	Yes: usually transplants aim for something that lawmakers aspire legitimately (Chapter 4); malicious transplants are the exception
International interests?	'ought'	Idealist view of comparative law, including role of natural law and universalism	Uncertain: less frequently considered; criticisms against this position
	'is'	Measurable benefits of lower transaction costs and mutual learning etc Costs of exploitation etc	Yes: trend that this is done, also with easier access to comparative information (Chapter 4)

mean that each and every transplant should then be supported, as we will see in the following sections.

3. Suitability of transplant

Suitability of the legal transplant means that the interest identified in the previous section can be fulfilled by using the transplant. If there are multiple interests, each of them needs to be assessed in preparation for the balancing stage (Section 5, below). This section divides this assessment into three steps: general capacity of the legal transplant to realise the interest (or interests), its suitability in the transplant unit, and considerations of time and costs. Some of these topics relate to the way transplants 'work' in a particular context (Chapter 5) but some also to possible design choices (Chapter 7).

(a) General capacity of transplant to realise interest

As far as interests are based on normative approaches to law associated with 'ought' positions (eg, deontology), the general capacity of a transplant to realise this interest simply means that the corresponding rules account for it. In other words, this is based on the view that law is not a mere tool to achieve something else but that it has an intrinsic value. For example, such a position is sometimes suggested for principles of the 'rule of law'.[134] Similarly, it is said that simply perceiving law as a means of development should be replaced by the position of 'law as development'.[135]

Other normative approaches typically include an 'is' element in the sense that it matters whether the transplant can, empirically, realise the respective interest. As legal transplants can concern many elements of the law, and as their use can be based on many different motivations,[136] some interests may be of a rather intangible nature. For example, the transplant may concern a particular innovative legal theory, improvements in the clarity of the law, or the adoption of new forms of legal learning. Still, even here, empirical findings can help: for example, research on cross-citations between courts has examined how far such citations are due to 'soft' motivations, such as improving its mode of reasoning or bolstering the acceptance of its argument.[137] It is also conceivable that sometimes a theory is chosen that is not objectively advantageous but that is just 'easier to understand' and 'appears to approximate most closely to existing concepts';[138] thus, in such a case, the decision to transplant may be presented as a trade-off since the objective quality may be worse while there is expected to be a good 'fit' in the transplant unit.[139]

In many other situations, the general quality of a law is directly tied to a particular aim. The mainstream view of the interconnected fields of law and development, law and economics, development economics, and new institutional economics is that we know that certain laws generally matter for a country's economic development.[140] For example, empirical quantitative studies have

[134] See eg Brian Z Tamanaha, *On the Rule of Law* (Cambridge: CUP, 2004) 137; Ronald J Daniels and Michael Trebilcock, 'The Political Economy of Rule of Law Reforms in Developing Countries' (2004) 26 *Michigan Journal of International Law* 99, 104.

[135] Ada Ordor, 'Tracking the Law and Development: Continuum Through Multiple Intersections' (2015) 8 *Law and Development Review* 333, 335.

[136] See Chapter 3 at Section B and Chapter 4.

[137] See Folker de Witte and others, 'Decoding Judicial Cross-Citations: How Do European Judges Engage with Foreign Case Law?' (2024) 72 *American Journal of Comparative Law* 292, 311–3.

[138] Eoin Carolan, 'Diffusing Bad Ideas: What the Migration of the Separation of Powers Means for Comparative Constitutionalism and Constitutional Transplants' in Sue Farran and others (eds), *The Diffusion of Law* (Farnham: Ashgate, 2015) 213.

[139] For the notion of 'fit' see Chapter 5 at Section C 1.

[140] See eg Mariana Mota Prado and Michael Trebilcock, *Advanced Introduction to Law and Development* (Cheltenham: Edward Elgar, 2nd edn, 2021); Robert D Cooter and Hans-Bernd Schäfer, *Solomon's Knot: How Law Can End the Poverty of Nations* (Princeton, NJ: Princeton University Press, 2011); Kenneth W Dam, *The Law-Growth Nexus: The Rule of Law and Economic Development* (Washington, DC: Brookings Institution Press, 2006); Daron Acemoglu and James A Robinson, *Why Nations Fail: The Origins of Power, Prosperity, and Poverty* (London: Profile Books, 2012). Specifically for the connection to new institutional economics see Sara Blanco Contreras, 'Los trasplantes institucionales en el campo del derecho. Una nueva perspectiva para la nueva economía institucional' (2016) 3(2) *Iberian Journal of the History of Economic Thought* 170.

typically found that indicators of the rule of law and property rights (including measures of risks of expropriation and political stability) are more decisive for economic development than, for example, geographic and cultural differences.[141] To be sure, according to other quantitative research, other factors than the law were found to be more decisive.[142] Furthermore, more qualitative and historical research emphasises the crucial role of culture and politics. For example, with respect to culture, it is said that social norms and ideas channel development through many means, not only law,[143] and that effective law reform needs to nurture changes to 'cultural norms and practices that impede human rights, reinforce entrenched power structures, and perpetuate traditional inequalities'.[144] With respect to politics, it is argued that the underlying problems of developing countries are often due to systemic political problems,[145] and that the economic success of East Asian countries in the post-war period mainly exemplifies the role of a strong and active state.[146]

In assessing this debate, it is possible to focus on the methodological challenges to make general causality claims in the social sciences and empirical legal studies.[147] In the present context, it is important to note that the external validity of such quantitative research is, by its very nature, restricted to the units and time period under investigation.[148] Thus, any such findings do not exempt from analysis whether a transplant really works in a particular place

[141] Daron Acemoglu, Francisco A Gallego, and James A Robinson, 'Institutions, Human Capital, and Development' (2014) 6 *Annual Review of Economics* 875; Daron Acemoglu, Simon Johnson, and James A Robinson, 'Institutions as Long Run Causes of Economic Growth' in Philippe Aghion and Steven N Durlauf (eds), *Handbook of Economic Growth, volume IA* (Amsterdam: Elsevier, 2005) 385; Dani Rodrik, Arvind Subramanian, and Francesco Trebbi, 'Institutions Rule: The Primacy of Institutions over Geography and Integration in Economic Development' (2004) 9 *Journal of Economic Growth* 131.

[142] See the discussion in Siems (n 15) 263–4.

[143] See Kevin E Davis and Michael J Trebilcock, 'The Relationship Between Law and Development: Optimists versus Skeptics' (2008) 56 *American Journal of Comparative Law* 895, 897 (summarising this view). For book-length treatments associated with this position see Steven Pinker, *Enlightenment Now: The Case for Reason, Science, Humanism, and Progress* (New York: Penguin, 2018); Deirdre Nansen McCloskey, *Bourgeois Equality: How Ideas, Not Capital or Institutions, Enriched the World* (Chicago, IL: University of Chicago Press, 2016).

[144] Lan Cao Cao, *Culture in Law and Development: Nurturing Positive Change* (New York: OUP, 2016) 186–7.

[145] Eg William Easterly, *The Tyranny of Experts: Economists, Dictators, and the Forgotten Rights of the Poor* (New York: Basic Books, 2014).

[146] See eg Franklin Allen and Jun QJ Qian, 'Comparing Legal and Alternative Institutions in Finance and Commerce' in James J Heckman, Robert L Nelson, and Lee Cabatingan (eds), *Global Perspectives on the Rule of Law* (Abingdon: Routledge, 2010) 118; Katharina Pistor and Philip A Wellons, *The Role of Law and Legal Institutions in Asian Economic Development, 1960–1995* (New York: OUP, 1999).

[147] See eg Christoph Engel, 'Empirical Methods for the Law' (2018) 174 *Journal of Institutional and Theoretical Economics* 5; Daniel E Ho and Donald B Rubin, 'Credible Causal Inference for Empirical Legal Studies' (2011) 7 *Annual Review of Law and Social Science* 17.

[148] For the challenge of 'context' in empirical comparative law see eg Mathias Siems, 'The European Advantage in Empirical Comparative Law' (2025) 2 *European Journal for Empirical Legal Studies*, https://doi.org/10.62355/ejels.24727 accessed 23 October 2025.

and time. Relatedly, one problem associated with some empirical studies of the 'law and finance school'[149] is that they were based on inaccurate representations of the law, including the notion of grouping laws into legal families (also known as 'legal origins'); this led to incorrect conclusions about topics such as the role of shareholder protection for financial markets and the possible advantage of the common law over the civil law.[150] Some of these studies have also been associated with the World Bank's Doing Business Reports which have now been withdrawn due to data irregularities.[151]

Thus, such empirical studies should be treated with a dose of scepticism. Lawmakers too have experienced that changing behaviour through legal means may be difficult. For example, recent attempts to raise birth rates by various forms of legal incentives have so far largely been unsuccessful.[152] However, this should also not lead to the opposite conclusion that law can never fulfil certain aims. Rather, as some of the studies cited above also indicate, legal change and its impact should not be seen in an isolated manner but in the context of other social, cultural, political, and economic changes. Naturally, it also depends on the precise law, circumstances, and desired effect whether it is more or less likely that law matters, which also implies that the choice and design of the transplant can make all the difference. In the policy diffusion literature, Shipan and Volden list as helpful policy attributes that are observable, have a relative advantage, are not too complex, and have 'trialability'.[153] Thus, the position taken here is that it is possible to evaluate the general capacity of a transplant to realise a particular interest whilst acknowledging that this evaluation may not lead to a definite result but to the finding of a more or less likely effect.

(b) Transplant can work in transplant unit

Chapter 5 distinguished three dimensions in examining how the transplanted law may or may not 'work': that it is known and understood, that it is complied

[149] See the list of studies in Gerhard Schnyder, Mathias Siems, and Ruth V Aguilera, 'Twenty Years of "Law and Finance": Time to Take Law Seriously' (2021) 19 *Socio-Economic Review* 377, 402–6.

[150] Siems (n 15) 235–53. For a discussion of these claims see also Simon Deakin and Katharina Pistor (eds), *Legal Origin Theory* (Cheltenham: Edward Elgar, 2012); Emma Phillips, 'The War on Civil Law—The Common Law as a Proxy for the Global Ambition of Law and Economics' (2006–2007) 24 *Wisconsin International Law Journal* 915.

[151] See https://archive.doingbusiness.org/en/doingbusiness accessed 23 October 2025.

[152] See eg from the *Financial Times*: 'The Baby Gap: Politicians want more children. Their policies are failing' (29 January 2025); 'Falling birth rates raise prospect of sharp decline in living standards' (15 January 2025); 'China steps up campaign for single people to date, marry and give birth' (25 December 2024); 'Why Hungary's lavish family subsidies failed to spur a baby boom' (19 August 2024); 'Why family-friendly policies don't boost birth rates' (29 March 2024).

[153] Shipan and Volden (n 86) 52 (specifically for problem areas where the learning-based spread of good policies could go wrong). For design questions see also Chapter 7.

with and/or enforced, and that it has the desired influence on society. These topics will be revisited in this subsection, as applied to the normative question of whether it is desirable to use legal transplants.

With respect to normative 'ought' standards, a distinction may be made between those standards that may be seen as universal (eg, Kant's Categorical Imperative) and those that are specific about particular cultures (eg, religious beliefs). In the former case, the suitability of the transplant is straightforward, while in the latter case a supporter would need to show that rules based on such standards are morally (or ethically) suitable in another culture. For example, the latter may consider research from comparative sociology and cross-cultural psychology in order to examine whether cultures share similar notions of what may constitute 'good law'.[154] In some cases, research may also show that the underlying reasons why certain norms exist are more generalisable than expected. For example, it has been found that prohibitions of interest payments on loans are not merely due to certain religious beliefs but typical for many small-scale societies and their need for reciprocity.[155]

Common to these and other normative positions is the requirement that the transplant can be expected to be known and understood in the transplant unit. In some cases, this may be difficult. For example, Rodolfo Sacco writes that 'a legal system cannot borrow elements that are expressed in terms that are foreign to its own doctrine'.[156] However, considering the findings of Chapter 5, experience generally shows that, after some time, foreign-inspired law is usually known and understood, even if the origin and transplant units appear to be quite different.[157] Thus, the challenge may often be less about the general suitability, but more about the ease of transmitting the knowledge about the law (and thus questions of timing and costs, discussed in the next subsection).

For transplants driven by normative approaches that include an 'is' element, it also matters that the law is complied with and/or enforced and that it has the expected societal effect. As regards compliance and enforcement, Chapter 5

[154] See generally Roger Cotterrell, 'Is it So Bad to Be Different? Comparative Law and the Appreciation of Diversity' in Esin Örücü and David Nelken (eds), *Comparative Law: A Handbook* (Oxford: Hart Publishing, 2007) 169 ('Legal sociologists have shown that there are also strikingly different popular ideas in different countries about the purposes of law and what is to be expected from it') and eg Rodrigo Míguez Núñez, 'Pour une déconstruction du concept de propriété dans les Andes centrales' (2010) 62 *Revue internationale de droit comparé* 981 (on incompatibility of 'possessive individualism' with the culture of the high Andean region).

[155] Sally Falk Moore, 'Legal Systems of the World: An Introductory Guide to Classifications, Typological Interpretations, and Bibliographic Resources' in Leon Lipson and Stanton Wheeler (eds), *Law and the Social Sciences* (New York: Russell Sage, 1986) 11, 26.

[156] Rodolfo Sacco, 'Legal Formants: A Dynamic Approach to Comparative Law (Installment II of II)' (1991) 39 *American Journal of Comparative Law* 343, 400.

[157] See Chapter 5 at Section C 2.

observed that the path towards an effective 'law in practice' can be challenging, but also found that, after some time, transplanted law is often complied with and enforced. Variations depend on aspects such as the 'fit' with existing legal rules and traditions (notably, courts and other enforcement institutions).[158] Moreover, in some cases, it is deliberate that the transplanted law deviates from existing traditions as it aims to change the law in practice. For example, writing about constitutional transplants, Gábor Halmai suggests 'a dialectic relationship between constitutional law and constitutional culture: the former is based on the latter, and it also influences it'.[159] We have also seen that, in some instances, countries have deliberately changed their alignment with a particular legal family.[160] From a normative perspective, such change can be justified if outdated traditions are ultimately responsible for the problems of a particular unit.[161]

Furthermore, as regards compliance, it is often beneficial that the application of the law in the transplant unit is somehow different from that in the origin unit. As it is said that 'repetitions are favourable to variations',[162] it can be part of a learning process that transplanted rules are modified in both their design and application. It is also often in the interest of the transplant unit to modify their use. The literature refers to many situations where this is recommended or where it has happened. For example, a book on indigenous and transplanted institutions in Africa suggests a 'reconciliation paradigm' as a way to reform laws while also ensuring the loyalty of the local population.[163] In order to ensure compliance with transplanted Western laws in Muslim-majority countries, an article suggests a form of legal hybridity which incorporates modernisation with 'reasonable interpretations of rules and legal process compliance with Islamic law'.[164] A book on the implementation of a provision of international law analyses how different forms of implementation in three countries can lead to legal transplants on these variations.[165] And

[158] See Chapter 5 at Section C 3.

[159] Gábor Halmai, 'Constitutional Transplants' in Roger Masterman and Robert Schütze (eds), *The Cambridge Companion to Comparative Constitutional Law* (Cambridge: CUP, 2019) 580, 601.

[160] See Chapter 3 at Section B 2.

[161] Similarly, as regards the critical potential of legal history: Markus D Dubber, 'Legal History as Legal Scholarship: Doctrinalism, Interdisciplinarity, and Critical Analysis of Law' in Markus D Dubber and Christopher Tomlins (eds), *The Oxford Handbook of Legal History* (Oxford: OUP, 2018) 99; Anna di Robilant, 'Big Questions Comparative Law' (2016) 96 *Boston University Law Review* 1325, 1334.

[162] Gabriel Tarde, *The Laws of Imitation* (New York: Henry Holt and Company, 1903) 7.

[163] Mamadou Dia, *Africa's Management in the 1990s and Beyond: Reconciling Indigenous and Transplanted Institutions* (Washington, DC: World Bank, 1996).

[164] Maliheh Zare, 'Creating Laws for Economic Growth in a Hybrid Islamic Legal System' (2019) 28 *Southern California Interdisciplinary Law Journal* 429.

[165] Sean Whittaker, *The Right of Access to Environmental Information* (Cambridge, CUP, 2021).

examples from common law countries show that, despite a baseline of similarities, transplant countries engage in 'ad-hoc engineering' in order to improve the way the transplant works.[166]

Turning to the desired influence on society, the main challenge is that it cannot be assumed that the transplant will simply work in the same way in the transplant unit as in the origin one. In the literature, this is sometimes presented in a manner that the society of the transplant unit is mainly seen as an impediment to the transplant.[167] However, this misses important differentiations. To start with, it is also conceivable that society is already in line with the possible new law, but that the current law is lagging behind (and this is precisely what the transplant is meant to fix).[168] Another variant is that the transplant unit does not simply use the transplant to improve on a particular measure (higher GDP, less crime, etc), but use it with the aim to 'disrupt' society in some manner (eg, related to certain technologies, such as allowing or banning Uber, Airbnb, AI, nuclear power etc),[169] and thus, in this case, the mismatch with current society is deliberate. Another relevant differentiation is the prevalence of diverse interests between different societal groups which not only matters for the balancing stage (and, thus, Section 5, below) but also for their societal effectiveness as different groups may have different preferences towards the use of transplanted rules.[170]

As regards the question of whether, in practice, transplants usually 'work' from a societal perspective, Chapter 5 has shown that this is often the case.[171] This does not deny the risk of failed transplants. Thus, from a normative perspective, it can be helpful if adjustments to the transplant reduce this risk. In some cases, this has been shown to be difficult,[172] but it would go too far to say that the diversity of societal interests typically makes transplant undesirable. Comparative law scholarship has shown that different societies often face similar problems. For example, without claiming legal universality, it has been said that:

[166] May Fong Cheong, Divyangana Dhankar, and Shaun Star, 'Legal Transplantation of Minors' Contracts in India and Malaysia: "Weak" Watson and a "Misfitted" Transplant' (2023) 23 *Oxford University Commonwealth Law Journal* 17, 19; Joshua Getzler, 'Transplantation and Mutation in Anglo-American Trust Law' (2009) 10 *Theoretical Inquiries in Law* 355, 363.

[167] Notably, views associated with a 'mirror theory' of law and society; see Chapter 5 at Section B 2.

[168] See already Chapter 4 at Section C 3 (c).

[169] For transplants being motivated to change society see also Chapter 4 at Section B 2.

[170] See eg Roger Cotterrell, 'Is There a Logic of Legal Transplants?' in David Nelken and Johannes Feest (eds), *Adapting Legal Culture* (Oxford: Hart Publishing, 2001) 71 (distinguishing between instrumental, traditional, belief, and affective communities as having weak or strong bonds, drawing on earlier classifications by Max Weber).

[171] See Chapter 5 at Section C 4.

[172] Eg, in the case of legal transplants in Afghanistan, see ibid.

> 'The battle of the rule of law against arbitrary government takes place in every human society, when those with power seek to expand their discretion (and control), and their subjects resist . . . Struggle for freedom usually begins with the demand for written laws, to constrain the discretion of those in authority, then proceeds to the pursuit of just laws, a much more difficult undertaking'.[173]

Thus, there is often a benefit of using tested ideas, which also means that foreign law should not be borrowed blindly or manipulatively. As regards the choice and design of legal transplants, decisions about legal transplants should follow evidence-based lawmaking.[174] This needs to consider all significant short and long-term consequences of the transplanted law. In the context of this chapter, such findings thus also relate to the efficiency (and not only effectiveness) of the legal transplant in terms of time and costs (discussed in the next subsection), as well as the balancing of all possible interests which are expected to benefit from or suffer due to the legal transplant (Section 5, below).

(c) Time dimension and costs

If the reasons for a transplant are entirely based on 'ought' arguments, time and costs are unlikely to be a decisive counterargument. However, this is different for the more common positions that transplants are also meant to achieve certain interests whose estimated success depends on 'is' findings. In Chapter 5, the question of whether transplants 'work' did not consider the time and costs involved in this process. However, for the decision to support or oppose a transplant, they can play a crucial role. They can appear in two forms: the time and cost to adopt the transplant, and the subsequent time and cost to support its operation (eg, training lawyers in the new law, making it known to the public, monitoring its use).

To assess the relevance of these costs, it is also necessary to know the corresponding benefits of the transplant. The impact assessment of legislation is common practice in many countries, regional organisations, and international bodies.[175] As legal transplants can concern a variety of objects

[173] Mortimer Sellers, 'An Introduction to the Rule of Law in Comparative Perspective' in Mortimer Sellers and Tadeusz Tomaszewski (eds), *The Rule of Law in Comparative Perspective* (Heidelberg: Springer, 2010) 1, 2.

[174] See also Chapter 7.

[175] See eg Claire A Dunlop and Claudio M Radaelli (eds), *Handbook of Regulatory Impact Assessment* (Cheltenham: Edward Elgar, 2016); for the OECD: https://www.oecd.org/en/publications/regulatory-impact-assessment_7a9638cb-en.html accessed 23 October 2025; for the EU see references in n 237.

and motivations,[176] some benefits can be difficult to be assessed precisely, for example, the effect of adopting a foreign legal theory by courts or legal academia. Another challenge is the time dimension as there may be uncertainty about possible trajectories. For example, while one projection may be that the transplant leads to a linear benefit every year, it could also happen that, after some time, societal circumstances change and, thus, there are diminishing returns, or, conversely, the transplant creates increasing returns as new laws can build on the previous achievements. In normal circumstances, it is therefore reasonable if the assessment of costs and benefits of the transplant focusses on the foreseeable future (rather than pursuing a type of futurology[177] about the evolution of the law's effect); yet, for some policy questions, it is unavoidable to engage in long-term projections (eg, climate change and other global risks).

There can also be cases where the comparison needs to consider whether the 'fit' of the transplant[178] really needs to be as good as possible. For example, assume that it would be possible to choose and design a transplant that would closely fit the current law but that this would take significant time and costs. Here, it can be the case that the more suitable transplant is one that can be readily and quickly adopted even if it leads to lower benefits.

To assess suitability, another comparison is with a hypothetical new home-grown law. Here, it is possible that either the transplant or this home-grown law is more costly and slowly. On the one hand, identifying a suitable transplant, translating the law into the local context, and making it work may be more costly and slow than 'simply' enacting one's own law. On the other hand, taking a ready-made law from elsewhere may be cheap and quick compared to drafting one's own law from scratch.[179] Thus, a careful analysis is needed in order to assess which of the two scenarios is more likely to occur in a particular case. Assuming that the benefits of the two options are quantifiable, it can be attempted to convert the time dimension into financial measures by assuming a credit taken by the lawmaker to pay for these hypothetical costs and any interest payments. As far as such a calculation is not feasible, any more subjective measure (eg, a survey of citizens about having more today or later) may

[176] See Chapters 3 and 4.

[177] For discussion of such a challenge see also Christian Tarsney, 'The Epistemic Challenge to Longtermism' (2023) 201 *Synthese* 195.

[178] See generally Chapter 5 at Section C 1.

[179] For a modelling approach of such options see Peter Grajzl and Valentina Dimitrova-Grajzl, 'The Choice in the Lawmaking Process: Legal Transplants vs. Indigenous Law' (2009) 5 *Review of Law and Economics* 615.

be affected by the human failing to delay gratification.[180] Moreover, here again, we have the question about the length of the time horizon. The longer the time horizon the less certain it is to assume that any costs will be recovered, or it may also be possible that in the long run societal changes would, in any case, require a different law than the one enacted at the present moment.

In many of these considerations, we therefore face the problem of assessing the uncertainty of evaluating the costs and benefits of possible transplants and its alternatives. Past experience from the origin unit or other transplant units may be used to approximate these measures. Still, as there are always some differences in context, some uncertainty is unavoidable. Employing an economic analysis of the law, the response could be to estimate probabilities in order to compare these options (eg, a 100% probability to gain 91 would be preferable to a 90% probability to gain 100 as 0.9 x 100 = 90). Alternatively, it could be suggested that lawmakers should be risk averse, also considering that there may be further negative unintended consequences due to the transplant. However, it is proposed here that it is often preferable to be more optimistic. Regulatory research has shown that people and firms are fairly adaptable and that unintended consequences can also be positive.[181] Moreover, insights from comparative law show that mixing laws through foreign influence is something that all legal systems of the world have managed to achieve, even if this has sometimes been challenging (eg, in transition economies). As, in today's world, information is more readily available across borders, it also becomes easier to identify beneficial transplants and assess their costs and benefits. Thus, while it is important to consider the uncertain time and costs involved in a transplant, this should not be an argument to reject them as a matter of course.

(d) Conclusion

Table 6.4 summarises the findings for the suitability of transplants. It shows in the third column that, while there is variation across the different variants and themes, experience shows that many transplants can indeed be regarded as suitable. This is the case for both 'ought' and 'is' arguments, whereby 'is'

[180] See eg Jacek Buczny, 'Delay of Gratification' in Bernardo J Carducci and Christopher S Nave (eds), *The Wiley Encyclopedia of Personality and Individual Differences: Models and Theories* (Hoboken, NJ: John Wiley & Sons, 2020) 153; Renée M Tobin and William G Graziano, 'Delay of Gratification: A Review of Fifty Years of Regulation Research' in Rick H Hoyle (ed), *Handbook of Personality and Self-Regulation* (Hoboken, NJ: John Wiley & Sons, 2010) 47.

[181] Richard L Revesz and Michael A Livermore, *Retaking Rationality: How Cost-Benefit Analysis Can Better Protect the Environment and Our Health* (Oxford: OUP, 2008) 55–147 (as fallacies of some forms of cost-benefit analysis).

Table 6.4 Evaluating the suitability of a transplant

Sub-topic	**Possible relevance of 'ought' and 'is'**		**Does experience show likely support for transplants?**
Transplant can achieve interest?	'ought'	Laws which pursue intrinsic normative interests	Yes, if these normative interests are successfully pursued
	'is'	Empirical effect of law	Yes: empirical research on law's effect can be considered; to estimate effect, transplant needs to be well-chosen (see also Chapter 7)
Can it work in transplant unit?	'ought'	Normative interests sometimes regarded as universal	Yes, if these normative interests are successfully pursued
	'is'	Role of legal and extralegal context Adjustments often inevitable; use of evidence-based lawmaking	Yes: some legal irritation and acontextual borrowing, but often transplants 'work' (see Chapter 5); also design choices can help (Chapter 7)
Temporary delay and costs acceptable?	'ought'	Long-term horizon of aims	Yes: normative interests support long-term perspective
	'is'	Distinction between different time horizons Experience from origin unit and prior transplant units	Uncertain: experience with transplants is usually positive in the long-run (see also Chapters 4 and 5); time and costs can be considered in design (Chapter 7)

arguments tie this topic to empirical findings and measurements as far as possible; yet, even in situations where there are no hard data on the possible benefits and costs, it is not excluded to make use of a legal transplant.

4. Principled objections against transplant

The principled objections discussed here are related to the position of the 'general opponents' of legal transplants.[182] However, the following asks more specifically how far such objections could be relevant for specific cases of legal transplants. The discussion of this section also relates to the subsequent section as it is possible that an objection may not exclude the transplant on its

[182] See Section B 2.

own, but that it may still be considered in the general balancing of whether or not a transplant should be used.

(a) Domestic character of this law

While some normative positions associated with 'ought' arguments support legal transplants (some even in a universalist spirit),[183] communitarian positions may object to transplants on the basis of the domestic character of the law. In this regard, the use of the term 'domestic character' is meant to have a wide meaning, referring to arguments about the national character of the law but also laws that are said to closely reflect, for example, a particular religion or culture. To be sure, given the inexistence of cultures that have been completely autochthonous,[184] it is unlikely for anyone to suggest that there should never be any non-domestically grown elements in the law. Yet, we have already seen that there are, for example, the positions that courts should not consider foreign case law and that particular areas of law are so culturally embedded that transplants should not happen.[185] Other examples are that the allegedly deep divide between civil and common law countries (presented as irreconcilable 'world-views')[186] may speak against transplants across legal families, the reluctance of laws based on religious rationales to draw on secular traditions (and, possibly, vice versa),[187] and the argument that the autonomous nature of regional and international legal systems may speak against using ideas and concepts from domestic legal systems.[188]

In support of such positions, which, at least in some cases, regard the domestic character of the law as a reason against a transplant, reference may also

[183] See Section C 2 (b).

[184] This has been tried by the Tokugawa shogunate from 1603 to 1868 in Japan, but even then the writing system was Chinese-influenced; the People's Republic of Albania from 1946 till 1976 was also fairly but not completely isolated; today, the population of the North Sentinel Island in the Indian Ocean lives in self-isolation, though their language is said to belong to the broader group of Ongan languages, indicating past contacts with other populations.

[185] See Section B 2, as well as Chapter 4 at Section C 3 (d) and Chapter 5 at Section C 4 (a).

[186] Pierre Legrand, 'European Legal Systems are Not Converging' (1996) 45 *International and Comparative Law Quarterly* 52, 60. For the role of legal families in the transplant literature see also Chapter 3 at Section C 1, Chapter 4 at Section C 3 (a), and Chapter 5 at Section C 2 (b) and 4 (b).

[187] For an overview of the relationship between law and religion see Siems (n 15) 180–3.

[188] For discussion of this point see eg Elena Corcione, 'Is There a Role for Domestic Law in the Interpretation of the European Convention on Human Rights? Why Autonomous Concepts are Not that Autonomous After All' (2023) 3 *The Italian Review of International and Comparative Law* 491; Jan Engberg, 'Autonomous EU Concepts: Fact or Fiction?' in Susan Šarčević (ed), *Language and Culture in EU Law: Multidisciplinary Perspectives* (London: Routledge, 2015) 169. For an example from the EU see Opinion of Advocate General Bobek, 15 April 2021, Case C-561/19, *Consorzio Italian Management, Catania Multiservizi SpA v Rete Ferroviaria Italiana SpA*, para 95 (for the 'acte clair theory' writing that '(t)he more questionable element is the transplantability of what was a distinctively French doctrine, crafted in a very different context for a different purpose, into a sui generis EU-type of proceedings').

be made to insights from other academic fields. Referring to psychology, even general supporters of transplants acknowledge that people 'are attached to their own laws' due to 'habitual acquiescence',[189] and that legal transplants can 'leave behind a sense of inauthenticity'.[190] In a similar sense, there is the view that countries and cultures have a distinct 'character', for instance exemplified in national character studies,[191] with some anthropologists rejecting human universals while favouring differences or even uniqueness,[192] and with various philosophies emphasising the importance of the common consciousness of a people.[193] Reflecting on differences as regards the relationship between society and law, the legal anthropologist Simon Roberts also wrote:

> 'Societies differ widely as to the kinds of behaviour which are approved or tolerated and hence also in the amount of tension and quarrelling that will be felt acceptable. The possibilities can be seen as ranged along a continuum. At one end are societies in which subdued, self-effacing conduct is expected of the members. Here, peace and quiet and sustained harmonious interpersonal relations represent dominant values, and urgent appeals for unity are made wherever a quarrel shows signs of developing . . . Elsewhere, at the opposite end of the scale, loud, aggressive behaviour may be approved and a high value attached to individual ascendancy and achievement . . . There, persistent disputes may be tolerated, ignored or even enjoyed.'[194]

Thus, beyond problems of 'fit' (and, thus, the suitability of transplants, discussed in the previous section), sceptics of transplants may argue that often there is simply a lack of any common ground due to different notions about the function of law.

However, better reasons speak against such strongly sceptical positions. To start with, it is possible to refer to a (legitimate) 'is'/'ought' argument,[195]

[189] Bentham (n 4) 184 and Section B 1.

[190] David Nelken, 'Beyond the Metaphor of Legal Transplants?: Consequences of Autopoietic Theory for the Study of Cross-Cultural Legal Adaption' in Jiří Přibáň and David Nelken (eds), *Law's New Boundaries: The Consequences of Legal Autopoiesis* (Dartmouth: Ashgate, 2001) 265, 295.

[191] For a critical overview of these studies see Howard J Wiarda, *Political Culture, Political Science, and Identity Politics: An Uneasy Alliance* (Farnham: Ashgate, 2014) 45–64. For an empirical study on this topic see A Terracciano and others, 'National Character Does Not Reflect Mean Personality Trait Levels in 49 Cultures' (2005) 310 *Science* 96.

[192] Eg, American Anthropological Association, 'Statement on Human Rights' (1947) 40 *American Anthropologist* P539 (rejecting the concept of universal human rights). For the further debate in anthropology see Siems (n 15) 435–8.

[193] See eg Khanal (n 16) 38–42, 66–7 (referring to European but also Chinese, Hindu, Buddhist, and Islamic philosophy).

[194] Simon Roberts, *Order and Dispute: An Introduction to Legal Anthropology* (New Orleans, LA: Quid Pro Books, 2nd edn, 2013) 35–6.

[195] See Section C 1 (a).

namely that 'is' statements about group differences—including legal traditions and cultures—do not necessarily mean that these differences need to be maintained. Moreover, as far as there is a link between 'is' and 'ought', the fact that there are certain historical groups (nations, cultures, legal traditions, etc) needs to consider the historical context in which these groups have been formed. In other words, there is a limited external validity of historical information,[196] with the consequence that we may well make different choices today.

There is also the risk of essentialising group differences. To illustrate, Stephen Greenblatt's 'manifesto' of cultural mobility calls it a 'fantasy that once upon a time there were settled, coherent, and perfectly integrated national or ethnic communities' (while also noting the persistence of cultural identities).[197] Amongst his recommendations is that research should closely consider the concrete structures created by historical circumstances, including the relationship between 'the sensation of rootedness' and the reality of cultural mobility.[198] Normatively, this recommendation may also use the insight that mixed cultural phenomena are often beneficial: in the words of Matt Ridley 'ideas needed to meet and mate' and, 'imagine if the man who invented the railway and the man who invented the locomotive could never meet or speak to each other'.[199] By contrast, according to Olúfẹ́mi Táíwò, the purifying search for 'authenticity' by means of decolonisation is said to have 'lost its way';[200] for example, in his words, 'decolonisers' are associated with the position that there is a 'static idea of a precolonial Africa' with harmful implications such as 'an essential incompatibility between multiparty democracy and so-called traditional African statecraft'.[201]

In the legal sphere, the frequency of legal transplants in human history also shows that it is a myth to present the world as consisting of countries with their own 'pure laws'. This also extends to legal families as research has, for example, shown that (even) the common law has intercultural origins, and thus the potential to counter the '"clash of cultures" ideology'.[202] With respect to regional and international norms, presenting them as completely autonomous is contrasted by their frequent interconnections with the domestic legal orders.[203]

[196] Siems (n 15) 136.

[197] Stephen Greenblatt, 'Cultural Mobility: An Introduction' in Stephen Greenblatt (ed), *Cultural Mobility: A Manifesto* (Cambridge: CUP, 2010) 1, 2.

[198] Stephen Greenblatt, 'A Mobility Manifesto' in Greenblatt (ed) (n 197) 250, 251–2.

[199] Matt Ridley, *The Rational Optimist: How Prosperity Evolves* (London: HarperCollins, 2010) 6–7.

[200] Olúfẹ́mi Táíwò, *Against Decolonisation: Taking African Agency Seriously* (London: Hurst, 2022).

[201] Táíwò (n 200) 169.

[202] Marc Tizoc González, 'John Makdisi on the Intercultural Origins of the Common Law' (2019) 14 *Intercultural Human Rights Law Review* 167.

[203] Alban Spielkamp, *Dialogische Rechtsentwicklung im europäischen Verwaltungsrecht: Strukturen transnationaler Rechtsrezeptionen am Beispiel der Verwaltungstransparenz* (Tübingen: Mohr Siebeck, 2025) 57.

The previous chapter moreover explained that legal transplants are evidence of the pervasiveness of mixtures of laws, whereby this connects again to similar concepts in other social sciences, such as cultural hybridity, pluralism, and bricolage.[204]

Finally, arguments referring to the 'domestic character' of the law often imply that the lawmaker should, at least, not 'outsource' its responsibility to a non-domestic unit.[205] This relates to the way transplants should happen procedurally—and thus also the topic of the next subsection. Notably, it may indeed be a problem if there are involuntary elements leading to the transplant. In the case of voluntary transplants, however, lawmakers treat foreign law as merely having an informational value.[206] Thus, here, the fact that a lawmaker revisits the old law by considering a legal transplant may precisely be a means to realise contemporary domestic ownership of the law.[207] In the case of judicial transplants, it matters that courts incorporate foreign ideas within their general framework of judicial argumentation.[208] Or, it may even be the case that the consideration of foreign law is really only a means of 'constructing and criticising theories in one's own legal system';[209] in particular, this is plausible as far as citations of foreign case law refer to the reasoning of foreign courts (or other authorities) and not simply their result.[210] Thus, here too, it is not the case that courts outsource their responsibility to foreign legal authorities.

To conclude, the argument of the domestic character of the law is unlikely to be a strong principled objection against transplants. Only in rare cases, it may be relevant, say, where a particular religious law has peculiar rules that require certain behaviours such as the consumption of foods, and it would be irreconcilable to consider rules from other religions in this regard. But if we consider the relationship between religious and secular rules, it may already get more complex. For example, assuming an example where there are health concerns over certain foods, a transplant into the religion-based legal order may be considered, while it would then be the task of the balancing stage (discussed in Section 5, below) to determine whether or not the transplant should actually happen.

[204] See Chapter 5 at Section C 2 (a).
[205] See also Section B 2.
[206] Siems (n 15) 301.
[207] For a similar argument see Şafak Uğurlu, 'Türk Hukuk Devrimi ve Bu Devrimde Ankara Huku Mektebi'nin Yeri ve Önemi' (2009) 85 *Turkiye Barolar Birligi Dergisi* 414, 419 (how the Kemalist introduction of a secular state realised national sovereignty).
[208] Damiano Canale, 'L'argomento comparatistico. Un contributo allo studio del ragionamento giuridico' (2016) (1) *Ars interpretandi* 47. See also Chapter 7 at Section C 1.
[209] Coendet (2016) (n 14) 495. For details see Coendet (2012) (n 14).
[210] de Witte and others (n 137) 311–3.

(b) Procedural considerations

Procedures play a role in many normative approaches to law, though with a different emphasis. In instrumental approaches, they mainly matter in the way that good procedures are expected to achieve certain aims. In other normative approaches, procedural considerations have a more central role. For example, civic republicanism is said to regard 'active political participation as a core aspect of a good life', while discourse theory aims for a position whereby through means of 'acceptance of all concerned in practical discourse' conflicts are resolved consensually.[211] Regarding the latter theory, it has also been suggested that legal transplants can be 'conceptualized as regulatory conversations' and that this understanding may impact on the way in which their success is evaluated.[212]

In the policy diffusion literature, Shipan and Volden list a number of problems that may arise due to deficiencies in the political process and biases in policymaking. These include, for example, lack of expertise, time and incentives, short-termism, political opportunism, selective use of information, and the role of special interest groups.[213] Reference can also be made to a previous chapter which discussed whether lawmakers are more likely to follow private or public interests in their decision to transplant a particular law.[214] Yet, many of these topics are not specific about legal transplants (or policy diffusion) as they also need to be considered for home-grown laws. Likewise, given the wide understanding of 'law' in this book,[215] it should be noted that general procedures differ widely between, for example, legislation, soft law, case law, contracts, etc. Thus, given that the present analysis aims to specifically explore the normative desirability of a transplant, the following focusses on procedural considerations that are specific, or at least more typical, to legal transplants. For this analysis, it will also be shown that some 'is' considerations can help us with the decision of whether transplants should be supported procedurally.

To start with, legal transplants should be based on a diligent comparative law analysis that considers multiple options and is fully aware of differences in context.[216] This is not the case as far as lawmakers simply take the 'most obvious' foreign model, for example, that of a larger unit which shares the same

[211] See Hesselink (n 61) 44–54 (eg referring to Aristotle and Habermas).
[212] John Gillespie, 'Towards a Discursive Analysis of Legal Transfers into Developing East Asia' (2008) 40 *New York University Journal of International Law and Politics* 657, 688. See also Chapter 5 at Section B 3.
[213] Shipan and Volden (n 86) 52.
[214] See Chapter 4 at Section C 3 (c).
[215] See Chapter 3 at Section B 1.
[216] For details see Chapter 7 at Section C 2.

language and has already served as a model in the past. To be sure, even in such a case of 'superficial comparative law', it is not excluded that the choice and fit of the model is better than if a thorough comparative legal analysis had identified an obscure rule from a remote unit. As already mentioned, there is sometimes also a trade-off between time and quality if the transplant unit needs to enact a new law quickly.[217] Thus, it is unlikely that the mere superficiality of a comparative analysis will lead to a negative assessment of a legal transplant.

A further procedural element may be that the public of the transplant unit is supportive of the transplant.[218] In some studies, such general support has indeed been confirmed,[219] while it is also said that 'governments and civil society from time to time [successfully] resist foreign models'.[220] A link to the topic of the previous paragraph is the question of whether the public may have preferences towards the laws of a particular unit. Here, a concern may be that many legal systems of the Global South may still draw on legal models from the former colonisers; however, 'is' information is again helpful as international surveys show that the populations of these countries often have a positive view about the former colonisers today.[221]

This leads to a further consideration, namely that some of the opponents of legal transplants argue that many transplants are still largely involuntary.[222] This claim is not confirmed in this book as it has shown that there is a trend towards voluntary transplants.[223] Still, there are of course cases where, even today, due to military occupation, economic power, or other reasons transplants are largely or partially externally imposed. Such cases are also analysed in the policy transfer literature as it discusses links to foreign policy and international relations.[224] The key question is whether any element of involuntariness can ever be justified? In the past, this was often said to be the case. For example, in the nineteenth century, Rudolf von Jhering criticised as a 'deadly sin' that

[217] See Section C 3 (c), as well as Chapter 4 at Section B 2.

[218] For details, in particular variations between types of units and objects, see Chapter 7 at Section C 1 (c).

[219] See Chapter 4 at Section C 3 (b).

[220] Osmany Porto de Oliveira, 'A Prelude to Policy Transfer Research' in Osmany Porto de Oliveira (ed), *Handbook of Policy Transfer, Diffusion and Circulation* (Cheltenham: Edward Elgar, 2021) 1, 9.

[221] Andy Baker and David Cupery, 'Animosity, Amnesia, or Admiration? Mass Opinion Around the World Toward the Former Colonizer' (2023) 53 *British Journal of Political Science* 1132.

[222] See Section B 2.

[223] Chapter 4.

[224] See eg Magdaléna Hadjiisky, Leslie A Pal, and Christopher Walker, 'Introduction: Traversing the Terrain of Policy Transfer: Theory, Methods and Overview' and Laure Delcour, 'Competition in Policy and Institutional Transfer: the EU and Russia in the "Contested Neighbourhood"' in Magdaléna Hadjiisky, Leslie A Pal, and Christopher Walker (eds), *Public Policy Transfer: Micro-Dynamics and Macro-Effects* (Cheltenham: Edward Elgar, 2017) 1, 8–9 and 174.

countries such as China and Japan wanted to isolate themselves from the rest of the world, and he even saw it as justified that the 'Anglo-Saxon race' imposed its law on the indigenous population of North America.[225] Today, the mainstream view presents the colonial empires as having been simply 'wicked' and 'unethical'.[226] By contrast, a controversial article by Bruce Gilley suggests that there may be 'the case for colonialism' today. Specifically, he mentions that forms of governance which include foreign powers may initially not need to rely on public support but 'simply [. . .] the ability of the intervening state to win compliance from key actors and get the job done', akin to his claim that 'colonialism spread in order to better manage ungoverned encounters with the West'.[227]

Assessing this question, it is clear that even Gilley, despite the provocative title of his paper, would not suggest a return of colonial empires but rather focusses on cases of mixtures between domestic and foreign control. In development policy, this is indeed fairly common. For example, a book by Simon Chesterman (cited by Gilley) mentions how state-building activities by the UN installed 'transitional administrations' which assumed 'temporary sovereign powers in East Timor and Kosovo'.[228] Likewise, donor countries often play a key role in shaping the laws of developing countries. How benevolent or malevolent such influence is can depend on the internal structures of these origin units, be it countries or international organisations: for example, how legal norms shape the way donor countries promote the rule of law abroad.[229] Moreover, from a normative perspective, the length and depth of the involvement matters. For example, the 'battle of advisors' in the rule of law promotion by Western countries[230] may consist of merely providing information about one's own law, the use of forms of 'soft power', but also military and economic pressure. Thus, in some cases, foreign influence on its own should indeed lead

[225] von Jhering (n 10) 6–7 (own translation).

[226] For a challenge to this position see Nigel Biggar, *Colonialism: A Moral Reckoning* (London: HarperCollins, 2023), deriving from the former Oxford-based project on 'ethics and empire' (see https://web.archive.org/web/20220327090728/https://www.mcdonaldcentre.org.uk/ethics-and-empire accessed 23 October 2025).

[227] Bruce Gilley, 'The Case for Colonialism' (2018) 31 *Academic Questions* 167, 180. For the controversy surrounding this article see Rhoda E Howard-Hassmann and Neil McLaughlin, 'Ideacide: How On-Line Petitions and Open Letters Undermine Academic Freedom and Free Expression' (2022) 44 *Human Rights Quarterly* 451.

[228] Simon Chesterman, *You, the People: The United Nations, Transitional Administration, and State-Building* (Oxford: OUP, 2004) viii.

[229] Till Patrik Holterhus (ed), *The Law Behind Rule of Law Transfers: On Rule Based Interactions of Legal Orders in a Globalized World* (Baden-Baden: Nomos, 2019).

[230] See eg Frank Schimmelfennig, 'A Comparison of the Rule of Law Promotion Policies of Major Western Powers' in Michael Zürn, André Nollkaemper, and Randall Peerenboom (eds), *Rule of Law Dynamics: In An Era of International and Transnational Governance* (Cambridge: CUP, 2012) 111.

to a negative assessment of a partially voluntary/involuntary transplant. In other cases, the ultimate assessment depends on the balancing stage (see the next section) as well as other questions, such as the suitability of a transplant (notably, how far it benefits the transplant unit).

Finally, it has been discussed within the context of 'malicious legal transplants'[231] how far the various units and groups involved in the transplant process can prevent such malicious transplants. For example, third countries, international organisations, but also citizens, companies, and interest groups of either the origin or the transplant unit may, ideally, prevent malicious legal transplants.[232] Thus, together with the previous analysis of this section, it can be seen that both the promotion and the prevention of transplants can involve a variety of agents. It is difficult to determine abstractly when and how the influence of certain persons or groups may be beneficial, neutral, or harmful. Still, it may be concluded that domestic ownership of the transplant should in principle be guaranteed, while also considering that foreign legal influence may sometimes be a source for good in promoting beneficial and preventing malicious legal transplants.

(c) Conclusion

The summary of this section in Table 6.5 shows that the character of law objection is not usually a hurdle. By contrast, the analysis of procedural considerations has shown that there is sometimes a lack of attention to such issues (which also points towards the importance of questions of transplant design, discussed in the following Chapter 7).

5. Balancing of interests and objections

The literature on legal transplants and related topics sometimes notes that the choice of using a transplant may be challenging due to the diverse considerations at stake. For example, Barbara Dufková's book on *Success in Legal Transplanting* mentions the benefits to society or certain persons but also the goals of the transplant and considerations of efficiency.[233] David Nelken writes that conflicting interests may involve 'different governments or different

[231] See Section C 2 (a).
[232] Siems (n 95) 114–18.
[233] Barbara Dufková, *Success in Legal Transplanting* (Prague: Charles University, 2022) 34–41 (as part of 'result-oriented effects').

Table 6.5 Evaluating the principled objections against a transplant

Sub-topic	Possible relevance of 'ought' and 'is'		Does experience show likely support for transplants?
Character of law objection?	'ought'	Communitarian views due to national, cultural or religious identities	Yes: other normative positions more universal
	'is'	Possible relevance due to unit's legal and cultural history	Yes: evidence shows that (legal) cultures are not pure, borrowing is common and not authoritative (see also Chapters 3 and 4)
Procedural objection?	'ought'	Procedural normative positions (eg, civic republicanism)	Uncertain: foreign influence may harm legitimacy; yet, procedures can ensure domestic ownership
	'is'	Identifying degree of reflection and voluntariness of transplant Measures of public opinion	Uncertain: choice of transplants often unreflective; but also studies showing public support and trend towards voluntary transplants (see also Chapter 4)

economic interests, or among members of governmental and nongovernmental organizations, parliamentarians, judges, lawyers other professionals—as well as the various parties likely to be most affected by the law'.[234] In the policy diffusion literature, a study found that US states were more likely to transplant criminal justice policies that were more favourable to privileged than marginalised groups of society;[235] yet, in other literature, it is suggested that the strategic use of legal and policy models from elsewhere can be a successful tool by politically weaker actors.[236]

A possible response based on normative positions related to 'ought' arguments could be that the lawmaker should simply identify the 'one correct' 'ought' position, which should then provide clear guidance. An alternative position more associated with 'is' arguments is to scrutinise all possible effects of

[234] David Nelken, 'The Meaning of Success in Transnational Legal Transfers' (2001) 19 *Windsor Yearbook of Access to Justice* 349, 363.

[235] Graeme Boushey, 'Targeted for Diffusion? How the Use and Acceptance of Stereotypes Shape the Diffusion of Criminal Justice Policy Innovations in the American States' (2016) 110 *American Political Science Review* 198.

[236] John Braithwaite and Peter Drahos, *Global Business Regulation* (Cambridge: CUP, 2000) 578, 582. The 'emancipatory' and 'counter-hegemonic' potential of law is also discussed in the critical literature, see references in Siems (n 15) 163, 285.

a legal transplant in detail. For example, in regulatory impact assessment, the lawmaker may be expected to rate a wide range of possible economic, social, and environmental impacts according to their likelihoods and magnitude.[237] If, in such a case, all impacts are positive, the decision is an easy one; however, if this is not the case, the question about the evaluation of the transplant remains ambiguous.

Thus, often, it is necessary that lawmakers balance all interests at stake. This is not unique to legal transplants. Indeed, contrary to a 'monist' view, it is often said to be more plausible to adopt a plural normative position. Jonathan Haidt elaborates on this point from the perspective of moral psychology given that people frequently combine different motivations for their moral judgement (specifically: care, fairness, loyalty, authority, and sanctity).[238] But even more narrow positions are often plural in nature. Applying a multi-dimensional consequentialist perspective, the philosopher Martin Peterson finds that 'clashes between conflicting moral aspects are irresolvable and that moral rightness and wrongness are, as a consequence of this, non-binary properties' (ie they may be 'somewhat right and somewhat wrong').[239] By contrast, the interdisciplinary political theory of ordoliberalism starts with a Kantian understanding of freedom as autonomy and self-determination, but is then also pluralist in the way it incorporated both individualistic and social considerations.[240]

For the topic of this section, this general nature of the problem of balancing means that normative decisions about a voluntary transplant can, in principle, follow a similar balancing process as other lawmaking decisions by the transplant unit. Some aspects may, however, require additional considerations in evaluating the use of a legal transplant, following from the themes identified in the previous sections. For example, it can be the case that using a transplant is more costly than a home-grown law (given its initial mismatch with existing laws and society), while it can help that a law from another unit has already been tested (ie the transplant unit can draw on the experience from the origin and other transplant units).[241] As far as a transplant is motivated

[237] EU Commission, Impact Assessment Guidelines, SEC(2005) 791. Today, this is integrated in the 'Better regulation: guidelines and toolbox', available at https://commission.europa.eu/law/lawmaking-process/planning-and-proposing-law/better-regulation/better-regulation-guidelines-and-toolbox_en accessed 23 October 2025. See also https://commission.europa.eu/law/lawmaking-process/planning-and-proposing-law/impact-assessments_en accessed 23 October 2025.

[238] Jonathan Haidt, *The Righteous Mind: Why Good People are Divided by Politics and Religion* (London: Penguin, 2012) 118–79, 368.

[239] Peterson (n 54) vii.

[240] Jochen Mohr, 'Die Interdependenz der Ordnungen als rechts- und wirtschaftsphilosophische Konzeption' (2018) 73 *JuristenZeitung* 685, 690–1.

[241] See Section C 3 (a) to (c).

by international interests,[242] it can happen that these interests clash with domestic interests. For example, it may be that a transplant leads to a lowering of global environmental pollution while increasing a country's unemployment rate. Thus, in such a case, the lawmaker may face the challenge of justifying the transplant to its domestic audience, while it is also conceivable that it may manage to do so by implementing social security measures and convincing the public about the benefit of also considering international interests.

Specifically for legal transplants, the principled objections discussed in the previous section can feature as part of the general balancing. Similar to the finding of that section, it would be unrealistic to impose a requirement of 'purity' according to which the domestic character of the law would always need to be fully maintained, and any degree of foreign pressure would spoil the desirability of the transplant. As regards the domestic character of the law, contentious cases are likely to be those where the nature of the law has some in-built features according to which foreign considerations should not be considered. The previous section mentioned the case of religious laws. Another example may be rules of a particular international organisation which has the explicit task of focussing on one set of interests (eg, economic, environmental, humanitarian). But, sometimes, it could still be useful to deviate from this narrowness given that legal norms should consider the legal order as a whole.[243] For example, it has been suggested that there should be judicial cross-fertilization of environmental concerns into the trade framework of the WTO.[244] Yet, in other cases, it may be harmful to the legitimacy of a particular international legal framework.

The most contentious normative aspect may be to accept some degree of involuntariness as regards the transplant if, according to the other criteria, the transplant is normatively beneficial. For example, consider the situation that an organisation such as the World Bank puts pressure on a country to enact a particular law that is shown to benefit this country's population.[245] It is suggested here that it is acceptable to support the transplanted law in such a case, in particular if it can be ensured that domestic interests have been considered.

[242] Section C 2 (b).

[243] For the German view of the 'unity of the legal order' see eg Manfred Baldus, *Die Einheit der Rechtsordnung: Bedeutungen einer juristischen Formel in Rechtstheorie, Zivil- und Staatsrechtswissenschaft des 19. und 20. Jahrhunderts* (Berlin: Duncker & Humblot, 1995). But see also Andreas Fischer-Lescano and Gunther Teubner, 'Regime-Collisions: The Vain Search for Legal Unity in the Fragmentation of Global Law' (2004) 25 *Michigan Journal of International Law* 999.

[244] Elizabeth Trujillo, 'A Dialogical Approach to Trade and Environment' (2013) 16 *Journal of International Economic Law* 535.

[245] See Chapter 4 at Section C 3 (b).

Table 6.6 Evaluating the balancing of aims and objections

Possible relevance of 'ought' and 'is'		Does experience show likely support for transplants?
'ought'	Various normative positions	Uncertain: no clear standard on how to determine conflicting recommendations; normative pluralism may be seen as acceptable
'is'	Possible to examine different types of effects	Yes: regulatory impact assessments do not answer choice between different aims but, assuming voluntary transplants, decision can be similar to other lawmaking in transplant unit; use of experience in origin or other transplant units; problematic cases may still have positive effect

A different question, going beyond the transplantation of the law, is whether, geopolitically, it is seen as appropriate how international organisations (or other units) use their power and influence.

The summary in Table 6.6 indicates some of the ambiguities that decisions about legal transplants entail at the stage of balancing aims and objections. Yet, it also notes that some of these challenges can be overcome, in particular as far as 'is' considerations play a role in the decision-making process.

D. Conclusion

Is it desirable to use legal transplants? This chapter has shown that some authors express general positions on whether legal transplants should take place. Considering the stance of the general opponents, this chapter has acknowledged that transplants have sometimes been used maliciously, and that the involuntariness of some transplants is not simply a matter of the past. However, today, clear negative cases are the exception. As also shown in the other chapters of this book, legal systems have always incorporated foreign ideas, and the use of transplants typically happens voluntarily today.

Of course, this does not imply that legal transplants are always the best solution to any challenge a country or other unit may face. In other words, any normative evaluation needs to consider the specific circumstances in which a transplant is proposed, as well as the time and cost involved in this process. This insight that context matters is confirmed by the findings of Chapter 5 on how transplants 'work'. It also connects to the subsequent Chapter 7 on the way transplants should be designed, in particular the need for an evidence-based approach to lawmaking.

The main part of this chapter explored what criteria should be used to assess the question of whether a law should be transplanted. It did so by way of distinguishing between 'is' and 'ought' dimensions, while also noting that 'is' and 'ought' are closely entangled and that, in reality, we often have laws based on a plurality of different normative positions. Having examined the criteria of legitimate interest, suitability of the transplant, principled objections, and balancing, it found that, in practice, we reach more often a positive than a negative conclusion about the desirability of a legal transplant. Thus, in today's world, lawmakers should be open to the use of legal transplants.

The importance of the context in which a decision about a transplant needs to be taken also includes the temporal context and thus the impact of future developments. For example, it seems reasonable to assume that the ease of access to comparative information will increase further. As regards the interests that a transplant aims to pursue, the growing interconnectedness of the world and its global challenges could mean that international interests increasingly play a role, blurring the lines between origin and transplant units. However, according to some, there is also a trend towards 'nationalism, nativism and in the extreme cases, isolationism',[246] which may thus sharpen the differences of normative approaches to law across the world.

[246] Margaret YK Woo, 'Comparative Law in a Time of Nativism' (2018) 41 *Hastings International and Comparative Law Journal* 1, 29. In the first years of the 2020s, this trend seems to have accelerated; see eg 'How people in 24 countries feel about their political parties' (*Pew Research Center*, 15 September 2025), available at https://www.pewresearch.org/short-reads/2025/09/15/how-people-in-24-countries-feel-about-their-political-parties/.

7

How Should the Design of Transplants be Pursued?

A. Introduction

It has rightly been said that 'legal transplants' are (simply) 'a reality we cannot run away from'.[1] Thus, beyond the normative issue of whether it is desirable to use legal transplants (Chapter 6), a key question is how the design of legal transplants should be pursued. Asking this question is also in line with the findings of the positive chapters of this book. For example, we have seen that transplants can come in various shapes and forms (Chapter 3), that today they are usually voluntary (Chapter 4), and that their 'working' depends on the details of law and their implementation (Chapter 5). Thus, these findings too point towards the need—and challenge—to design legal transplants in an intelligent way.

The topic of designing legal transplants can be connected to various streams of legal research. The most general term is that of 'legal design'. It was initially used as an extension of the notion of 'contract design'[2] but has also now emerged as a more general field in which authors explain, for example, uses of design for socio-legal research and legal education.[3] Questions of 'constitutional design' have been discussed within the context of comparative constitutional law,[4] and

[1] Maria Reyes, 'The Challenges of Legal Transplants in a Globalized Context: A Case Study on "Working" Examples' (Working Paper, 2014), available at https://ssrn.com/abstract=2530811 accessed 23 October 2025.

[2] Gerlinde Berger-Walliser, Robert C Bird, and Helena Haapio, 'Promoting Business Success Through Contract Visualization' (2011) 17 *Journal of Law, Business & Ethics* 55. See also Marcelo Corrales Compagnucci, Helena Haapio, and Mark Fenwick (eds), *Research Handbook on Contract Design* (Cheltenham: Edward Elgar, 2022).

[3] Amanda Perry-Kessaris, *Doing Sociolegal Research in Design Mode* (London: Routledge, 2021); Emily Allbon and Amanda Perry-Kessaris (eds), *Design in Legal Education* (London: Routledge, 2022). See also Michael Doherty, 'Introducing the Legal Design Journal: A Home Where New Ideas Can Grow' (2024) 1 *Legal Design Journal* 1.

[4] Eg, Ran Hirschl, *Comparative Matters: The Renaissance of Comparative Constitutional Law* (Oxford: OUP, 2014) 176–9; Tom Ginsburg (ed), *Comparative Constitutional Design* (Cambridge: CUP, 2012); Sujit Choudhry (ed), *Constitutional Design for Divided Societies: Integration or Accommodation?* (Oxford: OUP, 2008). For examples see also Section C 2 (b).

Legal Transplants. Mathias Siems, Oxford University Press. © Mathias Siems 2026.
DOI: 10.1093/9780191991981.003.0007

the design of legal transplants has also been a topic within the field of legislative drafting.[5] Other research uses the phrase 'legal engineering' in referring to the way lawmakers aim to change society through law.[6] However, writing about the way to evaluate the success of legal transplants, David Nelken notes that an 'engineering approach to law varies greatly in its relevance (. . .) as between one legal culture and another'.[7] The concept of legal engineering also seems to be limited to a mere instrumental use of law. By contrast, the question about the design of a legal transplant in this chapter will include any possible use of law, ie not only instrumental but also laws seen as having an intrinsic value.

The topic of this chapter provides various points of connection to research in other academic fields. For example, development economics, as well as law and economics, may be able to 'help avoid potentially unusable or unworkable transplants',[8] and there is also a rich literature on evidence-based law-making, including the use of randomised controlled trials.[9] Some of the policy transfer literature explicitly analyses how lessons from other countries should be drawn.[10] It has also been argued that one should assess the possibility of policy transfer/diffusion within the general context of policy learning, notably how far it presents a case of (bounded) 'rational policy-making'.[11] Even more generally, reference can be made to the diffusion of innovations: here, the literature explains the typical evolution of the innovation-development process,[12]

[5] Eg, Helen Xanthaki, 'Legal Transplants in Legislation: Defusing the Trap' (2008) 57 *International and Comparative Law Quarterly* 659; Nicola Lupo and Lucia Scaffardi (eds), *Comparative Law in Legislative Drafting: The Increasing Importance of Dialogue Amongst Parliaments* (The Hague: Eleven, 2014).

[6] Eg, Jan M Smits, 'Legal Engineering in an Age of Globalisation—Is There a Future for Jurisdictional Competition?' in Eleanor Cashin Ritaine (eds), *Legal Engineering and Comparative Law, Volume 2* (Zurich: Schulthess, 2008) 51, 52; Giovanni Sartori, *Comparative Constitutional Engineering: An Inquiry into Structure, Incentives and Outcomes* (New York: NYU Press, 2nd edn, 1997). For a different usage: David Howarth, *Law as Engineering: Thinking About What Lawyers Do* (Cheltenham: Edward Elgar, 2013).

[7] David Nelken, 'The Meaning of Success in Transnational Legal Transfers' (2001) 19 *Windsor Yearbook of Access to Justice* 349, 360.

[8] Kerstin Mechlem, 'Legal Reform in Developing Countries: The Use of Comparative Law and Law-and-Economics' in Jean-Jacques Dethier (ed), *Governance, Decentralization and Reform in China, India and Russia* (Boston: Kluwer Academic Publishers, 2001) 311, 334.

[9] See Section C 1 (a).

[10] See Section B 1.

[11] Oliver James and Martin Lodge, 'The Limitations of "Policy Transfer" and "Lesson Drawing" for Public Policy Research' (2003) 1 *Political Studies Review* 179. See also Pierre Squevin and others, 'Closer Than They Look at First Glance: A Systematic Review and a Research Agenda Regarding Measurement Practices for Policy Learning' (2021) 3 *International Review of Public Policy* 146. For bounded rationality see also Kurt Weyland, *Bounded Rationality and Policy Diffusion: Social Sector Reform in Latin America* (Princeton, NJ: Princeton University Press, 2006).

[12] The classical work is Everett M Rogers, *Diffusion of Innovations* (New York: Free Press of Glencoe, 1962; 5th edn, 2003) 144 (for diffusion and adoption). For the so-called 's-curve' in this process see already n 194 and n 195 in Chapter 4.

including the role of hubs,[13] as well as the possibility of increasing the likelihood of diffusion through design.[14]

This chapter proceeds as follows. In Section B, transplant design is discussed as a series of steps that the transplant unit may be advised to undertake. Section C presents this book's own recommendations for key topics of transplant design, followed by the concluding Section D. A challenge of this analysis is how far it is feasible to generalise about transplants of any type: thus, the steps discussed in Section B mainly focus on legal transplants by legislatures, while the recommendations of Section C can, mutatis mutandis, apply to any type of transplants, be it by legislatures, courts, contracting parties, legal academia, etc.

B. Identifying steps of transplant design

Some of the literature presents the question about the right design of legal transplants in a number of steps that lawmakers can, or should, follow. While using such a blueprint is not without its limitations,[15] these suggestions are a useful starting point for key topics that the design of transplants may need to consider.

1. Steps and criteria suggested in literature

In a narrow sense, the transplant design begins with the moment where the idea of using a foreign model is introduced in the lawmaking process and it ends with the enactment of the law. However, we have seen in the previous chapters that the 'causes of causes' of legal transplants can go back further in time and that the effect of transplants may often only be apparent at a later stage (possibly, after some modifications).[16] Thus, some of the literature, outlined in Table 7.1, presents this topic in a longer time frame.

[13] Albert-László Barabási, *Linked: How Everything Is Connected to Everything Else and What It Means for Business, Science, and Everyday Life* (New York: Basic Books, 2014) 55–64, 135.

[14] James W Dearing and others, 'Designing for Diffusion of a Biomedical Intervention' (2023) 44 *American Journal of Preventive Medicine* S70.

[15] Similarly, for a blueprint of the methods of comparative law: Mathias Siems, *Comparative Law* (Cambridge: CUP, 3rd edn, 2022) 40–3.

[16] See Chapter 4 at Section C and Chapter 5 at Section C.

Table 7.1 Transplant design and related topics in the literature

	Trigger in transplant unit	Background analysis	Law proposal		Law enacted	Legal application			Socio-legal outcomes and evaluation	
Hirsch 1968			Planning (and enactment) by legislature (Hirsch 1981: legal idea as object)			Execution by courts	Sign-posting by legal academia	Realisation through interpretation by highest court		
Rose 2005	Groups make case for legal change	Choice of models considered	Abstract generalised model	Examine how to make model fit	Decide on adoption	Application, also if modified			Evaluate outcome	
Seidman & Seidman 2006	Identification of behaviours causing a problem	Explanation of causes of those behaviours							Correction of causes	Monitoring and evaluation
Xanthaki 2008	(same social need)	Transplant question	Transplant concept	Transplant research design						
Frankenberg 2010		Foreign model	De-contextualised model as 'global reservoir'	Recontextualise model						
Wörner-Schönecker 2022	Preparation stage				Incorporation	Adoption by legal community		Application and enforcement		
	Status quo in transplant unit	Analyse type of transplant and transfer	Identify risks	Identify how to avoid problems						
Noori et al 2023	Recipient preparation	Identifying and learning from practices from abroad			Transferring to recipient	Policy adoption and implementation (eg policy localisation; monitoring and evaluation)				
Al-Umuri 2020	*What and why? Problem and current law in transplant unit*	*From where? Deep understanding of foreign model*		*How? Context in transplant unit to ensure effectiveness of transplant*						
de Jong et al 2002	*Voluntary adoption – Use in times of regime transformation*	*Consider multiple models*	*Consider using generic model*	*Consider similarity of units – Adapt to localcircumstances*						

The 1968 article by Ernst Hirsch[17] may have been the first that explicitly dealt with different phases of the transplantation process. Hirsch uses the Turkish case[18] as an illustration, including his own involvement. He also seems to regard this case as an example of how steps should evolve. In substance, his main focus is on the legal application of the law after its enactment (step 1). Specifically, he mentions how courts may struggle to interpret the new law (step 2), how legal academia may then provide guidance (step 3), which may eventually lead to clarifications by the highest courts (step 4). Elsewhere, Hirsch explored the decision of the lawmaker to draw on foreign law in more detail: here, his main argument is that a transplant should not simply be a translation of foreign law but focus on the underlying legal idea.[19] In other words, a good design asks for a degree of abstraction, which we will also see in some of the other views.

The second publication in Table 7.1 is the 2005 book by the political scientist Richard Rose on 'learning from comparative public policy'. He calls this book 'a study in political engineering, that is, the application of social science knowledge to the world in which policymakers must make choices'.[20] The 'ten steps in lesson-drawing' are presented in a condensed form in the table. They show that Rose is relatively detailed about the process leading to the transplant, including the influence of interest groups and the choice of models. He also mentions, as a final point, the need to 'evaluate a lesson's outcome prospectively and, if it is adopted, as it evolves over time';[21] by contrast, there is less emphasis than in the work by Hirsch on the way courts and legal academics may shape the new law.

The 2006 article by Ann and Robert Seidman focusses on legal transplants and development;[22] yet, its main four steps derive from work that the authors have proposed more generally for assessing legislation.[23] These steps are therefore generic in their instrumental use of the law with a particular focus on the way a new law may be able to change the behaviours which account for the underlying problem. Thus, this asks for a contextual understanding of the way

[17] Ernst E Hirsch, 'Vier Phasen im Ablauf eines zeitgenössischen Rezeptionsprozess' (1968) 69 *Zeitschrift für Vergleichende Rechtswissenschaft* 182, reprinted in Ernst Hirsch, *Rezeption als sozialer Prozeß: erläutert am Beispiel der Türkei* (Berlin: Duncker & Humblot, 1981) 29–89.

[18] See generally Chapter 5 at Section C 3 (b).

[19] Hirsch (n 17) (1981), 11–12, 19. See also Chapter 3 at Section B 2.

[20] Richard Rose, *Learning from Comparative Public Policy* (London: Routledge, 2005) xi.

[21] For the full list see Rose (n 20) 8.

[22] Ann Seidman and Robert B Seidman, 'Law in Aid of Development: Hasty Legal Transplants and the Fatal Race' (2006) 1 *The Journal of Comparative Law* 282.

[23] Ann Seidman, Robert B Seidman, and Nalin Abeyesekere, *Assessing Legislation: A Manual for Legislators* (Boston, MA: Boston University School of Law, 2002), available at http://www.legislativeconsulting.com/resources-new/ accessed 23 October 2025.

law should be designed. Another noteworthy point is that this taxonomy includes, as a final step, the suggestion to 'regularly monitor and evaluate the new structure'.

Helen Xanthaki's 2008 article on 'legal transplants in legislation' also draws on general literature, in this case, the research on legislative drafting.[24] It is then specifically interested in the phase in which the legal transplantation is pursued. For this purpose, it distinguishes between the question of which foreign model may be used ('transplant question'), the identification of both a generic and concrete concept that can be transplanted ('transplant concept'), and, then, the actual question of whether the transplant should be adopted, including the analysis of differences and similarities between the units ('transplant comparative research design').[25] In other work, Xanthaki suggests that a legal transplant needs to fulfil the same social need as in the origin country, drawing on the functionalism of traditional comparative law.[26] However, this may overlook cases where a transplant has the aim of changing society in a particular manner (ie the main motivation of the transplant is that, at present, society is different between both units).[27]

The 2010 publication by Günter Frankenberg is also specifically focussed on the moment of legal transplantation.[28] It resembles the positions of Hirsch and Xanthaki in that it also identifies the need for an abstraction of the foreign law. However, Frankenberg presents this abstraction as being part of a 'global reservoir' and, for that reason, he also calls his proposal 'IKEA theory', regarding this process as being akin to choosing from a variety of standardised models and then reassembling them at home.[29] With respect to the actual steps, Frankenberg presents the abstraction as two steps (see Table 7.1), namely de-contextualisation and its subsequent inclusion in a global reservoir, while a comment by Ralf Michaels treats those as three steps, adding the

[24] See now also Ittai Bar-Siman-Tov and Helen Xanthaki, 'Legislation, Legisprudence and Comparative Law' in Jan M Smits and others (eds), *Elgar Encyclopedia of Comparative Law* (Cheltenham: Edward Elgar, 3rd edn, 2023) 530.

[25] Helen Xanthaki, 'Legal Transplants in Legislation: Defusing the Trap' (2008) 57 *International and Comparative Law Quarterly* 659.

[26] Helen Xanthaki, *Legislative Drafting for the EU: Transposition Techniques as a Roadmap for Better Legislation and a Sustainable EU* (Cheltenham: Edward Elgar, 2024) 153; Helen Xanthaki, 'On Transferability of Legislative Solutions: The Functionality Test' in Constantin Stefanou and Helen Xanthaki (eds), *Drafting Legislation: A Modern Approach* (London: Routledge, 2008) 3.

[27] See further Section C 2 (a) and (d).

[28] Günter Frankenberg, 'Constitutional Transfer: The IKEA Theory Revisited' (2010) 8 *International Journal of Constitutional Law* 563. See also Günter Frankenberg, 'Constitutions as Commodities: Notes on a Theory of Transfer' in Günter Frankenberg (ed), *Order from Transfer: Comparative Constitutional Design and Legal Culture* (Cheltenham: Edward Elgar, 2013) 1; Günter Frankenberg, *Comparative Constitutional Studies: Between Magic and Deceit* (Cheltenham: Edward Elgar, 2018) 117–55.

[29] Frankenberg (n 28) (2018), 117 fn 24.

unaltered transfer of the abstract rule to the transplant country as a further step.[30] From a normative perspective, Michaels notes that Frankenberg actually views this form of transfer critically, and that it may indeed be worrying how, in this process, 'global capitalism' turns 'laws into commodities'.[31] Compared to other positions, however, this IKEA strategy at least has the advantage that a transplant may, potentially, also work where the context of the two units is dissimilar. In other literature, Michele Spanò notes that the IKEA conceptualisation can be helpful as it encourages a focus on the social actors that matter for the transplant process.[32]

A monograph by Maximilian Wörner-Schönecker distinguishes between preparation, incorporation, adoption, and application of the law,[33] drawing on work by other scholars.[34] Wörner-Schönecker then elaborates on the process of preparation prior to the actual transplant. This includes an 'attention grid' for the transplant unit to follow. To start with, it should identify the characteristics of the situation at hand, namely the status quo in the transplant unit, the type of legal transplant, and the modalities of the planned transfer. Subsequently, the lawmaker should identify the risks of the transplantation and the means to tackle any problems that may arise, say, due to differences in context.[35] Thus, while the first part of the attention grid is theoretical, the subsequent parts are meant to use prior experiences in order to assess the design of the transplant and any related questions about its implementation.

The final publication of Table 7.1 which presents legal (or policy) transplantation in stages is by Negar Noori and colleagues.[36] Its substantive topic is the use of policy transplantation for smart city development. Yet, the article also contains a general scheme of four phases, namely 'recipient preparation', 'identifying and learning from practices from abroad', 'transferring policy to

[30] Ralf Michaels, '"One Size Can Fit All": Some Heretical Thoughts on the Mass Production of Legal Transplants' in Günter Frankenberg (ed), *Order from Transfer: Comparative Constitutional Design and Legal Culture* (Cheltenham: Edward Elgar, 2013) 56, 59. For the steps Frankenberg draws on Edward Said, see already Chapter 5 at Section B 3.

[31] Michaels (n 30) 58 and 77. See also Section C 3 (c).

[32] Michele Spanò, 'BILLY o del pluralism procedural. Un programma di ricercarca' (2014) 11 *Jura Gentium (Special Issue Pluralismo giuridico)* 124. See also Section B 2, as well as more generally Chapter 4 at Section B 3.

[33] Maximilian Wörner-Schönecker, *Rechtstransfers: Eine Analyse anhand von Typologien* (Tübingen: Mohr Siebeck, 2022) 36–7.

[34] Marina Kurkchiyan, 'What to Expect from Institutional Transplants? An Experience of Setting up Media Self-regulation in Russia and Bosnia' (2012) 8 *International Journal of Law in Context* 115, 123–4; Beata Kviatek, *Explaining Legal Transplants: Transplantation of EU Law into Central Eastern Europe* (Nijmegen: Wolf Legal Publishers, 2015) 120.

[35] Wörner-Schönecker (n 33) 162–77.

[36] Negar Noori and others, 'Transplanting Good Practices in Smart City Development: A Step-wise Approach' (2023) 40 *Government Information Quarterly* 101802. See also Negar Noori, *Policy Transplantation for Smart City Initiatives* (PhD Thesis, Rotterdam, 2021).

recipient', and 'policy adoption and implementation'. In the elaboration of these general headings, further details are proposed. For example, in the first phase, policymakers should map the goals and analyse the status quo, and in the second one, they should establish networks with other policy makers and identify good and bad practices. Particular emphasis is put on the final phase as it includes the monitoring and evaluation of the policy, which may lead to its adjustments or even termination.

Other authors also identify various criteria, yet they do not present them in a series of steps. In the policy diffusion literature, Charles Shipan and Craig Volden suggest that the 'learning-based spread of good policies' requires the use of observable experiments, time to learn, and expertise and incentives.[37] In the legal literature, Randall Peerenboom's article on 'successful legal transplants' mentions the importance of processes whilst listing several criteria that the transplant unit should consider. These criteria range from the relevance of general differences between countries (eg, legal families, political system, economic system) to topics such as the strengths and weaknesses of current legal institutions, the areas of law under consideration, the motivations for the law reform, as well as regional and geopolitical factors.[38] Thus, many of these criteria refer to topics that, in this book, have already featured in the previous chapters, for example, the questions why transplants take place and how they work,[39] while they can also play a role for questions of transplant design.

In other publications, criteria may be presented in a way that they are seen as akin to a series of steps. In an Australian PhD thesis, Mohammad Al-Umari mentions the issues 'what to transplant, why to transplant, from where to transplant and how to transplant' and then lists a number of criteria that concern, on the one hand, the transplant unit (eg, the problem at hand, the shortcomings of the current law, the cultural and political context), and, on the other hand, the foreign law (eg, its ability to deal with the problem, its historical background, its strength, and weaknesses).[40] As shown in Table 7.1, these points relate, in one way or another, to the preparatory phase of the transplant.

An example from political science is by Martin de Jong and colleagues. They developed six propositions about the use of institutional transplantation,

[37] Charles R Shipan and Craig Volden, *Why Bad Policies Spread (and Good Ones Don't)* (Cambridge: CUP, 2021) 20–6.

[38] Randall Peerenboom, 'Toward a Methodology for Successful Legal Transplants' (2013) 1 *The Chinese Journal of Comparative Law* 4.

[39] See Chapters 4 and 5.

[40] Mohammad Al-Umari, *Evaluation of the Transplantability of the Doctrine of Proper Law of the Contract from Australian Law into the Jordanian Legal System* (PhD thesis, UWA Law School, 2020) 28, 45, available at https://doi.org/10.26182/608c-xs31 accessed 23 October 2025.

namely that transplants should (i) be voluntary, (ii) not simply be copied but adapted to local circumstances, (iii) follow the consideration of multiple models, (iv) usually be based on like-to-like transplantations, (v) concern 'general and abstract policy lessons, ideas and ideologies' rather than 'specific legal frameworks or procedures', and (vi) often be used in times of regime transformations.[41] Again, this complements the previous literature. However, as regards the fifth point, it may be objected that adopting specific laws may sometimes be the most effective strategy if those laws are well-tested and/or time-constraints make the drafting of tailor-made laws too costly.[42]

To conclude, the positions shown in Table 7.1 are complementary in the sense that most authors focus on some of the steps needed to enact and implement legal transplants. As far as these positions differ, it is clear that authors from political sciences (as well as those who draw on such research) focus on other aspects than legal scholars (say, Hirsch and Wörner-Schönecker). There are also some substantive differences, at least in emphasis: for example, whether the model of a transplant should be fairly generic or whether contextual differences are likely to be a key challenge, or whether the advice is given in an optimistic spirit that legal transplants have the potential to solve problems or whether there is more emphasis on challenges and risks. Indeed, as the use of transplants can vary, notably its object and units, any advice about design needs to be sensitive to the specifics of a particular case. This will also be apparent in the remainder of this chapter.

2. Own position

The design of legal transplants should not only be in the hands of lawmaking bodies. The following distinguishes between these lawmaking bodies, 'lawyers and other experts', and 'stakeholders and the general public'. The group of lawyers and other experts is important as transplants often require a deep comparative understanding of the laws of various units.[43] Thus, beyond the use of general types of expertise that can help lawmaking (whatever it may

[41] Martin de Jong, Virginie Mamadouh, and Konstantinos Lalenis, 'Drawing Lessons about Lesson Drawing' in Martin de Jong, Konstantinos Lalenis, and Virginie Mamadouh (eds), *The Theory and Practice of Institutional Transplantation: Experiences With the Transfer of Policy Institutions* (Deventer: Kluwer Academic Publishers, 2002) 283, 284–91. Similarly, for international lawmaking, Martin de Jong and Suzan Stoter, 'Institutional Transplantation and the Rule of Law: How this Interdisciplinary Method Can Enhance the Legitimacy of International Organisations' (2009) 2 *Erasmus Law Review* 311, 319–22.

[42] See Chapter 6 at Section C 3.

[43] See further Section C 1 (a).

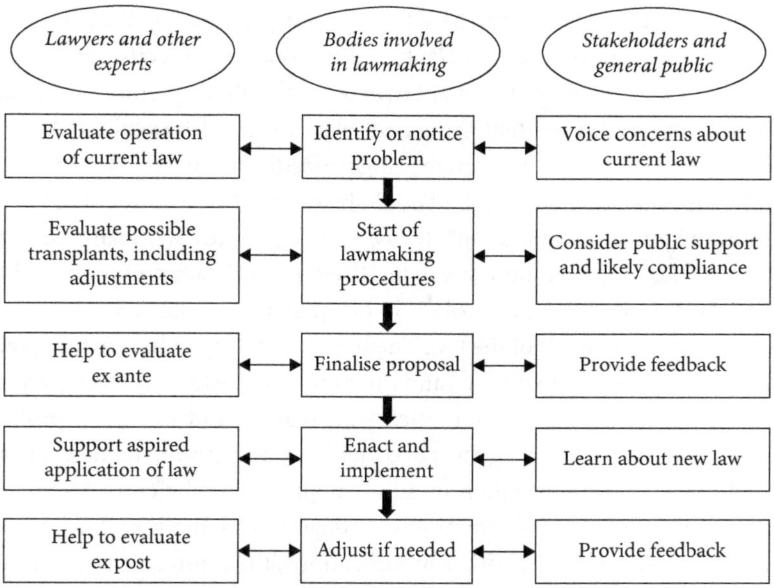

Figure 7.1 Main stages in designing legal transplants

be: eg, economics or moral ethics),[44] there is a particular case to be made that expert involvement needs to play a key role in the design of legal transplants. Similarly, while stakeholders and the general public may initiate any new law or be involved in any type of lawmaking, legal transplants are potentially more contentious as they deviate from the (allegedly) typical starting point of home-grown laws.[45]

Figure 7.1 distinguishes between these three groups and between five broad steps. The figure also shows multiple interactions between the law-making bodies and the two other groups. For example, the lawmaking body may involve them in order to improve the quality and legitimacy of the law, or these groups may, using their own initiative, interact with the respective law-making body.

The first step displayed in Figure 7.1 is the recognition of a 'problem' that the transplant plans to address. This can be anything from a practical social or economic problem to a wish to improve the clarity of the law.[46] Starting with this step is not meant to imply that the problem may not already have been contemplated at previous moments. The identification of a 'problem' may not,

[44] See already Chapter 6 at Sections A and C 1.
[45] See generally Chapter 6 at Section C 4 (a) and 5.
[46] See further Section C 2 (a).

depending on the subject matter, be self-evident but depend on the skills of the lawmaker and its willingness to listen to public concerns. Specifically, for legal transplants, it can be suggested that lawmakers should implement structures that facilitate the ability of identifying and selecting 'good' transplants.[47]

In the second step, the actual lawmaking procedures start, and this may give rise to the idea that a legal transplant could be used, while also keeping in consideration the option of not using a transplant. This is further analysed in the third step as the proposed new law is finalised. In both steps, experts and the general public should play a key role.[48] In particular, these steps require a thorough comparative analysis of the law. The natural starting point are the foreign laws as they are, namely, to understand their content, history, and operation in practice and then consider a hypothetical transplant in addressing the problem at hand, while also considering any costs (widely understood, including resistance by the public).[49] Subsequently, adjustments should be considered. This can be based on forms of abstraction (as suggested by the literature, see the previous subsection) but also other modifications, including, for example, different ways of implementing and enforcing the law.[50] In particular in the third step, the transplant unit also needs to address the actual formulation of the new law, including possible challenges of translation.[51]

The fourth step consists of the enactment and implementation of the law, which typically also involves courts or enforcement institutions. Experts such as lawyers and law professors may help in the communication and application of the law, while the law should also become known to the general public and any relevant stakeholders. In some cases, this may then lead to the fifth step, namely the need for adjustments of any possible type. These final two steps are, in many respects, the same for any new law. However, if the new law concerns a legal transplant, it is possible that particular challenges arise due to the foreign element that is intended to generate a positive effect.[52]

The necessary caveat of suggesting these five steps is that, in a specific situation, more factors and details can come into play. Thus, rather than attempting to further refine (or complicate) such a step-based scheme, the following section focusses on a selection of key topics that the design of many transplants should consider.

[47] For example, through Law Commissions, see Section C 1 (a). For the role of such prior conditions see also Chapter 8 at Section C.

[48] See further Section C 1 (a) and (c).

[49] See further Section C 1 (c) and 2 (a) and (d).

[50] See further Section C 3 (a) and (c).

[51] See further Section C 3 (b).

[52] See further Section C 1 (d).

C. Key topics of transplant design

This section presents twelve recommendations for the design of legal transplants. Similar to the analysis of the previous chapter, this advice is of a normative nature, while it also considers the importance of positive factors that matter for normative questions.[53] The recommendations are divided into three subsections of four recommendations each: procedural considerations, choice of models, and details of the law. These recommendations are meant to cover the design of any type of transplant and, thus, not only cases of domestic legislation but also case law, international laws, soft laws, legal ideas, etc. They are also open in the sense that different bodies may be involved in the transplant process (eg, the government and different parliamentary bodies for legislative transplants).[54]

This wide scope poses the obvious challenge that, due to the diversity of objects of transplants, units and actors involved, the design of a transplant is likely to differ in many details. Thus, the following cannot aim to provide a comprehensive set of criteria. Rather, it should be understood as 'just' identifying key recommendations that are likely to matter for many legal transplants. In other words, these recommendations should not be read as implying that they are always sufficient in all situations. They also need to be adjusted depending on the precise unit and body that is designing the transplant.

1. Procedural considerations

It is suggested here that, principally, experts should play a key role in the design of legal transplants, while also ensuring domestic ownership and public accountability. Implementation and evaluation of transplants may revisit their design and use if needed.

(a) Experts should play a key role in transplant design

Recent years have seen many critical voices on the role of experts in policy making, and even social life more generally. For example, William Easterly's book on the 'tyranny of experts' challenges the expert-led development policy by international development organisations and Western countries,[55] David

[53] For the entanglement of 'is' and 'ought' see already Chapter 6 at Section C 1 (b).

[54] Similar Figure 4.1 in Chapter 5 at Section C 1 and 3.

[55] William Easterly, *The Tyranny of Experts: Economists, Dictators, and the Forgotten Rights of the Poor* (New York: Basic Books, 2014).

Kennedy's 'world of struggle' criticises the growing global 'expert rule' that is detached from its distributive consequences,[56] and Jeffrey Friedman's 'power without knowledge' presents a critique of technocracy as not (even) delivering on its own promise to use policies that can work in practice.[57] The views of experts have recently also been challenged in the context of events such as the Brexit referendum campaign, climate change, and the responses to the Covid pandemic;[58] yet, reference can also be made to critiques from both the left and the right that go back to the 1960s and 1970s.[59]

The status of experts also has its supporters. Steven Pinker, for example, criticises both the postmodernist left and populist right in abandoning the achievements of the Enlightenment—reason, science, and humanism,[60] and Garett Jones suggests that we should find the 'right dose of democracy' with some topics better left outside full democratic participation.[61] Another response is that it matters who should be seen as an 'expert', with some suggesting a democratisation of expertise, notably campaigns by environmental and patient rights movements.[62] Yet, applied more generally, such an extension would make expert involvement identical to stakeholder participation (which, of course, also matters, see the following subsections). Experts should also be valued due to their contributions to a 'design informed by factual evidence and expert knowledge'.[63] Thus, while such a position does not limit the scope of experts to particular persons, it points toward the underlying reasons why experts should play a key role in lawmaking.

For legal transplants, the analysis of the previous chapters indicates the need for the involvement of persons with expertise in comparative law, broadly understood. Following on from Chapter 4, the knowledge about a possible transplant

[56] David Kennedy, *A World of Struggle: How Power, Law, and Expertise Shape Global Political Economy* (Princeton, NJ: Princeton University Press, 2016).

[57] Jeffrey Friedman, *Power Without Knowledge: A Critique of Technocracy* (Oxford: OUP, 2020). See also Alessandra Arcuri and Florin Coman-Kund (eds), *Technocracy and the Law: Accountability, Governance and Expertise* (Abingdon: Routledge, 2021).

[58] For the first two examples see Gil Eyal, *The Crisis of Expertise* (Cambridge: Polity Press, 2019). For the third one see Thomas S Harrington, *The Treason of the Experts: Covid and the Credentialed Class* (Austin, TX: Brownstone Institute, 2023).

[59] Gil Eyal and Thomas Medvetz, 'Introduction' in Gil Eyal and Thomas Medvetz (eds), *The Oxford Handbook of Expertise and Democratic Politics* (Oxford: OUP, 2023) 3.

[60] Steven Pinker, *Enlightenment Now: The Case for Reason, Science, Humanism, and Progress* (New York: Penguin, 2018).

[61] Garett Jones, *10% Less Democracy: Why You Should Trust Elites a Little More and the Masses a Little Less* (Stanford, CA: Stanford University Press, 2020).

[62] Steven Epstein, 'The Meaning and Significance of Lay Expertise' in Gil Eyal and Thomas Medvetz (eds), *The Oxford Handbook of Expertise and Democratic Politics* (Oxford: OUP, 2023) 76.

[63] Gaby Umbach, 'Evidence and expertise in 21st century policy-making' (*EUI Ideas*, 17 November 2020), available at https://euideas.eui.eu/2020/11/17/evidence-and-expertise-in-21st-century-policy-making/ accessed 23 October 2025.

needs to be correctly identified and any perceived qualities of the transplant need to be real qualities.[64] Chapters 5 and 6 further indicate that transplants need to be sensitive to questions of context and timing and, thus, here too, comparative law expertise is often crucial.[65] The list of reasons on 'what can go wrong' in policy transfer by Shipan and Volden also indicates the need for such expert involvement. Among others, this list mentions that the learning process goes wrong if lawmakers 'lack expert staff and committees', they view 'limited examples as representative', 'rely too much on availability', and fail to consider compatibility with current practices and time to learn.[66] With such involvement, it is also clear that expert advice can also lead to the conclusion that a particular issue is unlikely to be fixed by legal means.[67]

Who exactly the comparative law experts are and how and when they should be involved depends on the circumstances. As far as legislation is concerned, detailed analysis is found in an edited book on the use of comparative law in legislative drafting.[68] For example, it identifies a divide between 'transplant friendly' legislators with institutionalised forms of incorporating comparative insights, legislators 'partially interested in transplanting', which sometimes rely on research services, ad hoc committees or reports, and 'transplanting hostile' legislators.[69] More specifically, a chapter of this book suggests that Law Commissions of the English model and professional research units can provide expertise to legislators, who are unlikely to have the time and resources to conduct comparative law research themselves.[70] Another chapter also found that fundamental decisions about the original design of a unit and its lawmaking procedures may play an important role (eg, the EU being a plural system and relying on standing committees for legislative drafting).[71] For transplants by courts too, many differentiations may be made. For example, it is likely to not only matter whether judges have direct expertise beyond their legal system but also how far foreign insights are presented through the parties of a trial,

[64] See Chapter 4 at Section C 3.

[65] See also Section C 2 and 3.

[66] Shipan and Volden (n 37) 52 (specifically the points 4, 5, 10, 11, 12, and 13).

[67] Similar to the evaluation of whether a specific transplant can effectively achieve a particular aim, see Chapter 6 at Section C 3 (a). See also Zeynep Özlem Üskül Engin, 'Medeni Kanun ve Toplumsal Dönüşüm' in Fethi Gedikli (ed), *I. Turk Hukuk Tarihi Kongresi Bildirileri* (Istanbul: XII Levha Yayinlari, 2014) 31, 42 (for the ability of the transplanted Turkish Civil Code to change only some aspects of society).

[68] Lupo and Scaffardi (n 5).

[69] Nicola Lupo and Lucia Scaffardi, 'Introduction: The Uses of Comparative Law in Legislative Drafting', in Lupo and Scaffardi (n 5) 1, 11–5.

[70] Daphne Barak-Erez, 'Legislation as Transplantation' in Lupo and Scaffardi (n 5) 17, 25–6.

[71] Robert L Tsai, 'Conclusion. The Migration of Legal Ideas: Legislative Design and the Lawmaking Process' in Lupo and Scaffardi (n 5) 197, 302–3.

legal academia, reports, or model rules.[72] Similar to legislatures, some supreme courts have also established designated comparative law units to support their work.[73]

The involvement of experts should also go beyond comparative law expertise, notably as far as empirical information plays a role. Only some aspects of this general topic can be sketched here. The previous chapter mentioned observational studies that found that certain laws promote wealth and prosperity.[74] Others argue that a robust way of showing the effect of laws needs to be based on experiments, such as randomised controlled trials;[75] yet, the downside is that experiments may have limited external validity. It has also been suggested that experimental insights may not have produced clear findings in many fields, while their use can still be helpful if one avoids considering them in a binary manner (also noting that the actual implementation of laws plays a key role).[76] Beyond the use of social science methods to estimate the likely effect of laws, behaviourally informed policy-making can shape the substance of legal rules, as many initiatives show.[77] Another line of research, which is interested in the way 'policy learning' happens, also includes the role of experts.[78] In this regard, it is rightly said that expertise should not be limited to problem solving but also include forms of reflective learning.[79]

An inevitable topic for future transplants will be the role of Artificial Intelligence (AI) for the design of legal transplants. There are already some

[72] See eg Thomas Coendet, *Rechtsvergleichende Argumentation: Phänomenologie der Veränderung im rechtlichen Diskurs* (Tübingen: Mohr Siebeck, 2012) 179.

[73] For France see Paolo Passaglia, 'Comparative Law and the French Constitutional Council' in Giuseppe Franco Ferrari (ed), *Judicial Cosmopolitanism: The Use of Foreign Law in Contemporary Constitutional Systems* (Leiden: Brill Nijhoff, 2019) 263, 280–3. For Italy see https://www.cortecostituzionale.it/diritto-comparato accessed 23 October 2025.

[74] See Chapter 6 at Section C 3 (a).

[75] For an overview see Abhijit Vinayak Banerjee, Esther Duflo, and Michael Kremer, 'The Influence of Randomized Controlled Trials on Development Economics Research and on Development Policy' in Kaushik Basu, David Rosenblatt, and Claudia Sepúlveda (eds), *The State of Economics, the State of the World* (Cambridge, MA: MIT Press, 2019) 439.

[76] Megan T Stevenson, 'Cause, Effect, and the Structure of the Social World' (2023) 103 *Boston University Law Review* 2001. For further discussion see the articles in 'Does Evidence Matter? Research meets the real world' (*Vital City*, 2024/7), available at https://www.vitalcitynyc.org/issues/issue-7 accessed 23 October 2025.

[77] See eg Marianna Baggio and others, 'The Evolution of Behaviourally Informed Policy-making in the EU' (2021) 28 *Journal of European Public Policy* 658; Holger Straßheim, 'The Rise and Spread of Behavioral Public Policy: An Opportunity for Critical Research and Self-Reflection' (2020) 2 *International Review of Public Policy* 115.

[78] Claire A Dunlop and Claudio M Radaelli, 'Systematising Policy Learning: From Monolith to Dimensions' (2013) 61 *Political Studies* 599, 603–4 (in the variant of 'epistemic learning').

[79] Claudius Messner, 'Border Troubles. Some Uncertainties of Legal Transfer' (2020) 5 *International Journal of Legal Discourse* 151, 178–9.

attempts to employ AI in lawmaking, for example, to identify inconsistencies of existing laws, to help with the formulation of legislative proposals, to consolidate consultation responses, or to facilitate the transcription of parliamentary debates.[80] Whatever their merit, expertise is likely to remain essential for legal transplants, possibly in combination with using AI to support the screening for suitable transplants, their real and hypothetical functionality and shortcomings, as well as their empirically most likely effects.

(b) Maintain domestic ownership despite the use of foreign knowledge

The previous subsection implicitly assumed that the transplant unit acts entirely voluntarily. Yet, we have seen in the previous chapters that, even today, there may be forms of pressure, be it by other units or foreign agents.[81] Here, a radical position would be that such transplants should simply not happen. By contrast, this book takes the view that some external influence, leading to the influx of foreign knowledge, does not exclude the possible endorsement of a transplant.[82] However, it needs to be ensured that ultimate domestic ownership is maintained.

Terminologically, the domestic-foreign divide is meant to refer to laws that are enacted by countries but also other units, and they may also concern all types of legal objects.[83] For example, for a soft law proposed by an international organisation, the transplantation of soft laws by other organisations or countries would make use of such 'foreign knowledge'.

The specific phrase 'domestic ownership' derives from discussion in the field of development policy. Following the criticism of 'structural adjustment' requirements used by the IMF and the World Bank, these and other development organisations started emphasising that any influence on developing countries should respect their ownership in reforming their legal system.[84] How far this shift in terminology has been meaningful is a matter of debate.[85]

[80] References in Fotios Fitsilis, Jörn von Lucke, and Franklin De Vrieze, 'Inception, Development and Evolution of Guidelines for AI in Parliaments' (2025) 13 *The Theory and Practice of Legislation* 405. Nicoletta Rangone and Luca Megale, 'Risks Without Rights? The EU AI Act's Approach to AI in Law and Rule-Making' (2025) 16 *European Journal of Risk Regulation* 1082. See also the example of Albania, discussed in Section C 2 (a).

[81] See Chapter 4 at Sections B 3 and C 3 (b).

[82] See Chapter 6 at Section C 4 and 5.

[83] See generally Chapter 3 at Sections B and C, as well Chapter 6 at Section C 4 (a).

[84] See eg Malin Hasselskog, 'What Happened to the Focus on the Aid Relationship in the Ownership Discussion?' (2022) 155 *World Development* 105896; Jeremy Gould (ed), *The New Conditionality: The Politics of Poverty Reduction Strategies* (London: Zed, 2005).

[85] Palash Kamruzzaman, *Poverty Reduction Strategy in Bangladesh: Rethinking Participation in Policy Making* (Bristol: Bristol University Press, 2014) 81–110; Marte Briseid and others, 'Domestic Ownership or Foreign Control? A Content Analysis of Poverty Reduction Strategy Papers from Eight Countries' (Crisis States Research Centre, Occasional Paper No 5, 2008).

Indeed, the metaphor of 'ownership' is unlikely to produce a clear conclusion in the common situation where multiple sources of influence interact to produce a policy outcome. In a similar sense, Virginia Harper Ho discusses how transnational networks of public and private actors may lead to transplant-like regulatory innovations.[86] Still, it makes sense to use 'ownership' as the ultimate decision on the transplant should be taken by the transplant unit, even if involuntary elements occur in the preceding phase. This is meant to be a minimum standard; thus, it does not exclude that other reasons may speak against a particular form or direction of influence on the transplant unit.

The requirement of ownership can also be applied to judicial transplants. Previous chapters already addressed various aspects of this topic.[87] In the context of this chapter, the recommendation is that foreign case law should be treated as having an informational value only. Notably, this implies the use of foreign precedents as persuasive but not binding authorities. Considering foreign case law can also be a legitimate means of gaining deeper insights into general ideas about the law, including the understanding of one's own legal system.[88] For further details, differences between their use in courts can be due to their general design. For example, the extent of using judicial transplants also depends on their general use of judicial discretion and creativity,[89] and, in some countries, special rules exist on the way authorities may or may not be cited in judgments.[90]

This dependency on general procedural rules is not unique to judicial transplants. It can also matter for domestic legislation and, even more so, for the lawmaking of international organisations. For example, the World Bank is required to follow 'considerations of economy and efficiency [. . .] without regard

[86] Virginia E Harper Ho, 'Beyond Transplant: A Network Innovation Model of Transnational Regulatory Change' (2023) 71 *American Journal of Comparative Law* 513.

[87] See Chapter 1 at Section B 2, Chapter 3 at Section B 2, and Chapter 6 at Sections B 2, C 1 (b), and 4 (a).

[88] See Chapter 6 at Section C 4 (a).

[89] Similarly, Daphne Barak-Erez, 'The Institutional Aspects of Comparative Law' (2009) 15 *Columbia Journal of European Law* 477, 490 ('this controversy emerges as a variation on the dispute about judicial discretion').

[90] References to foreign case law are allowed in the UK Practice Directions issued by the Lord Chief Justice [2001] 2 All ER 510, Section 39(1)(c) of the Constitution of the Republic of South Africa 1996, and in the Hong Kong Basic Law, Article 84 (but only to other common law jurisdictions). In France, Cour de Cassation, *Motivation enrichie: le guide de redaction* (2023), available at https://www.courdecassation.fr/toutes-les-actualites/2023/09/25/motivation-enrichie-le-guide-de-redaction accessed 23 October 2025, deals with legal reasoning more generally. In Italy, Article 118 of the *Disposizioni per l'attuazione del codice di procedura civile* (RD 18/12/1941, n 1368, as amended) prohibits the citation of 'legal authors'. In the US, some states unsuccessfully tried to prohibit the citation of foreign authorities, see Holly Tao, 'Congress, Courts, and Control over Persuasive Sources of Law' (2015/16) 51 *Gonzaga Law Review* 235.

to political or other non-economic influences or considerations'.[91] Thus, in this context, 'domestic ownership' means that it may not be acceptable to disregard these rules by way of incorporating certain transplants from other units (while it would, of course, be possible to change these procedural rules). Another example is a situation where a contract explicitly stipulates that its interpretation should not draw on the rules of a certain country or unit. Similarly, the previous chapter already mentioned that religious laws may, due to their own understanding, exclude the use of foreign models.[92]

(c) Transplants should generally be transparent and enjoy public support

The recommendations for transparency of the transplant and public support also require some clarifications and qualifications. To start with, the analysis of the preceding subsection may be read as arguing that, given the mere informational value of foreign ideas, disclosing the origins of such information may not be relevant. The previous subsection also referred to differences in judicial styles and, for that reason too, it may be acceptable that, for example, in the French judicial style, we have a 'bifurcation' between very short judgments and a more substantive discourse (including references to foreign case law) which is only sometimes available in the reports of the reporting judge or the opinions of the advocate general.[93]

However, better reasons exist which speak in favour of transplants generally being transparent. As the previous subsection also referred to the need to ensure domestic ownership, public accountability means that the use of a transplant should usually not be concealed. In particular, this is the case as far as transplants need to have the support of the public and/or key stakeholders (as discussed in the second part of this subsection). Moreover, as the design of transplants requires prudent choices about the foreign model and the details of the law,[94] these choices should be open to public scrutiny and feedback. Finally, from a more general perspective, it can be argued that the transparent use of transplants can create a fruitful dialogue between lawmakers (possibly, but not necessarily, leading to a marketplace for good legal ideas[95]).

[91] For the different units of the World Bank: IBRD Articles of Agreement, Articles 4(10), 3(5)(b); IDA Articles of Agreement, Articles 5(6), 5(1)(g); IFC Articles of Agreement, Article 3(9).

[92] See Chapter 6 at Section C 4 (a).

[93] Mitchel Lasser, *Judicial Deliberations: A Comparative Analysis of Judicial Transparency and Legitimacy* (Oxford: OUP, 2009) 27–61, but see also the recent changes, cited above at n 90.

[94] See Section C 2 and 3.

[95] See Chapter 6 at Section C 2 (b).

This general support for transparency can allow for some exceptions. Providing full and accurate information can create unnecessary costs, for example where the actual origins of an idea are complex and not relevant for the functioning of these rules. In some cases, there can also be a trade-off, namely if a good legal idea can only succeed if its origins are not disclosed. Two prominent examples are from the second part of the twentieth century. In the communist countries of Central and Eastern Europe, transplants from the 'capitalist' West were not openly acknowledged.[96] The same applied to the influence of German law in Israel soon after the Second World War: here, while many senior lawyers and judges had received their legal training in Germany, it was not seen as opportune to mention the German sources of legal ideas which shaped parts of Israeli law.[97] Another example may be transplants at the international level where it is recommended that 'explicit reference to controversial world hegemons or rogue states is to be avoided'.[98]

This final aspect leads to the other topic of this subsection, namely how far public support should be a required element in the design of legal transplants. In the case of judicial transplants, it is clear that judges are expected to decide cases on the basis of the law, even if public opinion were to take a different view on a particular issue. However, it is also evident that judges do 'care about what other people think of them',[99] not least since their legitimacy would suffer otherwise. For legislation, it can also be said that, in a system of representative democracy, members of parliaments have a free mandate that does not require them to simply follow public opinion. Yet, of course, the wishes of the public matter in practice, not least due to the desire of politicians to maximise their prospects of re-election. If the public are sceptical about a transplant as challenging their sociocultural identity, it is at least good advice that the lawmakers explain and, if necessary, convince the public why this law should be enacted. Similar arguments can be made for other types of units and objects. For example, soft laws by international organisations can be expected to be drafted in a manner that considers the views of the relevant stakeholders.

Thus, it is suggested here that, in general, it is good advice that the proposed transplant is supported by the general public and the relevant stakeholders (as it

[96] Jutta Mues, *Rechtstransfer: Zur theoretisch-methodischen Komplexität der Interaktion normativer Ordnungen* (Frankfurt: Peter Lang, 2015) 61.

[97] See Fania Oz-Salzberger and Eli Salzberger, 'The Secret German Sources of the Israeli Supreme Court' (1998) 3 *Israel Studies* 159; also Nili Cohen, 'German Law in Israeli Courts' (2018) *Comparative Studies in the Humanities* 195, 202–4 (on more recent growth of explicit references).

[98] de Jong and Stoter (n 41) 322.

[99] Lawrence Baum, 'Judges and their Audiences' in Lee Epstein and Stefanie A Lindquist (eds), *The Oxford Handbook of US Judicial Behavior* (Oxford: OUP, 2017) 343.

was also already found in the previous chapter that public opposition may be a reason against a transplant[100]). However, this is not a strict requirement. In particular, as far as details of the law are concerned, it is unlikely that the precise design of a transplant will be of much interest to the general public or stakeholders. As far as these interests are relevant, it is also reassuring that some studies have confirmed general public support for legal transplants.[101] Thus, if there is opposition, it may often have more to do with the substance of a particular law than the fact that it originates from another unit.

(d) Implement, evaluate, and, if necessary, react after transplant is enacted

Previous chapters have shown that the effect of transplants ranges from overfit, full effect, partial effect, adverse effect, and no effect,[102] and that the way a transplant 'works' may only emerge after some time.[103] Determinants for these variations are partly the result of the substance of the transplanted law (see the following two sections) but also procedural considerations after the transplant is enacted.

The implementation of any laws can be challenging; yet, there are some aspects that are specific to legal transplants.[104] To start with, the transplant unit may need to provide special training for judges and other lawyers in order to make them accurately understand and apply the foreign elements of the new law. In some cases, it may also be the case that the application of the law should not be exactly the same as in the origin unit. For example, according to Jack Hiller and Bernhard Grossfeld, the judicial application of the transplanted law must be creative,[105] and Esin Örücü discusses how, after the transplant, 'local tuning' needs to happen by persons and institutions of the transplant unit.[106] Thus, in such cases, the result is often an application that mixes foreign and domestic elements.[107]

[100] See Chapter 6 at Section C 4 (b) and 5.

[101] Katerina Linos, *The Democratic Foundations of Policy Diffusion: How Health, Family, and Employment Laws Spread Across Countries* (Oxford: OUP, 2013) 36–66; Åse B Grødeland and William L Miller, *European Legal Cultures in Transition* (Cambridge: CUP, 2015).

[102] Chapter 3 at Section D 2.

[103] Chapter 5 at Section C.

[104] Similarly, Athanase C Papachristos, *La réception des droits privés étrangers comme phénomène de sociologie juridique* (Paris: LGDJ, 1975) 77 (gap between law and society larger if legal change triggered by reception). For legal transplants and the relationship between law and society see also Chapter 5 at Section B.

[105] Jack Hiller and Bernhard Grossfeld, 'Comparative Legal Semiotics and the Divided Brain: Are We Producing Half-Brained Lawyers?' (2002) 50 *American Journal of Comparative Law* 175, 179.

[106] Esin Örücü, *The Enigma of Comparative Law: Variations on a Theme for the Twenty-First Century* (Leiden: Martinus Nijhoff, 2004) 93–106.

[107] For transplants leading to mixtures see also Chapter 5 at Section C 2 (a). For the adjustment to local conditions see also Section C 3 (a).

As for all laws, there should also be an evaluation of the way the transplanted law is received.[108] For transplants in particular, this needs to consider that the aspired effect of a transplant may only occur after some time.[109] Details also depend on the type of law and unit, for example, whether the way it 'works' may be assessed through the collection of data on the intended outcomes, surveys of the affected population, interviews, or other ethnographic research.[110] Such evaluation may also consider why, due to behavioural reasons, transplanted laws may not have the desired effect. John Linarelli provides two examples where this can be the case. Domestic lawyers may need to overcome the feeling of 'loss aversion' as they may fear that their expertise and prestige deteriorates, and both lawyers and citizens may show a form of 'identity-protective cognition', namely that they align the application of the new law with their prior experiences with the risk that this may contradict the desired meaning of the transplanted law.[111]

Any problems of implementation and/or negative evaluation should then lead to a reaction by the lawmaker. A first option can be that the transplant has been incomplete. For example, the transplant unit may realise that it also needs to transplant other elements of the law from the origin unit, say certain means of law enforcement.[112] Second, it may modify the transplanted law. This can happen with the aim of making the transplant 'work' more effectively. It can also have the aim of reducing the effect of the transplant if the 'overfit' of a transplant is harmful to the transplant unit.[113] Emphasising the openness for possible modifications is important as there are some instances of transplants that have remained unchanged, even after the origin unit deviated from it.[114] Third, the transplant unit may decide to reverse the decision to use the transplant. Here too, however, some research has identified forms of petrification where laws which have long been repealed in their place of origin still exist in transplant units.[115]

[108] See generally eg Frédéric Varone, Steve Jacob, and Pirmin Bundi (eds), *Handbook of Public Policy Evaluation* (Cheltenham: Edward Elgar, 2023).

[109] See generally Chapter 5 at Section C.

[110] For different methods see also the examples in Chapter 5 at Section C 4 (b).

[111] John Linarelli, 'Behavioural Comparative Law: Its Relevance to Global Commercial Law-making' in Orkun Akseli and John Linarelli (eds), *The Future of Commercial Law: Ways Forward for Change and Reform* (Oxford: Hart Publishing, 2019) 69, 91–2.

[112] For such a recommendation see also Section C 3 (d).

[113] See the (non-legal) example by David Nelken, 'The Meaning of Success in Transnational Legal Transfers' (2001) 19 *Windsor Yearbook of Access to Justice* 349, 351 fn 2 ('Some transplants, such as the introduction of rabbits into Australia, can be "too successful"'). For the idea of overfitting legal transplants see also Chapter 3 at Section D 2 and Chapter 5 at Section C 1.

[114] See, eg, for France and Latin America: Siems (n 15) 97–8.

[115] Justine K Collins, *Tracing British West Indian Slavery Laws: A Comparative Analysis of Legal Transplants* (Abingdon: Routledge, 2021) 204 ('To date the legal systems of the islands still mirror

Another response to possible challenges of implementation is to use innovative forms of law that have in-built adjustment mechanisms. At a general level, this has been discussed as 'experimentalist governance' being 'based on framework rule-making and revision through a recursive review of implementation experience in different local contexts'.[116] For transplants in particular, it may sometimes be possible to experiment with a transplanted law by way of introducing it as an additional option to the existing law. Such a form of 'menu law' has, for example, happened in the company law of many countries as they introduced a second type of board model.[117] With a different terminology, it has been noted that Canadian law provides the indigenous population with some choice between traditional customary laws and the transplanted Western laws.[118] In such cases, the real-life application of the transplanted rules can then be compared with their real-life application of the, still present, prior rules. However, such an experimental way to test laws is not feasible for all legal topics; thus, often, a choice between models needs to be made.

2. Choice of models

It is suggested that both comparative law and research from other disciplines should guide the choice of the legal transplant. While the popularity of models and the similarity of units may be considered heuristically, it should not limit the scope of possible models.

(a) Make good use of comparative law

It is widely accepted that comparative law can contribute to the choice of a transplant from another unit, sometimes called 'applied comparative law'.[119]

England and there are old laws, now outdated within the metropole, which are still applicable in the West Indies'); Mathias Siems, 'Malicious Legal Transplants' (2018) 38 *Legal Studies* 103, 106–7 (example from English law in India).

[116] Charles F Sabel and Jonathan Zeitlin, 'Experimentalist Governance' in David Levi-Faur (ed), *The Oxford Handbook of Governance* (Oxford: OUP, 2012) 169.

[117] Martin Gelter and Mathias Siems, 'Letting Companies Choose Between Board Models: An Empirical Analysis of Country Variations' (2021) 43 *University of Pennsylvania Journal of International Law* 137.

[118] Ghislain Otis, 'Individual Choice of Law for Indigenous People in Canada: Reconciling Legal Pluralism with Human Rights?' (2018) 8 *UC Irvine Law Review* 101; Ghislain Otis, 'L'individu comme arbitre des tensions entre pluralisme juridique et droits fondamentaux chez les peuples autochtones' (2015) 2 *Revue de droit constitutionnel appliqué* 171.

[119] For this term see David L Finnegan, 'Applied Comparative Law and Judicial Reform' (2006) 8 *Thomas M Cooley Journal of Practical and Clinical Law* 97; Esin Örücü, 'Developing Comparative

For example, Konrad Zweigert and Hein Kötz hold 'that the comparatist is in the best position to follow his comparative researches with a critical evaluation', and add that '[i]f he does not, no one else will do it';[120] according to Jan Smits, comparative law has an important role to play to respond to the question 'what the law ought to be';[121] and, according to Esin Örücü, 'by giving examples of successful transplants [. . .] comparative law can show [. . .] the best road towards law reform'.[122]

For actual practices, George Mousourakis suggests that contemporary lawmaking often investigates multiple jurisdictions in order to integrate them into the drafting of new legislation.[123] However, how this happens in practice is often said to be not particularly good. For example, an analysis of examples from Chile observes that references to foreign law are 'scattered' and do not follow any particular method.[124] For Poland, it has been said that transplants have often been quite mechanical and lacking an in-depth analysis.[125] An example from Mexico is said to show how the lawmaker presented foreign law in a distorted manner in order to support its plans.[126] With respect to judicial transplants, an extensive analysis of supreme courts in Europe concludes that cross-citations are often made without thorough analysis of the foreign law.[127] A global project on foreign precedents in constitutional courts also found that, if at all, courts tend to engage in a form of 'judicial bricolage' rather than 'judicial comparativism'.[128] Similarly, another author mentions the general 'risk

Law' in Esin Örücü and David Nelken (eds), *Comparative Law: A Handbook* (Oxford: Hart Publishing, 2007) 43, 45.

120 Zweigert and Kötz (n 9) 47.

121 Jan M Smits, *The Mind and Method of the Legal Academic* (Cheltenham: Edward Elgar, 2012) 44, 77–8.

122 Örücü (n 106) 93.

123 George Mousourakis, *Traversing Legal Traditions: Perspectives on Comparative Law and Legal History* (Cham: Springer, 2nd edn, 2025) 74.

124 María Elisa Morales Ortiz, 'Two Examples of Legal Transplants in Chilean Consumer Law' (2023) 11 *Latin American Legal Studies* 58.

125 Adam Sulikowski, '„Prawo petycji" a „prawo do składania petycji". Warunki sensowności rozróżnienia' in Ryszard Balicki and Mariusz Jabłoński (eds), *Teoretyczne i praktyczne aspekty realizacji prawa petycji* (Wrocław: E-Wydawnictwo, 2015) 27, 30.

126 Sabrina Ragone, 'Giurisdizioni costituzionali e politica: tendenze e crisi recenti nel diritto comparato' (2025) 45 *Quaderni costituzionali* 67, 79–80 (for the introduction of judicial elections).

127 Folker de Witte and others, 'Decoding Judicial Cross-Citations: How Do European Judges Engage with Foreign Case Law?' (2024) 72 *American Journal of Comparative Law* 292, 303–11.

128 Tania Groppi, Marie-Claire Ponthoreau, and Irene Spigno (eds), *Judicial Bricolage: The Use of Foreign Precedents by Constitutional Judges in the 21st Century* (Oxford: Hart Publishing, 2025). See also Piotr Chybalski, '"Chilling Effect" in the Judicial Decisions of the Polish Constitutional Tribunal as an Example of a Legal Transplant' (2022) 48 *Review of European and Comparative Law* 209, 230 (case study concluding 'lack of thorough research' by Polish court).

of misunderstanding foreign laws', while also drawing a distinction between (proper) comparative legal reasoning and (naively) using a 'mere transplant'.[129]

As a general guidance, good use of comparative law requires the usual steps of a comparative analysis, namely, to describe, compare, and evaluate.[130] Thus, this involves a thorough understanding of possible foreign legal models, including, for example, their normative aims and the way they work in practice. The comparison between the models, as well as the current law of the transplant unit, would then try to understand why units have developed different laws on a particular topic. Finally, the evaluative stage needs to analyse the use of a hypothetical transplant (including possible modifications and adjustments),[131] while also considering (full) 'originality' of lawmaking as a counterfactual.[132] This final stage also connects to previous findings of this book, notably evaluations on the way transplants 'work', their underlying normative aims, and potential suitability within the context of the transplant unit,[133] involving both experts and, if appropriate, the general public.[134]

From the perspective of comparative law, a prior publication presented three ways comparative law can contribute to the quest for 'better law'.[135] First, comparative insights may help to improve law 'technically'. This variant is related to a functional-technical perspective of comparative law, in particular if it is plausible to accept a presumption of relatively similar results (*praesumptio similitudinis*).[136] Thus, here, the foreign model may, for example, be used as it provides more legal certainty, ie clearer legal rules and concepts, for instance, through codification.[137] It can also be the case that the foreign law is better able to balance the interests at stake, for example, if it employs general principles, with the details being left to the judiciary. Furthermore, we may consider a situation where the transplant does not change the substance or form of the

[129] Thomas Coendet, 'Legal Reasoning: Arguments from Comparison' (2016) 102 *Archiv für Rechts- und Sozialphilosophie* 476, 499, 505. In the policy literature, Dolowitz and Marsh (n 5) 17 also refer to the risk of 'uninformed transfer'.

[130] See, with further references, Siems (n 15) 15–29.

[131] See Section C 3.

[132] For this contrast see Miguel Ángel Ciuro Caldani, 'Originalidad y Recepción en el Derecho' (1987) 9 *Boletín del Centro de Investigaciones de Filosofía Jurídica y Filosofía Social* 33; Miguel Ángel Ciuro Caldani, 'Nuevamente sobre los efectos de la recepción jurídica en la cultura argentina' (2006) 29 *Revista del Centro de Investigaciones de Filosofía Jurídica y Filosofía Social* 49. See also Chapter 6 at Section C 3 (c) (for the option to consider a 'new home-grown law').

[133] See Chapter 5 at Section C and Chapter 6 at Sections C 2 and 3.

[134] See Section C 1.

[135] For the following see Mathias Siems, 'Bringing in Foreign Ideas: The Quest for Better Law in Implicit Comparative Law' (2014) 9 *The Journal of Comparative Law* 119.

[136] For this presumption see Zweigert and Kötz (n 9) 40. For further discussion see Siems (n 15) 36–7,45–7.

[137] See Chapter 4 at Sections B 2 and C 3 (d). For such considerations as legitimate interests see Chapter 6 at Section C 2 (a).

rules fundamentally, but that it has the advantage that it brings its language closer to the 'international mainstream' of other units.[138]

Second, comparative law may help to identify laws that meet a particular aim more successfully. This variant is based on a form of 'socio-legal functionalism', namely that laws typically have the aim of addressing a particular problem or to pursue a particular policy.[139] For example, a transplanted law (or, say, a foreign-inspired reform of law enforcement) may be able to achieve such an aim more fully, while also ensuring that the switching costs do not exceed these benefits. Complications can arise due to complexities of the function of the law. For example, consider a situation where all units agree on some general normative aims, say, to promote wealth or happiness, but that it is contentious how this should be understood in a more specific manner. Thus, there can be situations where, despite a similar general aim, the use of a transplant also implies a normative shift in the transplant unit.

Third, the transplant unit can explicitly choose a foreign model in order to change the normative aims pursued by law in the transplant unit. For example, at the level of ideas, it can happen that the transplant unit compares itself with other units and comes to the conclusion that it wants to adjust its normative priorities.[140] However, this variant can also be connected to more instrumental uses of legal rules. For example, a unit wishing to modernise its society may choose a transplant with the aim of having laws that can lead it to an 'imagined future'.[141] It is also possible that the society has already changed: thus, here, the normative shift by following the path of a more modern foreign law has the aim of responding to changed societal circumstances.[142]

(b) Consider insights from other disciplines

Many scholars recommend that comparative law should become more interdisciplinary. For example, according to John Reitz, 'since law is but a part of the seamless whole of human culture, there is in principle scarcely any field of

[138] For such an aim see Chapter 4 at Section B 4, as well as Chapter 6 at Section C 2 (b).

[139] In this sense also James Gordley, 'The Functional Method' in Pier Giuseppe Monateri (ed), *Methods of Comparative Law* (Cheltenham: Edward Elgar, 2012) 107, 109. For a skeptical position see Ralf Michaels, 'The Functional Method of Comparative Law' in Mathias Reimann and Reinhard Zimmermann (eds), *The Oxford Handbook of Comparative Law* (Oxford: OUP, 2nd edn, 2019) 345, 379–81.

[140] See Chapter 6 at Section C 2 and 5.

[141] David Nelken, 'Comparatists and Transferability' in Pierre Legrand and Roderick Munday (eds), *Comparative Legal Studies: Traditions and Transitions* (Cambridge: CUP, 2003) 437, 456. For such cases of transplants being motivated to change or even disrupt society see also Chapter 4 at Section B 2 and Chapter 6 at Section C 3 (b).

[142] See Chapter 4 at Section B 2.

study that might not shed some light on the reasons for or significance of similarities and differences among legal systems'.[143] This potential for an interdisciplinary perspective extends to the topic of legal transplants, as already shown in the many references to research from other disciplines throughout this book. Such a perspective should also be used for the design of transplants,[144] including the choice of models. For this purpose, this subsection continues with the three categories outlined in the previous subsection in order to show how other disciplines than law can contribute to the decision of which model the transplant unit may choose.[145]

First, recommendations for the technical improvement of law may be thought to lie primarily in the domain of comparative law, but other disciplines can also provide some contributions. This can concern social scientific methods that make sense of the text and structure of the law. For example, studies may use tools of network analysis in order to compare the complexity of legal texts,[146] or forms of natural language processing in order to examine their readability.[147] While such findings would not automatically indicate that a particular law would be better, they may still be indicators that can inform the choice of a transplant. It is also possible that other disciplines may be able to show that these technicalities have implications for extra-legal factors. For example, Max Weber associated the civil law's use of a formally rational legal system of codified rules with a successful capitalist economy[148]—and this question of whether the common law or the civil law model of codified versus case law may be advantageous has also been the topic of empirical research, to be discussed in the following subsection.

[143] John C Reitz, 'How to Do Comparative Law' (1998) 46 *American Journal of Comparative Law* 617, 627. For similar statements in the literature see Siems (n 15) 9. More generally see Jaakko Husa, *Interdisciplinary Comparative Law: Rubbing Shoulders with the Neighbours or Standing Alone in a Crowd* (Cheltenham: Edward Elgar, 2022).

[144] See already Sections A, B 1, and C 1.

[145] Based on Siems (n 135).

[146] Eg, Corinna Coupette and others, 'Measuring Law Over Time: A Network Analytical Framework with an Application to Statutes and Regulations in the United States and Germany' (2021) 9 *Frontiers in Physics* 658463.

[147] For literature on 'Natural Legal Language Processing' see https://nllpw.org/resources/ accessed 23 October 2025. For examples from comparative law: Mike Madden, 'Judging Readability: A Study of Opinions by Apex-Court Judges from Australia, Canada, South Africa, the United Kingdom, and the United States' (2023/24) 21 *The Scribes Journal of Legal Writing* 15; Jan M Smits, 'Do Small Jurisdictions Have a More Complex Law? A Numerical Experiment in Constitutional and Private Law' in Alexis Albarian and Olivier Moréteau (eds), *Le droit compare et . . . /Comparative Law and . . .* (Aix-en-Provence: Presses Universitaires d'Aix-Marseille, 2016) 473.

[148] Max Weber, *Economy and Society* (Berkeley, CA: University of California Press, 1968 [original from 1922]). For Max Weber as a comparative lawyer see Ahmed A White, 'Max Weber and the Uncertainties of Categorical Comparative Law' in Annelise Riles (ed), *Re-thinking the Masters of Comparative Law* (Oxford: Hart Publishing, 2001) 40.

Second, a good deal of empirical work from other disciplines examines what laws can achieve a particular aim more successfully. This book already mentioned the examples of observational studies that found that certain laws tend to promote wealth and prosperity.[149] Research on constitutional engineering[150] has also explored the impact of specific legislatory choices, for example that the extent to which a country is a 'consensus democracy' is associated with less violence and more extensive social welfare,[151] that parliamentarism is more conducive to stability and development than presidentialism,[152] and that proportional representation leads to larger government spending and more frequent political compromise than more majoritarian voting systems.[153] The use of experiments[154] includes, for example, a study that the common law rule of not generally requiring specific performance of contracts leads to less trade by the participants of the experiment.[155] Some quasi-experiments also show which rules are better able to promote certain aims. For example, a study on changes to minimum capital requirements in the law of private companies in some European countries used the unchanged law of public companies as a control group, finding a positive effect on the incorporation of new companies.[156]

Third, we already saw in the previous chapter that the decision about law's normative aims is a topic that, at its core, requires input from other fields of research, such as ethics and political theory.[157] As regards the choice of models, reference can, for example, be made to research challenging the view of economic development as the main aim of development policy. Intellectually, this may point towards views such as Amartya Sen's call for elementary 'capabilities' which not only considers income and wealth but also education, social security, personal liberties, equal opportunities, and fairness.[158] A real-life example of this alternative development vision is Bhutan, which has explicitly

[149] See Chapter 6 at Section C 3 (a).

[150] See generally n 6.

[151] Arend Lijphart, *Patterns of Democracy: Government Forms and Performance in Thirty-Six Countries* (New Haven, CT: Yale University Press, 1999) 244, 258–71, 293–300.

[152] Juan J Linz, 'The Perils of Presidentialism' (1990) 1 *Journal of Democracy* 51.

[153] Torsten Persson and Guido Tabellini, *The Economic Effect of Constitutions* (Cambridge, MA: MIT Press, 2003).

[154] Including randomised controlled trials, see Section C 1 (a).

[155] Christoph Engel and Lars Freund, 'Behaviorally Efficient Remedies—An Experiment' (MPI Collective Goods Preprint, No 2017/17), available at https://ssrn.com/abstract=2988653 accessed 23 October 2025.

[156] Reiner Braun and others, 'Does Charter Competition Foster Entrepreneurship? A Difference-in-Difference Approach to European Company Law Reforms' (2013) 51 *Journal of Common Market Studies* 399.

[157] See Chapter 6 at Sections A and C 1.

[158] Amartya Sen, *Development as Freedom* (New York: Knopf, 1999).

endorsed 'happiness' as a development goal.[159] There are also classifications from comparative politics that can guide the choices countries may make. For example, Gøsta Esping-Andersen's 'three worlds of welfare capitalism' distinguishes between the liberal welfare systems of Anglo-Saxon countries, a conservative-corporatist category of most continental European countries and the social-democratic Scandinavian countries, and Peter Hall and David Soskice's 'varieties of capitalism' distinguishes between liberal market economies, such as the UK and the US, on the one hand and co-ordinated market economies, such as Germany and Japan, on the other.[160]

(c) Popularity of models should only be used heuristically

We have seen in Chapter 3 that the laws of certain units tend to be popular choices for legal transplants. For example, there is a strong influence of major jurisdictions from the Global North in other parts of the world, and there are examples that the rules and ideas from the common law (including US law) have been attractive models in civil law countries.[161] Of course, this does not imply that the design of transplants necessarily should consider such popularity; yet, knowledge of popular models may have a heuristic value.

In detail, a possible 'Global North advantage' may be based on their strength in protecting property rights and the rule of law, as noted in the literature,[162] and as shown in various indicators.[163] Reference may also be made to the claim that human rights are largely of Western origins,[164] and, here too, indicators usually confirm that human rights are better protected in the Global North.[165] Beyond any substantive qualities, it may also be said that the legal systems of

[159] Kent Schroeder, *Politics of Gross National Happiness: Governance and Development in Bhutan* (Cham: Palgrave Macmillan, 2018). For other countries see Trevor TW Wan, 'Constitutionalization of Happiness: A Global and Comparative Inquiry' (2023) 24 *German Law Journal* 1209.

[160] Gøsta Esping-Andersen, *The Three Worlds of Welfare Capitalism* (Princeton, NJ: Princeton University Press, 1990); Peter A Hall and David Soskice (eds), *Varieties of Capitalism: The Institutional Foundations of Comparative Advantage* (Oxford: OUP, 2001). For further discussion of these categories see Siems (n 15) 428–9.

[161] Chapter 3 at Section C 1, above. The role of a model's popularity is also discussed in the literature on the diffusions of innovations, see Section A.

[162] See generally Chapter 6 at Section C 3 (a), as well as Chapter 5 at Section C 4 (b) (for the example of Singapore).

[163] See eg https://internationalpropertyrightsindex.org/ accessed 23 October 2025; https://www.worldbank.org/en/publication/worldwide-governance-indicators accessed 23 October 2025; https://worldjusticeproject.org/rule-of-law-index/ accessed 23 October 2025. For the contentious role of such indicators see, with further references, Siems (n 15) 368–76.

[164] See discussion in Siems (n 15) 340–3.

[165] See eg https://ourworldindata.org/human-rights accessed 23 October 2025; https://cirights.com/ accessed 23 October 2025; http://www.humanrightsdata.com/ accessed 23 October 2025. For the ratification of human rights treaties see https://indicators.ohchr.org/ accessed 23 October 2025.

the Global North benefit from network effects, stemming from their relatively long history but also their frequent use in many contemporary legal systems.

A main critique is that laws of the Global North (or specifically 'the West') are one-sided in that their main orientation may be a 'capitalist' focus on privatisation, property rights, ease of doing business, and the corresponding disregard of social rights, inequality, and the natural environment.[166] By contrast, the use of other models may provide some advantages:

> 'Think about the role of workers in the former Yugoslavian corporate governance, or the variety of alternative visions of property in Andean cultures, or the institutional settings that allow the social capital represented by elderly people be put to value in many African societies, or the legal institutions of solidarity and long term commitment in Islamic finance, or the open access to culture and social knowledge in the traditional Asian resistance to intellectual property rights.'[167]

Similar statements can be found elsewhere. For example, Patrick Glenn refers to the respect for the environment in chthonic legal traditions,[168] and Ezra Vogel points towards the higher levels of co-operation in the Japanese economic and political model as a lesson for the US.[169] At a more general level, we also find calls for 'reverse legal transplants' from the Global South to the Global North,[170] and, even more generally, the plea to more closely consider 'epistemologies of the [Global] South'.[171] Finally, reference can be made to the early work on imitation by Gabriel Tarde, according to which, it makes the individual freer and more rational to choose from 'more numerous and diversified' options.[172]

[166] See eg Ugo Mattei and Laura Nader, *Plunder: When the Rule of Law is Illegal* (Oxford: Wiley-Blackwell, 2008); Fritjof Capra and Ugo Mattei, *The Ecology of Law: Toward a Legal System in Tune with Nature and Community* (Oakland, CA: Berrett-Koehler, 2015).

[167] IUC Global Legal Standards Research Group, 'IUC Independent Policy Report: At the End of the End of History – Global Legal Standards: Part of the Solution or Part of the Problem?' (2009) 9(3) *Global Jurist* article 2, 14.

[168] H Patrick Glenn, *Legal Traditions of the World* (Oxford: OUP, 5th edn, 2014) 375. For transplants of the 'rights of nature' see also Chapter 3 at Section C 1.

[169] Ezra F Vogel, *Japan as Number One: Lessons for America* (Cambridge MA: Harvard University Press, 1979) 254. See also the seminal work by Chalmers Johnson, *MITI and the Japanese Miracle* (Stanford, CA: Stanford University Press, 1982).

[170] Sital Kalantry, 'Reverse Legal Transplants' (2020) 99 *North Carolina Law Review* 49 and the further literature cited in Chapter 3 at Section C 1.

[171] Boaventura de Sousa Santos, *The End of the Cognitive Empire: The Coming of Age of Epistemologies of the South* (Durham, NC: Duke University Press, 2018); Boaventura de Sousa Santos, *Toward a New Legal Common Sense: Law, Globalization, and Emancipation* (Cambridge: CUP, 3rd edn, 2018) 112–13.

[172] Gabriel Tarde, *The Laws of Imitation* (New York: Henry Holt and Company, 1903) 83 ('We should also observe, however, that as the suggestions of example become more numerous and diversified

As to the choice of a specific legal transplant, it follows that it depends on the details of the circumstances of whether or not a model from the Global North should be adopted. For example, even a fairly optimistic law and economics analysis of transplants in developing countries acknowledges that 'there are no standard legal reforms that can be applied without a thorough knowledge of specific national circumstances'.[173] We have also already seen that there are no pure legal systems: even the laws of the Global North are mixtures,[174] and mixtures also emerge due to the impact of transplants on other jurisdictions.[175] Moreover, as far as global legal indicators play a role, it has been argued that they should be adapted to the realities of a plural legal world.[176]

The question about a 'common law advantage' can start with the position suggested by law and economics scholars that judge-made law has an inbuilt tendency to produce efficient rules.[177] According to some, this translates into an advantage of the common law over the civil law,[178] as also claimed in some empirical studies as common law countries are said to have higher 'legal adaptability'[179] and experience faster economic growth than civil law countries.[180] Other empirical studies suggest that the substance of the law from common law countries is superior. Notably, this is the case for the 'law and finance' line of research by Rafael La Porta and colleagues, according to which differences in the law between 'English legal origin' countries (ie common law countries) and other legal origins (ie civil law countries) explain differences in economic performance in many areas of law.[181]

around an individual, each of them loses in intensity, and the individual becomes freer to determine his choice according to the preference of his own character, on the one hand, and on the other, according to certain logical laws which I will discuss elsewhere. Thus it is certain that the progress of civilisation renders subjection to imitation at once more personal and more rational.').

173 Mechlem (n 8) 311. The criticism of 'prepacked reforms' also features prominently in the literature critical of 'law and development', see eg David M Trubek, 'The Owl and the Pussy-cat: Is There a Future for Law and Development?' (2007) 25 *Wisconsin International Law Journal* 235, 238.

174 See Chapter 2 at Section A and Chapter 3 at Section C 1.

175 See Chapter 5 at Section C 2 (a).

176 Siddharth Peter de Souza, *Designing Indicators for a Plural Legal World* (Cambridge: CUP, 2022).

177 For the foundational literature on this topic see Alain Marciano (ed), *Law and Economics: A Reader* (Abingdon: Routledge, 2009) 331–440.

178 Richard B Cappalli, 'At the Point of Decision: The Common Law's Advantage over the Civil Law' (1998) 12 *Temple International and Comparative Law Journal* 87.

179 Thorsten Beck, Asli Demirguc-Kunt, and Ross Levine, 'Law and Finance: Why Does Legal Origin Matter?' (2003) 31 *Journal of Comparative Economics* 653. For a different view see Mathias Siems, 'Legal Adaptability in Elbonia' (2006) 2 *International Journal of Law in Context* 393.

180 Paul G Mahoney, 'The Common Law and Economic Growth: Hayek Might be Right' (2001) 30 *Journal of Legal Studies* 503. Similarly, Carmine Guerriero, 'Endogenous Legal Traditions and Economic Outcomes' (2016) 44 *Journal of Comparative Economics* 416.

181 Rafael La Porta, Florencio Lopez-de-Silanes, and Andrei Shleifer, 'The Economic Consequences of Legal Origins' (2008) 46 *Journal of Economic Literature* 285.

These strong statements about a common law advantage may be a surprise to comparative law scholars who usually hold that formal differences between civil law and common law often lead to similar outcomes.[182] Indeed, the alleged empirical advantage of the common law has been challenged by other empirical studies: for example, the comparative coding of the law in some of the 'law and finance' studies has shown to be incorrect,[183] it has been found that other differences than the law are often more important explanatory variables,[184] and, in some comparative studies, results on the empirical effect of the law have remained inconclusive.[185] Furthermore, in challenging the argument about the importance of courts, a study has found that, in securities law, it is mainly good public enforcement, and not private litigation, which stimulates financial market development.[186]

Some research also suggests that there can be cases of a 'civil law advantage'. For example, the judicial design of civil law countries with more active judges may be more suitable for emerging legal systems, since the latter countries tend to have few experienced trial lawyers.[187] According to some empirical studies, civil law countries perform better if one uses measures of low inequality as dependent variables.[188] Civil law countries may in particular have an advantage in terms of legal certainty due to their more systematic approach to legislation and legal thought.[189] Thus, it is clear that any *a priori* plausible advantage of

[182] See eg Caslav Pejovic, 'Civil Law and Common Law: Two Different Paths Leading to the Same Goal' (2001) 32 *Victoria University of Wellington Law Review* 819 and Luke Nottage, 'Comment on Civil Law, and Common Law: Two Different Paths Leading to the Same Goal' (2001) 32 *Victoria University of Wellington Law Review* 843, as well as the '*praesumptio similitudinis*' discussed in (a).

[183] See Chapter 6 at Section C 3 (a).

[184] Eg, Daniel M Klerman and others, 'Legal Origin or Colonial History?' (2011) 3 *Journal of Legal Analysis* 379; Menzie D Chinn and Hiro Ito, 'What Matters for Financial Development? Capital Controls, Institutions, and Interactions' (2006) 81 *Journal of Development Economics* 163; Mark J Roe and Jordan I Siegel, 'Political Instability: Effects on Financial Development, Roots in the Severity of Economic Inequality' (2011) 39 *Journal of Comparative Economics* 279.

[185] Simon Deakin, Prabirjit Sarkar, and Mathias Siems, 'Is There a Relationship Between Shareholder Protection and Stock Market Development?' (2018) 3 *Journal of Law, Finance, and Accounting* 115; John Armour and others, 'Shareholder Protection and Stock Market Development: An Empirical Test of the Legal Origins Hypothesis' (2009) 6 *Journal of Empirical Legal Studies* 343.

[186] Howell E Jackson and Mark J Roe, 'Public and Private Enforcement of Securities Laws: Resource-Based Evidence' (2009) 93 *Journal of Financial Economics* 207.

[187] Charles H Koch, 'The Advantages of the Civil Law Judicial Design as the Model for Emerging Legal Systems' (2004) 11 *Indiana Journal of Global Legal Studies* 139.

[188] Illan Barriola, Bruno Deffains, and Olivier Musy, 'Law and Inequality: A Comparative Approach to the Distributive Implications of Legal Systems' (2023) 75 *International Review of Law and Economics* Article 106139; John Ferguson and others, 'Shareholder Protection, Income Inequality and Social Health: A Proposed Research Agenda' (2017) 41 *Accounting Forum* 253; Giuseppe Maggio, Alessandro Romano, and Angela Troisi, 'The Legal Origin of Income Inequality' (2014) 7 *Law and Development Review* 1.

[189] For discussion of this point see Mathias Siems, 'Comparative Legal Certainty: Legal Families and Forms of Measurement' in Mark Fenwick, Mathias Siems, and Stefan Wrbka (eds), *The Shifting Meaning of Legal Certainty in Comparative and Transnational Law* (Oxford: Hart Publishing, 2017) 115.

either the common law or the civil law should not replace a thorough analysis of choosing a transplant from a particular unit.

(d) Similarity between units should only be used heuristically

It is often said that it helps if the transplant and origin units are relatively similar. For example, we have seen that, according to 'realists', the effectiveness of a transplant depends on the society of the transplant unit.[190] What is more, a particularly favourable socio-cultural or legal context can mean that the transplanted law works even better than in the origin unit.[191] In the steps suggested in the literature (see Table 7.1, above), some authors also refer to the similarity between units. For instance, Al-Umari writes, in relation to the question 'from where to transplant', that the 'transplantation between legal systems that share the same culture and speak the same language is easier than transplantation between fundamentally different legal system'.[192] The merit of similarity can also be about existing legal similarities, namely that there are often complementarities between different areas of law and, thus, say, if two countries have similar company laws, it makes sense that they also have similar labour laws.[193]

More specifically, it may be suggested that units should usually stay within their own legal family. For example, this can refer to the work of Daniel Berkowitz and colleagues, which argues that choosing a transplant of the same legal family is economically beneficial,[194] as well as Gunther Teubner's finding that transplanting the civil law concept of 'good faith' into English law led to a 'legal irritant'.[195] Such arguments may also be valid beyond domestic laws. For example, according to Francesco Duina, regional agreements of civil law countries tend to aim for harmonisation and standardisation while those of common law countries more often embrace the principle of mutual recognition;[196] thus, here too, transplants across models may not be advisable.

Furthermore, similarities within one region may be a reason to favour intra-regional over extra-regional transplants. For example, Thomas Wilhelmsson

[190] See Chapter 5 at Section B 3. See also Chapter 4 at Section C 3 (a) (for one of the reasons why transplants take place).

[191] Mathias Siems, 'The Curios Case of Overfitting Legal Transplants' in Maurice Adams and Dirk Heirbaut (eds), *The Method and Culture of Comparative Law* (Oxford: Hart Publishing, 2014) 133. See also Chapter 3 at Section D 2 and Chapter 5 at Section C 1.

[192] Al-Umari (n 40) 28.

[193] Beth Ahlering and Simon Deakin, 'Labour Regulation, Corporate Governance and Legal Origin: A Case of Institutional Complementarity?' (2007) 41 *Law and Society Review* 865, 876, further discussed in Section C 3 (d).

[194] Discussed in Chapter 5 at Section C 4 (b).

[195] Discussed in Chapter 5 at Section C 3 (b).

[196] Francesco Duina, 'Making Sense of the Legal and Judicial Architectures of Regional Trade Agreements Worldwide' (2016) 10 *Regulation & Governance* 368.

suggests that, in the EU, the 'movement of legal ideas' should be an important part of the process of Europeanisation given that 'due to the relative similarities between the Member States both legally, societally and culturally, the use of experience from other Member States [. . .] encounters fewer hurdles than the use of materials from a legally and societally more distant environment'.[197] In other parts of the world, there are frequent calls to stimulate a (Global) 'South-South dialogue'.[198] It has also been suggested that countries from the Global South can share their experiences in dealing with laws from the Global North. For example, as the colonial history of Africa has led to the frequent problem of competing land claims, successful models from other African countries are likely to be the best guide for any law reform on this matter.[199]

However, legal transplants can, and sometimes should, also be used among relatively different units. The previous chapters have shown that transplants are possible between any units, and that they can 'work well' if they happen across legal families or other types of groups.[200] Thus, one should not overstate the differences between common and civil law,[201] or the capacity of units to adjust to foreign laws. Moreover, the use of a model from a relatively dissimilar unit may precisely have the aim of deviating from the current law in order to change society in a particular direction.[202] This can be the case if the two units are countries, but also in other situations. For example, in the literature on regional co-operation, it is discussed whether regional institutions should only be enacted after there has been (some) economic, social, and cultural convergence, or whether these institutions may rather be a means to create strong economic ties and a regional identity.[203] There is also now a rich literature on how forms of transnational and international law have diminished the attachment to particular domestic models. For example, authors refer to the impact of 'new global governance structures', 'transnational legal processes', and soft forms of 'international corporate law' to challenge

[197] Thomas Wilhelmsson, *Free Movement of Legal Ideas: Towards a Dynamic Europeanisation of Private Law* (Oxford: Hart Publishing, 2024) 119.
[198] See Chapter 3 at Section C 1.
[199] Sandra Evers, Marja Spierenburg, and Harry Wels (eds), *Competing Jurisdictions: Settling Land Claims in Africa* (Leiden: Brill Evers, 2005). This can also mean a transplant of models from the past (ie a diachronic legal transplant), see Chapter 4 at Section B 2.
[200] See Chapter 3 at Section C 2 and Chapter 5 at Section C 2 to 4.
[201] Siems (n 15) 73–80.
[202] ie the third variant discussed in Section C 2 (a) and (b).
[203] See eg Richard Baldwin, 'Sequencing Asian Regionalism: Theory and Lessons from Europe' (2012) 27 *Journal of Economic Integration* 1; Jeffrey T Checkel, 'Regional Identities and Communities' in Tanja A Börzel and Thomas Risse (eds), *The Oxford Handbook of Comparative Regionalism* (Oxford: OUP, 2016) 559.

the notion that foreign influence can only happen within groups of similar countries.[204]

To conclude, it is plausible that transplant units may want to rely on 'cognitive shortcuts' in selecting a particular law to transplant[205] and, in this regard, the similarity between units may sometimes be a suitable criterion. However, as one of the previous subsections also asks to 'make good use of comparative law', it is generally good advice that the laws of dissimilar units should also be taken under consideration. Which unit is then chosen, will depend on the aim that a transplant wants to achieve, as well as the costs and benefits that the choice of a more or less familiar model may entail.

3. Details of the law

The following suggests that legal transplants should usually adjust to local conditions, including closely considering the legal language in which the transplanted law is drafted. However, there can also be situations where it is less relevant to consider the context of the origin unit or where comprehensive transplantation is advisable.

(a) Adjustment to local conditions of transplant unit is often necessary

The relevance of context not only plays a role for the choice of the transplant (see the previous section) but also its adjustment in the transplant unit. This has already been mentioned in the previous chapters as they referred to the options of copying, emulation, and combination as forms of transplantation[206] and discussed that, whether or not a transplant 'works', may depend on adjustments to the local conditions of the transplant unit.[207]

In this chapter, we have seen that some of the steps suggested in the literature include the recommendation for local adjustment.[208] Similar suggestions are made by other authors in various contexts. For example, Antonio Gidi uses

[204] Michele Graziadei, 'Comparative Law as the Study of Transplants and Receptions' in Mathias Reimann and Reinhard Zimmermann (eds), *The Oxford Handbook of Comparative Law* (Oxford: OUP, 2nd edn, 2019) 442, 454; Jedidiah J Kroncke, 'Law and Development' in Jan M Smits and others (eds), *Elgar Encyclopedia of Comparative Law* (Cheltenham: Edward Elgar, 3rd edn, 2023) 391, 397; Mariana Pargendler, 'The Rise of International Corporate Law' (2021) 98 *Washington University Law Review* 1765.

[205] Cf Kurt Weyland, *Bounded Rationality and Policy Diffusion: Social Sector Reform in Latin America* (Princeton, NJ: Princeton University Press, 2006) 30 ('policy-makers commonly rely on cognitive shortcuts that are crucial for processing overabundant, uncertain information').

[206] See Chapter 3 at Section D 1.

[207] See the 'intermediate cases' in Chapter 5 at Section C.

[208] Eg, Rose, Frankenberg, Al-Umiri, and de Jong and others discussed in Section B 1.

the term 'responsible transplant' as referring to the example of the successful adjustment of the US class action to the Brazilian context.[209] In his discussion about the 'free movement of legal ideas' in Europe, Thomas Wilhelmsson suggests adjustments to the 'real context' in which such ideas will be used.[210] Eliška Vejchodská and Andreas Hendricks' analysis of a transplant of local public administration from Munich to Prague refers to differences between the cities as obstacles to be overcome in order to ensure the 'smooth adoption' of the transplanted model.[211] Chenguang Wang writes that China closely considers local cultural norms by 'selective borrowing and transplantation rather than wholesale absorption' as it aims to tackle 'particular problems or issues'.[212] And Catherine Dupré praises the way the Hungarian Constitutional Court incorporated the German case law on the right to human dignity in a creative manner.[213]

The adjustment of the transplanted law can involve multiple elements. To start with, the transplantation process needs to consider the existing legal context. Thus, this is a topic where the expertise of comparative lawyers is essential, though there is apparently an attempt to use AI in Albania in order to facilitate the incorporation of EU law.[214] It also connects to the importance of legal language and thus the topic of the following subsection. Moreover, the social, cultural, and economic context of the transplant unit can make adjustments necessary. Thus, here, experts from other disciplines also have a key role.[215] Specifically, the design of the transplant needs to compare the costs and benefits of possible adjustments with the existing rules (and with each other).

[209] Antonio Gidi, 'Class Actions in Brazil: A Model for Civil Law Countries' (2003) 51 *American Journal of Comparative Law* 311, 314. See also Antonio Gidi, *Las acciones colectivas y la tutela de los derechos difusos, colectivos e individuales en Brasil: un modelo para países de derecho civil* (Mexico City: UNAM, 2004).

[210] Wilhelmsson (n 197) 120.

[211] Eliška Vejchodská and Andreas Hendricks, 'Munich's Developer Obligations as a Legal Transplant to the Czech Institutional Context' (2023) 94 *Town Planning Review* 193, 212 (eg, differences in trust in public institutions and in power distributions within city governance).

[212] Chenguang Wang, 'Legal Transplantation and Legal Development in Transitional China' in Hassane Cissé and others (eds), *The World Bank Legal Review, Volume 4: Legal Innovation and Empowerment for Development* (Washington DC: World Bank Publications, 2013) 161, 174, 176.

[213] Catherine Dupré, *Importing the Law in Post-Communist Transitions: The Hungarian Constitutional Court and the Right to Human Dignity* (Oxford: Hart Publishing, 2003) 63–154. However, in recent years, this has changed: see eg Gábor Halmai and Nóra Chronowski, 'The Decline of Human Dignity and Solidarity through the Misuse of Constitutional Identity: The Case of Hungary since 2010' in Daniel Bedford and others (eds), *Human Dignity and Democracy in Europe: Synergies, Tensions and Crises* (Cheltenham: Edward Elgar Publishing, 2022) 177.

[214] See Albi Nani, 'From Code to Candidacy: Albania's Accelerated European Union Application with ChatGPT' (2025) 4(3) *Digital Socoiety*, https://doi.org/10.1007/s44206-024-00158-3.

[215] See eg Liesel Spencer, 'Comparative Legal Geography: Context and Place in "Legal Transplants"' in Tayanah O'Donnell, Daniel F Robinson, and Josephine Gillespie (eds), *Legal Geography: Perspectives and Methods* (London: Routledge, 2020) 149, 152 (on 'how incorporating legal geography can produce a more nuanced, place-sensitive legal transplant methodology').

Such adjustments can concern substantive changes to the legal rules but also the way the transplanted law will be applied and enforced.[216] Adjustments can also be about changing the legal form: for example, a rule that is part of statute law in one unit may be transplanted in an adjusted manner by case law in another one.[217]

Thus, adjustment of the transplant to local conditions is indeed often necessary. However, there can also be cases where this is not recommended. This too follows from previous findings of this book. Prior chapters mentioned the case where a good fit would take significant time and costs: thus, here, it may be recommended to use a transplant that can be readily and quickly adopted even if it is less beneficial.[218] Another exception to the rule is where the transplant has the aim of changing society in a particular manner: thus, in such a situation, a mismatch with society is deliberate,[219] while modifications from the law of the origin unit may still be made if this is needed to induce such a transformative effect.

(b) Transplants should closely consider the role of legal language

There is a good deal of literature which has discussed the relationship between comparative law and translation (including translation studies).[220] Specifically for the topic of legal transplants, an article by Roman Uliasz explains the risks that can arise due to reasons related to the language of the transplanted law but also how these risks can be mitigated.[221] Further literature suggests that legal transplants and convergence 'facilitate the emergence of the language of the global law'[222] and thus a possible reduction of linguistic differences and problems.

When units share the same language, it is possible that no particular linguistic problems arise. Specifically, this may be the case for transplants in fields that are already relatively similar between both units, for example, transplants

[216] For an example see Reinier H Kraakman and Bernard S Black, 'A Self Enforcing Model of Corporate Law' (1996) 109 *Harvard Law Review* 1911.

[217] See generally Chapter 3 at Section B 2. For a different view see Justice Barak-Erez (n 70) 29 ('legislation is not only the main, but also the ideal route for transplantation').

[218] See Chapter 3 at Section D 1, Chapter 5 at Section C 1, and Chapter 6 at Section C 3 (c).

[219] See Section C 2 (a), (b), and (d).

[220] Eg, Łucja Biel, 'Linguistic Approaches' in Mathias Siems and Po Jen Yap (eds), *The Cambridge Handbook of Comparative Law* (Cambridge: CUP, 2024) 91, 101–10; Jan Engberg, 'Comparative Law for Legal Translation: Through Multiple Perspectives to Multidimensional Knowledge' (2020) 33 *International Journal for the Semiotics of Law* 263; Simone Glanert (ed), *Comparative Law: Engaging Translation* (London: Routledge, 2014).

[221] Roman Uliasz, 'The Transplantation of Legal Concepts by Means of Language: A Private Law Perspective' (2023) 12 *Cambridge International Law Journal* 266.

[222] Marcus Galdia, 'The Comparative Element in Comparative Legal Linguistics' (2020) 43 *Comparative Legilinguistics* 57, 66.

between German and Austrian commercial law[223] or in the case law of common law countries.[224] However, in other situations, even within countries of the same language, challenges can arise, such as false friends, idiosyncratic terminologies, and differences in legal writing style.[225]

The special case of multilingual laws presents, on the one hand, an opportunity as they can show how it is possible to find translations of concepts that seem alien to a particular legal tradition. For instance, this has been observed for the use of the common law in French and the civil law in English in Canada.[226] On the other hand, there can be challenges. For example, it has been said about EU law that certain terms may derive from one of the legal languages, but that it would not be in the interest of the transplant unit to use this term in exactly the same manner, also considering how it should be translated into the other official EU languages.[227]

In the cases of transplants between units of different legal languages, the transfer can sometimes be relatively straightforward. For example, this may be the case for some transplants between countries of Romance languages as far as there is still a connection to Roman law or even the use of 'legal Latin'.[228] In other situations, the issue may arise on how to translate a particular term, often with the variant that the substance of the law has been modified in the transplant unit. An example is the transplant of a form of the common law 'trust' in civil law countries: here, some countries use the English term 'trust', others

[223] Austria's Civil Code is older and distinct from its German counterpart; yet, its commercial law is largely based on the German model; see eg Mathias Siems, 'The Divergence of Austrian and German Commercial Law—What Kind of Commercial Law Do We Need in a Globalised Economy?' (2004) *International Company and Commercial Law Review* 273.

[224] See generally Chapter 3 at Section B 2.

[225] See eg Christopher Hutton, *Word Meaning and Legal Interpretation: An Introductory Guide* (London: Palgrave Macmillan, 2014) (how common law jurisdictions differ in the definition and interpretation of words such as 'plant' or 'vehicle'); Rodolfo Sacco, 'Legal Formants: A Dynamic Approach to Comparative Law' (1991) 39 *American Journal of Comparative Law* 1, 16 (for the language of the Civil Codes of the former Western and Eastern Germany).

[226] Emmanuel Didier, 'La Common Law en français. Étude juridique et linguistique de la common law en français au Canada' (1991) 43 *Revue internationale de droit comparé* 7. See also Serge Lortie and Robert C Bergeron, 'Legislative Drafting and Language in Canada' (2007) 28 *Statute Law Review* 83.

[227] See eg Katia Peruzzo, 'Secondary Term Formation within the EU: Term Transfer, Legal Transplant or Approximation of Member States' Legal Systems?' (2012) 18 *The Journal of Specialised Translation* 175; Federico M Mucciarelli, '*E Pluribus Unum*? Language Diversity and the Harmonization of Company law in the European Union' (2019) 26 *Maastricht Journal of European and Comparative Law* 669; Agnieszka Doczekalska, *Język prawny w tworzeniu i transpozycji prawa Unii Europejskiej. Procesy hybrydyzacji* (Warsaw: Wolters Kluwer, 2021) 169–83.

[228] Paulina Kozanecka, Aleksandra Matulewska, and Paula Trzaskawka, *Methodology of Interlingual Comparison of Legal Terminology: Towards General Legilinguistic Translatology* (Poznań: Dissertationes legilinguisticae, 2017) 12 ('there is no denying the fact that the more genetically related the source and the target languages are, the less problematic the process of translation is'); Heikki ES Mattila, *Comparative Legal Linguistics* (Farnham: Ashgate, 2nd edn, 2013) 173–90 (on legal Latin in modern legal languages).

translate it or deliberately use terms with a somehow different connotation.[229] As regards the transplant design, the use of any of these options needs to consider the target audience in order to reduce the risk of misunderstandings by both lawyers and the general public. Moreover, the challenges of translations can be connected to the subsequent interpretation of the law. For example, if the legislation introduces a neologism on the occasion of a transplant, measures may be needed to support lawyers and courts in the understanding and application of the new legal terms.[230]

Beyond individual words, the translation of a transplanted legal text can follow different approaches. A functional approach aims for a translation so that the receiver (ie the reader of the translated text) reacts to the text as if the text had been written in the target language. A literal approach, by contrast, retains the original structure and idiosyncrasies of the source text aiming to be as faithful as possible to the original law. Finally, a cultural approach aims to get 'the best of both worlds': like a functional translation, it aims for a non-literal translation that reads well, while, like a literal translation, it also aims to be sensitive to the source language.[231] As far as a legal transplant has a clearly defined purpose, the choice between these options may often favour a functional approach.[232] There can also be cases, however, where a cultural approach is most suitable. For example, a paper on translating the common law from English into Chinese in Hong Kong suggests 'legal translation as cultural transfer' in order to achieve a successful transfer of the common law legal culture.[233]

(c) Sometimes the context of the origin unit may not matter

The general position of this book is that the context of the law is of fundamental importance for legal transplants. However, in some situations, it can make sense not to be too concerned about the context of the origin unit, namely where the transplant is about an abstract model that is only somehow related to a specific real model of a particular unit.

[229] See eg Kateřina Ronovská and Vlastimil Pihera, 'The Reception of the Trust in Civil Law Jurisdictions' in Mark Bennett and others (eds), *The Oxford Handbook of Comparative Trust Laws* (Oxford: OUP, forthcoming). For another example, see Przemysław Kusik, 'Legal Transplants and Legal Translation: A Case Study of the Borrowing of the U.S. Limited Liability Partnership into the Polish Legal System' (2024) 14 *Perspectives: Studies in Translation Theory and Practice* 92.

[230] See eg Uliasz (n 221) 273–79 (on the interpretation of laws deriving from EU laws).

[231] Siems (n 15) 157. See also Biel (n 220) 106–10.

[232] Similarly, Iwona Szymczak, 'Dobór ekwiwalentnych rozwiązań prawnych w procesie transplantacji prawa' (2015) 77(4) *Ruch Prawniczy, Ekonomiczny i Socjologiczny* 29 (functionally equivalent solutions for transplants requiring legal translation).

[233] Ling Wang and King Kui Sin, 'Legal Translation and Cultural Transfer: A Framework for Translating the Common Law into Chinese in Hong Kong' (2013) 26 *International Journal for the Semiotics of Law* 883.

An example of such a situation is the aforementioned 'IKEA theory', namely that, today, de-contextualised global models may sometimes be a transplant unit's most convenient choice.[234] Similar ideas can be found elsewhere. For example, Mariana Pargendler identifies transplants of international corporate law as being 'conceived in abstract form and detached from concrete institutional contexts' while still drawing inspiration from certain domestic law (notably from the US and the UK).[235] From the perspective of institutional research, Bruce Kogut also notes that certain codified knowledge may be 'institutionally neutral' and thus able to diffuse relatively easily across borders.[236]

As regards the design of transplants, the question may be raised whether this trend towards de-contextualised models is something that should be encouraged. It was already mentioned that there is some scepticism about the growing commodification of law.[237] However, ultimately, it depends on the normative quality of the model whether or not the transplant unit may be advised to choose them. For example, such an abstract model may be a good legal idea that is supported by legitimate domestic interests of the transplant unit, or it may promote legitimate international interests.[238] Moreover, a cautiously positive view can find some support in the recent literature on 'law and development'. Here, some authors, while being sceptical about universal laws, identify the trend that we should accept forms of 'middle-level generalisations' that justify some cross-border learning between countries.[239]

Beyond models related to existing legal systems, 'ideal models' can sometimes be sources for legal transplants. For example, the 'Weberian' aim for a professional and politically neutral civil service is an ideal model, although it was initially associated with the Prussian civil service.[240] Some authors go further and consider any idea about the law as a possible source of a 'transplant'. For example, Jaakko Husa writes about 'imaginary legal transplants' as a topic

[234] See Section B 1.

[235] Pargendler (n 204) 1775 (using the term 'legal implants').

[236] Bruce Kogut, *Knowledge, Options, and Institutions* (Oxford: OUP, 2008) 40–1.

[237] See Section B 1, as well as eg Tommaso Edoardo Frosini, 'Legislazione e comparazione' (2015) *Diritto pubblico comparato ed europeo* 63 (sceptical about use of law as a 'commercial good'); special issues by Ian J Murray and Tommaso Fia, 'Law, Commodification, and the Distribution of Resources' (2024) 24(3) *Global Jurist* 221 and 'Dialogue and Debate: Symposium on Commodification and EU Law' (2023) 2(2) *European Law Open* 372.

[238] For such legitimate interests see Chapter 6 at Section C 2. For 'legal ideas' as an object of transplants see also Chapter 3 at Section B 1.

[239] Wouter Vandenhole, 'Towards a Fourth Moment in Law: and Development?' (2019) 12 *Law and Development Review* 265, 278. Similarly, Mariana Mota Prado and Michael Trebilcock, *Advanced Introduction to Law and Development* (Cheltenham: Edward Elgar, 2nd edn, 2021) 251–3.

[240] Francis Fukuyama, *Political Order and Political Decay: From the French Revolution to the Present* (London: Profile Books, 2014) 59–60, 66–80. See also Siems (n 15) 425–6.

of comparative law and literature,[241] and Barbara Pasa and Gianni Sinni propose 'speculative design [. . .], storytelling and design fiction as tools for legal change'.[242] Such insights may, in some cases, indeed help lawmakers. However, as far as the design of legal transplant is concerned, some connection to an existing legal system should be maintained. For example, as far as forms of imagination and fiction idealise the model of a particular legal system,[243] they may be seen as a variant of foreign law (and, thus, also as a possible adjustment of the transplantation, as discussed in the first subsection above).

(d) Sometimes comprehensive transplantation is advisable

It may be tempting to proceed cautiously in transplanting foreign law, but sometimes the best strategy may be to do the precise opposite, namely, to engage in a fairly comprehensive transplantation. This latter strategy may thus argue for the use of simultaneous transplants across multiple areas of law. Here, the intuition is that if one just changes the provisions of one area of law, it leads to inconsistencies between this new law and other areas which have remained unchanged. From the perspective of (German) legal theory, this argument can refer to the notion of the 'unity of the legal order' which states that all elements of a particular legal system (say, the laws of a specific country) should be seen as interconnected in order to avoid contradictions and gaps.[244] From the perspective of comparative economics and politics, a similar argument can be made with reference to the notion of 'institutional complementarities';[245] for example, that there may be national level complementarities between various areas of law.[246]

A transplant may also need to be ambitious if a mere transplant of substantive rules is likely to remain underenforced. In Chapter 5, we have seen that

[241] Jaakko Husa, 'Comparative Law, Literature and Imagination: Transplanting Law into Works of Fiction' (2021) 28 *Maastricht Journal of European and Comparative Law* 371, 382–6.

[242] Barbara Pasa and Gianni Sinni, 'New Frontiers of Legal Knowledge: How Design Provotypes Can Contribute to Legal Change' in Rossana Ducato, Alain Strowel, and Enguerrand Marique (eds), *Design(s) for Law* (Milan: Ledizioni, 2024) 27, 48–57.

[243] Say, the US model of the jury in the 1957 film *12 Angry Men*, but see also Stanley Fish, *Law at the Movies: Turning Legal Doctrine into Art* (Oxford: OUP, 2024) 6–21 (challenging the positive presentation of the law in this movie).

[244] See eg Manfred Baldus, *Die Einheit der Rechtsordnung: Bedeutungen einer juristischen Formel in Rechtstheorie, Zivil- und Staatsrechtswissenschaft des 19. und 20. Jahrhunderts* (Berlin: Duncker & Humblot, 1995); Dagmar Felix, *Einheit der Rechtsordnung: Zur verfassungsrechtlichen Relevanz einer juristischen Argumentationsfigur* (Tübingen: Mohr Siebeck, 1998).

[245] Masahiko Aoki, *Toward a Comparative Institutional Analysis* (Cambridge, MA: MIT Press, 2001) 225; Peter A Hall and Daniel W Gingerich, 'Varieties of Capitalism and Institutional Complementarities in the Political Economy' (2009) 39 *British Journal of Political Science* 449.

[246] Ahlering and Deakin (n 193) (referring to labour and company law, as well as ownership structures between firms). For the problem of 'partial receptions of foreign law' in company law, see also Mathias Siems, *Convergence in Shareholder Law* (Cambridge: CUP, 2008) 333–4.

lack of compliance and enforcement has been problematic for some transplants in transition economies and developing countries.[247] The literature on policy transfer also refers to 'incomplete transfer' as a form of policy failure where the institutional structure that makes a policy a success in the origin unit has not been transferred.[248] By contrast, an evaluation of transplants in India mentions institutional features as being most important for the 'beneficial effect' of English law, such as 'an independent and impartial judiciary', 'a trained legal profession', and a system of higher courts 'to assure a uniform application of law'.[249]

Even more fundamentally, it has sometimes been attempted to comprehensively change a unit's legal system within a short time frame. Chapter 3 mentioned the examples of Rwanda and Sudan which deliberately changed their legal family.[250] However, and going even further, attempts to change a country's entire political, legal, and economic system in a 'big bang' may typically be less effective than a more gradual approach.[251] Thus, on the one hand, it may be recommended that lawmakers reject the notion that certain aspects of the law are immune to change. In a similar sense, a policy brief by the World Bank states:

> 'Legal culture is often considered as a given feature of the local environment to which proposed legal reform projects must adapt; many argue that legal and judicial reform programs must be tailored to fit local legal culture or they will fail. Other times, the prevailing legal culture itself may be the object of reform, rather than merely a constraint.'[252]

On the other hand, the way changes are pursued may proceed in a cautious manner. For example, it may often be good advice that reforms are sequenced, starting with lawmaking institutions, then law-enforcement institutions, then commercial laws, and then social and environmental standards.[253] Sequencing is also said to be important for the relationship between political and economic

[247] See Chapter 5 at Section C 3 (b).
[248] Dolowitz and Marsh (n 5) 17.
[249] Kurt Lipstein, 'The Reception of Foreign Law in India' (1957) 9 *International Social Science Bulletin* 85, 86–7 (reporting statements by senior Indian judges). See also Chapter 1 at Section B 2.
[250] See Chapter 3 at Section B 2.
[251] Michael J Trebilcock, 'Between Universalism and Relativism: Reflections on the Evolution of Law and Development' (2016) 66 *University of Toronto Law Journal* 330, 336–7. For an empirical study see Roberto Dell'Anno and Stefania Villa, 'Growth in Transition Countries: Big Bang versus Gradualism' (2013) 21 *Economics of Transition* 381.
[252] World Bank, 'Legal Culture and Judicial Reform' (27 April 2012), available at https://moj.gov.vn/en/Pages/Talking-Laws.aspx?ItemID=14 accessed 23 October 2025.
[253] Siems (n 15) 407.

reform. Here, the classical work by Seymour Martin Lipset indicated that economic development often stimulated democracy, ie democracy should be the second step;[254] yet, more recent findings indicate that democracy should be the first step as it typically leads to long-run prosperity and may also promote peace and reduce conflict.[255]

Overall, the transplant unit therefore needs to determine, first, whether or not an isolated transplant is feasible. Second, if this is unlikely to be the case, it needs to assess what other elements need to change in order to make the transplant a success. Third, it needs to decide in which sequence these changes should be enacted and implemented.

D. Conclusion

The literature on legal transplants shares a core interest in the questions of why transplants take place, how they work and whether they should be supported from a normative perspective. By contrast, the design of legal transplants has been discussed less frequently. This may be regarded as surprising as, in the nineteenth century, the emerging field of modern comparative law was often phrased as being interested in 'comparative legislation'.[256] Yet, it aligns with the conventional focus of legal scholarship on current and past laws.

This chapter aimed to remedy this shortcoming by drawing on some of the previous literature that has suggested various steps in which transplants can be implemented, and it then presented some general recommendations for the design of legal transplants. Constructively, it has shown that it is possible to provide recommendations on the way the search and design of legal transplants should be pursued. Thus, this finding challenges the claim that the use of transplants is bound to be based on arbitrary criteria.[257] While these recommendations included notes of caution, it is in any case clear that any

[254] Seymour Martin Lipset, 'Some Social Requisites of Democracy, Economic Development, and Political Legitimacy' (1959) 53 *American Political Science Review* 69.

[255] Eg Daron Acemoglu and others, 'Democracy Does Cause Growth' (2019) 127 *Journal of Political Economy* 47; Morton H Halperin, Joseph T Siegle, and Michael M Weinstein, *The Democracy Advantage: How Democracies Promote Prosperity and Peace* (New York: Routledge, 2010).

[256] For examples see Balázs Fekete, *Paradigms in Modern European Comparative Law: A History* (Oxford: Hart Publishing, 2021) 37 (Italian book from 1857 on 'scienza delle legislation comparate'), 38 (German and French journals on foreign legislation established 1829 and 1834), 43 (foundation of the French and British societies of comparative legislation in 1869 and 1894).

[257] Eg, the US Chief Justice John Roberts: 'if you don't find it in the decisions of France or Italy, it's in the decisions of Somalia or Japan or Indonesia, or wherever' (confirmation hearings, 13 September 2005, see https://opiniojuris.org/2005/09/13/judge-roberts-hearing-use-of-foreign-law-in-constitutional-cases/) accessed 23 October 2025.

lawmaking, whether it is based on transplants or not, happens under certain assumptions and risks (and thus it can never be fully excluded that a new law may fail). With respect to transplants, the 'foreignness' of the law can sometimes lead to heightened risks; however, if done intelligently, the experience of the transplant in the origin unit can reduce any risks that the enactment of the new law entails.

In many of the twelve recommendations of this chapter, it was highlighted that expertise in comparative law should play a key role. Many of the recommendations also emphasised the need to consider other academic disciplines than law, notably the aspiration for evidence-based lawmaking. More specifically, some of the recommendations may be seen as fairly uncontentious as they ask to consider, for example, the role of the context of the law. However, it should also be noted that the recommendations were often phrased in a manner that they allow for exceptions, for example, as they recommend that transplants should 'generally be transparent and supported by the general public', that the popularity of models and the similarity between units 'should only be used heuristically', and that the adjustments to the local conditions of the 'transplant unit is often [but not always] necessary'.

These latter examples show that the specifics of a particular transplant can make a difference in any design recommendations. Thus, while the recommendations presented in this chapter were presented in a manner that they can be applied to any possible legal transplant, future research may differentiate between types and further refine these recommendations. This indication of future research also provides a segway to the concluding chapter.

8
Conclusion

This concluding chapter has three aims. First, it summarises the contributions disciplines other than law should make to the literature on legal transplants. Second, it revisits the main substantive argument of this book, namely the case for legal transplants. Third, it discusses what this may mean for future use of, and research on, legal transplants.

A. Legal transplants as a cross-disciplinary topic

While the first chapter of this book mentioned the possible contributions of disciplines other than law at a general level,[1] the subsequent chapters addressed them in the context of each of the substantive topics. Thus, on the one hand, this section aims to summarise the contributions these disciplines can make to the research on legal transplants. On the other hand, it shows how, by including them, this book has identified blind spots in the current legal literature.

As regards the specific contributions from other disciplines, all chapters of this book incorporated work from political science. In particular, the book drew on research on policy transfer and diffusion but also research on institutions and legislative drafting (noting that these fields of research themselves have an interdisciplinary dimension). For example, this included the observation that policies can be objects of legal transplants, the reasons of coercion, competition, emulation, and learning to explain why transplants take place, quantitative work on the impact of transplants on policy outcomes, an analysis of why 'bad policies' may spread (too), and research on policy learning, legislative drafting, and the choices between different models of capitalism and welfare states.[2]

[1] Chapter 1 at Section C 2.

[2] Chapter 3 at Section B, Chapter 4 at Section B 2, Chapter 5 at Section C 4, Chapter 6 at Section C 2 (a), and Chapter 7 at Sections B 1 and C 2 (b).

Legal Transplants. Mathias Siems, Oxford University Press. © Mathias Siems 2026.
DOI: 10.1093/9780191991981.003.0008

The disciplines mentioned in the following have also featured prominently in many of the chapters. Historical research is, for example, relevant since cases of 'entangled history' can show why transplants happen and historical examples can indicate whether or not transplants 'work', while, more contentiously, some authors have used history to argue in favour or against transplants from a normative perspective.[3] Economic research, including such research in the field of development studies, has employed quantitative methods in order to show why transplants happen and what effect they can have, and it can also be relevant for the design of transplants (eg, randomised controlled trials, the normative variant of law and economics).[4] Sociology, social geography, cultural studies, and anthropology can show how individual agents shape the occurrence and operation of transplants, and it may also help to explain the relationship between legal transplants and different types of societies and cultures.[5]

Research from further disciplines has featured less frequently, but it has played a key role for some questions. For example, insights from international relations (IR) can help in understanding why transplants take place, while views related to postcolonial IR also connect to the normative discussion about legal transplants.[6] Ethics and moral philosophy played a role for the normative topics of the preceding two chapters, while some of it may also explain the motivations underlying legal transplants.[7] Psychology can potentially matter for a number of topics but it has mainly featured for the question of whether or not the general public may support foreign ideas.[8] Linguistics and translation studies can be relevant for the understanding of existing transplants but also their design.[9]

Incorporating these other disciplines into research on legal transplants can address some blind spots in the legal literature. To start with, such research, as presented in this book, has challenged legal scholarship as far as it regards Alan Watson as the main originator and proponent of this topic. The bibliometric analysis has shown that, across disciplines, the topics of legal transplants, policy diffusion and transfer, and diffusion of ideas rose in the 1990s and 2000s, regardless of Watson's book.[10] Both this analysis and the literature

[3] Chapter 4 at Section A, Chapter 5 at Sections A and C, and Chapter 6 at Section C 4 (a) and (b).
[4] Chapter 4 at Section C 3 (c), Chapter 5 at Section C 4 (b), and Chapter 7 at Section C 1 (a) and 2 (c).
[5] Chapter 4 at Section B 3, Chapter 5 at Sections B 2, C 2 (a), and 3 (a), and Chapter 7 at Section C 2 (b).
[6] Chapter 4 at Sections B 4 and C 3 (b) and Chapter 6 at Sections B 2 and C 4 (b).
[7] Chapter 6 at Section C 1 (a), Chapter 7 at Section C 2 (b), and Chapter 4 at Section B.
[8] Chapter 6 at Section C 4 (b) and Chapter 7 at Section C 1 (b).
[9] Chapter 5 at Section B 2 and 3 and Chapter 7 at Section C 3 (b).
[10] Chapter 2 at Section C.

in other disciplines have also challenged Watson's claim that the occurrence and effect of legal transplants can fruitfully be studied without considering the context of the law.[11] In other words, while the legal element of legal transplants distinguishes them from cultural, economic, technological, or other transplants, it also shares with them topics such as their rise in modern times despite the continuing role of local differences.

More generally, some of the other disciplines show that, different from conventional legal scholarship, we may sometimes be able to generalise about causal relationships (eg, economics, political science, international relations), while other disciplines point towards the need to consider precise contextual factors in detail (eg, history, anthropology, social geography).[12] Specifically, the chapters on why transplants take place and how they work, have shown the relevance of both quantitative and qualitative empirical research from these disciplines,[13] while the subsequent two normative chapters on supporting and designing transplants have drawn on both normative and empirical research from other disciplines.[14] Thus, all of this research outside legal scholarship can be helpful in demonstrating that the comparative law scholarship on legal transplants asks questions of an empirical and normative nature, while it lacks the tools to adequately answer them on its own.

Finally, these other disciplines can point towards certain substantive topics that are underexplored in the legal literature on legal transplants. To start with, research from political science and sociology is often interested in the agents (or actors) that account for the use of transplants but also shape their operation.[15] Thus, insights from such research challenge a presentation of transplants that focusses only on the law itself without considering the role of individuals and groups. Another frequent gap is that research on legal transplants typically follows the focus of comparative law on countries.[16] In this regard, research in other social sciences is more open to covering, for example, cities or other substate units, as well as international, regional and transnational laws. For the research on legal transplants, this opening not only matters for the inclusion of

[11] Chapter 2 at Section D, as well as the role of agents noted in this section.

[12] For this divide and its relationship to comparative law in general see Mathias Siems, *Comparative Law* (Cambridge: CUP, 3rd edn, 2022) 415–19.

[13] Chapter 4 at Sections B 3 and 4 and C 1 and 3 and Chapter 5 at Sections B 3 and C.

[14] Chapter 6 at Section C and Chapter 7 at Section C.

[15] Chapter 4 at Sections B 3 and C 3, Chapter 5 at Section C 3, Chapter 6 at Section C 4 (b), and Chapter 7 at Section C 1 (b).

[16] For a challenge to this position see eg Mathias Siems, 'The Power of Comparative Law: What Types of Units Can Comparative Law Compare?' (2019) 67 *American Journal of Comparative Law* 861.

these units but also points to the need to understand the complex interactions between multiple units and agents.[17]

Of course, interdisciplinarity should not only be a one-way street.[18] The bibliometric chapter has shown that 'legal transplants' do not feature prominently in the literature on policy transfer and policy diffusion.[19] This may partly be the result of the fragmentation of academic disciplines, but it may partly also be due to the narrow focus of some of the literature on legal transplants. Thus, in this regard too, this book has aspired to remedy this shortcoming in showing how its findings contribute to other disciplines.

B. Legal transplants: why they matter and why we need them

This book aimed to make a case for legal transplants, both from a positive and a normative perspective. This can be summarised in four main findings. First, today, transplants typically happen due to a voluntary decision taken by the transplant unit; thus, this challenged the position which regards some transplants as a form of neocolonialism.[20] Second, transplants generally 'work' well in the sense that the transplanted law is known, applied, and effective in most cases; thus, this finding disagreed with claims that transplants are said to be irrelevant or counterproductive.[21] Third, there are usually good normative arguments that can support the use of a legal transplant; thus, this confronted normative positions of nationalism and identity politics.[22] Fourth, this book provided guidance on how the design of legal transplants should be pursued; thus, this challenged the claim that the use of transplants is bound to be based on arbitrary criteria.[23]

These findings were presented in separate chapters, but they also interact in various ways, as will be summarised in the remainder of this section. First, the topic of why transplants take place (Chapter 4) responded to the question of what explains legal transplants as a dependent variable (ie the transplant being the outcome of other factors). Yet, it is clear that this question also connects to the question about the other causal relationship, namely whether a particular transplant is expected to be successful in pursuing the aim which it aspires to

[17] Chapter 4 at Section B 4.

[18] Similarly, Antonina Engelbrekt Bakardjieva, 'Economic and Legal Discourses on Legal Transplants: Lost in Translation?' (2015) 60 *Scandinavian Studies in Law* 111, 138 ('we are still a long way from a true and long-lasting interdisciplinary dialogue').

[19] Chapter 2 at Section D 2.

[20] Chapter 4 at Sections B 1 and D.

[21] Chapter 5 at Sections B 2 and D.

[22] Chapter 6 at Sections B 2 and D.

[23] Chapter 7 at Sections C and D.

achieve. Moreover, while the analysis of this chapter was of a positive nature in understanding the reasons for transplants, it also set the scene for the later normative analysis of why transplants should be pursued.

Second, the topic of whether and how transplants work (Chapter 5) included some differentiations between cases and situations to show when transplants may or may not work as expected. For example, it can matter why transplants take place—the topic of the previous chapter—as it is likely that involuntary transplants face higher risks of not working than voluntary ones. This chapter also indicated that there will often be modifications in the transplant unit which impact on the way the transplant works. Thus, this aspect connects to the analysis of the later chapter on the design of legal transplants, confirming that—while this book generally endorsed the use of legal transplants—it also noted that a naïve use of transplants can be risky.

Third, the analysis of whether it is desirable to use legal transplants (Chapter 6) discussed in some detail the relationship between 'is' and 'ought', concluding that normative evaluations cannot, and should not, detach themselves from positive findings. As a result, this chapter included many references to the chapters that considered the 'is' of transplants, ie why transplants take place and whether and how they work. In some cases, it may indeed be the case that such empirical insights are the main reason to choose a transplant, for example, where the aim (say, poverty reduction) is uncontroversial, but one unit has laws that have proven to be more effective in achieving this aim.

Fourth, the design of legal transplants (Chapter 7) has deliberately been the final of these four substantive chapters as it connected to the findings of the other three. It followed up from the frequent use of voluntary transplants and then considered that transplants are—and often should be—adjusted in order to ensure that they work in the transplant unit. This chapter also accepted that lawmakers may pursue different normative aims, as elaborated in the preceding chapter; yet, it then presented twelve recommendations that should guide the transplant unit in its design process.

Overall, the case for legal transplants consists of these four interconnected findings. Thus, while each chapter of this book presented a distinct argument, this interconnectedness also explains the use of this monograph as the best form to present a detailed general analysis of legal transplants.

C. An optimist's guide for legal transplants

There is no doubt that, sometimes, the use of legal transplants faces limitations or that it can lead to problems. Such failures of transplants can be explored by focussing on the agents involved in compliance and enforcement of the law and the difficulty of changing their behaviour.[24] Or, it is possible to identify deficiencies in lawmaking, for example, lack of expertise, time, and incentives, short-termism, political opportunism, selective use of information, and the role of special interest groups.[25] It is also clear that one should not be naïve about the idea of an efficient market for the best laws as there can be many limitations to the operation of such market-based forces, for example, lack of knowledge of foreign laws, legal parochialism, the prevalence of hegemonic jurisdictions, as well as non-market-based forms of legal evolution.[26]

Yet, such limitations and problems should not lead to resignation but rather, first of all, to the ambition to improve the design of legal transplants. The penultimate chapter of this book therefore presented general stages for the design of transplants and then also more specific recommendations.[27] Future research is encouraged to continue with this task. This focus on the careful design of legal transplants should, however, not lead to the automatic rejection of transplants that seem to be based on a shallow design. Notably, this is the case where the cost-benefit evaluation of a transplant leads to the conclusion that an imperfect transplant is preferable to the status quo or the delay of drafting one's own law.[28] Thus, the recommendations of this chapter should not be understood as dispensing from a focus on the contextual details of a particular transplant decision.

Another design topic, only briefly addressed in this book, concerns the conditions that make the enactment of certain legal transplants more likely. One of the normative chapters suggested that third countries, international organisations but also citizens, companies, and interest groups of either the origin or the transplant unit may be able to prevent 'malicious legal transplants'.[29] Expanding this argument, similar factors are likely to matter for 'good' legal transplants, ie transplants that should be supported from a normative perspective.[30] Thus, a future project could address this meta-level in further detail, namely how to create the conditions that make it more likely that lawmakers adopt the latter and not the former types of transplants.

[24] Chapter 5 at Section C 3 (c).
[25] Chapter 6 at Section C 4 (b).
[26] Chapter 6 at Section C 2 (b).
[27] Chapter 7 at Sections B 1 and C.
[28] Chapter 6 at Section C 3 (c) and Chapter 7 at Section C 3 (a).
[29] Chapter 6 at Section C 4 (b). For further details see Mathias Siems, 'Malicious Legal Transplants' (2018) 38 *Legal Studies* 103, 114–18.
[30] This can draw on different normative approaches see Chapter 6 at Section C 2 and 5.

Finally, what should be the role of scholarship vis-à-vis legal transplants? This book has shown that there has been a rise in research on legal transplants and that it has expanded its scope to new topics and approaches.[31] Indeed, it is valuable that authors pursue different types of projects (theoretical, empirical, normative, applied, critical, etc). My own position is that a form of 'legal cosmopolitanism' should be the way forward as it presents an openness to other experiences with the potential to integrate one's own and foreign legal cultures without endorsing universalism.[32] Thus, this position is sceptical of forms of exclusionary identity politics that apply an essentialist position of group identities and that reject the ability to understand or transplant legal ideas and rules across identity groups.[33] As also noted by others, legal systems should not be seen as 'closed frameworks' that foreigners can never enter[34] and 'borders of legal systems should not be seen as borders of knowledge acquisition'.[35] Thus, the promotion of legal transplants in this book favours an optimistic position that learning from others is both possible and valuable.

[31] For details see Chapter 2.

[32] Siems (n 12) 404–6; Mathias Siems and Po Jen Yap, 'Introduction: A New Handbook for Comparative Law in a Global Context' in Mathias Siems and Po Jen Yap (eds), *The Cambridge Handbook of Comparative Law* (Cambridge: CUP, 2024) 1, 6–7. See also Dominik Dworniczak and others, 'The Notion of Legal Transplants Beyond the Anglosphere: Decentring the Debate' (2025) 16 *Transnational Legal Theory* 357, 379–81.

[33] Mathias Siems, 'Identity Politics and Comparative Law' (2023) 30 *Maastricht Journal of European and Comparative Law* 719.

[34] Anne Peters and Heiner Schwenke, 'Comparative Law Beyond Post-modernism' (2000) 49 *International and Comparative Law Quarterly* 800, 816.

[35] Jaakko Husa, *Advanced Introduction to Law and Globalisation* (Cheltenham: Edward Elgar, 2018) 45.

Appendix

Annex 1: Books with 'legal transplants' or related concepts in the title

Category	Language	Publication [with comments if needed for the classification]
1. Case study, current law, one country	(a) English	John Stanley Gillespie, *Transplanting Commercial Law Reform: Developing a Rule of Law in Vietnam* (Aldershot: Ashgate, 2006)
		Penelope (Pip) Nicholson, *Borrowing Court Systems: The Experience of Socialist Vietnam* (Leiden: Martinus Nijhoff, 2007)
		Neil Chisholm, *Judicial Reform in Taiwan: Democratization and the Diffusion of Law* (Abington: Routledge, 2019)
		Catherine Dupré, *Importing the Law in Post-Communist Transitions: The Hungarian Constitutional Court and the Right to Human Dignity* (Oxford: Hart Publishing, 2003)
		Hélène Tyrrell, *Human Rights in the UK and the Influence of Foreign Jurisprudence* (Oxford: Hart Publishing, 2018)
		Bishal Khanal, *Legal Reform via Reception of Law* (Kathmandu: Bhrikuti Academic Publications, 2018) [mainly on Nepalese and some Indian law]
	(b) German	Jan von Hein, *Die Rezeption US-amerikanischen Gesellschaftsrechts in Deutschland* (Tübingen: Mohr Siebeck, 2008)
		Judith Schacherreiter, *Das Landeigentum als Legal Transplant in Mexiko: Rechtsvergleichende Analysen unter Einbezug postkolonialer Perspektiven* (Tübingen: Mohr Siebeck, 2014)
		Poonthep Sirinupong, *Same Same But Different: Grundgesetzimport und Verfassungsmutation in Thailand* (Baden-Baden: Nomos, 2022)
	(c) Italian	Pasquale Viola, *Costituzionalismo autoctono. Pluralismo culturale e trapianti giuridici nel subcontinente indiano* (Bologna: Bologna University Press, 2020)
	(d) Portuguese	Rafaela Coutinho Canetti, *Acordo de Leniência: Fundamentos do instituto e os problemas de seu transplante ao ordenamento jurídico brasileiro* (Belo Horizonte: Fórum, 2018)

Category	Language	Publication [with comments if needed for the classification]
2. Case study, current law, other focus	(a) English	Yuka Kaneko, *Insolvency Law Reforms in Asian Developing Countries: An Epitome of Legal Transplants* (Singapore: Springer, 2022)
		Amber Darr, *Competition Law in South Asia: Policy Diffusion and Transfer* (Cambridge: CUP, 2023)
		Pascale Fournier, *Muslim Marriage in Western Courts: Lost in Transplantation* (Abington: Routledge, 2010) [also published in French, see (2)(c), below]
		Leonardo Pierdominici, *The Mimetic Evolution of the Court of Justice of the EU: A Comparative Law Perspective* (London: Palgrave Macmillan, 2020)
		Thomas Wilhelmsson, *Free Movement of Legal Ideas: Towards a Dynamic Europeanisation of Private Law* (Oxford: Hart Publishing, 2024)
		Karen J Alter and Laurence R Helfer, *Transplanting International Courts: The Law and Politics of the Andean Tribunal of Justice* (Oxford: OUP, 2017)
		Simon Marsden, *Protecting the Third Pole: Transplanting International Law* (Cheltenham: Edward Elgar, 2019)
	(b) German	Attila Fodor, *Rechtsreform durch Normtransplantation in Mittel- und Osteuropa: Eine vergleichende Analyse der Rezeption von Neuen Pfandregistervorschriften in Ungarn und in Russland* (Berlin: Berliner Wissenschafts-Verlag, 2009)
		Alban Spielkamp, *Dialogische Rechtsentwicklung im europäischen Verwaltungsrecht: Strukturen transnationaler Rechtsrezeptionen am Beispiel der Verwaltungstransparenz* (Tübingen: Mohr Siebeck, 2025)
		David Fila, *Private Enforcement und Legal Transplants: Kartellschadensersatz in Lateinamerika aus EU-Perspektive* (Baden: Nomos, 2025)
	(c) French	Pascale Fournier, *Mariages musulmans, tribunaux d'Occident. Les transplantations juridiques et le regard du droit* (Paris: Presses de Sciences Po, 2013) [also published in English, see (a) above]
	(d) Italian	Jihane Benarafa, *Il Takaful oltre il legal transplant: l'etica islamica difronte al rischio assicurativo* (Turin: Giappichelli, 2024)
3. Case study, historical study	(a) English	Justine K Collins, *Tracing British West Indian Slavery Laws: A Comparative Analysis of Legal Transplants* (Abingdon: Routledge, 2021)
		Michael Ng, *Legal Transplantation in Early Twentieth-Century China: Practicing Law in Republican Beijing (1910s-1930s)* (Abingdon: Routledge, 2014)
		Tay-sheng Wang, *Legal Reform in Taiwan under Japanese Colonial Rule, 1895-1945: The Reception of Western Law* (Seattle, WA: University of Washington Press, 2000)

Category	Language	Publication [with comments if needed for the classification]
		Leonard Wood, *Islamic Legal Revival: Reception of European Law and Transformations in Islamic Legal Thought in Egypt, 1875–1952* (Oxford: OUP, 2016)
		Carol Weisbrod, *Kites and the Sabbath: Legal Transplants and Pluralism in Hawai'i* (Lake Mary, FL: Vandeplas Publishing, 2014)
		GW Bartholomew, *The Commercial Law of Malaysia: A Study in the Reception of English Law* (Singapore: Malayan Law Journal, 1965)
	(b) German	Georg von Below, *Die Ursachen der Rezeption des römischen Rechts in Deutschland* (Berlin: R Oldenbourg, 1905)
		Karl Michaelis, *Wandlungen des deutschen Rechtsdenkens seit dem Eindringen des fremden Rechts* (Berlin: Junker und Dünnhaupt Verlag, 1935)
		Helmut Coing, *Die Rezeption des Römischen Rechts in Frankfurt am Main* (Frankfurt: Vittoria Klostermann, 1939)
		Georg Dahm, *Zur Rezeption des römisch-italienischen Rechts* (Darmstadt: Wissenschaftliche Buchgesellschaft, 1955)
		Detlef Schumacher, *Das Rheinische Recht in der Gerichtspraxis des 19. Jahrhunderts: Ein Beitrag zur Auslegung rezipierter Rechtsnormen* (Stuttgart: W Kohlhammer Verlag, 1969)
		Zentaro Kitagawa, *Rezeption und Fortbildung des europäischen Zivilrechts in Japan* (Frankfurt: Metzner, 1970)
		Ernst Hirsch, *Rezeption als sozialer Prozeß: erläutert am Beispiel der Türkei* (Berlin: Duncker & Humblot, 1981)
		Jörg Fedtke, *Die Rezeption von Verfassungsrecht. Südafrika 1993–1996* (Baden-Baden: Nomos, 2000)
		Hülya Bandak, *Die Rezeption des schweizerischen Zivilgesetzbuches in der Türkei* (Bielefeld: Gieseking, 2008)
		Viktoria Draganova, *Recht durch Transfer: Der Anfang des bulgarischen Rechssystems 1878-1920* (Frankfurt: Vittoria Klostermann, 2014)
		Ruomeng Yang, *Die Rezeption der europäischen Privatrechte in China und die konfuzianische Tradition: Das Beispiel des Deliktsrechts im frühen 20. Jahrhundert* (Frankfurt: Peter Lang, 2015)
		Matthias Veicht, *Rezeption und Zivilrechtskodifikation in China seit 1900* (Tübingen: Mohr Siebeck, 2022)

Category	Language	Publication [with comments if needed for the classification]
	(c) Italian	Elia Ponti, *La recezione del diritto privato occidentale in Cina fra il 1840 e il 1949* (Milan: Unicopli, 2006)
	(d) Turkish	Gülnihal Bozkurt, *Batı Hukukunun Türkiye'de Benimsenmesi, Osmanlı Devletinden Türkiye Cumhuriyetine Resepsiyon Süreci 1839–1939* (Ankara: Türk Tarih Kurumu, 1996)
4. Multiple case studies, authored, current law	(a) English	Asif Salahuddin, *Transplant of Corporate Governance Regimes to South Asia: Are Legal Transplants Viable?* (Berlin: De Gruyter, 2026)
		Beata Kviatek, *Explaining Legal Transplants: Transplantation of EU law into Central Eastern Europe* (Nijmegen: Wolf Legal Publishers, 2015)
		Rosalind Dixon and David Landau, *Abusive Constitutional Borrowing: Legal Globalization and the Subversion of Liberal Democracy* (Oxford: OUP, 2021)
		Sir Basil Markesinis and Jörg Fedtke, *Judicial Recourse to Foreign Law: A New Source of Inspiration?* (London: Routledge-Cavendish, 2006)
		James L Nolan, *Legal Accents, Legal Borrowing: The International Problem-Solving Court Movement* (Princeton, NJ: Princeton University Press, 2009).
	(b) French	Conseil d'Etat, *L'influence internationale du droit français* (Paris: La Documentation française, 2001)
		Jacobo Rios Rodriguez, *L'influence internationale du droit français* (Paris: Savoirs et Connaissances, 2008)
	(c) German	Jens Drolshammer and Rolf Weber, *Wie das Recht auf Reisen geht: Eine Übersichtsdarstellung internationaler Rechtstransfers am Beispiel des schweizerischen Rechts- und Kulturraums* (Bern: Stämpfli, 2019)
	(d) Italian	Elisabetta Grande, *Imitazione e diritto: ipotesi sulla circolazione dei modelli* (Turin: Giappichelli, 2000)
	(e) Portuguese	Elisabetta Grande, *Imitação e Direito. Hipóteses Sobre a Circulação dos Modelos* (Porto Alegre: Sergio Antonio Fabris, 2009) [translation of Italian book, see above]
5. Multiple case studies, authored, historical study	(a) English	James Bryce (Viscount), *The Ancient Roman Empire and the British Empire in India: The Diffusion of Roman and English Law Throughout the World; Two Historical Studies* (Oxford: H Milford, OUP, 1914)
		Alan Watson, *Legal Transplants: An Approach to Comparative Law* (Edinburgh: Scottish Academic Press, 1974; Athens, GA: Georgia, University of Georgia Press, 2nd edn, 1993) [focus on reception of Roman law in different places] [for translations see next field]
		BH (Bruce Harvey) McPherson, *The Reception of English Law Abroad* (Brisbane: Supreme Court of Queensland Library, 2007)

Category	Language	Publication [with comments if needed for the classification]
	(b) Italian and Serbian	Alan Watson, *Il trapianto di norme giuridiche. Un «approccio» al diritto comparato* (Naples: Edizioni Scientifiche Italiane, 1984).
		Алан Вотсон, *Правни трансплантu, Напомена уз друго издање* (Belgrade: Правни фа- култет Универзитета у Београду, 2010).
6. Multiple case studies, edited, general titles	(a) English	William B Hamilton (ed), *The Transfer of Institutions* (Durham, NC: Duke University Press 1964)
		Robert Jagtenberg, Esin Örücü, and Annie J de Roo (eds), *Transfrontier Mobility of Law* (The Hague: Kluwer Law International, 1995)
		David Nelken and Johannes Feest (eds), *Adapting Legal Cultures* (Oxford: Hart Publishing, 2001)
		John Gillespie and Pip Nicholson (eds), *Law and Development and the Global Discourses of Legal Transfers* (Cambridge: CUP, 2012)
		Nicola Lupo and Lucia Scaffardi (eds), *Comparative Law in Legislative Drafting: The Increasing Importance of Dialogue amongst Parliaments* (The Hague: Eleven, 2014)
		Sue Farran and others (eds), *The Diffusion of Law: the Movement of Laws and Norms around the World* (Farnham: Ashgate, 2015)
		Mauro Bussani and Lukas Heckendorn Urscheler (eds), *Comparisons in Legal Development: The Impact of Foreign and International Law on National Legal Systems* (Zurich: Schulthess, 2016)
	(b) Italian	Fabio Rugge (ed), *Il trasferimento internazionale dei modelli istituzionali* (Bologna: Il Mulino, 2012)
	(c) French	Michel Doucet and Jacques Vanderlinden (eds), *La recéption des systèmes juridiques: implantation et destin: textes présentés au premier colloque international du Centre international de la common law en français (CICLEF)* (Brussels: Bruylant, 1994).
7. Multiple case studies, edited, current law	(a) English	Sujit Choudhry (ed), *The Migration of Constitutional Ideas* (Cambridge: CUP, 2006)
		Günter Frankenberg (ed), *Order from Transfer: Comparative Constitutional Design and Legal Culture* (Cheltenham: Edward Elgar, 2013)
		Anat Scolnicov (ed), *Constitutional Transplantations: The Diffusion and Adoption of Constitutional Ideas* (Oxford: Hart Publishing, 2026)
		Christa Jessel-Holst, Rainer Kulms, and Alexander Trunk (eds), *Private Law in Eastern Europe: Autonomous Developments or Legal Transplants?* (Tübingen: Mohr Siebeck, 2010)

Category	Language	Publication [with comments if needed for the classification]
		Andrew Harding, Jiaxiang Hu, and Maartje de Visser (eds), *Legal Education in Asia: From Imitation to Innovation* (Leiden: Brill Nijhoff, 2018)
		Vito Breda (ed), *Legal Transplants in East Asia and Oceania* (Cambridge: CUP, 2019)
	(b) German	Jörg-Martin Jehle, Volker Lipp, and Keiichi Yamanaka (eds), *Rezeption und Reform im japanischen und deutschen Recht* (Göttingen: Universitätsverlag, 2008)
		Werner Heun, Christian Starck, and Tzung-Jen Tsai (eds), *Rezeption und Paradigmenwechsel im öffentlichen Recht: Viertes Deutsch-Taiwanesisches Kolloquium Vom 7.-8. November 2008 in Taipeh* (Baden-Baden: Nomos, 2009)
		Werner F Ebke and others (eds), *Das Deutsche Wirtschaftsrecht unter dem Einfluss des US-amerikanischen Rechts* (Frankfurt: Verlag Recht und Wirtschaft, 2010)
		Yu-Cheol Shin (ed), *Rezeption europäischer Rechte in Ostasien* (Seoul: Bobmunsa, 2013)
		Eugenia Kurzynsky-Singer (ed), *Transformation durch Rezeption? Möglichkeiten und Grenzen des Rechtstransfers am Beispiel der Zivilrechtsreformen im Kaukasus und in Zentralasien* (Tübingen: Mohr Siebeck, 2014)
		Uwe Kischel (ed), *Der Einfluss des deutschen Verfassungsrechtsdenkens in der Welt: Bedeutung, Grenzen, Zukunftsperspektiven* (Tübingen: Mohr Siebeck, 2014)
		Romana Cierpial-Magnor, Arkadiusz Wudarski, and Martin Winner (eds), *Erfolge und Misserfolge des Rechtstransfers* (Vienna: Facultas, 2024)
	(c) Spanish	Daniel Bonilla Maldonado (ed), *Los mandarines del derecho: Trasplantes jurídicos, análisis cultural del derecho y trabajo pro bono* (Bogota: Siglo del Hombre Editores, 2017)
	(d) French	Hélène Ruiz Fabri and Lorenzo Gradoni (eds), *La circulation des concepts juridiques: le droit international de l'environnement entre mondialisation et fragmentation* (Paris: Société de législation comparée, 2009).
8. Multiple case studies, edited, historical study	(a) English	Mathias Reimann (ed), *The Reception of Continental Ideas in the Common Law World: 1820–1920* (Berlin: Duncker & Humblot, 1993)
		Katell Berthelot, Natalie Dohrmann, and Capucine Nemo-Pekelman (eds), *Legal Engagement: The Reception of Roman Law and Tribunals by Jews and Other Inhabitants of the Empire* (Rome: Publications de l'École française de Rome, 2021)

Category	Language	Publication [with comments if needed for the classification]
		Donal K Coffey and Stefan Vogenauer (eds), *Legal Transfer and Legal Geography in the British Empire* (Frankfurt: Max Planck Institute for Legal History and Legal Theory, 2025)
	(b) German	Vanessa Duss and others (eds) *Rechtstransfer in der Geschichte: Legal Transfer in History* (Munich: Jahrbuch junge Rechtsgeschichte, 2006)
9. General books	(a) English	Barbara Dufková, *Success in Legal Transplanting* (Prague: Charles University, 2022), available at https://dspace.cuni.cz/handle/20.500.11956/174718
		Diego López-Medina, *Comparative jurisprudence: reception and misreading of transnational legal theory in Latin America* (SJD thesis, Harvard University, 2001) [published in Spanish as: Diego Eduardo López Medina, *Teoría impura del derecho. La transformación de la cultura jurídica latinoamericana* (Bogota: Legis, 2004)]
	(b) German	Jutta Mues, *Rechtstransfer: Zur theoretisch-methodischen Komplexität der Interaktion normativer Ordnungen* (Frankfurt: Peter Lang, 2015)
		Maximilian Wörner-Schönecker, *Rechtstransfers: Eine Analyse anhand von Typologien* (Tübingen: Mohr Siebeck, 2022)
	(c) Spanish	Daniel Bonilla Maldonado (ed), *Teoría del derecho y trasplantes jurídicos* (Bogota: Siglo del Hombre Editores, 2009)
	(d) French	Athanase C Papachristos, *La réception des droits privés étrangers comme phénomène de sociologie juridique* (Paris: LGDJ, 1975)
10. Non-law books	(a) English	Cindy Skach, *Borrowing Constitutional Designs: Constitutional law in Weimar Germany and the French Fifth Republic* (Princeton, NJ: Princeton University Press, 2005)
		Katerina Linos, *The Democratic Foundations of Policy Diffusion: How Health, Family, and Employment Laws Spread Across Countries* (Oxford: OUP, 2013)
		Sören Stapel, *Regional Organizations and Democracy, Human Rights, and the Rule of Law: The African Union, Organization of American States, and the Diffusion of Institutions* (Basingstoke: Palgrave Macmillan, 2022)
		Marvin Wiegand, *The Reception of Learned Law in Fourteenth- and Fifteenth-Century Frisia* (Leiden: Brill, 2024)
		Mahmood Kooria, *Islamic Law in Circulation: Shāfiʿī texts Across the Indian Ocean and the Mediterranean* (Cambridge: CUP, 2022)

Annex 2: Details on data collection for Chapter 2

Section	Information for...	Details of search (examples if multiple years, data points etc)
B 1	Beckstrom and Kahn-Freund	Google Scholar search for "*Transplantation of Legal Systems: An Early Report on the Reception of Western Laws in Ethiopia*" and "*On Uses and Misuses of Comparative Law*": data on 'Cited by'
		Google Scholar search for "*On Uses and Misuses of Comparative Law*": 'Search within citing articles' for "*legal transplants*"
	Bentham and Walton	Google Scholar search for "*Of the Influence of Time and Place in Matters of Legislation*" and "*The Historical School of Jurisprudence and Transplantations of Law*": data on 'Cited by'
B 2	Watson and other authors	Google Scholar: settings – languages – English. Then search for "*La réception des droits privés étrangers comme phénomène de sociologie juridique*", "*Rezeption als sozialer Prozeß*", "*Imitazione e diritto. Ipotesi sulla circolazione dei modelli*" and "*Legal transplants: an approach to comparative law*": number of results
C 1	Figures 2.1 and 2.2	Google Ngrams: 1970–2022, English, Smoothing of 0: search for *legal transplant_INF,law transplant_INF,transplantation of law_INF*
		Google Ngrams: 1970–2022, English, Smoothing of 0: search for *legal transplants*1000/law,legal transplants/comparative law*
	Figure 2.3 and related data reported in text	Google Scholar search for "*transplantation of law*" *OR* "*transplantation of laws*" *OR* "*law transplants*" *OR* "*law transplant*" *OR* "*legal transplant*" *OR* "*legal transplants*" *OR* "*legal transplantation*" *OR* "*legal transplantations*": number of results (and then 'Custom range' time periods)
		Google Scholar search for *allintitle:* "*transplantation of law*" *OR* "*transplantation of laws*" *OR* "*law transplants*" *OR* "*law transplant*" *OR* "*legal transplant*" *OR* "*legal transplants*" *OR* "*legal transplantation*" *OR* "*legal transplantations*": number of results (and then 'Custom range' time periods)

Section	Information for . . .	Details of search (examples if multiple years, data points etc)
		Google Scholar search for *("transplantation of law" OR "transplantation of laws" OR "law transplants" OR "law transplant" OR "legal transplant" OR "legal transplants" OR "legal transplantation" OR "legal transplantations") (source:review OR source:journal)*: number of results (and then 'Custom range' time periods)
		Google Scholar search for *("law", "legal") (source:review OR source:journal)*: number of results (and then 'Custom range' time periods)
	Figure 2.4 and related data reported in text	Westlaw: World Journals with formulas such as:
		adv: "transplantation #of law" OR "transplantation #of laws" OR "law transplants" OR "law transplant" OR "legal transplant" OR "legal transplants" OR "legal transplantation" OR "legal transplantations"
		adv: ATLEAST5("transplantation #of law") OR ATLEAST5("transplantation #of laws") OR ATLEAST5("law transplants") OR ATLEAST5("law transplant") OR ATLEAST5("legal transplant") OR ATLEAST5("legal transplants") OR ATLEAST5("legal transplantation") OR ATLEAST5("legal transplantations") & DA(aft 1-1-2023 & bef 1-1-2024)
		adv: ATLEAST5("comparative law") & ATLEAST5("transplantation #of law") OR ATLEAST5("transplantation #of laws") OR ATLEAST5("law transplants") OR ATLEAST5("law transplant") OR ATLEAST5("legal transplant") OR ATLEAST5("legal transplants") OR ATLEAST5("legal transplantation") OR ATLEAST5("legal transplantations") & DA(aft 1-1-2023 & bef 1-1-2024)
C 2	Figures 2.5 and 2.6 and related data reported in text	Google Ngrams: 1970–2022, English, Smoothing of 0: search for *legal transplant_INF,legal diffusion,legal reception,reception of law_INF,diffusion of law_INF*
		Google Ngrams: 1950–1995, English, Smoothing of 0: search for *legal transplants,legal reception,reception of law,diffusion of law*
		Google Scholar search in 'Custom range' 1970-2023 for *("transplantation of law" OR "transplantation of laws" OR "law transplants" OR "law transplant" OR "legal transplant" OR "legal transplants" OR "legal transplantation" OR "legal transplantations") (source:review OR source:journal)*
		Google Scholar search in 'Custom range' 1970-2023 for *("legal reception" OR "reception of law" OR "reception of laws") (source:review OR source:journal)*

Section	Information for ...	Details of search (examples if multiple years, data points etc)
		Google Scholar search in 'Custom range' 1970-2023 for *("legal diffusion" OR "diffusion of law" OR "diffusion of laws") (source:review OR source:journal)*
		Westlaw: World Journals with formulas such as:
		adv: ATLEAST5("transplantation #of law") OR ATLEAST5("transplantation #of laws") OR ATLEAST5("law transplants") OR ATLEAST5("law transplant") OR ATLEAST5("legal transplant") OR ATLEAST5("legal transplants") OR ATLEAST5("legal transplantation") OR ATLEAST5("legal transplantations") & DA(aft 1-1-1970 & bef 1-1-2024)
		adv: ATLEAST5("diffusion #of law") OR ATLEAST5("diffusion #of laws") OR ATLEAST5("legal diffusion") & DA(aft 1-1-1970 & bef 1-1-2024)
		adv: ATLEAST5("reception #of law") OR ATLEAST5("reception #of laws") OR ATLEAST5("legal reception") & DA(aft 1-1-1970 & bef 1-1-2024)
	Figures 2.7 and related data reported in text	Google Ngrams: 1970–2022, English, Smoothing of 0: search for *legal transplants,policy transfer,policy diffusion*
		Google Scholar search in 'Custom range' 1970-2023 for *("policy transfer") (source:review OR source:journal)*
		Google Scholar search in 'Custom range' 1970-2023 for *("policy diffusion" OR "diffusion of policy" OR "diffusion of policies") (source:review OR source:journal)*
		Westlaw: World Journals with formulas such as:
		adv: ATLEAST5("legal transplants") & DA(aft 1-1-1970 & bef 1-1-2024)
		adv: ATLEAST5("policy transfer") & DA(aft 1-1-1970 & bef 1-1-2024)
		adv: ATLEAST5("diffusion of policy") OR ATLEAST5("diffusion #of policies") OR ATLEAST5("policy diffusion") & DA(aft 1-1-1970 & bef 1-1-2024)
	Figure 2.8	Google Ngrams: 1900–2022, English, Smoothing of 0: search for *legal transplants,cultural diffusion,circulation of ideas,cultural transfer,diffusion of ideas,mimetic theory*

Section	Information for . . .	Details of search (examples if multiple years, data points etc)
D 1	Figures 2.9 and related data reported in text	Google Scholar search for *"Watson" AND ("transplantation of law" OR "transplantation of laws" OR "law transplants" OR "law transplant" OR "legal transplant" OR "legal transplants" OR "legal transplantation" OR "legal transplantations") (source:review OR source:journal)* (and then 'Custom range' time periods) [and same for Legrand, Kahn-Freund and Bentham) Westlaw: World Journals with formulas such as: *adv: "Watson" & ATLEAST5("transplantation #of law") OR ATLEAST5("transplantation #of laws") OR ATLEAST5("law transplants") OR ATLEAST5("law transplant") OR ATLEAST5("legal transplant") OR ATLEAST5("legal transplants") OR ATLEAST5("legal transplantation") OR ATLEAST5("legal transplantations") & DA(aft 1-1-1970 & bef 1-1-2024)*
	Table 2.2 and related data reported in text	Google Scholar search in 'Custom range' 1970-2023 and the searchers such as: *"criminal law" (source:review OR source:journal)* and *"criminal law" AND ("transplantation of law" OR "transplantation of laws" OR "law transplants" OR "law transplant" OR "legal transplant" OR "legal transplants" OR "legal transplantation" OR "legal transplantations") (source:review OR source:journal)* Westlaw: World Journals with formulas such as: *adv: ATLEAST5("criminal law") & ATLEAST5("transplantation #of law") OR ATLEAST5("transplantation #of laws") OR ATLEAST5("law transplants") OR ATLEAST5("law transplant") OR ATLEAST5("legal transplant") OR ATLEAST5("legal transplants") OR ATLEAST5("legal transplantation") OR ATLEAST5("legal transplantations") & DA(aft 1-1-1970 & bef 1-1-2024)* *adv: ATLEAST5("criminal law") & DA(aft 1-1-1970 & bef 1-1-2024)*
	Table 2.3	Westlaw: World Journals with formulas such as: *adv: ATLEAST5("China") & ATLEAST5("transplantation #of law") OR ATLEAST5("transplantation #of laws") OR ATLEAST5("law transplants") OR ATLEAST5("law transplant") OR ATLEAST5("legal transplant") OR ATLEAST5("legal transplants") OR ATLEAST5("legal transplantation") OR ATLEAST5("legal transplantations") & DA(aft 1-1-1970 & bef 1-1-2024)* *adv: ATLEAST5("China") & DA(aft 1-1-1970 & bef 1-1-2024)*

Section	Information for ...	Details of search (examples if multiple years, data points etc)
D 2	Figure 2.10	Google Scholar search in 'Custom range' 2020-2020 search for *"legal transplants" OR "legal transplant" source:review OR source:journal*
	Table 2.4	Google Scholar search in 'Custom range' 2020-2021 search for *allintitle:("transplantation of law" OR "transplantation of laws" OR "law transplants" OR "law transplant" OR "legal transplant" OR "legal transplants" OR "legal transplantation" OR "legal transplantations") (source:review OR source:journal)*
	Table 2.5 and related data reported in text	JSTOR search for *(("legal transplant") OR ("legal transplants"))*: results limited to Journal and then numbers for each Subject (and date restrictions for time periods)
		JSTOR search for *((("policy diffusion") OR ("diffusion of policy")) OR ("diffusion of policies")) OR ("policy transfer"))*: results limited to Journal and then numbers for each Subject (and date restrictions for time periods)
		JSTOR search for *(("legal transplant") OR ("legal transplants")) OR (("policy diffusion")) OR (("diffusion of policy")) OR (("diffusion of policies")) OR (("policy transfer"))*: results limited to Journal and then numbers for each Subject (and date restrictions for time periods)

Index

For the benefit of digital users, indexed terms that span two pages (e.g., 52–53) may, on occasion, appear on only one of those pages.

Tables and figures are indicated by an italic *t* and *f* following the page number.